THE CULTURE OF
THE
TWENTIES

THE AMERICAN HERITAGE SERIES

THE AMERICAN HERITAGE SERIES

Under the General Editorship of
LEONARD W. LEVY and ALFRED YOUNG

THE CULTURE OF
THE
TWENTIES

Edited by LOREN BARITZ

State University of New York at Albany

THE BOBBS-MERRILL COMPANY, INC.

Indianapolis · New York

Foreword

Surely it is time to lay aside distorting images of the 1920's. The popular media often stereotype the period as the "Jazz Age": flappers, flaming youth (skirts above the knees!), bathtub gin, and the Charleston. A variant on this theme is the "Roaring Twenties," a time of smart operators and fast women, from Al Capone to "Peaches" Browning. Until recently, even historians tended to treat the period as a parenthesis between the supposedly more vital Progressive Era and the climactic reforms of the New Deal: an aberrant decade, fascinating and amusing, but somehow irrelevant.

Loren Baritz, an accomplished historian of American ideas, has assembled this anthology on the premise that the Twenties actually provided an "increasingly relevant legacy." He charts the development of this heritage in the cultural revolt of the times, the rebellion of the youth, the trenchant social criticism of the intellectuals—all of which his introductory essay interprets as products of a pervasive clash between the values of a new urban, urbane, and modern civilization, and the pieties of small town, provincial America.

His selections allow the figures of the dominant culture to

speak for themselves. Political fundamentalism is defended by Attorney General A. Mitchell Palmer, architect of the bogus "Red Scare," and by Hiram Wesley Evans, Imperial Wizard and Emperor of the Ku Klux Klan. The words of William Jennings Bryan and Aimee Semple McPherson represent religious fundamentalism, while business fundamentalism is championed by Herbert Hoover, and by Bruce Barton's incredibly vulgar portrayal of Jesus as a "go-getter."

Of necessity, those who challenged these prevailing doctrines are given the most space. The decade's rich harvest of social critics—among them Walter Lippmann, John Dewey, Joseph Wood Krutch, Lewis Mumford, and H. L. Mencken—deal with all these illiberal manifestations, and with the political apathy of the masses, the ugliness of American life, and the impact of "machine civilization" on the national culture. To name the subjects of their concern is to suggest their continuing relevance, whatever one thinks of their solutions. The words of two of the most famous dissenters are documented at moments of confrontation symbolic of the entire decade: Clarence Darrow cross-examining Bryan at the Dayton "monkey trial," and the radical pacifist Bartolomeo Vanzetti making his moving plea to the court before being unjustly sentenced to death.

Inevitably the creative writers dominate the anthology by the sheer brilliance of their prose. Ernest Hemingway, F. Scott Fitzgerald, and Edmund Wilson depict and comment critically on the literary scene, which in itself was a distinctive feature of the period. The writers also describe emerging moods and attitudes of the times: Samuel Hopkins Adams and Anita Loos, the new morality of the flapper; Hemingway and John Dos Passos, the anguish over the barbarism of the First World War; Sinclair Lewis, the revulsion with the values of the mid-American businessman booster, George Babbitt—what we now call "Babbittry."

It may have been a "Jazz Age," as Fitzgerald nostalgically remembers it in the final selection of the volume. Yet it is difficult not to conclude that the decade's best minds still have something to say to today's "age of soul" and "age of rock."

This volume is one of a series created to provide the essential primary sources of the American experience, especially of American thought. The series, when completed, will constitute a documentary library of American history, filling a need long felt among scholars, students, libraries, and general readers for authoritative collections of original materials. Some volumes will illuminate the thought of significant individuals, such as James Madison or Louis Brandeis; some will deal with movements, such as the Antifederalists or the Populists; others will be organized around special themes, such as Puritan political thought, or American Catholic thought on social questions. Many volumes will take up the large number of subjects traditionally studied in American history for which surprisingly there are no documentary anthologies; others will pioneer in introducing new subjects of increasing importance to scholars and to the contemporary world. The series aspires to maintain the high standards demanded of contemporary editing, providing authentic texts, intelligently and unobtrusively edited. It will also have the distinction of presenting pieces of substantial length which give the full character and flavor of the original. The series will be the most comprehensive and authoritative of its kind.

Alfred F. Young

Leonard W. Levy

Contents

I.

WAR: THE DISILLUSIONED

II.

POLITICAL FUNDAMENTALISM

III.

RELIGIOUS FUNDAMENTALISM

IV.

THE BUSINESS OF AMERICA

V.

THE YOUNGER GENERATION

VI.

THE WRITERS

VII.

THE SOCIAL CRITICS

VIII.

TECHNOLOGY

IX.

E P I L O G U E

Introduction

I

In his elegant and searching survey of the material implications of the work done at the Paris Peace Conference, John Maynard Keynes concluded that "we are at the dead season of our fortune." He believed that the war had produced the kind of emotional exhaustion that restricted vision, feeling, and thought to the limits of the self. According to Keynes, having implicated themselves so fully in the public realm during the war, men, especially in England and America, could no longer be moved by public events of whatever magnitude or intensity. In turning to the peace, such men turned from society; the men of a wounded world demanded the time now to attend to themselves. Thus it was, as Keynes put it in the final sentence of his book, that "the true voice of the new generation has not yet spoken, and silent opinion is not yet formed."[1] If Keynes was right, that "true voice" when it became audible might tell of somewhat unaccustomed things, might find the perhaps

[1] John Maynard Keynes, *The Economic Consequences of the Peace* (New York, 1920), pp. 297–298.

autonomous, perhaps isolated, perhaps alienated self a con-
tinuingly satisfying subject. Even if that should occur, however, the voice of the Twenties would not tell of things never
before heard in ways never before imagined. It did occur, and
it had a history. Thinking of the mid-Twenties, F. Scott Fitzgerald later remembered that "life . . . was largely a personal matter."[2] Fitzgerald, along with other writers, artists, and intellectuals who
flourished then, had a deep sense of the uniqueness of that
decade. Fitzgerald himself claimed to have found the most descriptive and characteristic label: he had baptized those years
"The Jazz Age."[3] And Gertrude Stein, following a lead given
her by the manager of a garage in Paris, gave Hemingway another, and more important, characterization: "All of you young
people who served in the war," she said. "You are a lost generation."[4]

The decade's writers seemed to agree with Keynes' worried
prophecy. Regardless of the attribute emphasized, many of the
most articulate spokesmen of the time eventually concluded
that they had occupied a parenthesis in historical time, one that
opened with the Armistice and closed with the Crash. The feeling of having come from nowhere and of being headed toward
no discoverable destination was described with sufficient power
to convince later generations that at least the cultural life of
the decade had in fact swung free in time. The writers of the
lost generation who occupied the Jazz Age in convincing themselves that they were rootless and aimless seem also to have
convinced others.

Though an important part of the brief in defense of their

[2]F. Scott Fitzgerald, *The Crack-Up,* ed. Edmund Wilson (New York,
1945), p. 70.
[3]F. Scott Fitzgerald to M. Perkins, May 21, 1931; *The Letters of F. Scott
Fitzgerald,* ed. Andrew Turnbull (New York, 1965), p. 225.
[4]Ernest Hemingway, *A Moveable Feast* (New York, 1964), p. 29.

uniqueness is true, it is too simple. Thinking for the moment only of Keynes' description of the retreat into privacy, and of Miss Stein's intended meaning about the loss of identity that came from war, one can easily—perhaps too easily—cast up an intellectual and emotional genealogy that would presumably prove that the ideas and tonalities of the Twenties had long been familiar in the American and European landscapes. The literature of disillusion has its own history, as does that of the feeling of cultural isolation. One need only open the American ledger to the pages devoted to Poe and Melville to see how rich and how clear that background is. The sense that the present generation has wearily climbed beyond earlier ones, that the present must suffer because of the stupidities of the past, that the son must break free from the father or lose his own authenticity, has characterized perhaps every single decade of the American story from the Puritans forward. The celebration of the private self and recoil from society may be found at the very heart of what most of the New England transcendentalists tried to say. None of this came new-born and fully developed from the forehead of Fitzgerald or anyone else.

It has been shown that a significant part of the generation immediately before World War I was itself in rebellion against many of the same aspects of middle-class American life that the men of the Twenties were to find inhibiting, stultifying, and suffocating.[5] This must mean that the war did not, as was so often assumed at the time and since, produce that pervasive wave of disillusion and, on occasion, pessimism that always seemed to rise to the surface of the Twenties. If similar disillu-

---

[5]See, for example, Henry F. May, *The End of American Innocence* (New York, 1959), *passim;* Christopher Lasch, *The New Radicalism in America, 1889–1963* (New York, 1965), pp. 253–254. The surge of poetry in the Twenties similarly began with the pre-war generation; see Conrad Aiken, "Poetry," *Civilization in the United States*, ed. Harold E. Stearns (New York, 1922), p. 217.

son existed before the war, how could the war be considered as its cause? As we shall see, the impeccable logic of that question may not turn out to be conclusive.

II

The stage was properly set by four quite different works that were all published in 1920. To understand the mood and thrust of each is to open the larger themes of that decade. In *Hugh Selwyn Mauberley,* Ezra Pound, with an electric condensation of rage and outrage, utterly rejected the war, repudiated the peace, and condemned that civilization whose rottenness was the cause of both. The corrupt complacencies of the antebellum world were replaced with new crimes. The political leaders of the world at peace were liars, and the young men who had died for their European countries had died "for an old bitch gone in the teeth."[6] The war, in Pound's view, was simply a catastrophic waste that was made necessary because of the power held by those pretty Victorians and Edwardians on both continents who would bleed the younger generation in order to conserve the corruption of the old.

Though Pound's temperature was higher than most, he spoke for a wide circle of articulate young people. The impact of that view on America was severe. George Santayana, in *Character and Opinion in the United States,* another work published in 1920, believed that recent experience had aged America, had functioned as a kind of puberty rite that symbolized the passage to adulthood, the passage from innocence to experience, from callowness to a sense of tragedy. As he saw it, America had been taught that it could no longer pretend to self-determination: "Hitherto America has been the land of universal good-

---

[6]Ezra Pound, *Hugh Selwyn Mauberley,* in Frederick J. Hoffman, *The Twenties: American Writing in the Postwar Decade* (New York, 1955), p. 438.

will, confidence in life, inexperience of poisons. Until yesterday
it believed itself immune from the hereditary plagues of mankind."[7]

The impact of this cultural shock on an individual can be
found in Fitzgerald's youthful and excited first book, *This Side
of Paradise*, also published in 1920. On the last page of this
novel, the narrator muses about the men at Princeton: "Here
was a new generation, shouting the old cries, learning the old
creeds, through a revery of long days and nights; destined
finally to go out into that dirty gray turmoil to follow love and
pride; a new generation dedicated more than the last to the
fear of poverty and the worship of success; grown up to find all
Gods dead, all wars fought, all faiths in man shaken."[8] If
Santayana was right, the discovery that America was suscepti-
ble to ugliness and pain meant, for the young Fitzgerald, an
instant world-weariness. American faith when shaken once
seemed completely destroyed. Pleasure was the residual goal,
along with the glamor and private power that formed the foundation of the Jazz Age.

Sinclair Lewis' *Main Street* completes this quartet of works
published in the first year of the Twenties. It was in many ways,
despite its occasionally cardboard characters, the single most
premonitory work. In the context of the three other works,
Lewis' intention can be put this way: Was the past dead in
fact? Had the war been rejected? Had America gone through
its rites of passage? Were Gods and faiths dead? There were
places in America, he answered, where none of this was true
in even the slightest degree. In the American small town the
terrible education suffered by an intellectual or artistic elite
was simply unavailable.

The mentality of non-metropolitan America did not have to
agonize about the tragic in modern life. The pieties and faiths

[7]George Santayana, *Character and Opinion in the United States* (Garden City, N.Y.: Doubleday Anchor, 1956), p. 89.
[8]F. Scott Fitzgerald, *This Side of Paradise* (New York, 1920), p. 282.

of a more comfortable past remained untouched and unyielding. Lewis telegraphed his attitude at once, in the opening lines of the foreword to the novel: "Main Street is the climax of civilization. That this Ford car might stand in front of the Bon Ton Store, Hannibal invaded Rome and Erasmus wrote in Oxford cloisters."[9] The small town and small city, against which so many American intellectuals, artists, and writers revolted in the Twenties, seemed—at least superficially—sufficiently secure not to take particular notice of the latest noise from America's bohemia. Evidently closed to new possibilities, to alternatives, the village, as Lewis sketched it, continued to define itself as both the center and goal of the universe.

Carol Kennicott, the often simultaneously rebellious and acquiescent heroine of *Main Street,* confessed that American mythology had acquainted her with only two traditions about the village. The first told that the small town was the essential repository of all virtue, the single habitat of "clean, sweet marriageable girls."[10] Ambitious boys might forsake their parental homestead in search of success or sophistication, but they would ultimately come to their senses, return to the village, rediscover the childhood sweetheart, marry, settle down, and live happily ever after. The other tradition described the town as rich in local color, picturesque, and infinitely amusing in its "whiskered rusticity." The truths that Carol discovered about Gopher Prairie tell what most of America's creative people thought of the American village, and consequently, of the American past:

It is an unimaginatively standardized background, a sluggishness of speech and manners, a rigid ruling of the spirit by the desire to appear respectable. It is contentment . . . the contentment of the quiet dead, who are scornful of the living for their restless walking.

[9]Sinclair Lewis, *Main Street* (New York, 1920), "Foreword."
[10]*Ibid.,* p. 264.

It is negation canonized as the one positive virtue. It is the prohibition of happiness. It is slavery self-sought and self-defended. It is dullness made God.

A savorless people, gulping tasteless food, and sitting afterward, coatless and thoughtless, in rocking-chairs prickly with inane decorations, listening to mechanical music, saying mechanical things about the excellence of Ford automobiles, and viewing themselves as the greatest race in the world.[11]

Though Carol believed that the prairie had a perhaps magnificent future, she finally concluded that she had somehow to resist its present. Urging a young man to break away, to go East, she also urged him to return in order to explain what the citizens of Gopher Prairie should do with the land they were clearing, "if," she said, "we'll listen—if we don't lynch you first!"[12]

What Carol demanded of her husband and of Gopher Prairie was the substitution of one kind of sublimation for another. Thinking of the wives of American villagers as a part of the oppressed classes of the world,[13] she thought "we want a more conscious life." She felt unable to continue living a life of postponement as "the politicians and priests and cautious reformers (and the husbands!)" continually advised. She demanded her own Utopia, and now: "All we want is—everything for all of us!"[14] She knew she would fail, and explained that this was why she would never be content. She did not have secret yearnings for the heady atmosphere of bohemia; she wanted everything, to be sure, but everything that would still comport with her own sense of decorum, a sense not entirely different from her husband's.

[11]*Ibid.*, p. 265.
[12]*Ibid.*, p. 343.
[13]Cf. F. Scott Fitzgerald to his daughter, October 5, 1940, in *Letters*, p. 96: ". . . I think the faces of most American women over thirty are relief maps of petulant and bewildered unhappiness."
[14]Lewis, *Main Street*, p. 201.

III

To encounter provincial America only in the writings of those who had declared war on it is finally to see merely a bizarre, pathetic, and infinitely comic phenomenon. Ludwig Lewisohn, Sherwood Anderson, and, above all, H. L. Mencken could conjure up the simple yokel whose five thumbs made him a lower order of creature, but that view is disabling in respect to the yokel's political strength. The American province, to put it most simply, was also committed to war, had a vast and dangerous arsenal, and won almost every major battle it had entered. It was in virtual control of America's public life during the Twenties, and the dismay of the writers and artists cannot be fully understood in any other context. They could dream of a world free of the province, but the present provincial hegemony made it impossible to predict what that world would be like. "Who knows," Walter Lippmann asked, "having read Mr. Mencken and Mr. Sinclair Lewis, what kind of world will be left when all the boobs and yokels have crawled back in their holes and have died in shame?"[15] And those creatures would refuse to crawl away without a bitter fight. One example will make the point; a newspaper editor and supporter of the Prohibition Party designed his early tirade to catch virtually all of the vibrations in America's provincial civilization:

Besodden Europe, worse bescourged than by war, famine and pestilence, sends here her drink-makers, her drunkard-makers, and her drunkards, or her more temperate but habitual drinkers, with all their un-American and anti-American ideas of morality and government; they are absorbed into our national life, but not assimilated; with no liberty whence they came, they demand unrestricted liberty among us, even to license for things we loathe; and through the ballot-box, flung wide open to them by foolish statesmanship that

[15]Walter Lippmann, *A Preface to Morals* (New York, 1929), p. 16.

covets power, their foreign control or conquest has become largely an appalling fact; they dominate our Sabbath, over large areas of country; they have set up for us their own moral standards, which are grossly immoral; they govern our great cities, until even Reform candidates accept their authority and pledge themselves to obey it; the great cities govern the nation; and foreign control or conquest could gain little more, though secured by foreign armies and fleets.[16]

Mencken's "yokel" might amuse the sophisticated, but the yokel might have found the sometimes frantic parody funny too. He must have known something about political power because, although he had to fight, he almost always won. The fight, for him, was to implement that phrase of Harding's: "not heroics but healing; not nostrums but normalcy; not revolution but restoration." As the intellectual could reject the war because the peace had not gone far enough, provincial Americans apparently grew restive because it had gone too far. The public policy the villager and the burgher demanded was all designed to create a known and presumably safer but seriously threatened earlier America. The legislation sought was intended to recreate that supposedly more congenial time when values were clearer, when religion was more secure, when intellectuals were supposedly more housebroken, when the farmer was supposedly dominant in the fields cleared from God's country.

William Jennings Bryan, the complete spokesman of rural and sometimes of provincial America, could seem thoroughly ludicrous to some, but he too knew something. He knew that the nation had changed, that urbanization and industrialism together with enormous immigration were generating political, economic, and even moral forces that were repugnant to the idyllic, Protestant, and democratic America he envisaged. He knew that something more important than the publication of the four books mentioned above occurred in 1920: for the first time

[16]Alphonso Alva Hopkins, quoted in Andrew Sinclair, *Prohibition, the Era of Excess* (Boston, 1962), p. 19.

in American history, according to the census bureau, more Americans were living in cities than in the countryside and villages combined. This single fact may explain some of the urgency in the battle of the small town and small city against continued uncontrolled change.

The massive power of non-metropolitan America may best be understood by viewing national policy and significant social phenomena as designed to arrest change or not, as intended to recapture the alleged simplicity and morality of a past but still desired rural civilization. "Foreign" influences in national or religious terms, urban power together with its pathology in crime and corruption, and the intellectual life constituted the dark trinity which the villager and the burgher were determined to destroy.

In simple economic terms, the American farmer suffered depression throughout most of the decade; in simple occupational terms, the Republican presidents represented business, not farmers or villagers. But in a wider perspective, the provincial mentality was virtually incarnate in Harding and Coolidge, and Hoover, too, spoke with and for the village in the special circumstance of his rival's thoroughly urban, Catholic, and wet background. It is true that rural political insurgency continued to sputter through the Twenties, but the dominant issues were no longer political. The collapsing alliance between old-time urban and rural reformers, the failure of national leadership, prosperity, exhaustion, boredom, and fear of change, together with Wilson's own example of defeat, all combined to wound if not destroy the earlier Progressive movement.[17] The small city— Zenith, Sinclair Lewis called it—exercised its power over the nation through its values, attitudes, and ideals; though it would

[17]See, for example, Arthur S. Link, "What Happened to the Progressive Movement in the 1920's?" *American Historical Review*, LXIV, 4 (July 1959), 833–851; Richard Hofstadter, *The Age of Reform* (New York, 1960), esp. pp. 272–301; Arthur M. Schlesinger, Jr., *The Crisis of the Old Order* (Boston, 1957), pp. 11–124.

be beset from perhaps desperate farmers on the one side, and the urban middle classes along with intellectuals on the other, it could generally rely on enough support in all quarters to ensure victory.

In their terms, the most abstract battle fought by villagers and their allies in small cities was the place and role of the United States in world affairs. Whether they were simple isolationists is an on-going debate.[18] We know, obviously, that the League of Nations was repudiated, though American participation, such as it was, increased throughout the decade. The Kellogg-Briand Pact intended to outlaw war through the moral pressure of world opinion. And American corporate interests extended to virtually every corner of the world. But public policy was not planned in the major cities; Zenith's George Babbitt, with his realtor's reflexes, could smile indulgently at the wishful thinking of the Kellogg-Briand Pact, could smile unreservedly in appreciation of the expansion and extension of American business (and therefore approve high protective tariffs), and he could bristle with indignation over the League with its supposed threat of "furrin" control.

The key to provincial desires and power, one that opens the door to almost everything else, is Prohibition, the single most revealing phenomenon of the time. It too, appropriately, went into effect in the first year of the decade, and was to last almost fourteen years. This "noble experiment" was preëminently the creature of the provincial, middle class, Protestant, white American. The alinement over the Eighteenth Amendment in the House of Representatives shows what happened. 197 representatives supported the Amendment; 129 were from towns of

---

[18]McGeorge Bundy, "Foreign Policy: From Innocence to Engagement," *Paths of American Thought*, ed. A. M. Schlesinger, Jr., and Morton White (Boston, 1963), pp. 293–308; George F. Kennan, *American Diplomacy* (Chicago, 1951), pp. 55–73; William Appleman Williams, "The Legend of Isolationism in the 1920's," *Science and Society*, XVIII (Winter 1954), 1–20.

xxvi   *Introduction*

less than 10,000, and 64 came from villages of less than 2,500. 190 representatives opposed the Amendment; 109 came from cities of over 25,000. "In fact," as the movement's most acute historian put it, "national prohibition was a measure passed by village America against urban America."[19] The war brought urban allies to the villager because of the identification of beer with the Kaiser, of alcohol with unpatriotic waste and selfishness during a national crisis. This alliance made the ratification of the Eighteenth Amendment possible. After the Volstead Act and with peace, the urban-village coalition broke, showing the determined core of Prohibitionism to be where it always was: in the Methodist and Baptist churches, in villages and towns all across the nation, among Southerners fearful of drunken Negroes and employers wanting sober laborers and afraid of drunken agitators, and among nativists who believed that swarthy and alien types would commit their worst excesses if given access to booze. An historian caught the basic strategy of the Prohibitionists: "The emotion which they exploited was fear: The fear of sin and God; the fear of race against race and skin against skin; the fear of venereal diseases; the fear of idiot children; the fear of violence suppressed by conscience and loosed by liquor; and the dark sexual fears of civilization."[20] The rich and middle class urbanite could get liquor if he wanted it, but had to contribute to Al Capone to do it, thereby confirming the dry villagers in all of their suspicions about urban corruption, the wages of sin, and the menace of foreigners. Nothing less than the protection of God and country was involved in Prohibition, and the provincial American was militant.

These same goals became the battle cry of the renewed Ku Klux Klan whose membership rose to approximately four mil-

[19]Sinclair, *Prohibition*, p. 163.
[20]*Ibid.*, p. 46.

lion in the Twenties. Prohibition and the Klan both aimed at restoring the values of an earlier America, values which were eroding under the waves of immigrants, cities, irreligion, science, and modernity in general. A dentist from Texas, Hiram Wesley Evans, became the national leader, the Imperial Wizard and Emperor, of the Klan in 1922, and a few years later published an article which shows that he viewed his organization as the only effective defense of traditional America, as a brake on noxious change, and as the true locus of patriotism.

Klansmen, according to Evans, "have enlisted our racial instincts for the work of preserving and developing our American traditions and customs."[21] He argued that the Klan had succeeded in limiting its earlier violence and internal corruption, and had now thrown its full weight against the results of the melting pot which, he said, the Klan considered "a ghastly failure" whose "very name was coined by a member of one of the races—the Jews—which most determinedly refuses to melt."[22] No alien and no "alien idea" could be tolerated in the America he envisaged. In order to purge successfully, the Klan had broken with liberalism because this persuasion "had provided no defense against the alien invasion, but instead had excused it—even defended it against Americanism. Liberalism," Evans said, "is today charged in the mind of most Americans with nothing less than national, racial and spiritual treason."[23] The Klan supposedly opposed the Catholic Church on political rather than religious grounds, and, following the lead of Madison Grant and Lothrop Stoddard, opposed the Negro and Eastern European Jews on racial grounds, and Western European Jews on religious grounds. All constituted a direct menace

[21]Hiram Wesley Evans, "The Klan's Fight for Americanism," *The North American Review*, CCXXIII (March–May 1926), 35. See Document 8.
[22]*Ibid.*, 40.
[23]*Ibid.*, 49.

for the white, Protestant, Anglo-Saxon American villager. Knowing that he and his kind were under some kind of attack for being villagers, Evans took the offensive:

We are a movement of the plain people, very weak in the matter of culture, intellectual support, and trained leadership. We are demanding, and we expect to win, a return of power into the hands of the everyday, not highly cultured, not overly intellectualized, but entirely unspoiled and not de-Americanized average citizen of the old stock. . . . This is undoubtedly a weakness. It lays us open to the charge of being 'hicks' and 'rubes' and 'drivers of second hand Fords.' We admit it. . . . The Klan does not believe that the fact that it is emotional and instinctive, rather than coldly intellectual, is a weakness. . . . [Emotions and instincts] are the foundations of our American civilization, even more than our great historic documents; they can be trusted where the fine-haired reasoning of the denatured intellectuals cannot.[24]

Evans was responding to all of the strains in the provincial mentality: the alleged moral superiority, evangelical and fundamentalist religion, anti-intellectualism, racism, nativism, and hypertrophy of patriotism. The imposition of quotas based on national origin (favoring those nations in which the villager's own family had probably originated) in the new immigration policies of the Twenties shows that Evans was, in many ways, merely giving voice to attitudes which small town America could and did enact into the law of the land. That the pressures for immigration restriction came from diverse interests and sections means that, once again, the villager and small city American could rely on outside support on specific issues. Intellectuals would protest that the idea of the great, blue-eyed blond Nordic was a groundless "myth,"[25] but, groundless or not, it con-

[24]*Ibid.*, 49–51.
[25]See, for example, C. E. Ayres, "The New Higher Criticism," *The New Republic*, XLV (December 9, 1925), 85–86.

tributed to the blood knowledge of the Klan, as well as to national attitudes toward immigration.

That myth lurks also in the background of the Red Scare of 1919 and the early Twenties, and the subsequent Palmer raids. A. Mitchell Palmer, the Attorney General, invented and initiated neither the fright nor the retribution. He was himself an expression of and vulnerable to the pressures from Zenith. Sharing the growing fear of revolution that would be caused by recent immigrants, Palmer once described those aliens arrested in his raids: "Out of the sly and crafty eyes of many of them leap cupidity, cruelty, insanity, and crime; from their lopsided faces, sloping brows, and misshapen features may be recognized the unmistakable criminal types."[26] The east side of New York was the most favored lair of the Leon Bronstein, alias Trotsky, type dedicated to the overthrow of Zenith, hence nation, hence God. At the very beginning of the decade, on January 2, the Palmer raids reached their height, with over 6,000 people taken into custody in the ensuing weeks.[27] If the alien could be deported, as legislation of May 1920 provided, and prevented from entering, as the new immigration policies provided, the old-stock American with his ideals and values would presumably be safer.

The alien threat was supposedly proved by the arrest and conviction of two semi-literate Italian radicals, Sacco and Vanzetti, confessed pacifists and draft-dodgers. Arrested for murder, in a trial dominated by the issues of patriotism and radicalism, they were actually convicted of being alien. Again sophisticated men protested, as Felix Frankfurter did: "By systematic exploitation of the defendants' alien blood, their imperfect knowledge of English, their unpopular social views, and their opposition to the war, the District Attorney invoked against them a riot of political passion and patriotic sentiment;

[26]Quoted in Stanley Coben, *A. Mitchell Palmer: Politician* (New York, 1963), p. 198.

[27]*Ibid.*, p. 227.

and the trial judge connived at—one had almost written, cooperated in—the process."[28] The fears of the American provinces, whether Muncie or elsewhere, determined that Sacco and Vanzetti should be executed.

These fears, as the Klan understood perfectly well, included the basic fear that alien gods would stalk the land, along with alien beer and ideologies, unless the Nordic American fought back. Religious Fundamentalism was perhaps the most authentic expression of this native fight, and Fundamentalism was a ligament that held Prohibition, the Klan, and nativism together. Billy Sunday's "booze sermon" demanded more than abstinence; he called for the deportation of foreigners involved in bootlegging, as well as other dissenters who refused to kiss the American flag.[29] Mencken (in the *American Mercury*) and Sinclair Lewis (in *Elmer Gantry*) poured scorn on the evangelists who wrapped the cross in the flag and carried it in a Bible, who baptized by the thousands, and who attacked booze, Darwin, and anarchy all in the same long breath. But Fundamentalism, as an intense folk movement, could fight back, claiming, as the Klan claimed, that too much education and piety were mutually exclusive.[30]

Fundamentalism's best champion was William Jennings Bryan, and his chosen field for his final battle was Dayton, Tennessee. The Scopes trial, with Bryan and Clarence Darrow facing each other, had to do with whether it was a punishable crime to teach evolution in the public schools, but it also had to do with the continuing struggle between small and large cities. Bryan had protested against the theory of evolution since the beginning of the twentieth century, but the fears that became exacerbated during the Twenties convinced him that direct action was then required. The silver-tongued orator

[28]Felix Frankfurter, "The Case of Sacco and Vanzetti," *The Atlantic Monthly*, CXXXIX, 3 (March 1927), 421. See Document 9.

[29]Sinclair, *Prohibition*, p. 290.

[30]Norman F. Furniss, *The Fundamentalist Controversy 1918–1931* (New Haven, 1954), especially pp. 39–41.

shared so much of the provincial mood that he, too, adopted
the usual aggressive apology for the lack of literary felicity of
his adherents, and he, too, mounted an attack against cleverness
and mind which must kill God. Early in the decade he accused
that generation of "mind-worship—a worship as destructive as
any other form of idolatry."[31] The head and the heart were at
war, which meant, to him, that America's folk religion was being
subverted by most of the dark forces of the city:

A scientific soviet is attempting to dictate what shall be taught in
our schools and, in so doing, is attempting to mould the religion of
the nation. It is the smallest, the most impudent, and the most tyrannical oligarchy that ever attempted to exercise arbitrary power.[32]

H. L. Mencken chortled, Darrow referred to Bryan's "fool
ideas," but Bryan was more than the incredible figure that
journalists and intellectuals exploited. Until he died a few days
after the Scopes trial, he was the voice of non-metropolitan
America, especially so in Fundamentalism.

The political and social power of the non-urban American
means, of course, that he was something other than the silly
clown that emerged from Mencken's pages. But Mencken also
knew that provincial America had muscle, that he and fellow
cosmopolites could not control the legislatures. These words,
obviously, are his: "Our laws are invented, in the main, by
frauds and fanatics, and put upon the statute books by pol-
troons and scoundrels."[33] But others, too, understood the pervasive public power of the small town, and wrote that it was
necessary at least "secretly" to acknowledge that fact:

The civilization of America is predominantly the civilization of
the small town. The few libertarians and cosmopolites who can con-

---

[31]Quoted in Lawrence W. Levine, *Defender of the Faith. William Jennings Bryan. The Last Decade, 1915–1925* (New York, 1965), p. 279.
[32]*Ibid.*, p. 289.
[33]H. L. Mencken, *Notes on Democracy* (New York, 1926), p. 129.

tinue to profess to see a broader culture developing along the Atlantic seaboard resent this fact, though they scarcely deny it. They are too intelligent, too widened in vision to deny it. They cannot watch the tremendous growth and power and influence of secret societies, of chambers of commerce, of boosters' clubs, of the Ford car, of moving pictures, of talking-machines, of evangelists, of nerve tonics, of the *Saturday Evening Post*, of Browning societies, of circuses, of church socials, of parades and pageants of every kind and description, of family reunions, of pioneer picnics, of county fairs, of firemen's conventions without secretly acknowledging it. And they know, if they have obtained a true perspective of America, that there is no section of this vast political unit that does not possess—and even frequently boast—these unmistakably provincial signs and symbols.[34]

Clearly enough, it was the strength, not the pathos or mere uncongeniality of the provinces, that made the writers and artists react in the ways they did. If it had been simply the latter, parody would have sufficed; but expatriation and high art aimed at the provinces are symptoms of the power of the enemy.

IV

One result of the political power of the American small town and small city was the decision on the part of many intellectuals and writers simply to withdraw from politics. The disgust with that political process which had led to war and to Versailles also contributed to political quiescence. Whether the enemy was Babbitt or Woodrow Wilson, or—more likely—both, the result was the same: Fitzgerald's concept of life as a "personal matter."

Joseph Freeman, later to become an editor of a politically radical journal, remembered a canoe trip he had taken with a friend; reciting Plato and Swinburne, neither could list the

[34]Louis R. Reid, "The Small Town," *Civilization*, ed. Stearns, p. 286.

terms of the Treaty of Versailles.[35] And much more extreme, but more indicative, George Jean Nathan, Mencken's partner in parody, exploded:

> The great problems of the world—social, political, economic and theological—do not concern me in the slightest. If all the Armenians were to be killed tomorrow and if half of Russia were to starve to death the day after, it would not matter to me in the least. What concerns me alone is myself, and the interests of a few close friends. For all I care the rest of the world may go to hell at today's sunset.[36]

The phenomenon of political retreat was sufficiently widespread to engage the attention of at least two important social analysts. By 1927 Walter Lippmann had concluded that the combination of party splintering and affluence had given rise to bewilderment, complacency, and cynicism. It was, he argued, one thing to feel disgust with politics, but another to be able to avoid it; affluence made the difference. Social questions concerning the Klan, Prohibition, Fundamentalism, immigration, evolution, and xenophobia continued to interest the electorate as phases in the war between province and city, but they were issues usually outside the formal political process. The economic boom, according to Lippmann, allowed these social issues to exist outside of politics,[37] as it allowed President Coolidge to announce that America's business was business.

John Dewey, in the same year, considered other reasons for this apathy. He also believed that the public was politically bewildered, but he concluded that the public had lost its political existence. The inability to identify with concrete issues resulted in the retreat from politics; the increasing complexity of Ameri-

---

[35]Joseph Freeman, *An American Testament* (New York, 1936), p. 154.

[36]George Jean Nathan, quoted in William E. Leuchtenburg, *The Perils of Prosperity 1914–1932* (Chicago, 1958), p. 150.

[37]Walter Lippmann, "The Causes of Political Indifference To-Day," *The Atlantic Monthly*, CXXXIX, 2 (February 1927), 261–268. See Document 11.

can life made such concrete issues increasingly hard to find and, more important, created a crippling discrepancy between current political needs and the traditional political machinery. That discrepancy made the traditional actions and pronouncements of political leaders seem increasingly irrelevant to what people cared most about.[38]

The present era of 'prosperity' may not be enduring. But the movie, radio, cheap reading matter and motor car with all they stand for have come to stay. That they did not originate in deliberate desire to divert attention from political interests does not lessen their effectiveness in that direction. The political elements in the constitution of the human being, those having to do with citizenship, are crowded to one side. In most circles it is hard work to sustain conversation on a political theme; and once initiated, it is quickly dismissed with a yawn. Let there be introduced the topic of the mechanism and accomplishment of various makes of motor cars or the respective merits of actresses, and the dialogue goes on at a lively pace.[39]

This complexity, furthermore, made decisions often too technical and specialized to create a devoted public, with the result that the public atomized. For this reason, no genuine community could be created, and that fact made a further advance in democratic efficiency impossible.[40] A genuine public, held together by political conviction and involvement, was a necessary and anterior condition to meaningful reform. As things stood, politics had degenerated into a mere reflex: "Only habit and tradition, rather than a reasoned conviction, together with a vague faith in doing one's civic duty, send to the polls a considerable percentage of the fifty percent who still vote."[41]

[38]John Dewey, *The Public and Its Problems* (New York, 1927), pp. 122–123, 134–135.
[39]*Ibid.*, p. 139.
[40]*Ibid.*, pp. 157–158.
[41]*Ibid.*, p. 135.

By now it is clear that Lippmann and Dewey had more in mind than the political withdrawal of scholars, writers, and artists. They were addressing a national problem that was manifested almost everywhere. The provincial American could retire with the conviction that he was the master of the legislature; the intellectuals and artists could thumb their noses at the public sector as they set out to explore what they believed to be more important terrain. But between the country village and Greenwich Village the rest of America lived. Relatively affluent, basically unchallenged, middle-class urban Americans constituted the middle term between the little old lady in Dubuque and the literary exile in Paris. This middle term was the world of the Jazz Age, flapper, speakeasy, and the rest. Reaching both forward and backward, it knew it was not truly of either world. It was the booming New Era, the Roaring Twenties. But it too was caught by the power of the village; it had to consume its booze secretly lest the village law cause embarrassment.

Urban America was not so far from its own rural or village past that the Red Scare would pass it by, that the Anti-Saloon League could find only a few urban adherents, that anti-immigration was a dead issue, that xenophobia generated no pressure. This middle America, as it were, would laugh with Mencken, frown with Sinclair Lewis, but without full certainty. It made best-sellers of both *Main Street* and *Elmer Gantry* along with Emily Post's *Etiquette* and, more revealing, Bruce Barton's *The Man Nobody Knows* (see Document 18). The most popular tunes, "Dinah" and "Ol' Man River," recalled the rural past, though Chaplin's popular comedies were invariably urban in spirit if not in setting.

This urban America, feeling somewhat free of older sexual restraints, could tolerate the fashions of the flapper. Held's cartoon character inspired this craze and was a point-by-point repudiation of the earlier ideal of femininity, the Gibson girl. The Gibson girl had flowing hair, the flapper bobbed hers; shoulders, breasts, and the waistline were emphasized before

the war, but the flapper bound her breasts flat and wore loosely
fitted blouses; legs were voluminously covered by the Gibson
girl, and the flapper raised her hemline above her knees and
rolled her stockings below them. The matter of sex created a vast urban market for a new
publishing adventure. The sex "confession" and picture maga-
zine made several fortunes. And yet, enough of the older morality survived to create incredible but by now familiar attitudes,
as a letter an editor sent as instructions to his authors will
show:

I intend to keep—a sex magazine, but sex need not necessarily mean
dirt. I want to stick to elementals, sex-elementals—the things closest
to the heart of the average woman or girl, whatever her ignorance
or sophistication. Above all, I mean to lift the moral tone of the
magazine. I believe that to treat sex trivially is to diminish its dramatic value, while sober treatment enhances it. Characters may do
anything they please but they must do it from some lofty, or apparently lofty, motive. If a girl falls, she must fall *upward*.[42]

The ostensible freedom of the flapper, her flat rejection of
the modishness of the past, was countered by the village ma-
tron's firm conviction about the relevance and applicability of
earlier standards and usages. The villager had to embark on no
quest for spiritual authority; morality, purity, and the home
were, for him, unshaken though under criticism from the city.
One civilized man, struggling to keep his spirit alive while he
was teaching at Ohio State, encountered, to his obvious dismay,
that provincial type: "thin-lipped, embittered by the poisons
that unnatural repression breeds, with a curious flatness about
the temples, with often, among the older men, a wiry, belligerent beard." He saw them with their ladies, "shallow-bosomed,

---

[42]Quoted in Ernest W. Mandeville, "Gutter Literature," *The New Republic*, XLV (February 17, 1926), 350.

ill-favored wives—stern advocates of virtue—walking on Sunday self-consciously to church."[43]

For intellectuals and artists, the brutality of the war that led only to the repugnant peace, together with the political prominence of provincial America, seemed to force them into themselves, seemed to produce precisely what Keynes had feared. Feeling betrayed by history in war and peace, and assaulted by the present in Prohibition, anti-evolution, and the rest, they tended to withdraw from society, actually to become exiles or to become unpolitical, perhaps anti-social, and probably alienated strangers at home. The lost generation was created by the war and non-urban America.

For the urban middle class, the brutality of the war could be forgotten in the bubbly ambience of the Jazz Age. Babe Ruth, mah jong, and crossword puzzles could, apparently, capture and hold attention. But affluence was the key; Fords and movie stars made their significant contribution to the de-politicization of the urban middle class. The sense, however, that the New Era was an intense moment of personal liberation, of sexual freedom for women as well as men, evidently places the urbanite at least partly in the camp of the exiles. The past was as dead, disabling, and irrelevant to the urbanite as to the exile, as the flapper showed when she contradicted Gibson in such perfect detail. Also besieged by the village, the middle class could acquiesce more easily than the exiles. But enough feeling of futility was generated to induce some city dwellers to embark on Fitzgerald's quest for cash and success. Privacy was the result, and, though for dramatically different reasons, the flapper and the exile both turned their backs on society in their respective celebrations of the autonomous and inviolate individual. And neither could find a usable social past.

The search, not for a usable past, but for an alternative to

[43]Ludwig Lewisohn, *Up Stream* (New York, 1922), p. 186.

the past is another of the revealing symptoms of the decade. The resulting conflict of generations gave at least one disillusioned intellectual grounds for measured optimism: "The most hopeful thing of intellectual promise in America today is the contempt of the younger people for their elders; they are restless, uneasy, disaffected." From this clash of old and new, the young would "attempt to create a way of life free from the bondage of an authority that has lost all meaning, even to those who wield it."[44] That this was an echo of a similar charge made by the pre-war generation—by Randolph Bourne in 1915, for example—should not obscure the fact that the special circumstances of the Twenties gave a new urgency and intensity to the paean to youth, to the condemnation of age. These circumstances similarly created the sense that since all guideposts were down the future could be newly charted. But those guideposts had once kept men from getting hopelessly lost; they once had given a certain security; they once had signified that at least part of the world was known. Freedom from the past was liberating, but also perhaps frightening.

The villager had succeeded in preventing a free experimental method in politics, to John Dewey's dismay. Sanctifying the political institutions of the nation, the American villager was preventing significant change, maintaining control, and participating in a widespread human process: "As supernatural matters have progressively been left high and dry upon a secluded beach, the actuality of religious taboos has more and more gathered about secular institutions, especially those connected with the nationalistic state."[45] This is simply a different way of saying that the small town had succeeded in dominating political institutions, thereby making the political process as such an anachronism for most intellectuals and artists.

[44]Harold E. Stearns, "The Intellectual Life," *Civilization*, ed. Stearns, p. 149. See Document 27. Cf., however, Lewis Mumford, "The Emergence of a Past, *The New Republic*, XLV (November 25, 1925), 18–19.
[45]Dewey, *The Public and Its Problems*, p. 170.

Walter Lippmann's *A Preface to Morals* was a key text that tied together the themes of the irrelevance of politics and society, the fearfulness of an unmapped terrain, and the concomitant retreat into self. He explained that the death of God had left men without satisfying explanations of what they were compelled to do, had left them unable to refer to a universe teleologically organized. When an earlier American:

believed that the unfolding of events was a manifestation of the will of God, he could say: Thy will be done. . . . [*sic*] In His will is our peace. But when he believes that events are determined by the votes of a majority, the orders of his bosses, the opinions of his neighbors, the laws of supply and demand, and the decisions of quite selfish men, he yields because he has to yield. He is conquered but unconvinced.[46]

Where the small town could control events, other Americans were conquered but unconvinced. Where the small town could not, other Americans were freer, but that too was a complicated freedom. Lippmann believed that the Twenties, for the first time in human history, made authoritative belief impossible for large masses of men. Massive and radical irreligion (always excepting provincial America) contributed to the destruction of those older guideposts that left men now free to walk new but obscure and therefore dangerous paths. Worrying that man's greater difficulties would only begin when he was free to do as he pleased, Lippmann got under the surface of the times:

The evidences of these greater difficulties lie all about us: in the brave and brilliant atheists who have defied the Methodist God, and have become very nervous; in the women who have emancipated themselves from the tyranny of fathers, husbands, and homes, and with the intermittent but expensive help of a psychoanalyst, are now enduring liberty as interior decorators; in the young men and women

[46]Lippmann, *Preface to Morals,* p. 10.

who are world-weary at twenty-two; in the multitudes who drug themselves with pleasure; in the crowds enfranchised by the blood of heroes who cannot be persuaded to take an interest in their destiny; in the millions, at last free to think without fear of priest or policeman, who have made the moving pictures and the popular newspapers what they are.[47]

By the end of the decade, Lippmann said, the problem for young urban America was no longer that of mounting an attack on the stupidities, pieties, and inhibitions of their close-kneed parents. That attack had already succeeded. The square dance was no longer audible over the bounce of the Charleston. The privacy of the back seat of their cars gave the young an opportunity to be sexually freer than ever before. Their rebellion for greater moral freedom had been won, but the young, according to Lippmann, had now to deal with the sobering consequences of this success: "When he has slain the dragon and rescued the beautiful maiden, there is usually nothing left for him to do but write his memoirs and dream of a time when the world was young."[48] The distinguishing characteristic of the young generation of the Twenties was therefore not merely the fact of rebellion against the ethical and moral codes of the past, but its disillusionment with its own rebellion. Such modern men, repelled by the village, bewildered by the present, were radically alone; following Fitzgerald's sigh over a world whose past faiths and Gods had died, Lippmann now probed a little deeper into the mood of the young:

They have seen through the religion of nature to which the early romantics turned for consolation. They have heard too much about the brutality of natural selection to feel, as Wordsworth did, that pleasant landscapes are divine. They have seen through the religion of beauty because, for one thing, they are too much oppressed by

[47]*Ibid.*, p. 6.
[48]*Ibid.*, p. 17.

the ugliness of Main Street. They cannot take refuge in an ivory
tower because the modern apartment house, with a radio loud-
speaker on the floor above and on the floor below and just across the
courtyard, will not permit it. They cannot, like Mazzini, make a religion of patriotism, because they have just been demobilized. They
cannot make a religion of science like the post-Darwinians because
they do not understand modern science. They never learned enough
mathematics and physics. They do not like Bernard Shaw's religion
of creative evolution because they have read enough to know that
Mr. Shaw's biology is literary and evangelical. As for the religion of
progress, that is preempted by George F. Babbitt and the Rotary
Club, and the religion of humanity is utterly unacceptable to those
who have to ride in the subways during the rush hours.[49]

The meaninglessness of society, the absurdity of a purposeless nature, and the richly textured mood of combined pleasure
and isolation, all coalesced to encourage exploration of the
increasingly fascinating world of the ego. Having just heard
about Freud, the modern man learned that there were things
about himself that even he did not know. The several pressures
of the decade pushed him inward. His own moods and motives,
preferences and aversions, were hugely more interesting than
the antics of villagers, and more interesting, too, than maintaining vigilance against an older generation that was too preoccu-
pied with making money to counter-charge. "His inferiority
complex and mine, your sadistic impulse and Tom Jones's,
Anna's father fixation, and little Willie's pyromania"[50] were, in
Lippmann's view, the substitute for tradition. Personal rather
than social history became relevant, and psychoanalysis was
the new way to make the past usable—the past of the individual, not the group. Sherwood Anderson summed this up in *Dark
Laughter:* "If there is anything you do not understand in human
life consult the works of Dr. Freud."[51] Guilt replaced con-

[49]*Ibid.*, p. 18.
[50]*Ibid.*, p. 18.
[51]Sherwood Anderson, *Dark Laughter* (New York, 1925), p. 230.

science, and Freud taught the rebels lesson after lesson, showing reason after dark reason why the rejection of the parental
code was essential to health. As the parent became the metaphor of the past, the child became that of the present. Such
personifications could not and were not intended to disguise
what was happening: the individual and his past were replacing
the world and its history.

The massive presentism that resulted was reflected in the
works of some of the leading intellectuals of the decade. The
presentism of the "New History" of Robinson and Beard, the
institutional economics of Veblen that demanded a repudiation
of classical economics, and Dewey's "reconstruction in philosophy" that rejected his empirical and classical predecessors in
philosophy—all attempted to start afresh, to re-design their
tools for modern tasks, and to bring serious thought to bear
seriously on the pervasive present.[52]

The idea of progress was one of the casualties of the war, the
peace, the village, and Freudianism. A humanistic celebration
of the steady and irrevocable march of civilization to higher
and higher plateaus of achievement became increasingly difficult for those who were now questioning the value of civilization itself. Emil Coué might make his incantation: "Day by day
in every way I am getting better and better,"[53] but, for some,
Coué's popularity merely proved that vulgarity was profitable.
Edison and Ford showed that technological progress was possible, but the war showed that men were not necessarily or even
probably served well as a result.[54] Cumulative disciplines
would continue to make progress, but who would win in a

[52]Morton White, *Social Thought in America* (Boston, 1957), pp. 182,
188–189.

[53]Frederick Lewis Allen, *Only Yesterday* (New York, 1946), p. 102.

[54]Clark A. Chambers, "The Belief in Progress in Twentieth-Century
America," *Journal of the History of Ideas*, XIX, 2 (April 1958), 204–208;
Sidney Kaplan, "Social Engineers as Saviors," *ibid.*, XVII, 3 (June 1956),
369.

struggle for survival between Darwin and Bryan? Social theories might grow increasingly sophisticated and ingenious, but Clemenceau, A. Mitchell Palmer, and Judge Webster Thayer (in whose court Sacco and Vanzetti were tried) seemed also to have something to say about how the world would be ruled, who would rule, and about the staying power of the past. The American economy could boom along with the proliferation of machines, but even the usually sanguine Dewey concluded that "we have harnessed this power to the dollar rather than to the liberation and enrichment of human life."[55] In the eyes of a widening circle of disaffected intellectuals and artists, modern America was a spiritual and cultural desert, committed to standardization and repression and blind to freedom and spontaneity. America was therefore a case study which showed that the older generation had used the idea of progress to camouflage its own failures.

None of this seems to have touched Herbert Hoover, the leading and most intelligent spokesman of non-metropolitan America. He published an important little book on *American Individualism* early in the decade that is a sensitive rendition of provincial values; by listing what he does not discuss, and by contradicting what he does, one may learn what the exiles, alienates, and even the flappers thought important. His optimism was unlimited because he believed that Americans were increasingly devoted to service: "Moral standards of business and commerce are improving; vicious city governments are less in number; invisible government has greatly diminished; public conscience is penetrating deeper and deeper; the rooting up of wrong grows more vigorous; the agencies for their exposure and remedy grow more numerous, and above all is the growing sense of service."[56] (The frequent reiteration of the ideal of "service" in the decade drove Mencken wild: "When a gang of real es-

[55]John Dewey, *Individualism Old and New* (London, 1931), p. 91.
[56]Herbert Hoover, *American Individualism* (Garden City, N. Y., 1922), p. 58. See Document 17.

tate agents . . . , bond salesmen and automobile dealers get together to sob for Service, it takes no Freudian to surmise that someone is about to be swindled."[57])

More than anything else, it was Hoover's "idealism" that connected him with the American village and separated him from serious writers and artists. Unaware of or perhaps despite the very wide rejection of idealism in both cultural and philosophical meanings, Hoover asserted that "the most potent force in society is its ideals." He was able to use both the meaning and the rhetoric that were most unacceptable to the cultural leaders: "From the instincts of kindness, pity, fealty to family and race; the love of liberty; the mystical yearnings for spiritual things; the desire for fuller expression of the creative faculties; the impulses of service to community and nation, are moulded the ideals of our people."[58]

Taking notice of the radical individualism of the period, as the intellectuals did too, Hoover made a virtue of necessity. American individualism, he said, was not rampant, was unique, because it was founded on the "great ideals" of the nation. The supposedly classless nature of America cleared the way for individual achievement even while the "emery wheel of competition" was whirling. Progress, about which he evidently had no or few doubts, was a result of "the yearning for individual self-expression," and individualism "alone admits the universal divine inspiration of every human soul."[59] Absolutely rejecting the idea that nature was purposeless, that historical fatality limited human choice, and that reason was an incompetent social and even personal guide, Hoover said that good ideas could replace bad ones, that reason could light the way to the implementation of eternal ideals. War was a conflict of ideas; irrationality and power were left out of his analysis.[60] For

[57]Mencken, *Notes on Democracy*, p. 176.
[58]Hoover, *American Individualism*, p. 16.
[59]*Ibid.*, pp. 9, 21, 26.
[60]*Ibid.*, p. 70.

Hoover, and for those whom he represented, Wilson's wartime career and the Treaty of Versailles did not prove anything about either the emptiness or the danger of idealism as such.

And yet the villagers took pride in dealing with actuality, at least on a certain level. That is what Harding meant in his diagnosis of what the American electorate wanted, and that is what Coolidge meant when he called the election of 1920 "the end of a period which has seemed to substitute words for things."[61] The "words" the villager meant included the words of intellectuals and the plans of reformers; the villager did not mean to repudiate national ideals which seemed to serve well even in the hard and actual world of the assembly lines.

In philosophy, idealism was repudiated by pragmatism and scientific realism. "New Realism" was formed on a rejection of the idealists' fusion of subject and object, on what was viewed as the obscurantism of idealist logic. John Dewey was the leading advocate of a new philosophy founded on exact science, not on the sovereignty of the human mind. The social implications of this philosophical recoil from idealism were drawn by one critic:

With all its incompleteness, Dewey's philosophy is undeniably that of the America of to-day. What shall we say of the future? No nation in the world has more abused its philosophies than ours. The inspirational elements of our idealisms have become the panderings of sentimentalists. The vitalizing forces of our pragmatisms threaten to congeal into the dogmata of cash-success. The war has intensified our national self-satisfaction. We tend to condemn all vision as radical, hence unsound, hence evil, hence to be put down.[62]

The peculiarly buoyant but often fretful zest of the creative people of the decade was largely a result of the feeling not that

[61]Quoted in Leuchtenburg, *Perils of Prosperity,* p. 89.
[62]Harold Chapman Brown, "Philosophy," *Civilization,* ed. Stearns, pp. 176–177.

the past had somehow to be abandoned, but that the best and most authentic expression of the time actually had already freed itself from the alleged suffocation of a social past. The individual, already almost sanctified in political and economic terms by the small town and its spokesman, already validated by Freudianism, already placed at the center of American philosophy, was to find his most elaborate and elevated position in the art and literature of the Twenties.

What was being done to and for the individual was sometimes made somewhat obscure by talk of freedom, adjustment, self-expression, and the war against Puritanism. But under most if not all of that rhetoric was the writers' quite open assumption: if the self could be freed from the oppression of the social past, from the repression of his private past, a new private world of self-determination would become newly accessible. This new world would still find it necessary to battle the old world of custom and tradition, but though the actual world might even probably remain unchanged, the now inviolate ego could feel for the limits of what it could do. Consigning society and history to the hell they caused and deserved, the liberated spirits of the time could themselves soar inward as they quite consciously rejected formal knowledge, economics, politics, and social service; as they quite consciously prayed at the shrines of the uncorrupted child, of the eternal present, of the equality of autonomous selves—male and female—and of freedom and paganism.[63] They were newly born into an idiot world whose power over them required their assent; refusing assent, they thought they had discovered how to prevent that world from taking what they would not give. They thought they had discovered how to nourish the self in a social madhouse, as e. e. cummings showed in *The Enormous Room* (see Document 2). Some chose a French or English setting out of their fear or conviction

[63]Cf. Malcolm Cowley, *Exile's Return: A Narrative of Ideas* (New York, 1951), pp. 60–61.

that America was stultifying or otherwise dangerous, but all sought that self whose discovery was, they believed, the basis of art.

Dada was merely the verge of freedom and privacy, the extreme and essentially unformulated assault on the morbid if not moribund civilization of the time, and the appropriate reflex of that eternal present. Moving from the avowedly destructive anti-rationalism of dada to the avowedly revolutionary unconscious of surrealism, the art of that moment was of a piece with the other cultural currents. Western man with his exquisite and urgent sublimatory necessities had created mind and civilization. Both led to outrageous war. By living inwardly one might escape these necessities, might re-discover the body and freedom known only by the uncivilized: children, Negroes, primitives, half-wits, and other heroes of the creative sub-culture of the Twenties. Freud, after all, had already explained that mind and freedom were mutually exclusive. In their war on mind, the American writers of the period, whether in Zurich, Paris, or New York, were responding to the same impulses that dada and surrealism understood. In their war on mind, these writers were laying siege to civilization itself: society and nation, history and time. The alternative to civilization was the self, and toward that they made their sometimes unsure, sometimes nervous, often frantic, and occasionally gay way.

V

Writers in America easily identified the hated past with the hated village. In the beginning, they suggested, all America was a village, and the contemporary village was a powerful reminder of the hold the past had on the present. Their enemy, with the double face of the philistine and the Puritan, was still strong enough to rule the land, though that fact mattered less and less. Of greater moment was the enemy's continued power to create and protect an environment absolutely hostile to the necessary private nourishment of those writers. One could presumably live with both Prohibition and the Klan, but the hegemonic village seemed also to pollute that part of the American atmosphere that was essential to art. So Van Wyck Brooks could conclude that America demanded the premature death of her artists:

> If America is littered with extinct talents, the halt, the maimed and the blind, it is for reasons with which we are all too familiar; and we to whom the creative life is nothing less than the principle of human movement, and its welfare the true sign of human health, look upon the wreckage of everything that is most precious to society and ask ourselves what our fathers meant when they extolled the progress of our civilization.[64]

Frustration was the price the village demanded of the artist; public America might be shoved into a corner of one's mind, but it still had power to drive the artist to his death. As Fitzgerald asked from his ineffective refuge in Paris: "Can you name a single American artist except James and Whistler (who lived in England) who didn't die of drink?"[65] The profound irrelevance of public America did not mean that one could succeed, in Hemingway's language, in concluding "a separate peace." Internal secession, expatriation, withdrawal, isolation, and alienation were solutions, but evidently expensive for some, prohibitively so for others.

Fitzgerald is a special case. He was not importantly involved in the writer's sometimes loving and sometimes bitter attack on traditional language, as, for example, were Gertrude Stein, James Joyce, all of the dadaists, e. e. cummings, and even Hemingway in his own way. Fitzgerald, at least at first blush,

[64]Van Wyck Brooks, "The Literary Life," *Civilization*, ed. Stearns, p. 192.

[65]F. Scott Fitzgerald to Marya Mannes, October 1925, in *Letters*, p. 489. See Document 25.

seems not to have been a man apart, seems rather to have been a perhaps simple reflection of dominant America. But his playful weariness, his brooding conviction of the hollowness of the very life he desired and depicted, and the iron inevitability of collapse in his best works, show him, obviously enough, to be preëminently a writer of his time and place.[66] Thus it was that the poet laureate of the Jazz Age could tell his editor: "My third novel, if I ever write another, will I am sure be black as death with gloom."[67]

Fitzgerald's fascination with youth, glamor, and power was clearly real. And it is partly accurate to label him with the now stock critical tag of the "eternal adolescent infatuated with the surfaces of material existence."[68] He made Jay Gatsby hope that hard cash could buy every desire of the insatiable heart, even the suspension of time or the eradication of the past. How is it then that, as he himself knew, his lovely, expensive, nineteen-year-old flappers came to ruin, his diamond mountains blew up, and his millionaires were damned? Fitzgerald, for all of his spiritual fraternizing with the flapper, for all of his personal needs, saw through the decade. He knew—and it was his most tense, painful, and creative knowledge—that he, and his most living characters, were inextricably involved in an unremitting search for what would turn out to be a fraud. Though he became disillusioned with the ideas of his own youth, he consistently refused to participate in American moralism about the evil of money and the corruptibility of power. Simultaneously accepting and rejecting the flapper and her friends, he could not turn away from society, as so many of the period's other writers were to do. His search for the possibilities of the self

---

[66]Cf. Henry San Piper, "Fitzgerald's Cult of Disillusion," *American Quarterly*, III, 1 (Spring 1951), 69–80.

[67]F. Scott Fitzgerald to M. Perkins, August 25, 1921, in *Letters*, p. 148.

[68]Irving Howe, "American Moderns," *Paths of American Thought*, ed. Schlesinger and White, p. 318. The following paragraph draws heavily on this essay.

was conducted not merely in society but in Society. Fitzgerald believed that Gatsby condemned himself to loneliness, fragility, and emptiness; this author's dependence on the self even in the face of the self's willed destruction was Fitzgerald's unique and powerful way of rendering the decade. To make and throw away a life because of an ideal of self, to be torn between enormous power and beatific dreams[69]—that was a fact to which he owed some of his best writing. Not rejecting society in his search for the self, Fitzgerald yet believed that the combat between them was mortal.

Hemingway's response to the Twenties was more typical of the contemporary writers' plight, as many of them understood it. Suffering what he felt to be a hideous psychic wound by the external world, Hemingway spent both his talent and his life in this period trying to learn to endure, but with some necessary dignity, with some acceptable sense of self, with some style appropriate to the problem. As the universe seemed always to be in an active conspiracy against manhood, so, for Hemingway, art was a way to fight back. Society and tradition might be rejected, but the rejection was active and necessary to his art.

Meaning was real only for the self. War, for instance, was less important than one's relationship to it, and one's experience of it. The world had come apart sufficiently, as the self perceived it, so that it was no longer necessary to demonstrate this fact. Starting with the assumption of meaninglessness, Hemingway, like other writers of the time, was convinced of the absurdity of attempting to supply meaning. Style and gesture became his personal substitute for meaning. The struggle to clarify the contours of the self replaced the earlier American literary struggle to clarify the contours of the cosmos.

Hemingway was so convinced of the emptiness of large meanings, of idealism as such, that he apparently believed it

[69]Lionel Trilling, *The Liberal Imagination* (Garden City, N.Y.: Doubleday Anchor, 1953), pp. 240, 242.

unnecessary to fight that battle. His taut language is itself an evidence of his rejection of the world of idealism, of concept, of rationalism, of civilization. Unlike American writers of the nineteenth century, he showed the results of his rejections rather than attempting to prove that they were right. Only occasionally would he become explicit, as in *A Farewell to Arms:* "Abstract words such as glory, honor, courage, or hallow were obscene beside the concrete names of villages, the numbers of roads, the names of rivers, the numbers of regiments and the dates."[70]

Personal involvement and especially risk destroyed abstraction. Perhaps one could learn through a precise scrutiny of the ego in danger or crisis, through scrutiny of probably raw nerve endings, and through awareness of the chill in the pit of the stomach. Things had a price, as Jake Barnes in *The Sun Also Rises* knew, and one had to pay: "Either you paid by learning about them, or by experience, or by taking chances, or by money." An attempt to impose or extract large meaning would necessarily destroy the involvement, and thereby necessarily obstruct learning. Endurance, not progress, was the point, as Barnes explained: "I did not care what it was all about. All I wanted to know was how to live in it."[71] Distance from experience would vitiate it; though life, in general terms, was not worth observing, it was worth participation if an opportunity for self-measurement could be found. So Jake Barnes explained the point of the bull fight to Brett Ashley: "the holding of his purity of line through maximum of exposure."[72] If the individual could nerve himself to will and execute maximum exposure, his personal authenticity would result in beauty, not necessarily truth. The code, the moral code, required both the risk and the gesture. The world of the other, of the non-self,

[70]Ernest Hemingway, *A Farewell to Arms* (New York, 1929), p. 191.
[71]Ernest Hemingway, *The Sun Also Rises* (New York, 1926), p. 153.
[72]*Ibid.*, p. 174.

was organized merely to destroy the true self, as Hemingway once explained in characteristic language:

If people bring so much courage to this world, the world has to kill them to break them, so of course it kills them. The world breaks every one and afterward many are strong at the broken places. But those that will not break it kills. It kills the very good and the very gentle and the very brave impartially. If you are none of these you can be sure it will kill you too but there will be no special hurry.[73]

Believing that, Hemingway exalted—a word he would reject —style. One could still summon courage and dignity in a meaningless world. Importantly, the style he exalted was moral— another word he would probably have rejected. His typically wounded hero achieves selfhood by facing, not trying to overcome, his wound. The conditions of modern life had so radically annihilated any community, that the individual with whatever strength or will or sensitivity he could summon had finally to discover in himself a psychic refuge, a way to endure. The appropriate style of endurance tended almost always to the inarticulate and the concrete. But, as Hemingway showed it, endurance was neither acquiescence nor humiliation. The *corrida*, as a substitute for society, requires endurance gracefully achieved. In the demand for such grace Hemingway's moral code of resistance to and defiance of society and social morality becomes clear. With a perfect *veronica* the individual can introduce a transitory but genuine beauty into an ugly and meaningless world.[74] But the inherent impermanence of such beauty meant that the threshold of satisfaction would be continually receding, and the sometimes aimless and comic, often frenzied reaching out for yet a new experience that would

[73]Hemingway, *Farewell to Arms*, pp. 258–259.

[74]Howe, "American Moderns," *Paths of American Thought*, ed. Schlesinger and White, pp. 315–317.

prove that nerves were yet capable of sensation, came increasingly to characterize Hemingway's work.

The decade's intellectual and literary finale came appropriately in 1929, in a humane and gentle but anguished lament by Joseph Wood Krutch. *The Modern Temper: A Study and a Confession* was, among other things, a direct summary of the difficulties of being alive and aware during the Twenties; it was, and is, an intellectual's despair at the intensity and magnitude of an intellectual's peculiar problems during a decade of America's history when the material conditions of life for a vast segment of the population were daily improving, when life was sufficiently well-managed so that those who were repelled by public life believed that they could afford to turn away.

Krutch feared that the scientists and industrialists who were satisfied with what they had thought and built, and who, as a result, necessarily suffered a coarsening of the grain, were in fact the fittest who would not merely survive but survive to rule. Others, more sensitively tuned, seized on a now superannuated humanism, trying desperately to ignore their own disbelief. The proposed retreat into self, into imagination perhaps, depended on ironic belief, an attitude Krutch thought appropriate only to proponents of a lost cause. Power seemed to ignore humanity, and humanism was out of touch with everything, even with itself: "Both our practical morality and our emotional lives are adjusted to a world which no longer exists. In so far as we adhere to a code of conduct," Krutch explained,

we do so largely because certain habits still persist, not because we can give any logical reason for preferring them, and in so far as we indulge ourselves in the primitive emotional satisfactions—romantic love, patriotism, zeal for justice, and so forth—our satisfaction is the result merely of the temporary suspension of our disbelief in the mythology upon which they are founded.[75]

[75] Joseph Wood Krutch, *The Modern Temper: A Study and a Confession* (New York, 1929), pp. 22–23. See Document 29.

Deracination was the major characteristic of modernity, and this was so in emotional as well as in other terms.

Modernity was, in a sense, unconnected with the past, and, as Krutch saw it, history was discontinuous. A more total adjustment was demanded by his decade than ever before. Extinction was the price of failure to understand—as the artists and writers of the period understood—and the failure to find a way to live with unprecedented uncertainties and necessities. Science, so far from providing answers, was itself part of the problem. With growing and spreading freedom, the objects— men, women, love—once summoned as the goal for which freedom was demanded had lost their significance, desirability, or meaning altogether.

Displaying something of the vogue of primitivism, new experience, and delicately wrought anti-intellectualism, Krutch thought that the future would fall to those who were then too deeply involved in living and loving to have time to think about how to live and love. Such people would come, he announced, "as the barbarians have always come, absorbed in the processes of life for their own sake, eating without asking if it is worth while to eat, begetting children without asking why they should beget them, and conquering without asking for what purpose they conquer."[76]

The modern mood, as it came through the filter of Krutch's critical intelligence, was desperate, rootless, aimless, disillusioned with everything including disillusion, and evidently secure in the knowledge that knowledge would not help. In often wonderful prose it told of the meaninglessness of language and mind, of the need somehow to act for goals no longer desired or believed real. It apparently longed to find a faith that could fire the imagination, and had lost faith in the possibility of faith. Above all (and it is strange to say of so simple a thing that it was above all), the modern man was ex-

[76]*Ibid.*, p. 237.

hausted. Exhausted not from a particular exertion, but chronically so. The burden of needing to ask not why to endure, but how, was obviously murderously heavy. When men added this burden to their other labors, they staggered into modernity.

One aspect of the grotesque humor of the Great Depression is that, in giving men a concrete task to perform, it did not solve but at least temporarily obscured the peculiarly modern anguish. That is probably why many of the most articulate American writers and scholars seem to have found new energy, new zest, and even a new joy in their work. It is too much to say that as the stock market declined, intellectual spirits rose. But enough is true to say that for some at least the Depression was a relief, a chance to engage a world larger than one's own skin, a time to deal with problems that were simpler because capable of some measure of solution. It was a time when village and city could combine in common cause, when material privation seemed almost able to re-create an American community, almost coterminous with the nation. And World War II continued the happy chance to ignore the increasingly relevant legacy of the Twenties.

With peace and returning affluence, with skirts rising again and traditional morality declining again, some of these now old questions re-asserted themselves. This time a larger group of young Americans would think about the discontinuities of history. By the mid-1960's they began seriously to repudiate conventional attitudes and reflexes. And, unlike their predecessors of the 1920's, this time many young people added a vital political dimension to their cultural awakening. This search for liberation from history did not begin in the Twenties and it will not end in the Sixties. But, at least in America, these two cultural moments are important steps in the endless funeral of the social fathers.

Rochester, New York
September 1966

Selected Bibliography

Especially useful bibliographies of the fiction, memoirs, and biographies of the 1920's are included in the works listed below that are marked with an asterisk. Works cited in the Introduction or used as selections in the anthology are not repeated in this bibliography.

I. GENERAL

Goldman, Eric F. *Rendezvous With Destiny.* New York: Alfred A. Knopf, 1952.

Kazin, Alfred. *On Native Grounds. An Interpretation of Modern American Prose Literature.* New York: Reynal & Hitchcock, 1942.

*May, Henry F. "Shifting Perspectives on the 1920's," *Mississippi Valley Historical Review,* XLIII (December 1956), 405–427.

Slosson, Preston. *The Great Crusade and After, 1914–1928.* New York: Macmillan, 1931.

Soule, George Henry. *Prosperity Decade. From War to Depression: 1917–1929.* New York: Rinehart, 1947.

II. POLITICAL ECONOMY

Adler, Selig. *The Isolationist Impulse: Its Twentieth Century Reaction.* New York: Abelard Schuman, 1957.

Chase, Stuart. *Men and Machines.* New York: Macmillan, 1929.

Cochran, Thomas. *The American Business System.* Cambridge: Harvard University Press, 1957.

Feis, Herbert. *The Diplomacy of the Dollar: First Era, 1919–1932.* Baltimore: Johns Hopkins Press, 1950.

Galbraith, John K. *The Great Crash, 1929.* Boston: Houghton Mifflin, 1955.

Giedion, Sigfried. *Mechanization Takes Command. A Contribution to Anonymous History.* New York: Oxford University Press, 1948.

*Hicks, John D. *Republican Ascendancy, 1921–1933.* New York: Harper & Brothers, 1960.

Moos, Malcolm Charles. *The Republicans: A History of Their Party.* New York: Random House, 1956.

*Neufeld, Maurice F. *A Bibliography of Labor Union History.* Ithaca, New York: Cornell University Press, 1958.

Prothro, James. *Dollar Decade: Business Ideas in the 1920's.* Baton Rouge: Louisiana State University Press, 1954.

Ripley, William Z. *Main Street and Wall Street.* Boston: Little, Brown, 1927.

Schlesinger, Arthur Meier, Jr. *The Age of Roosevelt.* Vol. 1. *The Crisis of the Old Order 1919–1933.* Boston: Houghton Mifflin, 1957.

Schriftgiesser, Karl. *This Was Normalcy: An Account of Party Politics During Twelve Republican Years, 1920–1932.* Boston: Little, Brown, 1948.

Schumpeter, Joseph. "The American Economy in the Interwar Period: The Decade of the Twenties," *American Economic Review*, XXXVI (May 1946), 1–10.

Shideler, James H. *Farm Crisis 1919–1923*. Berkeley: University of California Press, 1957.

White, William Allen. *A Puritan in Babylon: The Story of Calvin Coolidge*. New York: Macmillan, 1938.

III. LITERATURE

Geismar, Maxwell. *Writers in Crisis: The American Novel, 1925–1940*. Boston: Houghton Mifflin Co., 1942.

Hoffman, Frederick J. *Freudianism and the Literary Mind*. Baton Rouge: Louisiana State University Press, 1945.

*Jones, Howard Mumford. *Guide to American Literature and Its Backgrounds Since 1890*. Cambridge: Harvard University Press, 1953.

*Rideout, Walter B. *The Radical Novel in the United States, 1900–1954*. Cambridge: Harvard University Press, 1956.

*Spiller, Robert, *et al.*, eds. *Literary History of the United States*. Vol. III, *Bibliography*, edited by Thomas H. Johnson. Supplement edited by Richard M. Ludwig. 2nd ed. New York: Macmillan, 1962.

IV. SOCIAL AND INTELLECTUAL

Chalmers, David Mark. *Hooded Americanism. The First Century of the Ku Klux Klan, 1865–1955*. Garden City, N.Y.: Doubleday, 1965.

DeVoto, Bernard. *The Literary Fallacy*. Boston: Little, Brown, 1944.

Higham, John. *Strangers in the Land.* New Brunswick, N.J.: Rutgers University Press, 1955.

Leighton, Isabel, ed. *The Aspirin Age.* New York: Simon & Schuster, 1949.

Lynd, Robert S. & Helen M. *Middletown: A Study in Contemporary American Culture.* New York: Harcourt, Brace, 1929.

Merz, Charles. *The Dry Decade.* Garden City, N.Y.: Doubleday, Doran, 1931.

President's Research Committee on Social Trends. *American Civilization Today: A Summary of Recent Social Trends.* New York: McGraw-Hill, 1933.

Ward, John. "The Meaning of Lindbergh's Flight." *American Quarterly,* X, 1 (Spring 1958), 3–16.

Ware, Carolyn Farrar. *Greenwich Village 1920–1930.* Boston: Houghton Mifflin, 1935.

White, Morton. *Social Thought in America. The Revolt Against Formalism.* New York: Viking Press, 1949.

V. Radicalism

Draper, Theodore. *The Roots of American Communism.* New York: Viking Press, 1957.

*Egbert, Donald Drew, and Stow Persons, eds. *Socialism and American Life.* Vol. II, *Bibliography,* T.D.S. Bassett. Princeton: Princeton University Press, 1952.

Freeman, Joseph. *An American Testament. A Narrative of Rebels and Romantics.* New York: Farrar & Rinehart, 1936.

Joughin, George Louis, and Edmund M. Morgan. *The Legacy of Sacco and Vanzetti.* New York: Harcourt, Brace, 1948.

Murray, Robert K. *Red Scare: A Study in National Hysteria, 1919-1920.* Minneapolis: University of Minnesota Press, 1955.

Shannon, David A. *The Socialist Party of America: A History.* New York: Macmillan, 1955.

Editor's Note

All of the selections in this volume appear exactly as they did in the original, except that occasional repetitive or irrelevant passages were deleted; ellipses mark these deletions. The few identifications made by the editor appear either in square brackets within the text or as footnotes. Professor Paul Levine and Mr. Alan Cywar suggested specific items for inclusion; Miss Mary Lynn assisted in almost every stage of preparing the selections, headnotes, and bibliography for the printer, and did so with intelligence, efficiency, and good cheer. These colleagues made this a better anthology than it otherwise would have been.

THE CULTURE OF
THE TWENTIES

PART I

WAR: THE DISILLUSIONED

1 / JOHN DOS PASSOS

The Scene of Battle

An impersonal and anonymous death was one of the possibilities of modern, mechanized warfare. The Unknown Soldier, buried with all the pomp official Washington could display, symbolized all of the faceless and nameless dead. National hymns of gratitude were sung over the arbitrarily selected and carefully packaged carcass sent home from the war. Disillusioned with war, with Woodrow Wilson's failures to honor his own pledges about the peace, and with civilization itself, many of the writers of the decade between the Armistice and the Crash were sickened by their memories of the horrors civilized society had perpetrated on itself. John Dos Passos (1896–   ), in the last few pages of *1919*, the second volume of the trilogy *U.S.A.*, shows the new barbarism of war. Although this selection was written shortly after the Crash, Dos Passos had seen the war as a volunteer in an ambulance corps. His recoil from the mass butchery was a typical reaction, but the intensity and the swirling, cinematic prose are peculiarly his own.

THE BODY OF AN AMERICAN

Whereasthe Congressoftheunitedstates byaconcurrentresolution-adoptedon the4thdayofmarch lastauthorizedthe Secretaryofwar to cause to be brought to theunitedstatesthe body of an Americanwho-

"The Body of an American," from *1919* (New York: Harcourt, Brace, 1932), pp. 467–473. *Nineteen Nineteen* by John Dos Passos, copyright by John Dos Passos 1932 and 1960, published by the Houghton Mifflin Co. Reprinted by permission of the author.

wasamemberoftheamericanexpeditionaryforcesineurope   wholosthis-
lifeduringtheworldwarandwhoseidentityhasnotbeenestablished   for
burial inthememorialamphitheatreofthenationalcemeteryatarlington-
virginia

In the tarpaper morgue at Chalons-sur-Marne in the reek of
chloride of lime and the dead, they picked out the pine box
that held all that was left of
    enie menie minie moe plenty other pine boxes stacked up
there containing what they'd scraped up of Richard Roe
    and other person or persons unknown. Only one can go. How
did they pick John Doe?
    Make sure he aint a dinge, boys,
      make sure he aint a guinea or a kike,
    how can you tell a guy's a hunredpercent when all you've
got's a gunnysack full of bones, bronze buttons stamped with
the screaming eagle and a pair of roll puttees?
    . . . and the gagging chloride and the puky dirtstench of
the yearold dead . . .

The day withal was too meaningful and tragic for applause. Silence, tears, songs and prayer, muffled drums and soft music were
the instrumentalities today of national approbation.

John Doe was born (thudding din of blood in love into the
shuddering soar of a man and a woman alone indeed together
lurching into
    and ninemonths sick drowse waking into scared agony and
the pain and blood and mess of birth). John Doe was born
    and raised in Brooklyn, in Memphis, near the lakefront in
Cleveland, Ohio, in the stench of the stockyards in Chi, on Bea-
con Hill, in an old brick house in Alexandria Virginia, on Telegraph Hill, in a halftimbered Tudor cottage in Portland the
city of roses,
    in the Lying-In Hospital old Morgan endowed on Stuyvesant
Square,

across the railroad tracks, out near the country club, in a shack cabin tenement apartmenthouse exclusive residential suburb;

scion of one of the best families in the social register, won first prize in the baby parade at Coronado Beach, was marbles champion of the Little Rock grammarschools, crack basketballplayer at the Bonneville High, quarterback at the State Reformatory, having saved the sheriff's kid from drowning in the Little Missouri River was invited to Washington to be photographed shaking hands with the President on the White House steps;—

though this was a time of mourning, such an assemblage necessarily has about it a touch of color. In the boxes are seen the court uniforms of foreign diplomats, the gold braid of our own and foreign fleets and armies, the black of the conventional morning dress of American statesmen, the varicolored furs and outdoor wrapping garments of mothers and sisters come to mourn, the drab and blue of soldiers and sailors, the glitter of musical instruments and the white and black of a vested choir

—busboy harveststiff hogcaller boyscout champeen cornshucker of Western Kansas bellhop at the United States Hotel at Saratoga Springs office boy callboy fruiter telephone lineman longshoreman lumberjack plumber's helper,

worked for an exterminating company in Union City, filled pipes in an opium joint in Trenton, N.J.

Y.M.C.A. secretary, express agent, truckdriver, fordmechanic, sold books in Denver Colorado: Madam would you be willing to help a young man work his way through college?

President Harding, with a reverence seemingly more significant because of his high temporal station, concluded his speech:

We are met today to pay the impersonal tribute; the name of him whose body lies before us took flight with his imperishable soul . . .

as a typical soldier of this representative democracy he fought and died believing in the indisputable justice of his country's cause . . .

by raising his right hand and asking the thousands within the sound of his voice to join in the prayer:

Our Father which art in heaven hallowed be thy name . . .

Naked he went into the army;
they weighed you, measured you, looked for flat feet, squeezed your penis to see if you had clap, looked up your anus to see if you had piles, counted your teeth, made you cough, listened to your heart and lungs, made you read the letters on the card, charted your urine and your intelligence,
gave you a service record for a future (imperishable soul)
and an identification tag stamped with your serial number to hang around your neck, issued O D regulation equipment, a condiment can and a copy of the articles of war.
Atten'SHUN suck in your gut you c——r wipe that smile off your face eyes right wattja tink dis is a choirch-social? For-war-D'ARCH.

John Doe
and Richard Roe and other person or persons unknown
drilled hiked, manual of arms, ate slum, learned to salute, to soldier, to loaf in the latrines, forbidden to smoke on deck, overseas guard duty, forty men and eight horses, shortarm inspection and the ping of shrapnel and the shrill bullets combing the air and the sorehead woodpeckers the machineguns mud cooties gasmasks and the itch.
Say feller tell me how I can get back to my outfit.

John Doe had a head
for twentyodd years intensely the nerves of the eyes the ears the palate the tongue the fingers the toes the armpits, the nerves warmfeeling under the skin charged the coiled brain with hurt sweet warm cold mine must dont sayings print headlines:

Thou shalt not the multiplication table long division, Now is the time for all good men knocks but once at a young man's door, It's a great life if Ish gebibbel, The first five years'll be the Safety First, Suppose a hun tried to rape your my country right or wrong, Catch 'em young, What he dont know wont treat 'em rough, Tell 'em nothin, He got what was coming to him he got his, This is a white man's country, Kick the bucket, Gone west, If you dont like it you can croaked him
Say buddy cant you tell me how I can get back to my outfit?

Cant help jumpin when them things go off, give me the trots them things do. I lost my identification tag swimmin in the Marne, roughhousin with a guy while we was waitin to be deloused, in bed with a girl named Jeanne (Love moving picture wet French postcard dream began with saltpeter in the coffee and ended at the propho station);—
Say soldier for chrissake cant you tell me how I can get back to my outfit?

John Doe's
heart pumped blood:
alive thudding silence of blood in your ears down in the clearing in the Oregon forest where the punkins were punkin-color pouring into the blood through the eyes and the fall-colored trees and the bronze hoopers were hopping through the dry grass, where tiny striped snails hung on the underside of the blades and the flies hummed, wasps droned, bumblebees buzzed, and the woods smelt of wine and mushrooms and apples, homey smell of fall pouring into the blood,
and I dropped the tin hat and the sweaty pack and lay flat with the dogday sun licking my throat and adamsapple and the tight skin over the breastbone.

The shell had his number on it.

The blood ran into the ground.

The service record dropped out of the filing cabinet when the quartermaster sergeant got blotto that time they had to pack up and leave the billets in a hurry.
The identification tag was in the bottom of the Marne.

The blood ran into the ground, the brains oozed out of the cracked skull and were licked up by the trenchrats, the belly swelled and raised a generation of bluebottle flies,
    and the incorruptible skeleton,
    and the scraps of dried viscera and skin bundled in khaki

    they took to Chalons-sur-Marne
    and laid it out neat in a pine coffin
    and took it home to God's Country on a battleship
    and buried it in a sarcophagus in the Memorial Amphithea-
tre in the Arlington National Cemetery
    and draped the Old Glory over it
    and the bugler played taps
    and Mr. Harding prayed to God and the diplomats and the
generals and the admirals and the brasshats and the politicians
and the handsomely dressed ladies out of the society column of
the *Washington Post* stood up solemn
    and thought how beautiful sad Old Glory God's Country it
was to have the bugler play taps and the three volleys made
their ears ring.

    Where his chest ought to have been they pinned the Congres-
sional Medal, the D.S.C., the Medaille Militaire, the Belgian
Croix de Guerre, the Italian gold medal, the Vitutea Militara
sent by Queen Marie of Rumania, the Czechoslovak war cross,
the Virtuti Militari of the Poles, a wreath sent by Hamilton Fish,
Jr., of New York, and a little wampum presented by a deputation

of Arizona redskins in warpaint and feathers. All the Washing-
tonians brought flowers.

Woodrow Wilson brought a bouquet of poppies.

2 / E. E. CUMMINGS

Bureaucratic Dehumanization

e. e. cummings (1894–1962) joined an ambulance corps in France
during World War 1. One of his comrades (referred to as "B."
in the following selection) wrote some letters critical of the
French government, which the French censor caught; both men
were put in a concentration camp in La Ferté Macé, although no
charges had been made against cummings. At La Ferté Macé
cummings gathered material for *The Enormous Room*, his first
book, a description of his internment. Applauding the ability of
some of the other inmates to sustain their humanity, and aghast at
the almost mechanized stupidities of the bureaucrats in charge of
the prison, cummings depicted a surrealistic world in which a few
real individuals struggle to survive the stolid madness and cruelty
typical of twentieth-century governments. In *The Enormous Room*,
as well as in his many volumes of poetry (among which were *Tulips
and Chimneys*, 1922; *XLI Poems*, 1925; &, 1925; *IS 5*, 1926; and
Viva, 1931), in other prose (*Eimi*, 1932), and later in more poems
and in three plays (*Him*, 1927; *Anthropos*, 1930; *Santa Claus*, 1946)
—in all of his works, cummings consistently sought value and meaning in the intuitive individual whose authenticity resisted organized
society.

It must have been late in November when *la commission*
arrived. *La commission* . . . visited La Ferté *tous les trois mois*.

From Chap. XII: "Three Wise Men," *The Enormous Room* (New York:
Boni and Liveright, Inc., 1922), pp. 294–302. From *The Enormous Room*
by e. e. cummings. Copyright ℝ 1949 by e. e. cummings. Reprinted
by permission of Liveright Publishing Corporation, New York.

That is to say B. and I (by arriving when we did) had just escaped its clutches. I consider this one of the luckiest things in my life. *La commission* arrived one morning, and began work immediately. A list was made of *les hommes* who were to pass *la commission*, another of *les femmes*. These lists were given to the *planton* with The Wooden Hand. In order to avert any delay, those of *les hommes* whose names fell in the first half of the list were not allowed to enjoy the usual stimulating activities afforded by La Ferté's supreme environment: they were, in fact, confined to The Enormous Room, subject to instant call—moreover they were not called one by one, or as their respective turns came, but in groups of three or four; the idea being that *la commission* should suffer no smallest annoyance which might be occasioned by loss of time. There were always, in other words, eight or ten men waiting in the upper corridor opposite a disagreeably crisp door, which door belonged to that mysterious room wherein *la commission* transacted its inestimable affairs. Not more than a couple of yards away ten or eight women waited their turns. Conversation between *les hommes* and *les femmes* had been forbidden in the fiercest terms by *Monsieur le Directeur:* nevertheless conversation spasmodically occurred, thanks to the indulgent nature of The Wooden Hand. The Wooden Hand must have been cuckoo—he looked it. If he wasn't I am totally at a loss to account for his indulgence.

B. and I spent a morning in The Enormous Room without results, an astonishing acquisition of nervousness excepted. *Après la soupe* (noon) we were conducted *en haut,* told to leave our spoons and bread (which we did) and—in company with several others whose names were within a furlong of the last man called—were descended to the corridor. All that afternoon we waited. Also we waited all next morning. We spent our time talking quietly with a buxom, pink-cheeked Belgian girl who was in attendance as translator for one of *les femmes.*

This Belgian told us that she was a permanent inhabitant of La Ferté, that she and another *femme bonnête* occupied a room by themselves, that her brothers were at the front in Belgium, that her ability to speak fluently several languages (including English and German) made her invaluable to *Messieurs la commission*, that she had committed no crime, that she was held as a *suspecte*, that she was not entirely unhappy. She struck me immediately as being not only intelligent but alive. She questioned us in excellent English as to our offences, and seemed much pleased to discover that we were—to all appearances—innocent of wrong-doing.

From time to time our subdued conversation was interrupted by admonitions from the amiable Wooden Hand. Twice the door SLAMMED open, and *Monsieur le Directeur* bounced out frothing at the mouth and threatening everyone with infinite *cabinot,* on the ground that everyone's deportment or lack of it was menacing the aplomb of the commissioners. Each time The Black Holster appeared in the background and carried on his master's bullying until everyone was completely terrified—after which we were left to ourselves and The Wooden Hand once again.

B. and I were allowed by the latter individual—he was that day, at least, an individual and not merely a *planton*—to peek over his shoulder at the men's list. The Wooden Hand even went so far as to escort our seditious minds to the nearness of their examination by the simple yet efficient method of placing one of his human fingers opposite the name of him who was (even at that moment) within, submitting to the inexorable justice of *le gouvernement français.* I cannot honestly say that the discovery of this proximity of ourselves to our respective fates wholly pleased us; yet we were so weary of waiting that it certainly did not wholly terrify us. All in all, I think I have never been so utterly un-at-ease as while waiting for the axe to fall, metaphorically speaking, upon our squawking heads.

We were still conversing with the Belgian girl when a man

came out of the door unsteadily, looking as if he had submitted to several strenuous fittings of a wooden leg upon a stump not quite healed. The Wooden Hand, nodding at B., remarked hurriedly in a low voice:

'*Allez!*'

And B. (smiling at *La Belge* and at me) entered. He was followed by The Wooden Hand, as I suppose for greater security.

The next twenty minutes or whatever it was were by far the most nerve-racking which I had as yet experienced. *La Belge* said to me:

'*Il est gentil, votre ami,*'

and I agreed. And my blood was bombarding the roots of my toes and the summits of my hair.

After (I need not say) two or three million æons, B. emerged. I had not time to exchange a look with him—let alone a word—for The Wooden Hand said from the doorway:

'*Allez, l'autre américain,*'

and I entered in more confusion than can easily be imagined; entered the torture chamber, entered the inquisition, entered the tentacles of that sly and beaming polyp, *le gouvernement français.* . . .

As I entered I said, half-aloud: The thing is this, to look 'em in the eyes and keep cool whatever happens, not for the fraction of a moment forgetting that they are made of *merde,* that they are all of them composed entirely of *merde*—I don't know how many inquisitors I expected to see; but I guess I was ready for at least fifteen, among them President Poincaré lui-même. I hummed noiselessly:

'si vous passez par ma vil-le
n'oubliez pas ma maison:
on y mange de bonne sou-pe Ton Ton Tay-ne;
faite de merde et des onions, Ton Ton Tayne Ton Ton
    Ton,'

remembering the fine *forgeron* of Chevancourt who used to sing this, or something very like it, upon a table.—Entirely for the benefit of *les deux américains,* who would subsequently render 'Eats uh lonje wae to Tee-pear-raeree,' wholly for the gratification of a roomful of what Mr. A. liked to call 'them bastards,' alias 'dirty' Frenchmen, alias *les poilus, les poilus divins.* . . .

A little room. The *Directeur's* office? Or the *Surveillant's?* Comfort. O yes, very, very comfortable. On my right a table. At the table three persons. . . . Three persons: reading from left to right as I face them—a soggy, sleepy, slumpy lump in a gendarme's cape and cap, quite old, captain of gendarmes, not at all interested, wrinkled coarse face, only semi-*méchant,* large hard clumsy hands floppingly disposed on table; wily, tidy man in civilian clothes, pen in hand, obviously lawyer, *avocat* type, little bald on top, sneaky civility, smells of bad perfume or at any rate sweetish soap; tiny red-headed person, also civilian, creased, worrying, excited face, amusing little body and hands, brief and jumpy, must be a Dickens character, ought to spend his time sailing kites of his own construction over other people's houses in gusty weather. Behind the Three, all tied up with deference and inferiority, mild and spineless, Apollyon.

Would the reader like to know what I was asked?

Ah, would I could say! Only dimly do I remember those moments—only dimly do I remember looking through the lawyer at Apollyon's clean collar—only dimly do I remember the gradual collapse of the *capitaine de gendarmerie,* his slow but sure assumption of sleepfulness, the drooping of his soggy *tête de cochon* lower and lower till it encountered one hand whose elbow, braced firmly upon the table, sustained its insensate limpness—only dimly do I remember the enthusiastic antics of the little red-head when I spoke with patriotic fervour of the wrongs which La France was doing *mon ami et moi*—only dimly do I remember, to my right, the immobility of The Wooden Hand, reminding one of a clothing-dummy, or a life-size doll which might be made to move only by him who knew the proper combination. . . . At the outset I was asked: Did I want a translator? I looked and saw the *secrétaire,* weak-eyed

and lemon-pale, and I said '*Non.*' I was questioned mostly by
the *avocat,* somewhat by the Dickens, never by either the captain (who was asleep) or The *Directeur* (who was timid in the
presence of these great and good delegates of hope, faith, and
charity per the French Government). I recall that, for some
reason, I was perfectly cool. I put over six or eight hot shots
without losing in the least this composure, which surprised myself and pleased myself and altogether increased myself. As the
questions came for me I met them half-way, spouting my best
or worst French in a manner which positively astonished the
tiny red-headed demigod. I challenged with my eyes and with
my voice and with my manner Apollyon Himself, and Apollyon
Himself merely cuddled together, depressing his hairy body between its limbs as a spider sometimes does in the presence of
danger. I expressed immense gratitude to my captors and to
le gouvernement français for allowing me to see and hear and
taste and smell and touch the things which inhabited La Ferté
Macé, Orne, France. I do not think that *la commission* enjoyed
me much. It told me, through its sweetish-soap-leader, that my
friend was a criminal—this immediately upon my entering—
and I told it with a great deal of well-chosen politeness that I
disagreed. In telling how and why I disagreed I think I managed to shove my shovel-shaped imagination under the refuse
of their intellects. At least once or twice.

Rather fatiguing—to stand up and be told: Your friend is no
good; have you anything to say for yourself?—And to say a
great deal for yourself and for your friend and for *les hommes*
—or try your best to—and be contradicted, and be told 'Never
mind that, what we wish to know is,' and instructed to keep to
the subject; et cetera, ad infinitum. At last they asked each
other if each other wanted to ask the man before each other
anything more, and each other not wanting to do so, they said:
'*C'est fini.*'

. . . I had made an indisputably favourable impression upon
exactly one of my three examiners. I refer, in the present case,

to the red-headed little gentleman who was rather decent to me. I do not exactly salute him in recognition of this decency; I bow to him, as I might bow to somebody who said he was sorry he couldn't give me a match but there was a cigar-store just around the corner you know.

At '*C'est fini*,' The *Directeur* leaped into the lime-light with a savage admonition to The Wooden Hand—who saluted, opened the door suddenly, and looked at me with (dare I say it?) admiration. Instead of availing myself of this means of escape I turned to the little kite-flying gentleman and said:

'If you please, sir, will you be so good as to tell me what will become of my friend?'

The little kite-flying gentleman did not have time to reply, for the perfumed presence stated drily and distinctly:

'We cannot say anything to you upon that point.'

I gave him a pleasant smile which said, If I could see your intestines very slowly embracing a large wooden drum rotated by means of a small iron crank turned gently and softly by myself, I should be extraordinarily happy—and I bowed softly and gently to *Monsieur le Directeur* and I went through the door using all the perpendicular inches which God had given me.

Once outside I began to tremble like a *peuplier* in *l'automne* . . . '*L'automne humide et monotone.*'

—'*Allez en bas, pour la soupe,*' The Wooden Hand said not unkindly. I looked about me. 'There will be no more men before the commission until to-morrow,' The Wooden Hand said. 'Go get your dinner in the kitchen.'

I descended.

Afrique was all curiosity—what did they say? what did I say?—as he placed before me a huge, a perfectly huge, an inexcusably huge plate of something more than lukewarm grease. . . . B. and I ate at a very little table in *la cuisine*, excitedly comparing notes as we swallowed the red-hot stuff. . . . '*Du pain; prenez, mes amis,*' Afrique said. '*Mangez comme vous voulez,*' the Cook quoth benignantly, with a glance at us over his placid shoulder. . . . Eat we most surely did. We could have eaten the French Government.

The morning of the following day we went on promenade once more. It was neither pleasant nor unpleasant to promenade in the *cour* while somebody else was suffering in the Room of Sorrow. It was, in fact, rather thrilling.

The afternoon of this day we were all up in The Enormous Room when *la commission* suddenly entered with Apollyon strutting and lisping behind it, explaining, and poohpoohing, and graciously waving his thick wicked arms.

Everyone in The Enormous Room leaped to his feet, removing as he did so his hat—with the exception of *les deux améri-cains,* who kept theirs on, and The Zulu, who couldn't find his hat and had been trying for some time to stalk it to its lair. *La commission* reacted interestingly to The Enormous Room: the captain of gendarmes looked soggily around and saw nothing with a good deal of contempt; the scented soap squinted up his face and said 'Faugh' or whatever a French bourgeois *avocat* says in the presence of a bad smell (*la commission* was standing by the door and consequently close to the *cabinet*); but the little red-head kite-flying gentleman looked actually horrified.

'Is there in the room anyone of Austrian nationality?'

The Silent Man stepped forward quietly.

'Why are you here?'

'I don't know,' The Silent Man said, with tears in his eyes.

'NONSENSE! You're here for a very good reason and you know what it is and you could tell it if you wished, you imbecile, you incorrigible, you criminal,' Apollyon shouted; then, turning to the *avocat* and the red-headed little gentleman, 'He is a dangerous alien, he admits it, he has admitted it—DON'T YOU ADMIT IT, EH? EH?' he roared at The Silent Man, who fingered his black cap without raising his eyes or changing in the least the simple and supreme dignity of his poise. 'He is incorrigible,' said (in a low snarl) The *Directeur.* 'Let us go,

gentlemen, when you have seen enough.' But the red-headed
man, as I recollect, was contemplating the floor by the door,
where six pails of urine solemnly stood, three of them having
overflowed slightly from time to time upon the reeking planks.
. . . And The *Directeur* was told that *les hommes* should have a
tin trough to urinate into, for the sake of sanitation; and that
this trough should be immediately installed, installed without
delay—'O yes indeed, sirs,' Apollyon simpered, 'a very good
suggestion; it shall be done immediately; yes indeed. Do let
me show you the—it's just outside—' and he bowed them out
with no little skill. And the door SLAMMED behind Apollyon
and the Three Wise Men.

3 / ERNEST HEMINGWAY

Nausea

The toughness, economy, and control of the literary style of Ernest
Hemingway (1898–1961) made it one of the major literary forces
during and since the 1920's. Searching for personal authenticity in a
world gone mad with comfort and anonymity, Hemingway always
remained the tough guy from Oak Park, Illinois. His first book was
a collection of short stories (from which the following selection was
made), *In Our Time* (1924), followed by *The Sun Also Rises*
(1926), another collection, *Men Without Women* (1927), and *A
Farewell to Arms* (1929). In the revealing story, "Soldier's Home,"
Hemingway says much of what he was to repeat in longer works.
The central figure of the story, Harold Krebs, is forced to distort and
exaggerate his war experiences in order to retain attention; these
lies lead to nausea and turn him against his own experience. Experience unmediated by language is a primary goal of Hemingway (and
Krebs), and the problem of describing that goal in language explains part of the final style. The challenge of seeking honesty in a

sentimental and hypocritical world explains much of Krebs' deepening disgust with the small-town pieties of his clumsy mother and, through her, of his Babbitt-like father. Hemingway (and Krebs) had resolutely repudiated the posturing and deceit of a world for whose death he wished, but a world still sufficiently alive to determine his behavior and to dilute (if permitted) the purity of experience and sensation.

Krebs went to the war from a Methodist college in Kansas. There is a picture which shows him among his fraternity brothers, all of them wearing exactly the same height and style collar. He enlisted in the Marines in 1917 and did not return to the United States until the second division returned from the Rhine in the summer of 1919.

There is a picture which shows him on the Rhine with two German girls and another corporal. Krebs and the corporal look too big for their uniforms. The German girls are not beautiful. The Rhine does not show in the picture.

By the time Krebs returned to his home town in Oklahoma the greeting of heroes was over. He came back much too late. The men from the town who had been drafted had all been welcomed elaborately on their return. There had been a great deal of hysteria. Now the reaction had set in. People seemed to think it was rather ridiculous for Krebs to be getting back so late, years after the war was over.

At first Krebs, who had been at Belleau Wood, Soissons, the Champagne, St. Mihiel and in the Argonne did not want to talk about the war at all. Later he felt the need to talk but no one wanted to hear about it. His town had heard too many atrocity stories to be thrilled by actualities. Krebs found that to

"Soldier's Home," from *In Our Time* (New York: Charles Scribner's Sons, 1931), pp. 89–101. "Soldier's Home" is reprinted with the permission of Charles Scribner's Sons from *In Our Time* by Ernest Hemingway. Copyright 1925, Charles Scribner's Sons; renewal copyright 1953, Ernest Hemingway.

be listened to at all he had to lie, and after he had done this twice he, too, had a reaction against the war and against talking about it. A distaste for everything that had happened to him in the war set in because of the lies he had told. All of the times that had been able to make him feel cool and clear inside himself when he thought of them; the times so long back when he had done the one thing, the only thing for a man to do, easily and naturally, when he might have done something else, now lost their cool, valuable quality and then were lost themselves.

His lies were quite unimportant lies and consisted in attributing to himself things other men had seen, done or heard of, and stating as facts certain apocryphal incidents familiar to all soldiers. Even his lies were not sensational at the pool room. His acquaintances, who had heard detailed accounts of German women found chained to machine guns in the Argonne forest and who could not comprehend, or were barred by their patriotism from interest in, any German machine gunners who were not chained, were not thrilled by his stories.

Krebs acquired the nausea in regard to experience that is the result of untruth or exaggeration, and when he occasionally met another man who had really been a soldier and they talked a few minutes in the dressing room at a dance he fell into the easy pose of the old soldier among other soldiers: that he had been badly, sickeningly frightened all the time. In this way he lost everything.

During this time, it was late summer, he was sleeping late in bed, getting up to walk down town to the library to get a book, eating lunch at home, reading on the front porch until he became bored and then walking down through the town to spend the hottest hours of the day in the cool dark of the pool room. He loved to play pool.

In the evening he practiced on his clarinet, strolled down town, read and went to bed. He was still a hero to his two young sisters. His mother would have given him breakfast in bed if he had wanted it. She often came in when he was in bed and asked him to tell her about the war, but her attention always wandered. His father was non-committal.

Before Krebs went away to the war he had never been allowed to drive the family motor car. His father was in the real estate business and always wanted the car to be at his command when he required it to take clients out into the country to show them a piece of farm property. The car always stood outside the First National Bank building where his father had an office on the second floor. Now, after the war, it was still the same car.

Nothing was changed in the town except that the young girls had grown up. But they lived in such a complicated world of already defined alliances and shifting feuds that Krebs did not feel the energy or the courage to break into it. He liked to look at them, though. There were so many good-looking young girls. Most of them had their hair cut short. When he went away only little girls wore their hair like that or girls that were fast. They all wore sweaters and shirt waists with round Dutch collars. It was a pattern. He liked to look at them from the front porch as they walked on the other side of the street. He liked to watch them walking under the shade of the trees. He liked the round Dutch collars above their sweaters. He liked their silk stockings and flat shoes. He liked their bobbed hair and the way they walked.

When he was in town their appeal to him was not very strong. He did not like them when he saw them in the Greek's ice cream parlor. He did not want them themselves really. They were too complicated. There was something else. Vaguely he wanted a girl but he did not want to have to work to get her. He would have liked to have a girl but he did not want to have to spend a long time getting her. He did not want to get into the intrigue and the politics. He did not want to have to do any courting. He did not want to tell any more lies. It wasn't worth it.

He did not want any consequences. He did not want any

consequences ever again. He wanted to live along without consequences. Besides he did not really need a girl. The army had
taught him that. It was all right to pose as though you had to
have a girl. Nearly everybody did that. But it wasn't true. You
did not need a girl. That was the funny thing. First a fellow
boasted how girls mean nothing to him, that he never thought
of them, that they could not touch him. Then a fellow boasted
that he could not get along without girls, that he had to have
them all the time, that he could not go to sleep without them.

That was all a lie. It was all a lie both ways. You did not
need a girl unless you thought about them. He learned that in
the army. Then sooner or later you always got one. When you
were really ripe for a girl you always got one. You did not have
to think about it. Sooner or later it would come. He had learned
that in the army.

Now he would have liked a girl if she had come to him and
not wanted to talk. But here at home it was all too complicated.
He knew he could never get through it all again. It was not
worth the trouble. That was the thing about French girls and
German girls. There was not all this talking. You couldn't talk
much and you did not need to talk. It was simple and you were
friends. He thought about France and then he began to think
about Germany. On the whole he had liked Germany better.
He did not want to leave Germany. He did not want to come
home. Still, he had come home. He sat on the front porch.

He liked the girls that were walking along the other side of
the street. He liked the look of them much better than the
French girls or the German girls. But the world they were in
was not the world he was in. He would like to have one of
them. But it was not worth it. They were such a nice pattern.
He liked the pattern. It was exciting. But he would not go
through all the talking. He did not want one badly enough. He
liked to look at them all, though. It was not worth it. Not now
when things were getting good again.

He sat there on the porch reading a book on the war. It was

a history and he was reading about all the engagements he had been in. It was the most interesting reading he had ever done. He wished there were more maps. He looked forward with a good feeling to reading all the really good histories when they would come out with good detail maps. Now he was really learning about the war. He had been a good soldier. That made a difference.

One morning after he had been home about a month his mother came into his bedroom and sat on the bed. She smoothed her apron.

"I had a talk with your father last night, Harold," she said, "and he is willing for you to take the car out in the evenings."

"Yeah?" said Krebs, who was not fully awake. "Take the car out? Yeah?"

"Yes. Your father has felt for some time that you should be able to take the car out in the evenings whenever you wished but we only talked it over last night."

"I'll bet you made him," Krebs said.

"No. It was your father's suggestion that we talk the matter over."

"Yeah. I'll bet you made him," Krebs sat up in bed.

"Will you come down to breakfast, Harold?" his mother said.

"As soon as I get my clothes on," Krebs said.

His mother went out of the room and he could hear her frying something downstairs while he washed, shaved and dressed to go down into the dining-room for breakfast. While he was eating breakfast his sister brought in the mail.

"Well, Hare," she said. "You old sleepyhead. What do you ever get up for?"

Krebs looked at her. He liked her. She was his best sister.

"Have you got the paper?" he asked.

She handed him the Kansas City *Star* and he shucked off its brown wrapper and opened it to the sporting page. He folded the *Star* open and propped it against the water pitcher with his cereal dish to steady it, so he could read while he ate.

"Harold," his mother stood in the kitchen doorway, "Harold, please don't muss up the paper. Your father can't read his *Star* if it's been mussed."

"I won't muss it," Krebs said.

His sister sat down at the table and watched him while he read.

"We're playing indoor over at school this afternoon," she said. "I'm going to pitch."

"Good," said Krebs. "How's the old wing?"

"I can pitch better than lots of the boys. I tell them all you taught me. The other girls aren't much good."

"Yeah?" said Krebs.

"I tell them all you're my beau. Aren't you my beau, Hare?"

"You bet."

"Couldn't your brother really be your beau just because he's your brother?"

"I don't know."

"Sure you know. Couldn't you be my beau, Hare, if I was old enough and if you wanted to?"

"Sure. You're my girl now."

"Am I really your girl?"

"Sure."

"Do you love me?"

"Uh, huh."

"Will you love me always?"

"Sure."

"Will you come over and watch me play indoor?"

"Maybe."

"Aw, Hare, you don't love me. If you loved me, you'd want to come over and watch me play indoor."

Krebs' mother came into the dining-room from the kitchen. She carried a plate with two fried eggs and some crisp bacon on it and a plate of buckwheat cakes.

"You run along, Helen," she said. "I want to talk to Harold."

She put the eggs and bacon down in front of him and brought in a jug of maple syrup for the buckwheat cakes. Then she sat down across the table from Krebs.

"I wish you'd put down the paper a minute, Harold," she said.

Krebs took down the paper and folded it.

"Have you decided what you are going to do yet, Harold?" his mother said, taking off her glasses.

"No," said Krebs.

"Don't you think it's about time?" His mother did not say this in a mean way. She seemed worried.

"I hadn't thought about it," Krebs said.

"God has some work for everyone to do," his mother said. "There can be no idle hands in His Kingdom."

"I'm not in His Kingdom," Krebs said.

"We are all of us in His Kingdom."

Krebs felt embarrassed and resentful as always.

"I've worried about you so much, Harold," his mother went on. "I know the temptations you must have been exposed to. I know how weak men are. I know what your own dear grandfather, my own father, told us about the Civil War and I have prayed for you. I pray for you all day long, Harold."

Krebs looked at the bacon fat hardening on his plate.

"Your father is worried, too," his mother went on. "He thinks you have lost your ambition, that you haven't got a definite aim in life. Charley Simmons, who is just your age, has a good job and is going to be married. The boys are all settling down; they're all determined to get somewhere; you can see that boys like Charley Simmons are on their way to being really a credit to the community."

Krebs said nothing.

"Don't look that way, Harold," his mother said. "You know we love you and I want to tell you for your own good how matters stand. Your father does not want to hamper your freedom. He thinks you should be allowed to drive the car. If you want to take some of the nice girls out riding with you, we are only too pleased. We want you to enjoy yourself. But you are going to have to settle down to work, Harold. Your father doesn't care what you start in at. All work is honorable as he says. But you've got to make a start at something. He asked me to speak to you this morning and then you can stop in and see him at his office."

"Is that all?" Krebs said.

"Yes. Don't you love your mother, dear boy?"

"No," Krebs said.

His mother looked at him across the table. Her eyes were shiny. She started crying.

"I don't love anybody," Krebs said.

It wasn't any good. He couldn't tell her, he couldn't make her see it. It was silly to have said it. He had only hurt her. He went over and took hold of her arm. She was crying with her head in her hands.

"I didn't mean it," he said. "I was just angry at something. I didn't mean I didn't love you."

His mother went on crying. Krebs put his arm on her shoulder.

"Can't you believe me, mother?"

His mother shook her head.

"Please, please, mother. Please believe me."

"All right," his mother said chokily. She looked up at him. "I believe you, Harold."

Krebs kissed her hair. She put her face up to him.

"I'm your mother," she said. "I held you next to my heart when you were a tiny baby."

Krebs felt sick and vaguely nauseated.

"I know, Mummy," he said. "I'll try and be a good boy for you."

"Would you kneel and pray with me, Harold?" his mother asked.

They knelt down beside the dining-room table and Krebs' mother prayed.

"Now, you pray, Harold," she said.

"I can't," Krebs said.

"Try, Harold."

"I can't."

"Do you want me to pray for you?"

"Yes."

So his mother prayed for him and then they stood up and Krebs kissed his mother and went out of the house. He had tried so to keep his life from being complicated. Still, none of it had touched him. He had felt sorry for his mother and she had made him lie. He would go to Kansas City and get a job and she would feel all right about it. There would be one more scene before he got away. He would not go down to his father's office. He would miss that one. He wanted his life to go smoothly. It had just gotten going that way. Well, that was all over now, anyway. He would go over to the schoolyard and watch Helen play indoor baseball.

4 / THORSTEIN VEBLEN

The Legacy of Intervention

In the following selection, originally written for *The Freeman* magazine in 1922, Thorstein Veblen (1857–1929) discussed most of the reasons why many writers and intellectuals repudiated America's military and diplomatic intervention into European affairs. In his typically biting language, Veblen concluded that America's participation in the war resulted in an inconclusive peace that had kept the old ruling classes in power in Europe and that had converted America into a social madhouse. The peace Wilson had won, according to Veblen, merely sustained imperialism and capitalism, hindered the progress of science by encouraging superstition, and contributed to religious obscurantism, the Ku Klux Klan, the American Legion, and war profiteers. It made it possible, even necessary, for "morons" to assume the political leadership of the nation. The bulk of Veblen's critical forays into the meaning and drift of the modern political economy (*Theory of the Leisure Class*, 1889; *Theory of Business Enterprise*, 1904; *The Instinct of Workmanship*, 1914; *Imperial Germany and the Industrial Revolution*, 1915; *An Inquiry into the Nature of Peace*, 1917; *The Higher Learning in America*, 1918; *The Vested Interests*, 1919; *The Engineers and the Price System*, 1921; and *Absentee Ownership and Business Enterprise in Recent Times*, 1923) were better as criticism than construction, but his ironic and detached style, along with the inventiveness and strength of his mind, resulted in a body of work of permanent value. His assessment of the consequences of the war represented the feeling of a large body of increasingly disaffected writers and scholars.

It is evident now, beyond cavil, that no part of Europe is better off for America's having taken part in the great war. So also it is evident that the Americans are all the worse off for it. Europe is balancing along the margin of bankruptcy, famine, and pestilence, while America has gone into moral and industrial eclipse. This state of things, in both cases, is traceable directly to America's having taken part in the war, whatever may have been the ulterior determining circumstances that brought European politics to a boil in 1914.

As regards the state of Europe, the immediate effect of American intervention was to bring the war to an inconclusive settlement; to conclude hostilities before they were finished and thereby reinstate the *status quo ante* out of which the war had arisen; to save the Junkers from conclusive defeat. There is every reason to believe that in the absence of American intervention the hostilities would have been continued until the German nation had been exhausted and the German forces had

---

"Dementia Præcox," from *The Freeman*, V (June 21, 1922); reprinted in *Essays in Our Changing Order*, ed. Leon Ardzrooni (New York: Viking, 1934), pp. 423–436. From *Essays in Our Changing Order* by Thorstein Veblen. Copyright 1934, © 1962 by The Viking Press, Inc. Reprinted by permission of The Viking Press, Inc.

been broken and pushed back across their frontiers and across their own territory; which would have demoralised and discredited the rule of privilege and property in the Fatherland to such effect that the control of affairs would have passed out of the hands of the kept classes. The outcome should then have been an effectual liquidation of the old order and the installation of something like an industrial democracy resting on other ground than privilege and property, instead of the camouflage of a *pro forma* liquidation in 1918–19 and the resulting pseudo-republic of the Ebert Government. Noske could not have functioned and the Junkers would not have been war-heroes. It was the apprehension of some such eventuality that brought out the Lansdowne letters, which served warning on the kept classes of the Entente and prepared the way for an inconclusive peace—a compact to preserve the elements of dissension, the vested interests and national ambitions out of which the war arose.

There can be no grounded surmise as to what might have been the ulterior fortunes of any conceivable revolutionary establishments that so might have been set up in the German lands on some other basis than vested interests and national ambition; but it may at least be confidently believed that no such foot-loose establishment or group of establishments could have constituted a warlike menace to the rest of Europe, or even a practicable war-bogy. The outcome would presumably have been a serious peaceful menace to absentee ownership and imperial politics, throughout Christendom, but assuredly not a menace of war—Germany would have ceased to be a Power, in the usual minatory sense of the term. And when Germany, with Austria, had fallen out of line as a Power, the rest of the line of Powers would be in a precarious case for want of something formidable to lean against. A practicable Power has to rest its case on a nerve-shattering popular fear of aggression from without.

The American intervention saved the life of the German Empire as a disturber of the peace, by saving the German forces from conclusive defeat, and so saving the rule of the kept classes in Germany. It will be said, of course, by vainglorious Americans and by obsequious politicians of the Entente, that America's entrance into the war decided the case against the Central Powers; which is a sufficiently idle piece of stage-bravery. So also the German war-lords cover their shame with the claim that America turned their assured victory to defeat; but the reason for that claim is the need of it. When the whole adventure is seen in perspective it is evident that the defeat of the Germans was decided at the battle of the Marne in 1914, and the rest of the conflict was a desperate fight for negotiable terms on which the German war-lords hoped to save their face at home; and America's intervention has helped them save the remnants of their face.

If Imperial Germany had dropped out of the running, as a practicable war-Power, at the same time that Imperial Russia had gone into collapse, the French Government would have had no practicable war-scare at hand with which to frighten the French people into a policy of increased armament. On the same grounds coercion and submission would have ceased to characterise the administration of their internal affairs; the existing Government of French profiteers would have lost control; and expenditures would have been covered in part by taxes on income and capital, instead of the present deficit-financiering and constantly increasing debt. France would have returned to a peace-footing. At the same time the prosecution of hostilities through the winter 1918–19 would have carried the exhaustion of French resources and the inflation of French indebtedness to such a point as to ensure a drastic and speedy liquidation of their fiscal and commercial affairs, with a recapitalisation of assets at a reasonable figure, such as to permit French trade and industry to make a new start within a reasonable time.

What has just been said of the French case will hold true for the other Continental peoples in nearly the same degree, with some allowance for local circumstances. The case of the

British is not substantially different, except in degree, and except that the outcome of the war has enabled British imperialism to take on an added degree of jobbery and effrontery. The American intervention brought the war to a close before the exhaustion of resources and the inflation of capital and liabilities in Europe had reached the breaking-point, and thereby it has enabled the vested interests to keep their footing on a nominal capitalisation in excess of the earning-capacity of their assets, to maintain prices and restrict output; from which follows unemployment, privation, and industrial disorder. At the same time the inconclusive peace, with the resulting international intrigue, has enabled the politicians of the old line to retain control and continue the old line of warlike diplomacy and coercive administration—a state of things which could scarcely have come to pass except for the formidable intervention of America during the closing months of the war.

It may be said, of course, that the state of things in Europe was not brought on by the American intervention; that even if the contending Powers had been left to their own devices they might not have carried their emulation of the Kilkenny Cats through to the normal Kilkenny finish. Even if the Americans had not come in and upset the fighting-balance, the European statesmen might have seen their way to much the same sort of negotiated peace, with much the same view to renewed hostilities at a future date. Such an outcome would of course have been possible, though it would not seem probable; and in that event the Europeans would presumably have fallen into much the same evil case in which they now find themselves, under the rule of the statesmen of the kept classes. They would have been no worse off, and presumably no better.

But it still remains true that in such event the Americans would have been spared certain untoward experiences that have followed. Most of the war-debt, much of the increased armament, a good share of the profiteering incident to the war and the peace, and all of the income tax would have been avoided. It is true, American statesmen would still have continued to do the "dirty work" for American bankers in Nicaragua; they might still have seen their way to manhandle the Haitians and put the white man's burden on the black population of Liberia for the profit of American banks and politicians; it is even conceivable that they could still have backed the Polish adventures in Russia and have sent troops and supplies to the Murmansk and Siberia to annoy the horrid Bolsheviki; but there is at least a reasonable chance that, in such event, there would have arisen no "American Legion," no Ku-Klux-Klan, no Knights of Columbus, and no Lusk Commission. Presumably there would also have been relatively little of the rant and bounce of Red-Cross patriotism; no espionage act, no wholesale sentences or deportations for constructive sedition, and no prosecution of pacifists and conscientious objectors for excessive sanity. In short, there is a reasonable chance that in such event the Americans might have come through the period of the war in a reasonable state of buncombe and intolerance without breaking down into the systematised illusions of dementia præcox.

It will be said, of course, that the American intervention hastened the return of peace and thereby saved much property and very many lives of men, women, and children that would otherwise have been wasted in hostilities carried on to no effect for another four or five months; all of which is not reasonably to be questioned. But it is also not reasonably to be questioned that the past three or four years of dissension, disorder, privation, and disease that have been brought on by the precipitate conclusion of hostilities, have taken twice as heavy a toll in wasted time and substance and in wasted lives—not counting the debauch of waste and confusion which their unselfish participation in the war has brought upon the Americans.

Assuredly, none of these untoward consequences was aimed at or contemplated by the Administration when it shifted from a footing of quasi-neutrality to formal hostilities in 1917. Still

less was anything of the kind contemplated in that run of popular sentiment that came to the support of the Administration in
its declaration of war. So far as the case can be covered with
any general formula, America entered the war "to make the
world safe for democracy." It is only that, instead of what was
aimed at, the untoward state of things described above has
followed in the chain of consequence. The motives of the Americans in the case are not to be impugned. They were as nearly
blameless as might reasonably be expected under the circumstances. It is only that the unintended and unforeseen ulterior
outcome of the adventure has now, after the event, shown that
America's participation in the war was a highly deplorable
mistake. In so far, this unhappy turn of events has gone to
vindicate the protests of the pacifists and the conscientious objectors. Their arguments may have been unsound, and the conscientious objectors have at least found themselves on the
wrong side of the law, and their motives may have been un-
worthy as often as not. There is no call to argue the legalities or
the moralities of the case in this connection. It is only that now,
after the event, it has unhappily become evident that the course
of public policy against which they contended—perhaps un-
worthily—was not the wiser course to pursue. Their morals may
have been bad and their manners worse, and the courts have
decided, with great spontaneity, that their aim was criminal in
a high degree, and popular sentiment has borne out the sentiment of the courts in this matter, on the whole and for the time
being. Yet the turn of events has, unhappily, gone to show that,
barring the statutory infirmities of their case, these statutory
criminals were in effect contending for the wiser course. And
for so having, in some wrong-headed way, spoken for a wiser
course of action than that adopted by the constituted authorities, these statutory criminals have been and continue to be
subjected to cruel and unusual punishment. All of which invites
reflection on the vagaries of dementia præcox.

The current situation in America is by way of being something of a psychiatrical clinic. In order to come to an under-standing of this situation there is doubtless much else to be taken into account, but the case of America is after all not fairly to be understood without making due allowance for a certain prevalent unbalance and derangement of mentality, presumably transient but sufficiently grave for the time being. Perhaps the commonest and plainest evidence of this unbal-anced mentality is to be seen in a certain fearsome and feverish credulity with which a large proportion of the Americans are affected. As contrasted with their state of mind before the war, they are predisposed to believe in footless outrages and odious plots and machinations—"treasons, stratagems, and spoils." They are readily provoked to a headlong intolerance, and re-sort to unadvised atrocities as a defense against imaginary evils. There is a visible lack of composure and logical coherence, both in what they will believe and in what they are ready to do about it.

Throughout recent times the advance of exact knowledge in the material sciences has been progressively supplanting the received barbarian beliefs in magical and supernatural agen-cies. This progressive substitution of matter-of-fact in the place of superstition has gone forward unremittingly and at a con-stantly accelerated rate, being the most characteristic and most constructive factor engaged in modern civilisation. But during the past six or eight years, since the outbreak of the war, and even more plainly since its conclusion, the churches, high and low, have been gaining both in numbers and in revenues, as well as in pontifical unction. The logical faculty appears to have suffered a notable degree of prostration throughout the American community; and all the while it is the more puerile crudities of superstitious fear that have been making particular and inordinate gains. So, for example, it is since the outbreak of the war that the Rev. Billy Sunday has effectively come into his own, and it is since the peace that he has become such a power of obscurity as to command a price as an agency of intimidation and misrule. So also it is during these last few years of the same period of nervous prostration that the Fundamentalists are effectually making headway in their campaign of obscuration designed to reinstate the Fear of God in place of common-sense. Driven by a nerve-shattering fear that some climax of ghostly atrocities is about to be visited on all persons who are found lacking in bigotry, this grosser sort of devout innocents now impugn certain findings of material science on the ground that these findings are presumed to be distasteful to a certain well-known anthropomorphic divinity, to whom His publicity-agents impute a sadistic temper and an unlimited power of abuse. These evidences of a dilapidated mentality are growing more and more obvious. Meantime even a man of such signal good sense and humanity as Mr. Bryan is joining forces with the Rev. Billy Sunday in the propaganda of intolerance, while the gifts of so engaging a raconteur as Sir Conan Doyle are brought in to cover the flanks of this drive into intellectual twilight.

It may be said, of course, that such-like maggoty conceits are native to the religious fancy and are due to come into the foreground in all times of trouble; but just now the same fearsome credulity is running free and large through secular affairs as well, and its working-out is no more edifying in that department of human conduct. At the date when America formally entered the war, American popular sentiment had already been exposed to a protracted stress of apprehension and perplexity and was ready for alarms and excursions into intolerance. All manner of extravagant rumors met with ready belief, and, indeed, few were able to credit anything that was not extravagant. It was a period dominated by illusions of frightfulness and persecution. It was the peculiar misfortune of the American people that they were called into action only after their mental poise had been shattered by a long run of enervating perplexity and agitation. The measures taken under these circumstances were drawn on such lines of suspicion and intolerance as might be looked for under these circumstances. Differences of opinion were erected into statutory crimes, to which extravagant penalties were attached. Persons charged with these new-found statutory crimes were then convicted on a margin of legal interpretation. In effect, suspected persons were held guilty until proved innocent, with the doubt weighing against them. In one of these episodes of statutory frightfulness, that of the far-famed "Lusk Committee," some ten thousand persons were arrested on ungrounded suspicion, with extensive destruction of papers and property. The foreign-language press was laid under disabilities and the use of the mails was interrupted on general grounds of hysterical consternation. On the same grounds circulation and credence were given to extravagantly impossible fictions of Bolshevik propaganda, and the I.W.W. was by interpretation erected into a menace to the Republic, while the Secret Service kept faithfully on the job of making two suspicions grow where one grew before. Under cover of it all the American profiteers have diligently gone about their business of getting something for nothing at the cost of all concerned, while popular attention has been taken up with the maudlin duties of civil and religious intolerance.

The Republic has come through this era of spiritual dilapidation with an unbalanced budget and an increased armament by use of which to "safeguard American Interests"—that is to say, negotiate profitable concessions for American oil companies—a system of passports, deportations, and restricted immigration, and a Legion of veterans organised for a draft on the public funds and the cultivation of warlike distemper. Unreflecting patriotic flurry has become a civic virtue. Drill in patriotic—that is to say military—ritual has been incorporated in the ordinary routine of the public schools, and it has come to be obligatory to stand uncovered through any rendition of the "National Anthem"—a musical composition of which one could scarcely say that it might have been worse. The State constabularies have been augmented; the right of popular assembly freely interfered with; establishments of mercenary "gunmen," under the formal name of detective-agencies, have increased their output; the Ku-Klux-Klan has been reanimated and reorganised for extra-legal intimidation of citizens; and the American Legion now and again enforces "law and order" on the unfortunate by extra-legal measures. Meantime the profiteers do business as usual and the Federal authorities are busied with a schedule of increased protective duties designed to enhance the profits of their business.

Those traits in this current situation wherein it is different from the relatively sober state of things before the war, have been injected by America's participation in the war; and it is, in effect, for their failure to join hands and help in working up this state of things that the conscientious objectors, draft-evaders, I.W.W.'s, Communists, have been penalised in a manner unexampled in American history. This is not saying that the pacifists, conscientious objectors, etc., are not statutory criminals or that they foresaw such an outcome of the traffic against which they protested, or that they were moved by peculiarly high-minded or unselfish considerations in making their protest; but only that the subsequent course of events has unhappily brought out the fact that these distasteful persons took a stand for the sounder side of a debatable question. Except for the continued prevalence of a distempered mentality that still runs on illusions of persecution, it might reasonably have been expected that this sort of *de facto* vindication of the stand taken by these statutory criminals would be allowed to count in extenuation of their *de jure* fault. But the distemper still runs its course. Indeed, it is doubtless the largest, profoundest, and most enduring effect brought upon the Americans by America's intervention in the great war.

Typically and commonly, dementia præcox is a distemper of adolescence or of early manhood, at least such appears to be the presumption held among psychiatrists. Yet its occurrence is not confined within any assignable age-limits. Typically, if not altogether commonly, it takes the shape of a dementia perse-cutoria, an illusion of persecution and a derangement of the logical faculty such as to predispose the patient to the belief that he and his folks are victims of plots and systematic atroci-ties. A fearsome credulity is perhaps the most outstanding symptom, and this credulity may work out in a fear of atrocities to be suffered in the next world or in the present; that is to say a fear of God or of evil men. Prolonged or excessive worry ap-pears to be the most usual predisposing cause. Expert opinions differ as to how far the malady is to be reckoned as a curable disease; the standard treatment being rest, security, and nutri-tion. The physiological ground of such a failure of mentality appears to be exhaustion and consequent deterioration of nerve-tissue, due to shock or prolonged strain; and recuperation is notoriously slow in the case of nerve-tissue.

No age, sex, or condition is immune, but dementia præcox will affect adolescents more frequently than mature persons, and men more frequently than women; at least so it is said. Adolescent males are peculiarly subject to this malady, appar-ently because they are—under modern circumstances—in a peculiar degree exposed to worry, dissipation, and consequent nervous exhaustion. The cares and unfamiliar responsibilities of manhood fall upon them at that period, and under modern cir-cumstances these cares and responsibilities are notably exact-ing, complex, and uncertain. Given a situation of widespread apprehension, uncertainty, and agitation, such as the war-experience brought on the Americans, and the consequent derangement of mentality should be of a similarly widespread character—such as has come in evidence.

The peculiar liability of adolescent males carries the open suggestion that a similar degree of liability should also extend to those males of more advanced years in whom a puerile men-tality persists, men in whom a boyish temper continues into later life. These boyish traits may be seen in admirably systematised fashion in such organisations as the Boy Scouts. Much the same range of characteristics marks the doings and aspirations, individual and collective, of high-school boys, undergraduate students, and organisations of the type of the Y.M.C.A. In this connection it would perhaps be ungraceful to direct attention to the clergy of all denominations, where self-selection has resulted in a concentration on the lower range of the intellectual spectrum. One is also not unprepared to find a sensible infusion of the same puerile traits among military men. A certain truculent temper is conspicuous among the stigmata. Persons in whom the traits and limitations of the puerile mentality persist in a particularly notable degree are called "morons," but there are also many persons who approximate more or less closely to the moronic grade of mentality without being fully entitled to the technical designation. Such a degree of arrested spiritual and mental development is, in practical effect, no bar against entrance into public office. Indeed, a degree of puerile exuberance coupled with a certain truculent temper and boyish cunning is likely to command something of popular admiration and affection, which is likely to have a certain selective effect in the democratic choice of officials. Men, and perhaps even more particularly the women, will be sympathetically and affectionately disposed toward the standard vagaries of boyhood, and this sentimental inclination is bound to be reflected in the choice of public officials in any democratic community, where such choice is habitually guided by the play of sentiment. America is the most democratic of all nations; at least so they say. A run of persecutory credulity of the nature of dementia præcox should logically run swiftly and with a wide sweep in the case of such a community endowed with such an official machinery, and its effects should be profound and lasting.

PART 2

POLITICAL FUNDAMENTALISM

5

Prohibition

The Eighteenth Amendment to the Constitution, prohibiting the manufacture, sale, or transportation of alcoholic beverages, was adopted by Congress on December 18, 1917; it was ratified by the states in a little over a month and went into effect with the passage of the Volstead Act over the president's veto in January 1920. The debate in the House of Representatives on December 17, 1917, was, in several senses, a symptom of some of the issues that were to persist throughout the Twenties. Defenders of Prohibition were seeking ways to preserve what they believed to be traditional American values against the corrosion of time; they argued that Prohibition was necessary for the moral strength of the nation, to win the war, and to protect the families of drunkards. Opponents of Prohibition said that the issue was dangerously divisive during war, was anti-democratic, should be decided by local option, would result in a vast tax loss, and was rural aggression against the cities. After the beginning of the "noble experiment" the argument continued, largely as a result of the bootlegging and other crimes that were Prohibition's most significant although unintended consequence. From the moment of its implementation until repeal (with the Twenty-first Amendment in 1933), Prohibition was among provincial America's most important and irritating challenges to the advocates of change.

43

December 17, 1917

HOUSE OF REPRESENTATIVES

Mr. [Richard Wilson] AUSTIN [R.-Tenn.]. Mr. Speaker, Tennessee has successfully tried prohibition for six years. It has worked so well that both political parties are committed to it, and no political organization in that State would dare attempt to make a fight for its repeal. A law which has emptied the jails in Tennessee and virtually wiped out the criminal side of the dockets of the courts will do the same thing in every State in the American Union. [Applause.] King Alcohol has filled the world already with enough misery, with enough murders, with enough insane people, with enough unhappy wives and unfortunate children. Let us dedicate ourselves this day and this hour to the improvement of American manhood and womanhood by voting to make America the best country on the face of the earth. [Applause.] While our soldier boys are fighting to make the world free and safe, let the American Congress make the United States better physically, mentally, and morally. I predict that when the two great political parties in this country next assemble in their national conventions they will both adopt platforms favoring prohibition and woman suffrage. [Applause.]

Mr. [William] GORDON [D.-Ohio]. Would the people of States like New York, Pennsylvania, Ohio and Illinois, after having this amendment forced upon them by the legislatures of such States as New Mexico, Nevada, Wyoming, and Arizona be disposed to enact the necessary legislation to enforce it? The question answers itself.

These gentlemen from the rural districts who propose to assume the guardianship over the morals of the people who reside in the great and populous States of this Union are re-

From *Congressional Record,* 65th Cong., 2d sess., 1918, vol. 56, pt. 1, pp. 442, 444, 446, 448, 451.

minded that the great mass of the people of those States were born and have grown up in their own Commonwealths, are more familiar with the people and institutions of their own States than nonresidents possibly can be, and that the morals of the people, so far as the same are affected by what they eat and drink, are not likely to be improved by outside interference.

Mr. [Thomas] GALLAGHER [D.-Ill.]. Mr. Speaker, again the valuable time of this body is taken up and diverted from the consideration of many important legislative matters relating to the war and the general welfare of the country, again we are to interrupt and disturb business throughout the land, and many who are now doing a prosperous and successful business—and I do not mean saloonkeepers, either—will be ruined if the promoters of the pending measure have their way. A number of busy agitators and handsomely paid reformers are constantly at work keeping this prohibition wrangle before Congress and the country.

They are the same forces that upset and obstructed the plans of the administration at the late special session of Congress, and prevented the prompt enactment of a law for the conservation of food and fuel; as a result of needless controversy and delay at that time the poor and unfortunate in many sections of the country are to-day suffering because of the high and unreasonable prices demanded for food and fuel. There is a lobby here in the interest of prohibition, but none here in behalf of those who are suffering from hunger these cold winter days and freezing for want of coal.

If the people of the several States are anxious for prohibition, if they have such a desire as the promoters of this legislation claim to live in dry territory, there is no need of coming here demanding the passage of this joint resolution. The several States now have the power and can regulate by law the manufacture and sale of all intoxicating liquors. Congress has already stopped the manufacture and importation of whisky and has empowered the President to say whether light wines and beers shall be manufactured in the country. In view of all this, is it not a fact that we have all the law that is now necessary to make this country dry whenever it is essential to do so?

But this is not what the professional prohibitionists are after; they would stop the gathering of needed taxes, National, State, and municipal, that are now derived from the sale of liquor, ruin millions of dollars' worth of valuable property without recompense to the owners, destroy real estate values and rentals, make vineyards valueless, cause strikes and unrest among workmen and deprive them of opportunity to labor.

They would throw the entire country into violent and destructive political turmoil; bring about expensive, angry, and riotous election contests everywhere; disturb, hinder, and prolong legislative sessions in the various States; and destroy public interest in a cause that all should be interested in—that of winning this war.

I believe in temperance and favor laws that will regulate the liquor traffic. I also have some respect for the personal liberty and rights of others. I am against unjust and tyrannical laws. Merchants and manufacturers who contribute large sums of money to further this prohibition movement with an idea that they will receive greater efficiency from their employees may find in the end that it is simply money wasted, and if we knew now what it cost the Government to maintain a police force of United States marshals in many of the so-called prohibition States to prevent the manufacture and sale of liquor it might surprise many who favor this unnecessary legislation.

Many here who pretend they are anxious to pass this joint resolution that may change the organic act of the Nation to stop drunkenness and crime will assume a different attitude when the suffrage amendment is before us. We can then tell by the vote cast those who really favor law, order, and good government.

I hate hypocrisy and false pretense; there is more unfairness, deceit, and insincerity mixed up in the prohibition movement than any other I know of. A secret ballot here would show it. I am opposed to the pending resolution for national prohibition and will vote against it.

Mr. [John N.] TILLMAN [D.-Ark.]. Mr. Speaker, in this discussion it is neither my purpose nor desire to wantonly insult any man who may be engaged in the liquor business. The expression "Down with the saloon and up with the saloon keeper and the saloon patron" has obtained wide currency and generous approval in prohibition circles. But I shall not search for soft phrases in which to express an opinion of a traffic which is destroying men and women in this Republic alone at the rate of 100,000 a year, a traffic which fills the land with beggars and tramps, a traffic which draws from the pockets of the people of the United States two and one-half billion dollars annually and gives in return sorrow and suffering and tears and poverty.

King Alcohol collects from his vassal more of his substance than is required by any other potentate on earth, and when he has stripped him to his foolish hide he kicks him out of his palace into the street. The princes of earth, the executives of commonwealths, send abroad their taxgatherers once a year to collect from the people a small part of their earnings for government expenses, and they furnish officers to protect the life and preserve the peace and property of the citizen; they provide armies, hospitals, asylums, and pensions; but King John Barleycorn, who bestrides the narrow world like a colossus, haughty and heartless, the mightiest monarch of earth, greater than George the Fifth or William of Germany, greater than Sultan or Mikado, stations his collectors all over the land and gathers tribute from his thirsty subjects every hour in the day and every day in the year. Fair and generous rulers pension their servants, soldiers, and sailors when they become old or disabled, and provide for their widows and orphans if they fall while serving the State. Individuals and corporations do likewise, but you may serve this hard master till your money, character, happiness, and life are gone, and you will find that King John will not even provide a poorhouse to shelter your helpless wife and babies. If a subject flushed with the king's beverages, in lightsome sport or otherwise, kills a fellow man, King John does not draw from his well-filled purse money wherewithal to employ counsel to defend him, but he lets him hang, undefended, so far as he is concerned, when the real criminal is King John's agent, the man who sold the whisky. If a faithful subject, after paying tribute for many and many a weary year, at last yields to delirium tremens and dies a pauper's death, King John does not even give him swift burial in the potter's field. Pitiless King John! And yet men will march under his scarlet banner and give up honor, home, wife, and children that he may reign in guilty splendor. Men will serve this red despot and give him everything they have, even their bodies and their souls, and get not a pleasant look in return. The most arrogant, the least polite, the coldest mannered, the most disdainful citizen, is that haughty plutocrat, the American brewer, usually tainted with Teuton sympathies and damned by a German conscience. The average barkeeper—and it has been my ill fortune to meet him a few times in days long gone by—is as cold as the heart of the dead. One thing that can be said in his favor, however, he is always sober, because paradoxical as it may seem, saloon keepers want bartenders who do not drink. They will cheerfully sell you their wares, but they have too much sense to drink their own liquors. A cynical old miller of my town once said of the flour made by a rival mill that it was not fit for anything except to sell. In the eyes of the sensible barkeeper, whisky is good for nothing except to sell.

Royal King Alcohol, let us drink his health in pure water. Sweet, beautiful water. "Brewed in the running brook, the rippling fountain, and the laughing rill; brewed in the limpid cascade, as it joyfully leaps down the mountain side; brewed in the mountain top, whose granite peaks glitter like gold, bathed in the morning sun; brewed in the sparkling dewdrop; sweet, beautiful water; brewed in the crested waves of the ocean deep, driven by the storm, breathing its terrible anthem to the god of the seas; brewed in the fleecy foam of the whitened spray, as it hangs like a speck over the distant cataract; brewed in the clouds of heaven. Sweet, beautiful water! As it sings in the rain shower and dances in the hailstorm, as it comes sweeping down in feathery flakes, clothing the earth in a spotless mantle of white, always beautiful. Distilled in the golden tissues that paint the winter sky at the setting of the sun, and the silver tissues that veil the midnight moon. Sweet, health-giving, beautiful water; distilled in the rainbow of promise, whose warp is the raindrop of earth, and whose woof is the sunbeam of heaven; sweet, beautiful water." But the drunkard prefers Budweiser or Anheuser, Old Crow or Moonshine, to this blessed, God-made, health-giving beverage.

Oh, the miseries, the tears, the crimes, the deaths chargeable to this prince of destroyers. King John lays his heavy hand on the smallest and the greatest of earth, and they die his victims. The great son of Phillip conquered every foe save wine and death, and died like a dog. Lord Byron's brilliant mind and handsome face were debauched and destroyed by drink. The great Burns drank heavily, and going home one night from a drunken orgy he sank in a stupor by the roadside and thereby contracted an illness which soon stole the color from his splendid face and the glitter from his fine eyes, and long before his time this gifted son of Scottish song struck his colors to the pitiless foe that always conquers.

Who are for whisky? Those who make fortunes out of it.

Who are against it? The mothers of the land, because it destroys their loved ones. The ministers, because liquor undoes what they do. The officers of the law, because alcohol is the unapproachable chief of all causes of crime. The doctors advise against it because there is no more potent source of disease. The judges are against it because of its appalling record of misery, pauperism, and crime. Statesmen are against it because it is a menace to stable government. Educators are against it because it is a grim threat to every child in the land. Oh, I can call a cloud of witnesses to condemn it. . . .

6

Immigration Restriction

The debate in both the House of Representatives and the Senate over the first "Quota Law," restricting immigration into the United States, became an occasion for the legislators to define the meaning of America. Those in favor of restricting immigration, as well as those who wanted to continue the older and freer policies, agreed that American values were at stake in the debate. The opponents of free immigration argued that a continued influx of aliens would dilute what they called the American way of life, while the defenders of free immigration insisted that the very meaning of America depended, as it always had, upon free immigration. Radicalism, pauperism, and cheap labor were additional ingredients in the conflict. Underlying this debate was the growing tension between cosmopolitan and provincial America. The outcome was the passage of new legislation restricting immigration to 3 per cent of the nationalities represented in the census of 1910, but soon, in 1924, even more restrictive legislation was passed, cutting approximately in half the figures of 1920 and 1921. These debates disclosed the growing divergences in the United States and showed, too, that there was little hope for an immediate political or social armistice.

April 20, 1921
HOUSE OF REPRESENTATIVES

   Mr. [Lucian Walton] PARRISH [D.-Tex.].   We should stop immigration entirely until such a time as we can amend our im-

From *Congressional Record*, 67th Cong., 1st sess., 1921, vol. 61, pt. 1, pp. 511–512, 515.

migration laws and so write them that hereafter no one shall be admitted except he be in full sympathy with our Constitution and laws, willing to declare himself obedient to our flag, and willing to release himself from any obligations he may owe to the flag of the country from which he came.

It is time that we act now, because within a few short years the damage will have been done. The endless tide of immigration will have filled our country with a foreign and unsympathetic element. Those who are out of sympathy with our Constitution and the spirit of our Government will be here in large numbers, and the true spirit of Americanism left us by our fathers will gradually become poisoned by this uncertain element.

The time once was when we welcomed to our shores the oppressed and downtrodden people from all the world, but they came to us because of oppression at home and with the sincere purpose of making true and loyal American citizens, and in truth and in fact they did adapt themselves to our ways of thinking and contributed in a substantial sense to the progress and development that our civilization has made. But that time has passed now; new and strange conditions have arisen in the countries over there; new and strange doctrines are being taught. The Governments of the Orient are being overturned and destroyed, and anarchy and bolshevism are threatening the very foundation of many of them, and no one can foretell what the future will bring to many of those countries of the Old World now struggling with these problems.

Our country is a self-sustaining country. It has taught the principles of real democracy to all the nations of the earth; its flag has been the synonym of progress, prosperity, and the preservation of the rights of the individual, and there can be nothing so dangerous as for us to allow the undesirable foreign element to poison our civilization and thereby threaten the safety of the institutions that our forefathers have established for us.

Now is the time to throw about this country the most stringent immigration laws and keep from our shores forever those who are not in sympathy with the American ideas. It is the time now for us to act and act quickly, because every month's delay increases the difficulty in which we find ourselves and renders the problems of government more difficult of solution. We must protect ourselves from the poisonous influences that are threatening the very foundation of the Governments of Europe; we must see to it that those who come here are loyal and true to our Nation and impress upon them that it means something to have the privileges of American citizenship. We must hold this country true to the American thought and the American ideals.

Mr. [Albert B.] ROSSDALE [R.-N.Y.]. Will the gentleman yield to me one minute of his time to allow me to correct a statement in the speech of the gentleman from Texas [Mr. PARRISH]?

Mr. RAKER. I yield to the gentleman one minute.

Mr. ROSSDALE. Mr. Chairman, the gentleman from Texas [Mr. PARRISH] has stated that the indications are that 2,000,000 or possibly more people will enter the United States in the coming year. The estimated steamship facilities for bringing people from all over the world for a year are 809,000. Now, why this hysteria? The gentleman also assumes that all of these people over there are antagonistic to American ideals and interests. Has the gentleman ever come in contact with a lot of these immigrants and does he really know that they are of that type? I come from The Bronx, where there are a great many of these so-called foreigners, and I have an intimate knowledge of their political opinions and ideals, and I can say to the gentleman from Texas that if he had even a speaking acquaintance with them he would quickly learn that they breathe higher and purer ideals than he had any previous knowledge of. I invite the gentleman from Texas to come to The Bronx and find out for himself what splendid American citizens they make. [Applause.]

Mr. [Meyer] LONDON [Socialist-N.Y.]. Mr. Chairman and gentlemen, I have no hope of presenting even an outline of this subject. The world is still crazy. The war is not over. After preaching for thousands of years the fatherhood of God and the brotherhood of man, and then engaging for five years in slaughter, it is but natural that we should be in an abnormal state. While the killing of men's bodies has stopped, the poisoning of minds has just begun. This bill is a continuation of the war upon humanity. It is an assertion of that exaggerated nationalism which never appeals to reason and which has for its main source the self-conceit of accumulated prejudice.

At whom are you striking in this bill? Why, at the very people whom a short while ago you announced you were going to emancipate. We sent 2,000,000 men abroad to make the world "safe for democracy," to liberate these very people. Now you shut the door to them. Yes. So far, we have made the world safe for hypocrisy and the United States incidentally unsafe for the Democratic Party, temporarily at least. [Laughter.] The supporters of the bill claim that the law will keep out radicals. The idea that by restricting immigration you will prevent the influx of radical thought is altogether untenable. You can not confine an idea behind prison bars. You can not exclude it by the most drastic legislation. The field of thought recognizes no barriers. The fact that there was almost no immigration during the war did not prevent us from importing every abominable idea from Europe. We brought over the idea of deportation of radicals from France, not from the France of Rousseau, Jaurés, and Victor Hugo but from the France of the Bourbons. We imported the idea of the censorship of the press and the passport system from Russia, not from the Russia of Kropotkin and Tolstoy but from the Russia of Nicholas II. We have imported the idea of universal military service from Germany, not from the Germany of Heine, Boerne, and Freiligrath but from the Germany of the Kaiser. . . .

Ideas can neither be shut in nor shut out. There is only one

way of contending with an idea, and that is the old and safe
American rule of free and untrammeled discussion. Every attempt to use any other method has always proven disastrous.

While purporting to be a temporary measure, just for a year
or so, this bill is really intended to pave the way to permanent
exclusion.

To prevent immigration means to cripple the United States.
Our most developed industrial States are those which have had
the largest immigration. Our most backward States industrially
and in the point of literacy are those which have had no immigration to speak of.

The extraordinary and unprecedented growth of the United
States is as much a cause as the effect of immigration.

Defenders of this bill thoughtlessly repeat the exploded
theory that there have been two periods of immigration, the
good period, which the chairman of the committee fixes up to
the year 1900, and the bad period since. The strange thing
about it is that at no time in history has any country made
such rapid progress in industry, in science, and in the sphere of
social legislation as this country has shown since 1900.

The new immigration is neither different nor worse, and
besides that, identically the same arguments were used against
the old immigration.

By this bill we, who have escaped the horrors of the war, will
refuse a place of refuge to the victims of the war.

I repeat, this is an attempt at civilization. Progress is by no
means a continuous or uninterrupted process. Many a civilization has been destroyed in the tortuous course of history and
has been followed by hundreds or thousands of years of darkness. It is just possible that unless strong men who love liberty
will everywhere assert themselves, the world will revert to a
state of savagery. Just now we hear nothing but hatred, nothing
but the ravings of the exaggerated I—"I am of the best stock, I
do not want to be contaminated; I have produced the greatest

literature; my intellect is the biggest; my heart is the noblest"—
and this is repeated in every parliament, in every country, by
every fool all over the world. [Applause.]

May 2, 1921
Senate

Mr. [James Thomas] Heflin [D.-Ala.]. Mr. President, I
understand that as the pending bill is now written it will permit
about 300,000 immigrants annually to come into the United
States. I think the provision which is made in the bill as reported by the Senator from Vermont [Mr. Dillingham] is a
considerable improvement over the bill as it came from the
House. The provision of the House bill relative to permitting
those who are fleeing from foreign countries because of religious persecution would permit thousands and hundreds of
thousands of undesirable foreigners to come into our country.

We have tried for a long time to pass an immigration law
that would really restrict immigration and that would guard
our shores against the undesirable populations of foreign countries, but we have invariably discovered, after the law had been
enacted, that there were loopholes through which such people
could come. Undesirables have been coming and they are now
coming to this country. I submit, Mr. President, to the Senate
and to the country that if this Government ever intends to protect its life against the dangers that threaten it from this very
source that time is now. The daily newspapers have been filled
with headlines relative to the movements of red anarchists and
bolsheviki in the United States. I hold here in my hand the
notice of a circular which has been issued by them. This is from

From *Congressional Record,* 67th Cong., 1st sess., 1921, vol. 61, pt. 1,
pp. 915–917.

Ansonia, Conn., and is dated April 29. It appeared in the Washington Post of last Saturday, I believe. The article reads:

ANARCHIST CIRCULARS URGE REFUSAL TO OBEY LAWS.

ANSONIA, CONN., *April 29*

Radical literature again was distributed in this city during the night. Circulars bearing the caption, "The 1st day of May—the day of reckoning and liberation," and purporting to be issued by anarchist groups of the United States and Canada, were found this morning.

In them workers are advised to refuse to pay taxes and rents, refuse to obey laws, take possession of the land, factories, mills, and mines and to go armed to mass meetings or parades.

Mr. President, is this Government called upon to open the doors of this country to people who openly and notoriously advise the violation of our laws, the tearing down of our institutions and the taking over of private property? It seems to me that it is high time that Congress should pass a law that will keep out all people who are unfriendly to the American form of government. Several months ago one of these men who oppose our form of government, and while enjoying its hospitality, unfurled and burned the United States flag before an audience of his kind in the city of New York. I think some small fine was imposed upon him, but he is now again a free man. Is this Government called upon to open the doors of our country to such as he? Is this Government called upon to permit such as he to remain?

Mr. President, some months ago the boys who had returned from France with our flag, covered all over with the glory of their valor, while marching in a parade out in Centralia, Wash., celebrating Armistice Day, were fired upon from ambush and two of them killed. Is this Government called upon to permit any more of that kind from the criminal classes of Europe to land upon our shores?

Mr. President, it is high time for this Government to take

stock; it is high time that we were finding out here at home just "who is who" in America.

There was another story in the newspapers Saturday about one of these red anarchists who has been in this country for 17 years and yet he had never been naturalized. Think of it. He has been protected by our laws; he has enjoyed the blessings and benefits of the Government, which he is daily seeking to overthrow. Is there any good reason why we should pass a law that will permit such as he to come over here?

Mr. President, if I had my way about it, I would shut our immigration doors tightly for one year at least, and I would very rigidly restrict it for all time to come.

I am in favor of putting a commission of loyal Americans on the other side of the ocean to pass on prospective immigrants before they ever set foot upon the ship sailing for our shores. I am in favor, then, of having another such commission on this side to examine them and their credentials before they are permitted to set foot upon American soil.

Mr. President, it is no small thing to be a citizen of the United States. Time was when Rome had reached the zenith of her power that the proudest title a Roman could wear was that of a Roman soldier. To-day the proudest boast that mortal man can make is "I am an American citizen." And yet we have people in the United States, not long in the country, who threaten Members in the other branch of Congress and threaten Senators in this branch with punishment at the polls if they do not throw the doors open to all kinds of people coming from foreign countries. Political threats are used and local political power employed to secure the enactment of laws that will permit this stream of undeserved and undesirable people to continue to come into this country.

Thomas Jefferson warned us of this danger; Abraham Lincoln warned us of this danger; Gen. Grant warned us of this danger; a long line of illustrious leaders that I could mention have told us "Your danger is from within more than from without." Danger from within—How? you ask me. By people coming here who despise our form of government, who hate our institutions, and who spread the poison of their dangerous propaganda.

Senators, I repeat it is high time that we were taking stock; it is high time that we were passing a real immigration law that will keep such people out.

Not long ago I heard a Senator make a plea in behalf of liberal, easy immigration laws and he told us how in the old days we threw our doors open and how great and good people came to our shores. That is true; all of our ancestors came from across the sea; but the difference between the immigrants of that time and this, Mr. President, is that then the individual wanted to come here because he liked our form of Government; because he wanted to become a member of it; because he desired to enjoy its blessings and benefits; because he intended to support its institutions; to fight for it, if need be, and to die for it, if necessary. That is the difference between the old type that came then and some of the miserable horde that is coming now.

Mr. [Le Baron Bradford] COLT [R.-R.I.]. Mr. President—

The PRESIDING OFFICER. Does the Senator from Alabama yield to the Senator from Rhode Island?

Mr. HEFLIN. I am glad to yield to the Senator.

Mr. COLT. Does the Senator recall that 411,000 aliens waived exemption under the draft and enlisted in the late war under the banner of our country?

Mr. HEFLIN. If there were 400,000 of them who did waive exemption and were willing to fight, I dare say there were 5,000,000 of them who were shirking their responsibilities, dodging the draft law, and refusing to fight for the flag. We convicted a number of them who were openly and notoriously advising people to resist the draft law, who were telling them to paralyze the military arm of the Government in every way they could, and they were doing all in their power to defeat the purpose and the program of the Government.

Mr. COLT. Mr. President—

The PRESIDING OFFICER. Does the Senator from Alabama yield further to the Senator from Rhode Island?

Mr. HEFLIN. I yield to the Senator.

Mr. COLT. May I say further to the Senator that, of those who strove to avoid the draft, the percentage among the aliens was comparatively low? Indeed, I have seen it stated that it was less than among the native born. I merely make these statements in justice to the aliens. It does not seem to me that exaggerated statements should be made which the facts do not seem to warrant.

Mr. HEFLIN. Mr. President, I have to challenge that statement of the Senator. I do not agree with his statement that a larger percentage of native stock were disloyal and were guilty of slackerism than there were among the aliens in this country. I do not know where the distinguished Senator got his information, but evidently it came from some source not entirely friendly to the Government. I think it is a reflection upon the great body of American boys born here, native to the soil, to say that there were more of them who were guilty of trying to dodge their responsibility in time of war, refusing to follow their flag, than there were of aliens in America. . . .

Mr. President, in the old days, when the immigrant came, he came of his own accord, he worked and laid aside a little money in order to enjoy the great privilege of coming to the United States, of becoming citizens of this, the greatest Government on the globe, the freest and best Government in all the world. They were glad to come. They worked and stinted in order to get money to come. How is it now? Why, they have immigration agents now hired to go through foreign countries getting up people to come and fill up the ships that sail for America. These agents are paid money to do what? To get shiploads of people to go over to the United States. What kind of people? Any kind, just so they occupy space on a ship and pay money into the purses of the steamship companies of the United States and those of foreign countries, too.

Mr. President, are we to permit citizenship in this country to become in this fashion a mere matter of barter for the benefit of immigration agents and steamship companies? The cattlemen used to send their agents out into the country to buy and drive to the railroad station a carload of yearlings. They would then load them on the train and ship them to market. That is what the financiers of the immigration business are doing now with people whom they bring here and turn loose upon the people of the United States. They have agents going through Europe who display pictures of our savings banks, with the boys and girls from our factories rushing over with hands filled with greenbacks to deposit in the bank. They say to the foreigners: "America is the place. Get your tickets. The ship will sail soon. Don't fail to get your tickets." They fill these ships with people who make the business of the immigration agent profitable and pour money into the pockets of the steamship companies.

The steamship companies haul them over to America, and as soon as they step off the decks of their ships the problem of the steamship companies is settled, but our problem has but begun—bolshevism, red anarchy, black-handers, and kidnapers, challenging the authority and the integrity of our flag, and still we find people who want us to have loopholes in the law so that such may continue to come in.

I do not intend to vote for any such proposition. I would like to shut for a time the immigration door. Thousands come here who never take the oath to support our Constitution and to become citizens of the United States. They pay allegiance to some other country while they live upon the substance of our own. They fill places that belong to the loyal wage-earning citizens of America. They preach a doctrine that is dangerous and deadly to our institutions. They are no of service whatever to our people. They constitute a menace and danger to us every day, and I can not understand the seeming indifference that some national lawmakers exhibit upon this serious subject. This very question of immigration is the most vital question that affects us to-day.

Senators, if we permit this thing to go on the day is coming when you can draw a line through the United States and ask the native stock to get on one side and the foreign born on the other and they will outnumber us. They will be in the majority.

Mr. [John Sharp] WILLIAMS [D.-Miss.]. Mr. President—

The PRESIDING OFFICER. Does the Senator from Alabama yield to the Senator from Mississippi?

Mr. HEFLIN. I do.

Mr. WILLIAMS. The Senator speaks about the day coming when they will outnumber us. The day has already come, has it not, when they hold the balance of power and can decide a national election?

Mr. HEFLIN. That is true, absolutely true. They can get us divided on any great issue and get their forces in compact, concrete form and hold the balance of power and decide issues that affect the conduct and the life of the United States Government.

Mr. COLT. Mr. President—

The PRESIDING OFFICER. Does the Senator from Alabama yield to the Senator from Rhode Island?

Mr. HEFLIN. I yield.

Mr. COLT. May I ask the Senator if he has seen the recent statistics of the Census Bureau which show that for the 10 years from 1910 to 1920 the increase in the alien-born population of the United States was only 358,422?

Mr. WILLIAMS. But they were not the voters.

Mr. HEFLIN. No.

Mr. COLT. With a population, I might say, of 105,000,000 to 110,000,000, does the Senator think that an increase in alien population in 10 years of a little over 358,000 presents any great danger to American institutions?

Mr. WILLIAMS. Mr. President, if the Senator will permit me—

The PRESIDING OFFICER. Does the Senator from Alabama yield to the Senator from Mississippi?

Mr. HEFLIN.   I do.

Mr. WILLIAMS.   I hope the Senator will call attention to the fact that while that increase of 350,000 took place in one 10-year period, while we were isolated from Europe for the most part, there were 13,000,000 of foreign-born voters in the United States at the last election.

Mr. HEFLIN.   Think of that, Mr. President; if 13,000,000 of foreign-born voters participated in the last election that is as many, if not more, votes than Presidents Wilson and Taft and Roosevelt all polled in the presidential election of 1912.

Mr. WILLIAMS.   I beg the Senator's pardon. I meant 13,-000,000 of foreign-born population, with their due proportion of voters. Their due proportion is about 50 per cent in the case of foreigners.

Mr. HEFLIN.   Yes; about that.

Now, Mr. President, a great many of these foreigners went out of our country during the World War to fight against us. They were occupying places in this country, making money in our industrial establishments that some real, loyal Americans should have had, and when the war came on and our liberties were imperiled they went back to fight against the flag that had sheltered them and blessed and profited them while they were here. Every year foreigners in America send out of this country millions and millions of money. They send it back to the Governments over there; and these men that I am talking to you about are not citizens of the United States. They have never taken the oath to support that flag. There are thousands and hundreds of thousands of men in this country enjoying all the blessings and benefits that those who support our institutions enjoy, and yet when war comes they get out of the country and take up arms against the flag and the Government.

Mr. President, I want to suggest to the Senator from Rhode Island and to others on the other side that I hear a great deal said about protecting American labor against the cheap labor of Europe; that the standard of living is so much higher here,

American labor can not compete with cheap labor of Europe. I could never understand why you would build a tariff wall between the products of the cheap labor of Europe and the United States and then throw the doors to America open to thousands of cheap European laborers to come here and compete with American labor. Yes, come here and compete with the loyal American citizen who has a wife and children to support. If you want to protect these men, protect them by keeping out those who work for starvation wages and spread their dangerous doctrines around the industrial establishments of our country, and take the places of our men, and get money that ought to be going into the pockets of the loyal wage earners of America.

You are permitting people to come over here who never become citizens of this country. They go into our industrial establishments and take the places that should be filled by American workingmen. They get the places and American workingmen are walking the streets, idle and hungry. Senators, the time has come to stop this thing. We are seeking to keep these people out.

Some Members of the Congress, it seems, are opposed to this character of restriction. Some have constituents back home who say to them, "If you do not vote to permit these people to continue to come, we will beat you at the next election." I want to remind the American people, as I did on a former occasion in this Chamber, that it is high time that we were voting in Congress for the good of the Government of the United States.

Mr. President, in the Saturday Evening Post not long ago there was an article written by Kenneth L. Roberts in which he said that an American consul general in a European city said to him:

Every foreign Government understands that never in the history of the world was there such a movement of peoples as there is to America to-day. All the Governments understand that we have every

right to go into the case of every immigrant with extreme thorough-
ness, because it is becoming a matter of life and death for our people.
Why? Because our very existence is threatened. American institutions are threatened by this influx of the refuse and criminal hordes
of foreign countries.

Some time ago the chairman of the Committee on Immigration in the House, Congressman Burnett, of my State, said that
while in Italy he made inquiry about a dangerous band of
outlaws and cutthroats that he had heard of in Italy. The man
to whom he was speaking said: "They have all gone to America." The hearings in the House at that time disclosed that the
King of Denmark pardoned 700 criminals with the distinct
understanding that they would go to America. In other instances we are told that foreign countries make up purses to
send out of their countries undesirables, and they send them to
America. God help us to protect the great household of America from the dangers that threaten it.

What care we for wrongs and crimes,
It's dimes and dollars, dollars and dimes.

But they tell us that the immigration agents and steamship
companies make money out of it. Away with the interests of
America! "What care we for wrongs and crimes; it is dimes and
dollars, dollars and dimes." The steamship companies make
money out of it. Certain organizations, political and religious,
profit by it. On with the dizzy and dangerous dance they tell us.

I protest against it, Mr. President. I wish I had it in my
power to shut these doors tight for at least 12 months' time.
We know how upset and distracted the world is. We know
how much unrest and distress there is in the Old World, rent
and torn by war. People want to get away from conditions
over there. They want to leave behind them the big war debts.
And what is the suggestion made to them? Go to America. Who
is there to encourage them? The hired immigration agents. Who

is there to greet and receive them? The steamship companies, ready and anxious to bring them over and dump them down upon the shores of America.

In the name of the boys who fought and died in France, I protest against such a course. I plead for the preservation of the institutions of my country. I plead for the great army of wage earners of America, to protect and defend them against this horde of unfit foreigners who want to come here to take their places in our industrial establishments. I plead for the honor and glory of my flag and for the preservation and perpetuity of American institutions.

December 10, 1920
HOUSE OF REPRESENTATIVES

Mr. [John E.] RAKER [D.-Cal.]. Mr. Chairman and gentlemen of the House, I consider this bill as one of the necessary reconstruction bills following the World War. It is not a question of just what should be the amount or kind or character of immigration to this country. We need and always have required a reasonable amount of immigration. But it is apparent from the investigation of the committee that beyond all question there are now in the United States something like 15,000,000 people who are not American citizens. There are coming to the shores of America now all the way from 65,000 to 150,000 people a month. In other words, immigration at the present rate will amount to over a million and half a year. Our country is not determined as to just what it wants to do, and the people of the world are in the same condition, even more so than in this country. Hundreds and thousands of them are trying to get out from under the burden that has been placed on them by virtue of the war. They are not seeking necessarily the benefits

From *Congressional Record*, 66th Cong., 3rd sess., 1921, vol. 60, pt. 1, pp. 175–178, 180–181, 183.

of this country because they want to become citizens and be a part and parcel of America and to carry out the principles upon which this Government is founded. The great majority of those who have come already since the armistice and of those who are seeking admission now are dependents. They are not farmers or laborers, but are coming to live upon their relatives and friends and on the bounty of this country. The evidence shows that beyond all question. With the large number of contagious diseases that are prevalent in the Old World, many hundreds of persons afflicted with those diseases are bound to land on our shores, notwithstanding the inspection here, because the inspection as to physical and mental condition is exceptionally poor, on account of the fact that there are not enough inspectors or agents. Many of the immigrants who arrive here just practically walk off of the vessel on the landing planks and scatter promiscuously among the people of this country. So under the conditions which exist to-day it is better to let immigration be suspended, and to let us assimilate those who are here now, than to continue this overflow of the many, many undesirables who are coming at the present time. That is the purpose of the committee in reporting this bill. It excludes all. There is no discrimination against any country or race. All are excluded with the exception of Government officials and certain relatives of those who are now living in this country. We allow a man 24 years old to go abroad and be married if he desires and to bring his wife to this country. Notwithstanding these exceptions, the Secretary of Labor has the power to make investigations, and it is his duty, if there is any possible reason, notwithstanding the relationship of these people, why they should not be admitted to this country, to see that they are excluded, and that is one of the purposes of the bill.

Now, no one can object to a clearing up of this business. No one can object to putting our own house in order. No one, no matter how anxious he is for immigration, can object to our taking time to assimilate those who are here, to see that they are citizens; that they take unto themselves the principles of this country and study its institutions, in order that we may further extend our work of Americanization, so that those who have come to this country within the last 10 years may become citizens; that they may love, honor, respect, and assist in maintaining our Government; and that they may imbue their children with the same ideas. Instead of that we find communities in this country that are as foreign as to language and thought as any city in any foreign land to-day. That must be avoided, and now is the time to stop.

Mr. [Frederick W.] ROWE [R.-N.Y.]. Mr. Chairman, I am not so much afraid of the immigrant as some Members of this House appear to be. I have lived in the city of New York a great many years and have met and had business relations with a great many who came over as immigrants. Up to 1914 we received into this country a net of about a million a year. This year we will probably receive into this country 700,000 or 800,000. Of every two who come to this country one is going back. There is no great reason why we should take this up at this time. The people who come here are not of a poorer class than those who have come here during the last 20 years. I know considerable about the conditions. I was present at Ellis Island, went down on the ship that sent the 249 undesirables back to Europe, where they should have been sent long ago. I have been twice during the month of November to Ellis Island to see what the conditions were at that place. The last time I was over to Ellis Island I took with me a prominent citizen of the State of Iowa, because in the papers of Iowa he had read very often that undesirables were coming to this country, and wanted to see for himself the conditions at the island. That was about three weeks ago. The island was full of people and we had a splendid opportunity to examine the situation. We spent more than three hours there. When he came back on the boat and met several people at dinner that night I remember that the very first remark he made was to the effect that the immigrants whom he saw coming in at Ellis Island were of a much better class than one would believe from reading the newspapers of his own State or the papers of Chicago.

The fact is that in this country we need laboring men and women of certain classes. We are paying now in the city of New York for ordinary shovelers to dig trenches in which to lay a sewer or a water pipe from $4.50 to $6 a day. We are paying from $6 to $9 a day for hod carriers. It is not because we have not plenty of men in this country. The fact is that our people of the second generation in this country will not carry a hod or dig a trench. We need the men on the farms. We have a great need in this country of competent women to do housework, and there are in Europe men who are willing to do this hard work in America and women who are capable and willing to do the housework. I believe in restrictions. I would have a very careful examination. I would not have it made under labor-union organizations. They represent only about one-ninth of the laboring men in this country. They should not have the power of saying who shall come and how the laws of this country shall be administered in respect to who is to be permitted to come into the Nation. I want to have restrictions. I think that for a limited time we might stop immigration in this country long enough so that Ellis Island may be made a proper place in which to receive all of the immigrants who desire to come into the country.

Mr. [James V.] McCLINTIC [D.-Okla.]. Mr. Chairman and gentlemen of the committee, I feel that the Immigration Committee is entitled to the thanks of this body for bringing in a bill of this kind during the early part of this session. There is an old saying, "A stitch in times save nine," and this saying, in my opinion, is apropos of the condition that exists in the United States at the present moment with relation to the need of a law which will protect the citizens of this country from the foreign immigrants who are fleeing to our shores to escape the heavy taxation in the war-devastated regions of Europe.

Some time ago it was my privilege to visit Ellis Island, not as a member of the committee but as a private citizen interested in obtaining information relative to the situation which exists at that place. I stood at the end of a hall with three physicians, and I saw them examine each immigrant as they came down the line, rolling back the upper eyelid in order to gain some information as to the individual's physical condition. I saw them place the chalk marks on their clothing which indicated that they were in a diseased condition, so that they could be separated when they reached the place where they were to undergo certain examinations. Afterwards I went to a large assembly hall where immigrants came before the examiners to take the literacy test, and the one fact that impressed me more than anything else was that practically every single immigrant examined that day had less than $50 to his credit. . . .

Practically all of them were weak, small of stature, poorly clad, emaciated, and in a condition which showed that the environment surrounding them in their European homes were indeed very bad.

It is for this reason that I say the class of immigrants coming to the shores of the United States at this time are not the kind of people we want as citizens in this country. It is a well-known fact that the majority of immigrants coming to this country at the present time are going into the large industrial centers instead of the agricultural centers of the United States, and when it is taken into consideration that the large centers are already crowded to the extent that there is hardly sufficient living quarters to take care of the people it can be readily seen that this class of people, instead of becoming of service to the communities where they go, they will become charges to be taken care of by charitable institutions. The week I visited Ellis Island I was told that 25,000 immigrants had been unloaded at that port. From their personal appearance they seemed to be the offcasts of the countries from which they came. . . .

Mr. [William E.] Mason [R.-Ill.].   Mr. Chairman, I am not

in condition to do this subject justice, but I can not be silent—I think from a sense of duty—while this bill is so hurriedly passed through the House of Representatives. I want to say for my fellow immigrants [laughter] in the House—you are all immigrants; what have you got big heads about; every one of you. If this bill had been passed 50 or 100 years ago hardly any of the House would have been here. It would have kept the Pilgrim Fathers out. They had no passports. The meanest thing about this bill—and I say that with all respect to my good friends who framed it—is that the whole theory that this was to be the land of the free and the home of the brave and an asylum for the oppressed is destroyed by it. You must have a passport if you want to escape the rule of Lenin and Trotski.

You can not escape unless you get a passport from them, and this Government does not recognize the Soviet Government. It would have kept Kossuth out when he came to speak here for the liberty of Hungary. It would have kept Thomas Estrada Palma out, who came to speak for the liberty of Cuba. He could not get a passport from Spain, and to-day this little island of Cuba is blossoming, a beautiful, strong, young Republic. You propose to-day by this bill to say that no man, however good or strong of arm, that no man, however much in love with the principles of our Government, can come from India or Ireland or South Africa without a visé of the king. By article 10 we guaranteed the territory of all nations. The people knocked that out. You now propose to enact into law that provision by guaranteeing that the kings of the earth shall not be deprived of their right to govern the brain, blood, and bone of all their subjects. An honest, brave man fleeing from the power of the king you propose to deport and send him back to prison or the gallows if he lands on our soil without the consent of his master, the king.

To my colleagues on the Republican side, let me say to you, gentlemen, you are making a mistake personally and politically. But, bigger than that, you are making a mistake for your country. All of the treaties that we have will be amended or abrogated by this law, except possibly where there is a special treaty like that with Japan. We want peace and good fellowship. By this bill you turn the people of the world against us. You put into the mind of every man, woman, and child all over the world that this great country has suddenly drawn the cloak of seclusion about herself. You say by this bill, "Young man, have you got money?" "Yes." "Royal blood?" "Yes." "Do you want to go to school?" "Yes." "Come in." But if the Norwegian stands here with a strong hand and warm heart, in love with the doctrines of your country, you say to him, "Stay out unless you can go to school."

The trouble about this, my brother immigrants, is that the fault has been in the execution of the law we have. No man can come here who does not subscribe to our doctrines. The description given by my friend the gentleman from California as to granting of citizens' papers in our courts was not fair. I have seen them go through the United States courts. They are all examined. I saw them stand there. They did go fast before Judge Landis the other day, I noticed, but every one of them had been examined; their papers had been examined; the living witnesses were there as to their character and reputation.

The trouble in the immigration subject is where it has been all the while for eight years—inefficiency and incompetency in the execution of the laws. We do not need this law to shut out these people who want to come here. We do need—and the people have spoken—to give a new administration to this Government. And I hope and pray that the law we have will be enforced and that there be no more talk about the danger of the immigrants coming into this country and the danger and hysteria about the bolshevik. This country can take care of itself. All the Bolsheviki in the world can not hurt us. They may disturb us for a while, but the Bolsheviki can not come in here under the present law. The people have given you a new administration; we will have a new Attorney General; we will have a new administration of the department. Let us see what they can do. Let us see whether they can not protect the

American people from the things you are talking about. But to
me the most unsentimental, the most selfish, un-American, unpatriotic thing is the ungodly desire to crowd every man off the
earth because we do not want to compete with him. We get a
prejudice; and you know that largely the basis of this is the
prejudice against the Jews. Tell the truth about it. We are not
afraid to speak the truth, are we? There is a prejudice against
the Poles; there is a prejudice against the Germans; there is a
prejudice against the Irish.

It is a prejudice also against any nation in the world that is
seeking to adopt the doctrine of self-government, that has the
cruel hand of Great Britain at her throat. South Africa wants
to be heard. By unanimous vote of her Congress she declared
for self-determination. Within the memory of us here now, we
saw Great Britain kill that young republic. They want a chance
to come here. Her people want that chance. But they have got
to get a visé from the king, George.

There is war in Ireland. Ninety per cent of the people have
spoken for self-determination. They have established a de facto
government. We are not neutral. We refuse to recognize one
but do recognize the other. Some of them want to come here.
I remember my great leader, sir, in politics, was John A. Logan.
I remember that he saved the day at that critical hour in the
war, and I remember that he was the son of an Irish immigrant.
They want to come here. Here is this poor, brave woman, Mrs.
McSwiney; she could not be here 24 hours if we passed this bill,
without a visé from the king. He is not her king. The people of
that country have spoken. A larger percentage of Ireland are
back of De Valera to-day for president of Ireland than there
was back of George Washington when he established our Republic. A larger percentage are for that freedom to-day in Ireland than was back of Abraham Lincoln when he maintained
the Union—a larger percentage of the people. . . .

Just one illustration of this selfishness of us immigrants, the
Masons through Scotland and the Campbells from the same
country. A lot of you came along from Ireland and some from

Germany. You are here now and have gotten on your feet, and do not want anybody else to have a chance.

I read a legend once of an old stingy grouch who was in hell, and who appealed to an angel to help him. The angel said, "Name one good thing you ever did and I will try to help you." He said "I gave a carrot once to a poor boy." Immediately a carrot appeared before this grouch in hell. They got hold of him and began lifting him out of the pit, and just as they were going to deposit him out of hell-fire and damnation, he saw some other fellows clinging with him to the carrot. He said, "Get out of here. This is my carrot." And the angel very properly dropped them all back to hell, where they belonged. [Laughter.]

Gentlemen, this is not our carrot alone; it is not your world, your country alone; it is not my country. The people who have developed this country have come from all over the world. England is not the mother, but all of Europe. We have made this country. You have good laws; let us enforce them. Let us have a President in evidence on the 4th of March who will appoint men to see that those who come in here are sound of limb and of mind and can become good American citizens. It is a part of the world. It is not your country or mine alone; it is God's country. [Applause.]

Mr. [Lucian Walton] PARRISH [D.-Tex.]. . . . Not only are a large majority of the immigrants nonsupporting, but from past experience we know that a large per cent of them, at least, are not in sympathy with America and American institutions, and a good majority make up the criminal class that is causing so much concern throughout the entire United States. Mr. William Shadduck, foreman of Kings County grand jury, New York, recently reported the conditions actually existing in his county, and in this connection made use of these significant paragraphs:

A study of the record of our proceedings shows that all of the homicides and most of the graver, more desperate, and heinous crimes were committed by foreigners, who palpably have no understanding of the genesis or genius of American institutions. They not only have not been assimilated, but seemingly are unlikely under present conditions ever to be assimilable.

The facts as to many of these crimes show the presence in this city of foreign colonies whose existence is a perpetual menace to the lives and property of our law-abiding and law-loving citizens. From the testimony of witnesses, some of whom were participants in these heinous crimes, it has been clearly revealed that interracial hatred, with their attendant feuds and vendettas, have been transplanted to this country. These feuds have been aggravated and perpetuated by the increase and extension of these foreign colonies.

If the grand juries of the other sections of the United States where foreign elements predominate were to make reports, I have not the slightest doubt but that we would find great unanimity in their reports corroborating the report of the grand jury of New York. As a matter of fact every President who has fallen at the hand of the assassin has gone down by the murderous blow of a man of foreign extraction. . . .

The time once was in the history of this country when America was looked upon as the home of the downtrodden people of all the nations of the earth, but we have arrived at a new and different era in our history; new conditions have arisen among the people of the world. Beyond the seas there are being taught new and strange doctrines. Socialism, bolshevism, and anarchy are playing unusual parts in the history and welfare of those nations, and are threatening the very foundation of their governments. Bolshevism and anarchy may draw their slimy trail across the map of Europe and write their destructive doctrines into the history of the nations over there, but never with my vote or influence will they make their unholy imprint upon America or American institutions. . . .

Mr. [Adolph J.] SABATH [D.-Ill.]. The gentlemen from Minnesota, Kentucky, and Texas charge that the present immigration is undesirable and that the sections of this country to which this immigration goes are suffering from unemployment and lack of housing facilities.

Mr. Chairman, the charges that are being made against the present-day immigration are by gentlemen who come from sections who receive no immigration and who are not in position to know as much about that question as those who come from and live in the cities and in the States that absorb most of the present-day immigration. Is it not singular that up to this moment not a single gentleman coming from our great cities or our great States who, I am sure, are better acquainted with the immigration question than those from the rural districts, has said a word in behalf of this legislation; but, on the contrary, like myself, feel it is hasty, uncalled for, unnecessary, and unjustified.

7 / A. MITCHELL PALMER

The Red Scare

During the winter of 1919–1920, the Department of Justice attempted to sweep the United States free of radicals, especially alien labor and political leaders. Under the leadership of the Attorney General, A. Mitchell Palmer (1872–1936), a pre-war Progressive and a devout Quaker, mass arrests were made on a national scale, aliens were summarily deported, and a virulent case of hysteria infected many citizens. On January 2, 1920, for example, 2,700 people from 33 cities were arrested. Palmer was unable and perhaps unwilling to resist the pressures of the moment, and, as the following selection shows, he seriously believed that the United States was on the verge of an "internal revolution" led by radicals, aliens from Russia and Germany, with headquarters on the east side of New York City. He believed that strong actions were necessary, and concluded that finer distinctions and greater sophistication would simply hand the nation over to Trotsky and Lenin. Palmer's defensive arguments were confused and occasionally hysterical, but they accurately reflected the mood of most of the nation.

In this brief review of the work which the Department of Justice has undertaken, to tear out the radical seeds that have entangled American ideas in their poisonous theories, I desire not merely to explain what the real menace of communism is, but also to tell how we have been compelled to clean up the country almost unaided by any virile legislation. Though I have not been embarrassed by political opposition, I have been materially delayed because the present sweeping processes of arrests and deportation of seditious aliens should have been vigorously pushed by Congress last spring. The failure of this is a matter of record in the Congressional files.

The anxiety of that period in our responsibility when Congress, ignoring the seriousness of these vast organizations that were plotting to overthrow the Government, failed to act, has passed. The time came when it was obviously hopeless to expect the hearty co-operation of Congress, in the only way to stamp out these seditious societies in their open defiance of law by various forms of propaganda.

Like a prairie-fire, the blaze of revolution was sweeping over every American institution of law and order a year ago. It was eating its way into the homes of the American workman, its sharp tongues of revolutionary heat were licking the altars of the churches, leaping into the belfry of the school bell, crawling into the sacred corners of American homes, seeking to replace marriage vows with libertine laws, burning up the foundations of society.

Robbery, not war, is the ideal of communism. This has been demonstrated in Russia, Germany, and in America. As a foe, the anarchist is fearless of his own life, for his creed is a fanaticism that admits no respect of any other creed. Obviously it is the creed of any criminal mind, which reasons always from

From "The Case Against the 'Reds,' " *The Forum*, LXIII (February 1920), 173–176, 179–185.

motives impossible to clean thought. Crime is the degenerate factor in society.

Upon these two basic certainties, first that the "Reds" were criminal aliens, and secondly that the American Government must prevent crime, it was decided that there could be no nice distinctions drawn between the theoretical ideals of the radicals and their actual violations of our national laws. An assassin may have brilliant intellectuality, he may be able to excuse his murder or robbery with fine oratory, but any theory which excuses crime is not wanted in America. This is no place for the criminal to flourish, nor will he do so, so long as the rights of common citizenship can be exerted to prevent him.

It has always been plain to me that when American citizens unite upon any national issue, they are generally right, but it is sometimes difficult to make the issue clear to them. If the Department of Justice could succeed in attracting the attention of our optimistic citizens to the issue of internal revolution in this country, we felt sure there would be no revolution. The Government was in jeopardy. My private information of what was being done by the organization known as the Communist Party of America, with headquarters in Chicago, of what was being done by the Communist Internationale under their manifesto planned at Moscow last March by Trotzky, Lenine and others, addressed "To the Proletariats of All Countries," of what strides the Communist Labor Party was making, removed all doubt. In this conclusion we did not ignore the definite standards of personal liberty, of free speech, which is the very temperament and heart of the people. The evidence was examined with the utmost care, with a personal leaning toward freedom of thought and word on all questions.

The whole mass of evidence, accumulated from all parts of the country, was scrupulously scanned, not merely for the written or spoken differences of viewpoint as to the Government of the United States, but, in spite of these things, to see if the hostile declarations might not be sincere in their announced motive to improve our social order. There was no hope of such a thing. By stealing, murder and lies, Bolshevism has looted Russia not only of its material strength, but of its moral force. A small clique of outcasts from the East Side of New York has attempted this, with what success we all know. Because a disreputable alien—Leon Bronstein, the man who now calls himself Trotzky—can inaugurate a reign of terror from his throne room in the Kremlin; because this lowest of all types known to New York can sleep in the Czar's bed, while hundreds of thousands in Russia are without food or shelter, should Americans be swayed by such doctrines?

Such a question, it would seem, should receive but one answer from America.

My information showed that communism in this country was an organization of thousands of aliens, who were direct allies of Trotzky. Aliens of the same misshapen caste of mind and indecencies of character, and it showed that they were making the same glittering promises of lawlessness, of criminal autocracy to Americans, that they had made to the Russian peasants. How the Department of Justice discovered upwards of 60,000 of these organized agitators of the Trotzky doctrine in the United States, is the confidential information upon which the Government is now sweeping the nation clean of such alien filth. . . .

Under the appropriations granted by Congress to the Department of Justice, the maximum number of men engaged in the preparation of the violation of all United States laws is limited to about 500 for the entire country. Startling as this fact may seem to the reader who discovers it for the first time, it is the highest testimony to the services of these men, that the Department of Justice of the United States, is today, a human net that no outlaw can escape. It has been netted together in spite of Congressional indifference, intensified by the individual patriotism of its personnel aroused to the menace of revolution, inspired to superlative action above and beyond private interests.

One of the chief incentives for the present activity of the Department of Justice against the "Reds" has been the hope that American citizens will, themselves, become voluntary agents for us, in a vast organization for mutual defense against the sinister agitation of men and women aliens, who appear to be either in the pay or under the criminal spell of Trotzky and Lenine.

Temporary failure to seize the alien criminals in this country who are directly responsible for spreading the unclean doctrines of Bolshevism here, only increased the determination to get rid of them. Obviously, their offenses were related to our immigration laws, and it was finally decided to act upon that principle. Those sections of the Immigration Law applicable to the deportation of aliens committing acts enumerated in the Senate Resolution of October 14, 1919, above quoted, were found in the Act of Congress, approved October 16, 1918, amending the immigration laws of the United States.

By the administration of this law deportations have been made, the law being as follows:

Be it enacted by the Senate and House of Representatives of the United States of America in Congress assembled:

Sec. 1. That aliens who are anarchists; aliens who believe in or advocate the overthrow by force or violence of the Government of the United States or of all forms of law; aliens who disbelieve in or who are opposed to all organized government; aliens who advocate or teach the assassination of public officials; aliens who advocate or teach the unlawful destruction of property; aliens who are members of or affiliated with any organization that entertains a belief in, teaches, or advocates the overthrow by force or by violence of the Government of the United States or of all forms of law, or that entertains or teaches disbelief in or opposition to all organized Government, or that advocates the duty, necessity or propriety of the unlawful assaulting or killing of any officer or officers, either of specific individuals or of officers generally, of the Government of the United States, or of any other organized Government, because of his or their official character, or that advocates or teaches the unlawful destruction of property, shall be excluded from admission into the United States.

Sec. 2. That any alien who, at any time, after entering the United States, is found to have been at the time of entry, or to become thereafter, a member of any one of the classes of aliens enumerated in Sec. 1 of this Act, shall upon the warrant of the Secretary of Labor, be taken into custody and deported in the manner provided in the Immigration Act of Feb. 5, 1917. The provisions of this Section shall be applicable to the classes of aliens mentioned in this Act irrespective of the time of their entry into the United States.

Although this law is entirely under the jurisdiction of the Department of Labor, it seemed to be the only means at my disposal of attacking the radical movement. To further this plan, as Congress had seen fit to refuse appropriations to the Department of Labor which might have enabled it to act vigorously against the "Reds," I offered to co-operate with the immigration officials to the fullest extent. My appropriation became available July 19, 1919. I then organized what is known as the Radical Division.

Briefly this is a circumstantial statement of the present activities of the Department of Justice, co-operating with the Department of Labor, against the "Reds." They require no defense, nor can I accept as true the counter claims of the "Reds" themselves, who, apparently indifferent to their disgrace, violent in their threats against the United States Government, until they are out of sight and sound of it, betray the characterless ideas and purposes that Trotzky has impressed upon the criminal classes which constitute communism.

Behind, and underneath, my own determination to drive from our midst the agents of Bolshevism with increasing vigor and with greater speed, until there are no more of them left among us, so long as I have the responsible duty of that task, I have discovered the hysterical methods of these revolutionary humans with increasing amazement and suspicion. In the confused information that sometimes reaches the people, they are compelled to ask questions which involve the reasons for my acts against the "Reds." I have been asked, for instance, to what extent deportation will check radicalism in this country. Why not ask what will become of the United States Government if these alien radicals are permitted to carry out the principles of the Communist Party as embodied in its so-called laws, aims and regulations?

There wouldn't be any such thing left. In place of the United States Government we should have the horror and terrorism of bolsheviki tyranny such as is destroying Russia now. Every scrap of radical literature demands the overthrow of our existing government. All of it demands obedience to the instincts of criminal minds, that is, to the lower appetites, material and moral. The whole purpose of communism appears to be a mass formation of the criminals of the world to overthrow the decencies of private life, to usurp property that they have not earned, to disrupt the present order of life regardless of health, sex or religious rights. By a literature that promises the wildest dreams of such low aspirations, that can occur to only the criminal minds, communism distorts our social law.

The chief appeal communism makes is to "The Worker." If they can lure the wage-earner to join their own gang of thieves, if they can show him that he will be rich if he steals, so far they have succeeded in betraying him to their own criminal course.

Read this manifesto issued in Chicago:

THE COMMUNIST PARTY MANIFESTO

The world is on the verge of a new era. Europe is in revolt. The masses of Asia are stirring uneasily. Capitalism is in collapse. The workers of the world are seeing a new light and securing new courage. Out of the night of war is coming a new day.

The spectre of communism haunts the world of capitalism. Communism, the hope of the workers to end misery and oppression. The workers of Russia smashed the front of international Capitalism and Imperialism. They broke the chains of the terrible war; and in the midst of agony, starvation and the attacks of the Capitalists of the world, they are creating a new social order.

The class war rages fiercely in all nations. Everywhere the workers are in a desperate struggle against their capitalist masters. The call to action has come. The workers must answer the call!

The Communist Party of America is the party of the working class. The Communist Party proposes to end Capitalism and organize a workers' industrial republic. The workers must control industry and dispose of the product of industry. The Communist Party is a party realizing the limitation of all existing workers' organizations and proposes to develop the revolutionary movement necessary to free the workers from the oppression of Capitalism. The Communist Party insists that the problems of the American worker are identical with the problems of the workers of the world.

These are the revolutionary tenets of Trotzky and the Communist Internationale. Their manifesto further embraces the various organizations in this country of men and women obsessed with discontent, having disorganized relations to American society. These include the I.W.W.'s, the most radical socialists, the misguided anarchists, the agitators who oppose the limitations of unionism, the moral perverts and the hysterical neurasthenic women who abound in communism. The phraseology of their manifesto is practically the same wording as was used by the Bolsheviks for their International Communist Congress.

Naturally the Communist Party has bored its revolutionary points into the Socialist Party. They managed to split the Socialists, for the so-called Left Wing of the Socialist Party is now the Communist Party, which specifically states that it does not intend to capture the bourgeosie parliamentary state, but to conquer and destroy, and that the final objective, mass action, is the medium intended to be used in the conquest and destruction of the bourgeosie state to annihilate the parliamentary state, and introduce a revolutionary dictatorship of the Proletariat.

The Left Wing Socialists declared themselves when they issued a call for a convention held in Chicago, September 1, 1919, to organize a Communist Party. An effort was made at a convention of the Socialist Party of America in Chicago, August 30, 1919, to harmonize differences. Their first plan in harmonious endeavor was to refuse admission to their convention to members of the Left Wing, on the ground that the latter intended to capture it. At the Communist Convention of Left Wing Socialists on September 1, 1919, 129 delegates, representing 55,000 members, attended. Extensive Communist propaganda followed, including the establishment of a paper, "The Communist."

There is no legislation at present which can reach an American citizen who is discontented with our system of American Government, nor is it necessary. The dangerous fact to us is that the Communist Party of America is actually affiliated and adheres to the teaching program and tactics of the 3d Internationale. Consider what this means.

The first congress of the Communist Nationale held March 6, 1919, in Moscow, subscribed to by Trotzky and Lenine, adopted the following:

This makes necessary the disarming of the bourgeosie at the proper time, the arming of the laborer, and the formation of a communist army as the protectors of the rules of the proletariat and the inviolability of the social structure.

When we realize that each member of the Communist Party of America pledges himself to the principles above, set forth, deportation of men and women bound to such a theory is a very mild reformatory sentence.

If I were asked whether the American Federation of Labor had been betrayed by the "Reds," I should refer the inquiry to

the manifesto and constitution of the Communist Party of
America, in which, under the heading, "Revolutionary Constitution," the following paragraph appears:

But the American Federation of Labor, as a whole, is hopelessly
reactionary. At its recent convention the A. F. of L. approved the
Versailles Peace Treaty and the League of Nations, and refused to
declare its solidarity with Soviet Russia. It did not even protest the
blockade of Russia and Hungary! This convention, moreover, did all
in its power to break radical unions. The A. F. of L. is united with
the Government, securing a privileged status in the governing system
of State Capitalism. A Labor Party is being organized—much more
conservative than the British Labor Party.

It has been inferred by the "Reds" that the United States
Government, by arresting and deporting them, is returning to
the autocracy of Czardom, adopting the system that created the
severity of Siberian banishment. My reply to such charges is,
that in our determination to maintain our government we are
treating our alien enemies with extreme consideration. To deny
them the privilege of remaining in a country which they have
openly deplored as an unenlightened community, unfit for those
who prefer the privileges of Bolshevism, should be no hardship.
It strikes me an odd form of reasoning that these Russian
Bolsheviks who extol the Bolshevik rule, should be so unwilling
to return to Russia. The nationality of most of the alien "Reds"
is Russian and German. There is almost no other nationality
represented among them.

It has been impossible in so short a space to review the
entire menace of the internal revolution in this country as I
know it, but this may serve to arouse the American citizen to
its reality, its danger, and the great need of united effort to
stamp it out, under our feet, if needs be. It is being done. The
Department of Justice will pursue the attack of these "Reds"
upon the Government of the United States with vigilance, and

no alien, advocating the overthrow of existing law and order in this country, shall escape arrest and prompt deportation. It is my belief that while they have stirred discontent in our midst, while they have caused irritating strikes, and while they have infected our social ideas with the disease of their own minds and their unclean morals, we can get rid of them! And not until we have done so shall we have removed the menace of Bolshevism for good.

8 / *HIRAM WESLEY EVANS*

The KKK

The re-invigoration of the Ku Klux Klan in the Twenties was an unambiguous symptom of the frustrations and fears of provincial America. Under the leadership of Hiram Wesley Evans, a Texas dentist who became the Klan's Imperial Wizard and Emperor in 1922, the membership of the Klan rose to something under five million people and, equally significant, spread out to new areas, especially in the Midwest and Far West. Evans' explanation of the Klan in the following selection is simultaneously defensive and strident, the two moods increasingly characteristic of village America during this decade. He gave voice to a wide range of rural values and attitudes, including opposition to immigrants, radicalism, cosmopolitanism, liberalism, Jews, Catholics, urbanism, and, in general, all of the currents of the time that could be included under the label of "modernism"; the Klan defended what Evans called old-stock Americanism, white supremacy, and Protestantism. The reader must remember, of course, that Evans was writing to a partly hostile audience, so that much of his rhetoric must be carefully analyzed before it can be accepted as representing what he and his organization really stood for. With this warning in mind, this selection is the best statement of the Klan's credo that has ever been written.

The Ku Klux Klan on last Thanksgiving Day passed its tenth anniversary. In one decade it has made a place and won a record for achievement which are almost, if not quite, unique in the history of great popular movements. It has not merely grown from a handful to a membership of millions, from poverty to riches, from obscurity to great influence, from fumbling impotence to the leadership in the greatest cause now before the American people. All these are important, but not vital.

What is vital is that in these years the Klan has shown a power to reform and cleanse itself from within, to formulate and vitalize fundamental instincts into concrete thought and purposeful action, to meet changing conditions with adaptability but without weakness, to speak for and to lead the common people of America and, finally, to operate through the application of practical patriotism to public life with increasing success, and along the only constructive lines to be found in the present welter of our national thought.

By these things the Klan has proved not only its ability to live, but its right to life and influence. It has already lasted longer than any similar movement; its tenth birthday finds it stronger than ever before, with its worst weaknesses conquered or being eliminated, and so well prepared for the future that it may fairly be said to stand merely on the threshold of its life and service.

The greatest achievement so far has been to formulate, focus, and gain recognition for an idea—the idea of preserving and developing America first and chiefly for the benefit of the children of the pioneers who made America, and only and definitely along the lines of the purpose and spirit of those pio-

From "The Klan's Fight for Americanism," *The North American Review*, CCXXIII (March–May 1926), 33–47, 49–54, 60, 62–63. Reprinted by permission of *The North American Review*.

neers. The Klan cannot claim to have created this idea: it has long been a vague stirring in the souls of the plain people. But the Klan can fairly claim to have given it purpose, method, direction and a vehicle. When the Klan first appeared the nation was in the confusion of sudden awakening from the lovely dream of the melting pot, disorganized and helpless before the invasion of aliens and alien ideas. After ten years of the Klan it is in arms for defense. This is our great achievement.

The second is more selfish; we have won the leadership in the movement for Americanism. Except for a few lonesome voices, almost drowned by the clamor of the alien and the alien-minded "Liberal," the Klan alone faces the invader. This is not to say that the Klan has gathered into its membership all who are ready to fight for America. The Klan is the champion, but it is not merely an organization. It is an idea, a faith, a purpose, an organized crusade. No recruit to the cause has ever been really lost. Though men and women drop from the ranks they remain with us in purpose, and can be depended on fully in any crisis. Also, there are many millions who have never joined, but who think and feel and—when called on—fight with us. This is our real strength, and no one who ignores it can hope to understand America today.

Other achievements of these ten years have been the education of the millions of our own membership in citizenship, the suppression of much lawlessness and increase of good government wherever we have become strong, the restriction of immigration, and the defeat of the Catholic attempt to seize the Democratic party. All these we have helped, and all are important.

The outstanding proof of both our influence and our service, however, has been in creating, outside our ranks as well as in them, not merely the growing national concentration on the problems of Americanism, but also a growing sentiment against radicalism, cosmopolitanism, and alienism of all kinds. We have produced instead a sane and progressive conservatism along national lines. We have enlisted our racial instincts for the work of preserving and developing our American traditions and customs. This was most strikingly shown in the elections last fall, when the conservative reaction amazed all politicians—especially the LaFollette rout in the Northwest. This reaction added enormously to the plurality of the President, the size of which was the great surprise of the election.

I wish it might fairly be claimed that the Klan from the beginning had this vision of its mission. Instead the beginnings were groping and futile, as well as feeble; they involved errors which long prevented any important achievement. The chief idea of the founders seems to have been merely to start a new fraternal society, based on rather vague sentiments of brotherhood among white Americans, and of loyalty to the nation and to Protestantism. There was also a sentimental reverence for the Klan of the 'Sixties which led to revival of the old name and some of the ritual. There was finally the basic idea of white supremacy, but this was also at the time a mere sentiment, except as it applied to some Negro unrest.

But along with these ideas there shortly appeared others far from laudable. The Klan had remained weak, gaining barely 10,000 members in the first few years. Then the possibility of profit, both in cash and in power, was seen, and soon resulted in a "selling plan" based partly on Southern affection for the old Klan, partly on social conditions in the South, but chiefly on the possibility of inflaming prejudices. They began to "sell hate at $10 a package."

To us who know the Klan today, its influence, purpose and future, the fact that it can have grown from such beginnings is nothing less than a miracle, possible only through one of those mysterious interventions in human affairs which are called Providence. The fact is, as we see now, that beneath the stupid or dangerous oratory of those early leaders lay certain fundamental truths, quite unseen by them, and then hardly bigger than the vital germ in a grain of corn, but which matured automatically.

The hate and invisible government ideas, however, were what gave the Klan its first great growth, enlisted some 100,000 members, provided wealth for a few leaders, and brought down upon the organization the condemnation of most of the country, leaving it a reputation from which it has not yet recovered. But even before outside indignation had appeared there began an inside reaction, caused by abuses and excesses and by the first stirrings of the purposes which now dominate. Thus began the reform of the Klan by itself, which gained steadily until it won full control in 1922. It laid the basis for the astounding growth of the last three years, and for the present immense influence.

This reform did more than merely rectify the old abuses; it developed into full life the hidden but vital germs, and released one of the most irresistible forces in human affairs, the fundamental instinct of race pride and loyalty—what Lothrop Stoddard calls "the imperious urge of superior heredity." Closely associated with it are two other instincts vital to success among the northern races: patriotism, stimulated to unusual activity by the hyphenism revealed in the World War; and spiritual independence, a revival of the individualism which sprang up just as the Nordic races began to assert themselves in their great blossoming of the last four centuries, and which found its chief expression in Protestantism. These ideas gave direction and guidance to the reforms demanded by the rank and file three years ago. They have been further developed, made more definite and more purposeful, and they are the soul of the Klan today.

The direct reforms brought about were several. First was the stopping of any exercise of "invisible government." This was reinforced by a change in the oath, by which all Klansmen are sworn to uphold legally constituted officers in enforcing the law at all times. One result of this is to be seen in the decrease of lawlessness in Klan territory. We can justly claim credit for the remarkable improvement as regards lynching in the last two years.

The elimination of private profit for officers of the Klan came next and with it went a democratizing of the order. The Klan, being chiefly an organized crusade, cannot operate efficiently on a purely democratic basis, but the autocracy of the early years has been replaced by a system approximating that of the American Government in its early years; final power in the hands of the rank and file, but full power of leadership in the officers they choose.

Another most important reform was a complete change in the method of "propagation"—of recruiting and spreading our gospel. In the early days this had been done very secretively, a high percentage of money had gone to the kleagles—the "sales agents"—there had been a high-pressure appeal to sentimentality, hatred and the invisible government idea, and a tendency to emphasize numbers rather than quality of recruits. Today, instead, the evangelistic emphasis is put on Americanism, Protestant Christianity, and action through government machinery; an increasing number of the field agents are on salary, lists of possible members are carefully weeded out before any are approached, and those found worth while are won by personal work, backed by open discussion. This has, to be sure, cut down the number of new members accepted, but has greatly increased quality and loyalty, and it has brought amazing gains in strength, particularly in the Mid-West and North.

Most important of all has been the formulation of the true Klan purposes into definite principles. This has been a gradual process. We in the lead found ourselves with a following inspired in many ways beyond our understanding, with beliefs and purposes which they themselves only vaguely understood and could not express, but for the fulfillment of which they depended on us. We found ourselves, too, at the head of an army with unguessable influence to produce results for which responsibility would rest on us—the leaders—but which we had not foreseen and for which we were not prepared. As the solemn responsibility to give right leadership to these millions, and to make right use of this influence, was brought home to us, we were compelled to analyze, put into definite words, and give purpose to these half conscious impulses.

The Klan, therefore, has now come to speak for the great mass of Americans of the old pioneer stock. We believe that it does fairly and faithfully represent them, and our proof lies in their support. To understand the Klan, then, it is necessary to understand the character and present mind of the mass of old-stock Americans. The mass, it must be remembered, as distinguished from the intellectually mongrelized "Liberals."

These are, in the first place, a blend of various peoples of the so-called Nordic race, the race which, with all its faults, has given the world almost the whole of modern civilization. The Klan does not try to represent any people but these.

There is no need to recount the virtues of the American pioneers; but it is too often forgotten that in the pioneer period a selective process of intense rigor went on. From the first only hardy, adventurous and strong men and women dared the pioneer dangers; from among these all but the best died swiftly, so that the new Nordic blend which became the American race was bred up to a point probably the highest in history. This remarkable race character, along with the new-won continent and the new-created nation, made the inheritance of the old-stock Americans the richest ever given to a generation of men.

In spite of it, however, these Nordic Americans for the last generation have found themselves increasingly uncomfortable, and finally deeply distressed. There appeared first confusion in thought and opinion, a groping and hesitancy about national affairs and private life alike, in sharp contrast to the clear, straightforward purposes of our earlier years. There was futility in religion, too, which was in many ways even more distressing. Presently we began to find that we were dealing with strange ideas; policies that always sounded well, but somehow always made us still more uncomfortable.

Finally came the moral breakdown that has been going on

for two decades. One by one all our traditional moral standards went by the boards, or were so disregarded that they ceased to be binding. The sacredness of our Sabbath, of our homes, of chastity, and finally even of our right to teach our own children in our own schools fundamental facts and truths were torn away from us. Those who maintained the old standards did so only in the face of constant ridicule.

Along with this went economic distress. The assurance for the future of our children dwindled. We found our great cities and the control of much of our industry and commerce taken over by strangers, who stacked the cards of success and prosperity against us. Shortly they came to dominate our government. The *bloc* system by which this was done is now familiar to all. Every kind of inhabitant except the Americans gathered in groups which operated as units in politics, under orders of corrupt, self-seeking and un-American leaders, who both by purchase and threat enforced their demands on politicians. Thus it came about that the interests of Americans were always the last to be considered by either national or city governments, and that the native Americans were constantly discriminated against, in business, in legislation and in administrative government.

So the Nordic American today is a stranger in large parts of the land his fathers gave him. Moreover, he is a most unwelcome stranger, one much spit upon, and one to whom even the right to have his own opinions and to work for his own interests is now denied with jeers and revilings. "We must Americanize the Americans," a distinguished immigrant said recently. Can anything more clearly show the state to which the real American has fallen in this country which was once his own?

Our falling birth rate, the result of all this, is proof of our distress. We no longer feel that we can be fair to children we bring into the world, unless we can make sure from the start that they shall have capital or education or both, so that they need never compete with those who now fill the lower rungs of the ladder of success. We dare no longer risk letting our youth "make its own way" in the conditions under which we live. So even our unborn children are being crowded out of their birthright!

All this has been true for years, but it was the World War that gave us our first hint of the real cause of our troubles, and began to crystallize our ideas. The war revealed that millions whom we had allowed to share our heritage and prosperity, and whom we had assumed had become part of us, were in fact not wholly so. They had other loyalties: each was willing— anxious!—to sacrifice the interests of the country that had given him shelter to the interests of the one he was supposed to have cast off; each in fact did use the freedom and political power we had given him against ourselves whenever he could see any profit for his older loyalty.

This, of course, was chiefly in international affairs, and the excitement caused by the discovery of disloyalty subsided rapidly after the war ended. But it was not forgotten by the Nordic Americans. They had been awakened and alarmed; they began to suspect that the hyphenism which had been shown was only a part of what existed; their quiet was not that of renewed sleep, but of strong men waiting very watchfully. And presently they began to form decisions about all those aliens who were Americans for profit only.

They decided that even the crossing of salt water did not dim a single spot on a leopard; that an alien usually remains an alien no matter what is done to him, what veneer of education he gets, what oaths he takes, nor what public attitudes he adopts. They decided that the melting pot was a ghastly failure, and remembered that the very name was coined by a member of one of the races—the Jews—which most determinedly refuses to melt. They decided that in every way, as well as in politics, the alien in the vast majority of cases is unalterably fixed in his instincts, character, thought and interests by centuries of racial selection and development, that he thinks first for his own people, works only with and for them, cares entirely for their interests, considers himself always one of them, and never an American. They decided that in character, instincts, thought, and purposes—in his whole soul—an alien remains fixedly alien to America and all it means.

They saw, too, that the alien was tearing down the American standard of living, especially in the lower walks. It became clear that while the American can out-work the alien, the alien can so far under-live the American as to force him out of all competitive labor. So they came to realize that the Nordic can easily survive and rule and increase if he holds for himself the advantages won by strength and daring of his ancestors in times of stress and peril, but that if he surrenders those advantages to the peoples who could not share the stress, he will soon be driven below the level at which he can exist by their low standards, low living and fast breeding. And they saw that the low standard aliens of Eastern and Southern Europe were doing just that thing to us.

They learned, though more slowly, that alien ideas are just as dangerous to us as the aliens themselves, no matter how plausible such ideas may sound. With most of the plain people this conclusion is based simply on the fact that the alien ideas do not work well for them. Others went deeper and came to understand that the differences in racial background, in breeding, instinct, character and emotional point of view are more important than logic. So ideas which may be perfectly healthy for an alien may also be poisonous for Americans.

Finally they learned the great secret of the propagandists; that success in corrupting public opinion depends on putting out the subversive ideas without revealing their source. They came to suspect that "prejudice" against foreign ideas is really a protective device of nature against mental food that may be indigestible. They saw, finally, that the alien leaders in America act on this theory, and that there is a steady flood of alien ideas being spread over the country, always carefully disguised as American.

As they learned all this the Nordic Americans have been gradually arousing themselves to defend their homes and their own kind of civilization. They have not known just how to go about it; the idealist philanthropy and good-natured generosity which led to the philosophy of the melting pot have died hard. Resistance to the peaceful invasion of the immigrant is no such simple matter as snatching up weapons and defending frontiers, nor has it much spectacular emotionalism to draw men to the colors.

The old-stock Americans are learning, however. They have begun to arm themselves for this new type of warfare. Most important, they have broken away from the fetters of the false ideals and philanthropy which puts aliens ahead of their own children and their own race.

To do this they have had to reject completely—and perhaps for the moment the rejection is a bit too complete—the whole body of "Liberal" ideas which they had followed with such simple, unquestioning faith. The first and immediate cause of the break with Liberalism was that it had provided no defense against the alien invasion, but instead had excused it—even defended it against Americanism. Liberalism is today charged in the mind of most Americans with nothing less than national, racial and spiritual treason.

But this is only the last of many causes of distrust. The plain people now see that Liberalism has come completely under the dominance of weaklings and parasites whose alien "idealism" reaches its logical peak in the Bolshevist platform of "produce as little as you can, beg or steal from those who do produce, and kill the producer for thinking he is better than you." Not that all Liberalism goes so far, but it all seems to be on that road. The average Liberal idea is apparently that those who can produce should carry the unfit, and let the unfit rule them. This aberration would have been impossible, of course, if

American Liberalism had kept its feet on the ground. Instead it became wholly academic, lost all touch with the plain people, disowned its instincts and common sense, and lived in a world of pure, high, groundless logic.

Worse yet, this became a world without moral standards. Our forefathers had standards—the Liberals today say they were narrow!—and they had consciences and knew that Liberalism must be kept within fixed bounds. They knew that tolerance of things that touch the foundations of the home, of decency, of patriotism or of race loyalty is not lovely but deadly. Modern American Liberalism has no such bounds. If it has a conscience it hides it shamefacedly; if it has any standards it conceals them well. If it has any convictions—but why be absurd? Its boast is that it has none except conviction in its own decadent religion of Liberalism toward everything; toward the right of every man to make a fool or degenerate of himself and to try to corrupt others; in the right of any one to pull the foundations from under the house or poison the wells; in the right of children to play with matches in a powdermill!

The old stock Americans believe in Liberalism, but not in this thing. It has undermined their Constitution and their national customs and institutions, it has corrupted the morals of their children, it has vitiated their thought, it has degenerated and perverted their education, it has tried to destroy their God. They want no more of it. They are trying to get back to decency and common sense. . . .

The old stock "plain people" are no longer alone in their belief as to the nature of the dangers, their causes, and the folly of Liberal thought. Recently men of great education and mind, students of wide reputation, have come to see all this as the plain Americans saw it years before. This was stated by Madison Grant:

The Nordic race . . . if it takes warning in time, may face the future with assurance. Fight it must, but let the fight be not a civil war against its own blood kindred but against the dangerous foreign races, whether they advance sword in hand or in the more insidious guise of beggars at our gates, pleading for admittance to share our prosperity. If we continue to allow them to enter they will in time drive us out of our own land by the mere force of breeding.

The great hope of the future here in America lies in the realization of the working classes that competition of the Nordic with the alien is fatal, whether the latter be the lowly immigrant from Southern or Eastern Europe, or the more obviously dangerous Oriental, against whose standards of living the white man cannot compete. In this country we must look to such of our people—our farmers and artisans—as are still of American blood, to recognize and meet this danger.

Our present condition is the result of following the leadership of idealists and philanthropic doctrinaires.

The chief of Mr. Grant's demands, that the un-American alien be barred out, has already been partly accomplished. It is established as our national policy by overwhelming vote of Congress, after years of delay won by the aliens already here through the political power we gave them. The Klan is proud that it was able to aid this work, which was vital.

But the plain people realize also that merely stopping the alien flood does not restore Americanism, nor even secure us against final utter defeat. America must also defend herself against the enemy within, or we shall be corrupted and conquered by those to whom we have already given shelter.

The first danger is that we shall be overwhelmed, as Mr. Grant forecasts, by the aliens' "mere force of breeding." With the present birthrate, the Nordic stock will have become a hopeless minority within fifty years, and will within two hundred have been choked to death, like grain among weeds. Unless some means is found of making the Nordic feel safe in having children we are already doomed.

An equal danger is from disunity, so strikingly shown during the war, and from a mongrelization of thought and purpose. It is not merely foreign policy that is involved; it is all our thought at home, our morals, education, social conduct—everything. We are already confused and disunited in every way; the alien groups themselves, and the skilful alien propaganda, are both tearing steadily at all that makes for unity in nationhood, or for the soul of Americanism. If the word "integrity" can still be used in its original meaning of singleness of purpose or thought, then we as a nation have lost all integrity. Yet our old American motto includes the words ". . . divided we fall!"

One more point about the present attitude of the old stock American: he has revived and increased his long-standing distrust of the Roman Catholic Church. It is for this that the native Americans, and the Klan as their leader, are most often denounced as intolerant and prejudiced. This is not because we oppose the Catholic more than we do the alien, but because our enemies recognize that patriotism and race loyalty cannot safely be denounced, while our own tradition of religious freedom gives them an opening here, if they can sufficiently confuse the issue.

The fact is, of course, that our quarrel with the Catholics is not religious but political. The Nordic race is, as is well known, almost entirely Protestant, and there remains in its mental heritage an anti-Catholic attitude based on lack of sympathy with the Catholic psychology, on the historic opposition of the Roman Church to the Nordics' struggle for freedom and achievement, and on the memories of persecutions. But this strictly religious prejudice is not now active in America, and so far as I can learn, never has been. I do not know of a single manifestation in recent times of hostility to any Catholic because of his religion, nor to the Catholic Church because of its beliefs. Certainly the American has always granted to the Catholic not only full religious liberty, without interference or abuse either public or private, but also every civil, social and political equality. Neither the present day Protestant nor the Klan wishes to change this in any degree. . . .

The real indictment against the Roman Church is that it is, fundamentally and irredeemably, in its leadership, in politics, in thought, and largely in membership, actually and actively alien, un-American and usually anti-American. The old stock Americans, with the exception of the few such of Catholic faith—who are in a class by themselves, standing tragically torn between their faith and their racial and national patriotism —see in the Roman Church today the chief leader of alienism, and the most dangerous alien power with a foothold inside our boundaries. It is this and nothing else that has revived hostility to Catholicism. By no stretch of the imagination can it fairly be called religious prejudice, though, now that the hostility has become active, it does derive some strength from the religious schism.

We Americans see many evidences of Catholic alienism. We believe that its official position and its dogma, its theocratic autocracy and its claim to full authority in temporal as well as spiritual matters, all make it impossible for it as a church, or for its members if they obey it, to coöperate in a free democracy in which Church and State have been separated. It is true that in this country the Roman Church speaks very softly on these points, so that many Catholics do not know them. It is also true that the Roman priests preach Americanism, subject to their own conception of Americanism, of course. But the Roman Church itself makes a point of the divine and unalterable character of its dogma, it has never seen fit to abandon officially any of these un-American attitudes, and it still teaches them in other countries. Until it does renounce them, we cannot believe anything except that they all remain in force, ready to be called into action whenever feasible, and temporarily hushed up only for expediency.

The hierarchical government of the Roman Church is equally at odds with Americanism. The Pope and the whole hierarchy have been for centuries almost wholly Italian. It is nonsense to suppose that a man, by entering a church, loses his race or national loyalties. The Roman Church today, therefore, is just what its name says—Roman; and it is impossible for its hierarchy or the policies they dictate to be in real sympathy with Americanism. Worse, the Italians have proven to be one of the least assimilable of people. The autocratic nature of the Catholic Church organization, and its suppression of free conscience or free decision, need not be discussed; they are unquestioned. Thus it is fundamental to the Roman Church to demand a supreme loyalty, overshadowing national or race loyalty, to a power that is inevitably alien, and which at the best must inevitably inculcate ideals un-American if not actively anti-American. . . .

The facts are that almost everywhere, and especially in the great industrial centers where the Catholics are strongest, they vote almost as a unit, under control of leaders of their own faith, always in support of the interests of the Catholic Church and of Catholic candidates without regard to other interests, and always also in support of alienism whenever there is an issue raised. They vote, in short, not as American citizens, but as aliens and Catholics! They form the biggest, strongest, most cohesive of all the alien *blocs*. On many occasions they form alliances with other alien *blocs* against American interests, as with the Jews in New York today, and with others in the case of the recent opposition to immigrant restriction. Incidentally they have been responsible for some of the worst abuses in American politics, and today are the chief support of such machines as that of Brennan in Chicago, Curley in Boston and Tammany in New York. . . .

We are a movement of the plain people, very weak in the matter of culture, intellectual support, and trained leadership. We are demanding, and we expect to win, a return of power into the hands of the everyday, not highly cultured, not overly intellectualized, but entirely unspoiled and not de-Americanized, average citizen of the old stock. Our members and leaders are all of this class—the opposition of the intellectuals and liberals who held the leadership, betrayed Americanism, and from whom we expect to wrest control, is almost automatic.

This is undoubtedly a weakness. It lays us open to the charge of being "hicks" and "rubes" and "drivers of second hand Fords." We admit it. Far worse, it makes it hard for us to state our case and advocate our crusade in the most effective way, for most of us lack skill in language. Worst of all, the need of trained leaders constantly hampers our progress and leads to serious blunders and internal troubles. If the Klan ever should fail it would be from this cause. All this we on the inside know far better than our critics, and regret more. Our leadership is improving, but for many years the Klan will be seeking better leaders, and the leaders praying for greater wisdom.

Serious as this is, and strange though our attitude may seem to the intellectuals, it does not worry us greatly. Every popular movement has suffered from just this handicap, yet the popular movements have been the mainsprings of progress, and have usually had to win against the "best people" of their time. Moreover, we can depend on getting this intellectual backing shortly. It is notable that when the plain people begin to win with one of their movements, such as the Klan, the very intellectuals who have scoffed and fought most bitterly presently begin to dig up sound—at least well-sounding!—logic in support of the success. The movement, so far as can be judged, is neither hurt nor helped by this process.

Another weakness is that we have not been able, as yet, to bring home to the whole membership the need of continuous work on organization programmes both local and national. They are too prone to work only at times of crisis and excitement, and then to feel they can let down. Partly, of course, this is inherent in the evangelistic quality of our crusade. It is "strong medicine," highly emotional, and presently brings on a period of reaction and lethargy. All crusaders and evangelists know this: the whole country saw it after the war. The Klan will not be fully entrenched till it has passed this reaction period, and steadied down for the long pull. That time is only beginning for most of the Klan, which really is hardly three years old.

But we have no fear of the outcome. Since we indulge ourselves in convictions, we are not frightened by our weaknesses. We hold the conviction that right will win if backed with vigor and consecration. We are increasing our consecration and learning to make better use of our vigor. We are sure of the fundamental rightness of our cause, as it concerns both ourselves and the progress of the world. We believe that there can be no question of the right of the children of the men who made America to own and control America. We believe that when we allowed others to share our heritage, it was by our own generosity and by no right of theirs. We believe that therefore we have every right to protect ourselves when we find that they are betraying our trust and endangering us. We believe, in short, that we have the right to make America *American* and for Americans.

We believe also that only through this kind of a nation, and through development along these lines, can we best serve America, the whole world today, and the greater world yet unborn. We believe the hand of God was in the creation of the American stock and nation. We believe, too, in the right and duty of every man to fight for himself, his own children, his own nation and race. We believe in the parable of the talents, and mean to keep and use those entrusted to us—the race, spirit and nationhood of America!

Finally we believe in the vitality and driving power of our race: a faith based on the record of the Nordics throughout all history, and especially in America. J. P. Morgan had a motto which said, in effect, "Never bet against the future of America." We believe it is equally unsafe to bet against the future of any stock of the Nordic race, especially so finely blended and highly bred a stock as that of the sons of the pioneers. Handicaps, weaknesses, enemies and all, we will win!

Our critics have accused us of being merely a "protest move-ment," of being frightened; they say we fear alien competition, are in a panic because we cannot hold our own against the foreigners. That is partly true. We are a protest movement—protesting against being robbed. We are afraid of competition with peoples who would destroy our standard of living. We are suffering in many ways, we have been betrayed by our trusted leaders, we are half beaten already. But we are not frightened nor in a panic. We have merely awakened to the fact that we must fight for our own. We are going to fight—and win!

The Klan does not believe that the fact that it is emotional and instinctive, rather than coldly intellectual, is a weakness. All action comes from emotion, rather than from ratiocination. Our emotions and the instincts on which they are based have been bred into us for thousands of years; far longer than reason has had a place in the human brain. They are the many-times distilled product of experience; they still operate much more surely and promptly than reason can. For centuries those who obeyed them have lived and carried on the race; those in whom they were weak, or who failed to obey, have died. They are the foundations of our American civilization, even more than our great historic documents; they can be trusted where the fine-haired reasoning of the denatured intellectuals cannot.

Thus the Klan goes back to the American racial instincts, and to the common sense which is their first product, as the basis of its beliefs and methods. The fundamentals of our thought are convictions, not mere opinions. We are pleased that modern research is finding scientific backing for these convic-tions. We do not need them ourselves; we know that we are right in the same sense that a good Christian knows that he has been saved and that Christ lives—a thing which the intellectual can never understand. These convictions are no more to be argued about than is our love for our children; we are merely willing to state them for the enlightenment and conversion of others.

There are three of these great racial instincts, vital elements in both the historic and the present attempts to build an America which shall fulfill the aspirations and justify the heroism of the men who made the nation. These are the instincts of loyalty to the white race, to the traditions of America, and to the spirit of Protestantism, which has been an essential part of Americanism ever since the days of Roanoke and Plymouth Rock. They are condensed into the Klan slogan: "Native, white, Protestant supremacy."

First in the Klansman's mind is patriotism—America for Americans. He believes religiously that a betrayal of Americanism or the American race is treason to the most sacred of trusts, a trust from his fathers and a trust from God. He believes, too, that Americanism can only be achieved if the pioneer stock is kept pure. . . .

Americanism, to the Klansman, is a thing of the spirit, a purpose and a point of view, that can only come through instinctive racial understanding. It has, to be sure, certain defined principles, but he does not believe that many aliens understand those principles, even when they use our words in talking about them. Democracy is one, fairdealing, impartial justice, equal opportunity, religious liberty, independence, self-reliance, courage, endurance, acceptance of individual responsibility as well as individual rewards for effort, willingness to sacrifice for the good of his family, his nation and his race before anything else but God, dependence on enlightened conscience for guidance, the right to unhampered development—these are fundamental. But within the bounds they fix there must be the utmost freedom, tolerance, liberalism. In short, the Klansman believes in the greatest possible diversity and individualism within the limits of the American spirit. But he believes also that few aliens can understand that spirit, that fewer try to, and that there must be resistance, intolerance even, toward anything that threatens it, or the fundamental national unity based upon it.

The second word in the Klansman's trilogy is "white." The white race must be supreme, not only in America but in the world. This is equally undebatable, except on the ground that the races might live together, each with full regard for the rights and interests of others, and that those rights and interests would never conflict. Such an idea, of course, is absurd; the colored races today, such as Japan, are clamoring not for equality but for their supremacy. The whole history of the world, on its broader lines, has been one of race conflicts, wars, subjugation or extinction. This is not pretty, and certainly disagrees with the maudlin theories of cosmopolitanism, but it is truth. The world has been so made that each race must fight for its life, must conquer, accept slavery or die. The Klansman believes that the whites will not become slaves, and he does not intend to die before his time.

Moreover, the future of progress and civilization depends on the continued supremacy of the white race. The forward movement of the world for centuries has come entirely from it. Other races each had its chance and either failed or stuck fast, while white civilization shows no sign of having reached its limit. Until the whites falter, or some colored civilization has a miracle of awakening, there is not a single colored stock that can claim even equality with the white; much less supremacy.

The third of the Klan principles is that Protestantism must be supreme; that Rome shall not rule America. The Klansman believes this not merely because he is a Protestant, nor even because the Colonies that are now our nation were settled for the purpose of wresting America from the control of Rome and establishing a land of free conscience. He believes it also because Protestantism is an essential part of Americanism; without it America could never have been created and without it she cannot go forward. Roman rule would kill it.

Protestantism contains more than religion. It is the expression in religion of the same spirit of independence, self-reliance and freedom which are the highest achievements of the Nordic race. It sprang into being automatically at the time of the great "upsurgence" of strength in the Nordic peoples that opened the spurt of civilization in the fifteenth century. It has been a distinctly Nordic religion, and it has been through this religion that the Nordics have found strength to take leadership of all whites and the supremacy of the earth. Its destruction is the deepest purpose of all other peoples, as that would mean the end of Nordic rule. . . .

The Negro, the Klan considers a special duty and problem of the white American. He is among us through no wish of his; we owe it to him and to ourselves to give him full protection and opportunity. But his limitations are evident; we will not permit him to gain sufficient power to control our civilization. Neither will we delude him with promises of social equality which we know can never be realized. The Klan looks forward to the day when the Negro problem will have been solved on some much saner basis than miscegenation, and when every State will enforce laws making any sex relations between a white and a colored person a crime.

For the alien in general we have sympathy, opportunity, justice, but no permanent welcome unless he becomes truly American. It is our duty to see that he has every chance for this, and we shall be glad to accept him if he does. We hold no rancor against him; his race, instincts, training, mentality and whole outlook of life are usually widely different from ours. We cannot blame him if he adheres to them and attempts to convert us to them, even by force. But we must see that he can never succeed.

The Jew is a more complex problem. His abilities are great, he contributes much to any country where he lives. This is particularly true of the Western Jew, those of the stocks we have known so long. Their separation from us is more religious than racial. When freed from persecution these Jews have shown a tendency to disintegrate and amalgamate. We may hope that shortly, in the free atmosphere of America, Jews of this class will cease to be a problem. Quite different are the Eastern Jews of recent immigration, the Jews known as the Askhenasim. It is interesting to note that anthropologists now tell us that these are not true Jews, but only Judaized Mongols—Chazars. These, unlike the true Hebrew, show a divergence from the American type so great that there seems little hope of their assimilation. . . .

One of the outstanding principles of the Klan is secrecy. We have been much criticized for it, and accused of cowardice, though how any sane person can allege cowardice against men who stood unarmed while rioters beat and shot them down, as Klansmen were beaten and shot at Carnegie and other places, we cannot understand. Our secrecy is, in fact, necessary for our protection so long as the bitter intolerance and fanatic persecution lasts. Until the Klan becomes strong in a community, individual members have often found themselves in danger of loss of work, business, property and even life. There is also the advantage in secrecy that it gives us greater driving force, since our enemies are handicapped in not knowing just what, where or how great is the strength we can exert.

Both these reasons for secrecy will grow less in time, but it can safely be predicted that the Klan will never officially abandon its secrecy. The mask, by the way, is not a part of our secrecy at all, but of our ritual, and can never be abandoned. . . .

The future of the Klan we believe in, though it is still in the hands of God and of our own abilities and consecration as individuals and as a race. Previous movements of the kind have been short-lived, killed by internal jealousies and personal ambitions, and partly, too, by partial accomplishment of their purposes. If the Klan falls away from its mission, or fails in it, perhaps even if it succeeds—certainly whenever the time comes that it is not doing needed work—it will become a mere derelict, without purpose or force. If it fulfills its mission, its future power and service are beyond calculation so long as America has any part of her destiny unfulfilled. Meantime we of the Klan will continue, as best we know and as best we can, the crusade for Americanism to which we have been providentially called.

9 / FELIX FRANKFURTER

The Crime of Radicalism

In April 1920, a paymaster and a guard at a shoe factory in Massachusetts were murdered, and two Italian draft-dodgers and anarchists were convicted of the crimes in July 1921. Many people believed that Nicola Sacco and Bartolomeo Vanzetti were convicted not because they were guilty of murder but because they were foreigners and radicals. Defense committees were formed and secured a stay of execution while mass protests about the conviction were made in many parts of the world. The following selection by Felix Frankfurter (1882–1965), then a distinguished lawyer and later member of the U. S. Supreme Court, is a good example of the best arguments used by opponents of the conviction. Frankfurter was not challenging some minor legal technicality; he questioned the entire basis of the conviction, including the reliability of testimony, the prejudices of the time, and the competence of the judge. Despite all attempts to have a new trial, Sacco and Vanzetti were executed in the late summer of 1927. The debate about their guilt or innocence continues even now.

For more than six years the Sacco-Vanzetti case has been before the courts of Massachusetts. In a state where ordinary murder trials are promptly dispatched such extraordinary delay

From "The Case of Sacco and Vanzetti," *The Atlantic Monthly,* CXXXIX (March 1927), 409–411, 415–424, 426–428, 431–432. Copyright © 1927 by The Atlantic Monthly Company, Boston, Massachusetts 02116. Reprinted with permission.

in itself challenges attention. The fact is that a long succession of disclosures has aroused interest far beyond the boundaries of Massachusetts and even of the United States, until the case has become one of those rare *causes célèbres* which are of international concern. The aim of this paper is to give in the briefest compass an accurate résumé of the facts of the case from its earliest stages to its present posture. . . .

I

[Frankfurter here summarizes the events of Sacco and Vanzetti's alleged crime and their subsequent arrest and pre-trial examination.—Ed.]

Charged with the crime of murder on May 5, Sacco and Vanzetti were indicted on September 14, 1920, and put on trial May 21, 1921, at Dedham, Norfolk County. The setting of the trial, in the courthouse opposite the old home of Fisher Ames, furnished a striking contrast to the background and antecedents of the prisoners. Dedham is a quiet residential suburb, inhabited by well-to-do Bostonians, with a surviving element of New England small farmers. Part of the jury was specially selected by the sheriff's deputies from Masonic gatherings and from persons whom the deputies deemed 'representative citizens,' 'substantial' and 'intelligent.' The presiding judge was Webster Thayer of Worcester. The chief counsel for these Italians was a Westerner, a radical and a professional defender of radicals. In opinion, as well as in fact, he was an outsider. Unfamiliar with the traditions of the Massachusetts bench, not even a member of the Massachusetts bar, the characteristics of Judge Thayer unknown to him, Fred H. Moore found neither professional nor personal sympathies between himself and the Judge. So far as the relations between court and counsel seriously, even if unconsciously, affect the current of a trial, Moore was a factor of irritation. Sacco and Vanzetti spoke very broken English and their testimony shows how often they misunderstood the questions put to them. In fact, an interpreter had to be used, whose conduct raised such doubts that the defendants brought their own interpreter to check his questions and answers. The trial lasted nearly seven weeks, and on July 14, 1921, Sacco and Vanzetti were found guilty of murder in the first degree.

II

So far as the crime is concerned, we are dealing with a conventional case of pay-roll robbery. At the trial the killing of Parmenter and Berardelli was undisputed. The only issue was the identity of the murderers. Were Sacco and Vanzetti two of the assailants of Parmenter and Berardelli, or were they not?

On this issue there was at the trial a mass of conflicting evidence. Fifty-nine witnesses testified for the Commonwealth and ninety-nine for the defendants. The evidence offered by the Commonwealth was not the same against both defendants. The theory of the prosecution was that Sacco did the actual shooting while Vanzetti sat in the car as one of the collaborators in a conspiracy to murder. Witnesses testified to having seen both defendants in South Braintree on the morning of April 15; they claimed to recognize Sacco as the man who shot the guard Berardelli and to have seen him subsequently escape in the car. Expert testimony (the character of which, in the light of subsequent events, constitutes one of the most important features of the case . . .) was offered seeking to connect one of four bullets removed from Berardelli's body with the Colt pistol found on Sacco at the time of his arrest. As to Vanzetti, the Commonwealth adduced evidence placing him in the murder car. Moreover, the Commonwealth introduced the conduct of the defendants, as evinced by pistols found on their persons and lies admittedly told by them when arrested, as further proof of identification, in that such conduct revealed 'consciousness of guilt.'

The defense met the Commonwealth's eyewitnesses by other eyewitnesses, slightly more numerous and at least as well circumstanced to observe the assailants, who testified that the defendants were not the men they saw. Their testimony was confirmed by witnesses who proved the presence of Sacco and Vanzetti elsewhere at the time of the murder. Other witnesses supported Sacco's testimony that on April 15—the day that he was away from work—he was in Boston seeing about a passport to Italy, whither he was planning shortly to return to visit his recently bereaved father. The truth of that statement was supported by an official of the Italian consulate in Boston who deposed that Sacco visited his consulate at an hour that made it impossible for him to have been one of the Braintree murder gang. The claim of Vanzetti that on April 15 he was pursuing his customary trade as fish peddler was sustained by a number of witnesses who had been his customers that day.

From this summary it must be evident that the trustworthiness of the testimony which placed Sacco and Vanzetti in South Braintree on April 15 is the foundation of the case. . . .

[Here Frankfurter summarizes the evidence for and against Sacco and Vanzetti's presence at the scene of the crime.—Ed.]

The alibi for Vanzetti was overwhelming. Thirty-one eyewitnesses testified positively that no one of the men that they saw in the murder car was Vanzetti. Thirteen witnesses either testified directly that Vanzetti was in Plymouth selling fish on the day of the murder or furnished corroboration of such testimony.

What is the worth of identification testimony even when uncontradicted? The identification of strangers is proverbially untrustworthy. The hazards of this type of testimony are established by a formidable number of instances in the records of English and American trials. These instances are recent—not due to the brutalities of ancient criminal procedure.

In the Sacco-Vanzetti case the elements of uncertainty were intensified. All the identifying witnesses were speaking from casual observation of men they had never seen before, men of foreign race, under circumstances of unusual confusion. Thus, one witness, Cole, 'thought at the first glance that the man was a Portuguese fellow named Tony that he knew.' Afterward he was sure it was Vanzetti. Nor can we abstain from comment on the methods pursued by the police in eliciting subsequent identification. The recognized procedure is to line up the suspect with others, and so far as possible with individuals of the same race and class, so as not to provoke identification through accentuation. In defiance of these necessary safeguards, Sacco and Vanzetti after their arrest were shown singly to persons brought there for the purposes of identification, not as part of a 'parade.' Moreover, Sacco and Vanzetti were not even allowed to be their natural selves; they were compelled to simulate the behavior of the Braintree bandits. Under such conditions identification of foreigners is a farce.

After the conviction Judge Thayer himself abandoned the identification of Sacco and Vanzetti as the ground on which the jury's verdict rested. In denying a motion for a new trial, based on the discovery of a new eyewitness with better opportunities for observation than any of the other witnesses on either side, who, in his affidavit, swore that Sacco was not the man in the car, Judge Thayer ruled that this evidence:

would simply mean one more piece of evidence of the same kind and directed to the same end, and in my judgment would have no effect whatever upon the verdicts. These verdicts did not rest, in my judgment, upon the testimony of the eyewitnesses, for the defendants, as it was, called more witnesses than the Commonwealth to testify that neither of the defendants were in the bandit car.

The evidence that convicted these defendants was circumstantial and was evidence that is known in law as 'consciousness of guilt.'

III

'Consciousness of guilt' meant that the conduct of Sacco and Vanzetti after April 15 was the conduct of murderers. This inference of guilt was drawn from their behavior on the night of May 5, before and after arrest, and also from their possession of firearms. It is vital to keep in mind the evidence on which, according to Judge Thayer, these two men are to be sentenced to death. There was no claim whatever at the trial, and none has ever been suggested since, that Sacco and Vanzetti had any prior experience in holdups or any previous association with bandits; no claim that the sixteen thousand dollars taken from the victims ever found its way into their pockets; no claim that their financial condition or that of Sacco's family (he had a wife and child, and another child was soon to be born) was in any way changed after April 15; no claim that after the murder either Sacco or Vanzetti changed his manner of living or employment. Neither of these men had ever been accused of crime before their arrest. Nor did they during the three weeks between the murder and their arrest behave like men who were concealing the crime of murder. They did not go into hiding; they did not abscond with the spoils; they did not live under assumed names. They maintained their old lodgings; they pursued openly their callings within a few miles of the town where they were supposed to have committed murder in broad daylight; and when arrested Sacco was found to have in his pocket an announcement of a forthcoming meeting at which Vanzetti was to speak. Was this the behavior of men eluding identification?

What, then, was the evidence of guilty conduct against them?

1. Sacco and Vanzetti, as we have already explained, were two of four Italians who called for Boda's car at Johnson's garage on the evening of May 5. Mrs. Johnson gave the pretext of having to fetch some milk and went to a neighbor's house to telephone the police. She testified that the two defendants followed her to the house on the opposite side of the street, and when, after telephoning, she reappeared they followed her back. The men then left without taking the car, having been

advised by Mr. Johnson not to run it without the current year's number plate.

> Q. Now, Boda came there to get his car, didn't he? A. Yes.
> Q. There were no 1920 number plates on it? A. No.
> Q. You advised him not to take the car and run it without the 1920 number plates, didn't you? A. Yes.
> Q. And he accepted your view? A. He seemed to.
> Q. He seemed to. And after some conversation went away? A. Yes.

This was the whole of the testimony on the strength of which Judge Thayer put the following question to the jury:—

> Did the defendants, in company with Orciani and Boda, leave the Johnson house because the automobile had no 1920 number plate on it, or because they were conscious of or became suspicious of what Mrs. Johnson did in the Bartlett house? If they left because they had no 1920 number plates on the automobile, then you may say there was no consciousness of guilt in consequence of their sudden departure, but if they left because they were consciously guilty of what was being done by Mrs. Johnson in the Bartlett house, then you may say that is evidence tending to prove consciousness of guilt.

2. Following their departure from the Johnson house, Sacco and Vanzetti were arrested by a policeman who boarded their street car as it was coming into Brockton. Three policemen testified as to their behavior after being taken into custody. The following will serve as a sample:—

> I told them when we started that the first false move I would put a bullet in them. On the way up to the station Sacco reached his hand to put under his overcoat and I told him to keep his hands outside of his clothes and on his lap.
> Q. Will you illustrate to the jury how he placed his hands? A. He

was sitting down with his hands that way [indicating], and he
moved his hand up to put it in under his overcoat.
Q. At what point? A. Just about the stomach there, across his
waistband, and I says to him, 'Have you got a gun there?' He says,
'No.' He says, 'I ain't got no gun.' 'Well,' I says, 'keep your hands
outside of your clothes.' We went along a little further and he done
the same thing. I gets up on my knees on the front seat and I
reaches over and I puts my hand under his coat, but I did not see
any gun. 'Now,' I says, 'Mister, if you put your hands in there again,
you are going to get into trouble.' He says, 'I don't want no trouble.'

3. In statements made to the District Attorney and to the
Chief of Police at the police station after their arrest, both
Sacco and Vanzetti lied. By misstatements they tried to conceal
their movements on the day of their arrest, the friends they had
been to see, the places they had visited. For instance, Vanzetti
denied that he knew Boda.

What of this evidence of 'consciousness of guilt'? The testimony of the police that Sacco and Vanzetti were about to draw
pistols was emphatically denied by them. These denials, it was
urged, were confirmed by the inherent probabilities of the situ- .
ation. Did Sacco and Vanzetti upon arrest reveal the qualities
of the perpetrators of the Braintree murders? Would the ready
and ruthless gunmen at Braintree have surrendered themselves
so quietly into custody on a capital charge of which they knew
themselves to be guilty? If Sacco and Vanzetti were the holdup
men of Braintree, why did they not draw upon their expert skill
and attempt to make their escape by scattering shots? But, not
being gunmen, why should Sacco and Vanzetti have carried
guns? The possession of firearms in this country has not at all
the significance that it would have, say, in England. The extensive carrying of guns by people who are not 'gunmen' is a matter of common knowledge. Sacco acquired the habit of carrying
a pistol while a night watchman in the shoe factory, because, as
his employer testified, 'night watchmen protecting property do

have guns.' Vanzetti carried a revolver 'because it was a very bad time, and I like to have a revolver for self-defense.'

Q. How much money did you use to carry around with you? A. When I went to Boston for fish, I can carry eighty, one hundred dollars, one hundred and twenty dollars.

There were many crimes, many holdups, many robberies at that time.

The other evidence from which 'consciousness of guilt' was drawn the two Italians admitted. They acknowledged that they behaved in the way described by Mrs. Johnson; and freely conceded that when questioned at the police station they told lies. What was their explanation of this conduct? To exculpate themselves of the crime of murder they had to disclose elaborately their guilt of radicalism. In order to meet the significance which the prosecution attached to the incidents at the Johnson house and those following, it became necessary for the defendants to advertise to the jury their offensive radicalism, and thereby to excite the deepest prejudices of a Norfolk County jury picked for its respectability and sitting in judgment upon two men of alien blood and abhorrent philosophy.

Innocent men, it is suggested, do not lie when picked up by the police. But Sacco and Vanzetti knew they were not innocent of the charge on which they supposed themselves arrested, and about which the police interrogated them. For, when apprehended, Sacco and Vanzetti were not confronted with the charge of murder; they were not accused of banditry; they were not given the remotest intimation that the murders of Parmenter and Berardelli were laid at their door. They were told they were arrested as 'suspicious characters,' and the meaning which that carried to their minds was rendered concrete by the questions that were put to them.

Q. Tell us all you recall that Stewart, the chief, asked of you? A. He asked me why we were in Bridgewater, how long I knew Sacco,

if I am a radical, if I am an anarchist or Communist, and he asked me if I believe in the government of the United States.
Q. Did either Chief Stewart at the Brockton police station or Mr. Katzmann tell you that you were suspected of robberies and murder? A. No.
Q. Was there any question asked of you or any statement made to you to indicate to you that you were charged with that crime on April 15? A. No.
Q. What did you understand, in view of the questions asked of you, what did you understand you were being detained for at the Brockton police station? A. I understand they arrested me for a political matter. . . .
Q. . . . Why did you feel you were being detained for political opinions? A. Because I was asked if I was a Socialist. I said, 'Well—'
Q. You mean by reason of the questions asked of you? A. Because I was asked if I am a Socialist, if I am I. W. W., if I am a Communist, if I am a Radical, if I am a Black Hand.

Plainly their arrest meant to Sacco and Vanzetti arrest for radicalism.

Boston was one of the worst centres of the lawlessness and hysteria that characterized the campaign of the Department of Justice for the wholesale arrest and deportation of Reds. Its proximity to industrial communities having a large proportion of foreign labor and a history of past industrial conflicts lent to the lawless activities of the government officials the widespread support of influential public opinion. Mr. John F. Moors, himself a banker, has called attention to the fact that 'the hysteria against "the reds" was so great, at the time when these men were convicted, that even the most substantial bankers in this city [Boston] were carried away to the extent of paying for full-page advertisements about the red peril.' Sacco and Vanzetti were notorious Reds. They were associates of leading radicals; they had for some time been on the list of suspects of the Department of Justice; and they were especially obnoxious because they were draft-dodgers.

The terrorizing methods of the Government had very specific meaning for the two Italians. Two of their friends had already been deported. The arrest of the New York radical Salsedo, and his detention incommunicado by the Department of Justice, had been for some weeks a source of great concern to them. Vanzetti was sent to New York to confer with a committee having charge of the case of Salsedo and other Italian political prisoners. On his return, May 2, he reported to his Boston friends the advice which had been given him: namely, to dispose of their radical literature and thus eliminate the most damaging evidence in the deportation proceedings they feared. The urgency of acting on this advice was intensified by the tragic news of Salsedo's death after Vanzetti's return from New York. Though Salsedo's death was unexplained, to Sacco and Vanzetti it conveyed only one explanation. It was a symbol of their fears and an omen of their own fate.

On the witness stand Sacco and Vanzetti accounted for their movements on April 15. They also accounted for their ambiguous behavior on May 5. Up to the time that Sacco and Vanzetti testified to their radical activities, their pacifism, their flight to Mexico to avoid the draft, the trial was a trial for murder and banditry; with the cross-examination of Sacco and Vanzetti, patriotism and radicalism became the dominant emotional issues. Outside the courtroom the Red hysteria was rampant; it was allowed to dominate within. The prosecutor systematically played on the feelings of the jury by exploiting the unpatriotic and despised beliefs of Sacco and Vanzetti, and the judge allowed him thus to divert and pervert the jury's mind.

The opening question in the cross-examination of Vanzetti by the District Attorney discloses a motif that he persistently played upon:—

Q. (by Mr. Katzmann) So you left Plymouth, Mr. Vanzetti, in May, 1917, to dodge the draft, did you? A. Yes, sir.

Q. When this country was at war, you ran away, so you would not have to fight as a soldier? A. Yes.

This method was elaborated when Sacco took the stand:—

Q. (by Mr. Katzmann) Did you say yesterday you love a free country? A. Yes, sir.

Q. Did you love this country in the month of May, 1917? A. I did not say—I don't want to say I did not love this country.

Q. Did you go to Mexico to avoid being a soldier for this country that you loved? A. Yes.

Q. And would it be your idea of showing your love for your wife that, when she needed you, you ran away from her? A. I did not run away from her.

Q. Don't you think going away from your country is a vulgar thing to do when she needs you? A. I don't believe in war.

Q. You don't believe in war? A. No, sir.

Q. Do you think it is a cowardly thing to do what you did? A. No, sir.

Q. Do you think it is a brave thing to do what you did? A. Yes, sir.

Q. Do you think it would be a brave thing to go away from your own wife? A. No.

Q. When she needed you? A. No.

THE COURT. All I ask is this one question, and it will simplify matters very much. Is it your claim that in the collection of the literature and the books and papers that that was done in the interest of the United States?

MR. JEREMIAH MCANARNEY. I make no such broad claim as that. . . .

MR. KATZMANN. Well, he [Sacco] stated in his direct examination yesterday that he loved a free country, and I offer it to attack that statement made in his examination by his own counsel.

THE COURT. That is what I supposed, and that is what I supposed that remark meant when it was introduced in this cross-examination, but counsel now say they don't make that claim.

MR. KATZMANN. They say they don't make the claim that gathering up the literature on May 5 at West Bridgewater was for the purpose of helping the country, but that is a different matter, not released [*sic*] to May 5.

THE COURT. I will let you inquire further first as to what he meant by the expression.

Q. What did you mean when you said yesterday you loved a free country? A. Give me a chance to explain.

Q. I am asking you to explain now. A. When I was in Italy, a boy, I was a Republican, so I always thinking Republican has more chance to manage education, develop, to build some day his family, to raise the child and education, if you could. But that was my opinion; so when I came to this country I saw there was not what I was thinking before, but there was all the difference, because I been working in Italy not so hard as I been work in this country. I could live free there just as well. Work in the same condition but not so hard, about seven or eight hours a day, better food. I mean genuine. Of course, over here is good food, because it is bigger country, to any those who got money to spend, not for the working and laboring class, and in Italy is more opportunity to laborer to eat vegetable, more fresh, and I came in this country. When I been started work here very hard and been work thirteen years, hard worker, I could not been afford much a family the way I did have the idea before. I could not put any money in the bank; I could no push my boy some to go to school and other things. I teach over here men who is with me. The free idea gives any man a chance to profess his own idea, not the supreme idea, not to give any person, not to be like Spain in position, yes, about twenty centuries ago, but to give a chance to print and education, literature, free speech, that I see it was all wrong. I could see the best men, intelligent, education, they been arrested and sent to prison and died in prison for years and years without getting them out, and Debs, one of the great men in his country, he is in prison, still away in prison, because he is a Socialist. He wanted the laboring class to have better conditions and better living, more education, give a push his son if he could have a chance some day, but they [put] him in prison. Why? Because the capitalist class, they know, they are against that, because the capitalist class, they don't want our child to go to high school or college or Harvard College. There would be no chance, there would not be no—they don't want the working class educationed; they want the working class to be a low all the times, be underfoot, and not to be up with the head. So, sometimes, you see, the Rockefellers, Morgans, they give fifty—I mean they give five hundred thousand dollars to Harvard College, they give a million dollars for another school. Every day say, 'Well, D. Rockefeller is a great man, the best man in the country.' I want to ask him who is going to Harvard College? What benefit the working class they will get by those million dollars they give by Rockefeller, D. Rockefellers. They won't get, the poor class, they won't, have no chance to go to Harvard College because men who is getting $21 a week or $30 a week, I don't care if he gets $80 a week, if he gets a family of five children he can't live and send his child and go to Harvard College if he wants to eat everything nature will give him. If he wants to eat like a cow, and that is the best thing, but I want men to live like men. I like men to get everything that nature will give best, because they belong—we are not the friend of any other place, but we are belong to nations. So that is why my idea has been changed. So that is why I love people who labor and work and see better conditions every day develop, makes no more war. We no want fight by the gun, and we don't want to destroy young men. The mother has been suffering for building the young man. Some day need a little more bread, so when the time the mother get some bread or profit out of that boy, the Rockefellers, Morgans, and some of the peoples, high class, they send to war. Why? What is war? The war is no shoots like Abraham Lincoln's and Abe Jefferson, to fight for the free country, for the better education to give chance to any other peoples, not the white people but the black and the others, because they believe and know they are mens like the rest, but they are war for the great millionaire. No war for the civilization of men. They are war for business, million dollars come on the side. What right we have to kill each other? I been work for the Irish. I have been working with the German fellow, with the French, many other peoples. I love them people just as I could love my wife, and my people for that did receive me. Why should I go kill them men? What he done to me? He never done anything, so I don't believe in no war. I want to destroy those guns. All I can say, the Government put the literature, give us educations. I remember in Italy, a long time ago, about sixty years ago, I should say, yes, about sixty years ago, the Government they could not control very much those two—devilment went on, and robbery, so one of the government in the cabinet he says, 'If you want to destroy those devilments, if you want to take off all those criminals, you ought to give a chance to Socialist literature, education of people, emancipation. That is why I destroy governments, boys.' That is why my idea I love Socialists. That is why I like people who want education and living, building, who is good, just as much as they could. That is all.

Q. And that is why you love the United States of America? A. Yes. . . .

Q. So without the light of knowledge on that subject, you are condemning even Harvard University, are you, as being a place for rich men? . . .

Q. Did you intend to condemn Harvard College? (Objection overruled.) A. No, sir.

Q. Were you ready to say none but the rich could go there without knowing about offering scholarships? (Objection overruled.) . . .

[Frankfurter here includes part of the district attorney's examination of Vanzetti concerning his anarchism.—Ed.]

In 1921 the temper of the times made it the special duty of a prosecutor and a court engaged in trying two Italian radicals before a jury of native New Englanders to keep the instruments of justice free from the infection of passion or prejudice. In the case of Sacco and Vanzetti no such restraints were respected. By systematic exploitation of the defendants' alien blood, their imperfect knowledge of English, their unpopular social views, and their opposition to the war, the District Attorney invoked against them a riot of political passion and patriotic sentiment; and the trial judge connived at—one had almost written, coöperated in—the process. . . .

That the real purpose of this line of the prosecutor's cross-examination was to inflame the jury's passions is suggested by the professed ground on which, with the Court's sanction, it was conducted. The Commonwealth claimed that the alleged anxiety of Sacco and Vanzetti on the evening of their arrest and the lies they told could be explained only by the fact that they were the murderers of Parmenter and Berardelli. The defense replied that their conduct was clearly accounted for by the fact that the men were Reds in terror of the Department of Justice. To test the credibility of this answer the District Attorney proposed to examine Sacco and Vanzetti to find out whether they were really radicals or only pretending to be. In effect the Commonwealth undertook to show that the defendants were impostors, that they were spurious Reds. This it made not the least attempt to do. It never disputed their radicalism. Instead of undermining the claim of the defendants by which their conduct was explained, the District Attorney adopted their confession of radicalism, exaggerated and exploited it. He thereby wholly destroyed the basis of his original claim, for what reason was there any longer to suppose that the 'consciousness of guilt' was consciousness of murder rather than of radicalism?

IV

The deliberate effort to excite the emotions of jurors still in the grip of war fever is not unparalleled in the legal history of the times. During the year 1918–19 in the United States, forty-four convictions were reversed by appellate courts for misconduct of the trial judge or the public prosecutor; thirty-three of them for inflammatory appeals made by the district attorney on matters not properly before the jury. Appellate courts interfere reluctantly in such cases and only where there has been a flagrant abuse, so that we may safely assume the above figures indicate an even more widespread evil. What *is* unparalleled is that such an abuse should have succeeded in a Massachusetts court.

As things were, what wonder the jury convicted? The last words left with them by Mr. Katzmann were an appeal to their solidarity against the alien: 'Gentlemen of the jury, do your duty. Do it like men. Stand together, you men of Norfolk.' The first words of Judge Thayer's charge revived their memories of the war and sharpened their indignation against the two draft-dodgers whose fate lay in their hands: 'The Commonwealth of Massachusetts called upon you to render a most important service. Although you knew that such service would be arduous, painful, and tiresome, yet you, like the true soldier, responded to that call in the spirit of supreme American loyalty. There is no better word in the English language than "loyalty." ' It had been to the accompaniment of this same war motif that the jurors were first initiated into the case; by the license allowed to the prosecution it had remained continuously in their ears throughout the trial; and now by the final and authoritative voice of the Court it was a soldier's loyalty which was made the measure of their duty.

The function of a judge's charge is to enable the jury to find its way through the maze of conflicting testimony, to sift the relevant from the irrelevant, to weigh wisely, and to judge dispassionately. A trial judge is not expected to rehearse all the testimony; in Massachusetts he is not allowed to express his own opinion on it. But in drawing the disconnected threads of evidence and marshaling the claims on both sides he must exercise a scrupulous regard for relevance and proportion. Misplaced emphasis here and omission there may work more damage than any outspoken comment. By his summing up a judge reveals his estimate of relative importance. Judge Thayer's charge directs the emotions only too clearly. What guidance does he give to the mind? The charge occupies twenty-four pages; of these, fourteen are consumed in abstract legal generalities and moral exhortations. Having allowed the minds of the jurors to be impregnated with war feeling, Judge Thayer now invited them to breathe 'a purer atmosphere of unyielding impartiality and absolute fairness.' Unfortunately the passion and prejudice instilled during the course of a long trial cannot be exorcised by the general, placid language of a charge after the mischief is done. Every experienced lawyer knows that it is idle to ask jurors to dismiss from their memory what has been deposited in their feelings.

In this case the vital issue was identification. That the whole mass of conflicting identification testimony is dismissed in two pages out of twenty-four is a fair measure of the distorted perspective in which the Judge placed the case. He dealt with identification in abstract terms and without mentioning the name of any witness on either side. The alibi testimony he likewise dismissed in two paragraphs, again without reference to specific witnesses. In striking contrast to this sterile treatment of the issue whether or not Sacco and Vanzetti were in South Braintree on April 15 was his concrete and elaborate treatment of the inferences which might be drawn from the character of their conduct on the night of their arrest. Five pages of the charge are given over to 'consciousness of guilt,' set forth in great detail and with specific mention of the testimony given by the various police officials and by Mr. and Mrs. Johnson. The disproportionate consideration which Judge Thayer gave to this issue, in the light of his comments during the trial, must have left the impression that the case turned on 'consciousness of guilt.' As we have seen, Judge Thayer himself did in fact so interpret the jury's verdict afterward.

As to motive, the Court expatiated for more than a page on his legal conception and the undisputed claim of the Commonwealth that the motive of the murder of Parmenter and Berardelli was robbery, but made no comment whatever on the complete failure of the Commonwealth to trace any of the stolen money to either defendant or to connect them with the art of robbery. Undoubtedly, great weight must have been attached by the jury, as it was by the Court, to the identification of the fatal bullet taken from Berardelli's body as having passed through Sacco's pistol. The Court instructed the jury that Captain Proctor and another expert had testified that 'it was his [Sacco's] pistol that fired the bullet that caused the death of

Berardelli,' when in fact that was not Captain Proctor's testimony. Of course, if the jury believed Proctor's testimony as interpreted by Judge Thayer, Sacco certainly was doomed. In view of the temper of the times, the nature of the accusation, the opinions of the accused, the tactics of the prosecution, and the conduct of the Judge, no wonder the 'men of Norfolk' convicted Sacco and Vanzetti!

Hitherto the methods pursued by the prosecution, which explain the convictions, rested on inferences, however compelling. But recently facts have been disclosed, and not denied by the prosecution, to indicate that the case against these Italians for murder was part of a collusive effort between the District Attorney and agents of the Department of Justice to rid the country of Sacco and Vanzetti because of their Red activities. In proof of this we have the affidavits of two former officers of the Government, one of whom served as post-office inspector for twenty-five years, and both of whom are now in honorable civil employment. Sacco's and Vanzetti's names were on the files of the Department of Justice 'as radicals to be watched'; the Department was eager for their deportation, but had not evidence enough to secure it; and inasmuch as the United States District Court for Massachusetts had checked abuses in deportation proceedings, the Department had become chary of resorting to deportation without adequate legal basis. The arrest of Sacco and Vanzetti, on the mistaken theory of Chief Stewart, furnished the agents of the Department their opportunity. Although the opinion of the agents working on the case was that 'the South Braintree crime was the work of professionals,' and that Sacco and Vanzetti, 'although anarchists and agitators, were not highway robbers, and had nothing to do with the South Braintree crime,' yet they collaborated with the District Attorney in the prosecution of Sacco and Vanzetti for murder. For 'it was the opinion of the Department agents here that a conviction of Sacco and Vanzetti for murder would be one way of disposing of these two men.' Here, to be sure, is a startling allegation. But it is made by a man of long years of important service in the Government's employ. It is supported by the now admitted installation of a government spy in a cell adjoining Sacco's with a view to 'obtaining whatever incriminating evidence he could . . . after winning his confidence'; by the insinuation of an 'under-cover man' into the councils of the Sacco-Vanzetti Defense Committee; by the proposed placement of another spy as a lodger in Mrs. Sacco's house; and by the supplying of information about the radical activities of Sacco and Vanzetti to the District Attorney by the agents of the Department of Justice.

These joint labors between Boston agents of the Department of Justice and the District Attorney led to a great deal of correspondence between the agent in charge and the District Attorney and to reports between the agents of the Department and Washington. These records have not been made available, nor has their absence been accounted for. An appeal to Attorney-General Sargent proved fruitless, although supported by Senator Butler of Massachusetts, requesting that Mr. West, the then agent in charge, 'be authorized to talk with counsel for Sacco and Vanzetti and to disclose whatever documents and correspondence are on file in his office dealing with the investigation made by the Boston agents before, during, and after the trial of Sacco and Vanzetti.' The facts upon which this appeal was made stand uncontradicted. West made no denial whatever and the District Attorney only emphasized his failure to deny the facts charged by the two former agents of the Department of Justice by an affidavit confined to a denial of some of the statements of a former government spy. The charge that the principal agent of the Department of Justice in Boston and the District Attorney collaborated to secure the conviction of Sacco and Vanzetti is denied neither by the agent nor by the District Attorney. Chief Stewart of Bridgewater takes it upon himself to say that the officials of the Department 'had nothing whatsoever to do with the preparation of this case for trial.'

Instead of making a full disclosure of the facts, the representative of the Commonwealth indulged in vituperation against the
former officers of the Department of Justice as men who were
guilty of 'a breach of loyalty' because they violated the watch-
word of the Department of Justice, 'Do not betray the secrets
of your departments.' To which Mr. Thompson rightly replies,
'What are the secrets which they admit? . . . A government
which has come to value its own secrets more than it does the
lives of its citizens has become a tyranny. . . . Secrets, secrets!
And he says you should abstain from touching this verdict of
your jury because it is so sacred. Would they not have liked to
know something about the secrets? The case is admitted by that
inadvertent concession. There are, then, secrets to be admitted.'
Yet Judge Thayer found in these circumstances only opportunity to make innuendo against a former official of the Government well known for his long and honorable service, and an
elaborate denial of a claim that was never made. Not less than
twelve times Judge Thayer ridicules the charge of a conspiracy
between 'these two great Governments—that of the United
States and the Commonwealth of Massachusetts'! He indulges
in much patriotic protestation, but is wholly silent about the
specific acts of wrongdoing and lawlessness connected with the
Red raids of 1920. The historian who relied on this opinion
would have to assume that the charge of lawlessness and misconduct in the deportations of outlawed radicals was the trai-
torous invention of a diseased mind.

V

The verdict of guilty was brought in on July 14, 1921. The
exceptions which had been taken to rulings at the trial were
made the basis of an application for a new trial, which Judge
Thayer refused. Subsequently a great mass of new evidence
was unearthed by the defense, and made the subject of other

motions for a new trial, all heard before Judge Thayer and all denied by him. The hearing on the later motions took place on October 1, 1923, and was the occasion of the entry into the case of Mr. William G. Thompson, a powerful advocate bred in the traditions of the Massachusetts courts. The espousal of the Sacco-Vanzetti cause by a man of Mr. Thompson's professional prestige at once gave it a new complexion and has been its mainstay ever since. For he has brought to the case, not only his great ability as a lawyer, but the strength of his conviction that these two men are innocent and that their trial was not characterized by those high standards which are the pride of Massachusetts justice.

We have now reached a stage of the case the details of which shake one's confidence in the whole course of the proceedings and reveal a situation which undermines the respect usually to be accorded to a jury's verdict. By prearrangement the prosecution brought before the jury a piece of evidence apparently most damaging to the defendants, when in fact the full truth concerning this evidence was very favorable to them. Vital to the identification of Sacco and Vanzetti as the murderers was the identification of one of the fatal bullets as a bullet coming from Sacco's pistol. The evidence excluded the possibility that five other bullets found in the dead bodies were fired by either Sacco or Vanzetti. When Judge Thayer placed the case in the jury's hands for judgment he charged them that the Commonwealth had introduced the testimony of two experts, Proctor and Van Amburgh, to the effect that the fatal bullet went through Sacco's pistol.

Such was not the belief of Proctor; he refused to accede to this view in the course of the preparation of the case, and the District Attorney knew that such was not intended to be his testimony. . . .

[Frankfurter goes on to analyze the ambiguities in Captain Proctor's evidence for the prosecution on ballistics. It is emphasized that Proctor could not positively identify the murder bullet as having been fired from Sacco's gun.—Ed.]

The Judge next attempts to belittle the weight of Proctor's testimony two years after he was offered by the Commonwealth with elaborate reliance as a most important expert. We must dwell on one amazing statement of the Court. 'With his limited knowledge,' says Judge Thayer, 'Captain Proctor did not testify that the mortal bullet did pass through Sacco's pistol, but that from his examination of the facts it was simply consistent with it.' Why did not Judge Thayer say this to the jury when he charged them with determining the guilt or innocence of Sacco? Why did the Judge charge the jury that Captain Proctor *did* testify that the mortal bullet passed through Sacco's pistol? And why, having in October 1924, for the purpose of denying the Proctor motion, minimized the Proctor testimony by saying that Proctor testified that the passing of the mortal bullet through Sacco's pistol was 'simply consistent with' the facts, does he two years later, in order to show how strong the case was at the original trial, state that the 'experts testified in their judgment it [the mortal bullet] was *perfectly* consistent with' having been fired through the Sacco pistol? In charging the jury Judge Thayer misled them by maximizing the Proctor testimony as the prearrangement intended that it should be maximized. When the prearrangement was discovered and made the basis of a motion for a new trial, Judge Thayer depreciated Proctor's qualifications as an expert and minimized Proctor's actual testimony. Finally, when confronted with new evidence pointing seriously to guilt for the Berardelli murder, not only away from Sacco and Vanzetti, but positively in another direction, in order to give the appearance of impressiveness to the facts before the jury Judge Thayer again relies upon the weightiness of Proctor's expert testimony and maximizes Proctor's evidence at the trial, but not to the extent that he did

in charging the jury because Proctor's affidavit now prevents
him from doing so!

This is the attitude of mind which has guided the conduct
of this case from the beginning; this is the judge who has for
all practical purposes sat in judgment upon his own conduct. . . .

[Frankfurter appeals to the judicial standards set by the
Massachusetts Supreme Court, charging that Judge Thayer's
treatment of Proctor's evidence violates these standards.—Ed.]

VI

On May 12, 1926, the Supreme Court of Massachusetts
found 'no error' in any of the rulings of Judge Thayer. The
guilt or innocence of the defendants was not retried in the Supreme Court. That court could not inquire whether the facts as
set forth in the printed record justified the verdict. Such would
have been the scope of judicial review had the case come before the New York Court of Appeals or the English Court of
Criminal Appeal. In those jurisdictions a judgment upon the
facts as well as upon the law is open, and their courts decide
whether convictions should stand in view of the whole record.
A much more limited scope in reviewing convictions prevails
in Massachusetts. What is reviewed in effect is the conduct of
the trial judge; only so-called questions of law are open.

The merits of the legal questions raised by the exceptions
cannot be discussed here. Suffice it to say, with deference, that
some of the Supreme Court rulings are puzzling in the extreme.
One question of law, however, can be explained within small
compass, and that is the question which is the crux of the case:
Did Judge Thayer observe the standards of Anglo-American
justice? In legal parlance, was there abuse of 'judicial discretion' by Judge Thayer? What, then, is 'judicial discretion'? Is
it a legal abracadabra, or does it imply standards of conduct

within the comprehension of the laity in whose interests they are enforced? The present Chief Justice of Massachusetts has given an authoritative definition:—

Discretion in this connection means a sound judicial discretion, enlighted by intelligence and learning, controlled by sound principles of law, of firm courage combined with the calmness of a cool mind, free from partiality, not swayed by sympathy nor warped by prejudice nor moved by any kind of influence save alone the overwhelming passion to do that which is just. It may be assumed that conduct manifesting abuse of judicial discretion will be reviewed and some relief afforded.

This is the test by which Judge Thayer's conduct must be measured. The Supreme Court found no abuse of judicial discretion on the record presented at the first hearing before it. In other words, the Court was satisfied that throughout the conduct of the trial and the proceedings that followed it Judge Thayer was governed by 'the calmness of a cool mind, free from partiality, not swayed by sympathy nor warped by prejudice nor moved by any kind of influence save alone the overwhelming passion to do that which is just.'

The reader has now had placed before him fairly, it is hoped, however briefly, the means of forming a judgment. Let him judge for himself!

VII

Hitherto the defense has maintained that the circumstances of the case all pointed away from Sacco and Vanzetti. But the deaths of Parmenter and Berardelli have remained unexplained. Now the defense has adduced new proof, not only that Sacco and Vanzetti did *not* commit the murders, but also, positively, that a well-known gang of professional criminals *did* commit them. Hitherto a new trial has been pressed because of the character of the original trial. Now a new trial has

been demanded because an impressive body of evidence tends
to establish the guilt of others. . . .

[Frankfurter offers evidence that the Morelli gang of Providence committed the South Braintree payroll robbery.—Ed.]

. . . Every reasonable probability points away from Sacco and
Vanzetti; every reasonable probability points toward the Morelli gang.
How did these facts appear to Judge Thayer?

VIII

At the outset the scope of Judge Thayer's duty toward the
motion for a new trial based upon this new evidence must be
kept in mind. It was not for him to determine the guilt of the
Morellis or the innocence of Sacco and Vanzetti; it was not for
him to weigh the new evidence as though he were a jury, determining what is true and what is false. Judge Thayer's duty was
the very narrow one of ascertaining whether here was new material fit for a new jury's judgment. May honest minds, capable
of dealing with evidence, reach a different conclusion, because
of the new evidence, from that of the first jury? Do the new
facts raise debatable issues? Could another jury, conscious of
its oath and conscientiously obedient to it, be sufficiently impressed with the new evidence to reach a verdict contrary to
the one that was reached on a record wholly different from the
present, in view of evidence recently discovered and not adduceable by the defense at the time of the original trial? To
all these questions Judge Thayer says, 'No.' This amazing conclusion he reached after studying the motion 'for several weeks
without interruption' and set forth in an opinion of 25,000 words!
We wish for nothing more than that every reader who has proceeded thus far should study the full text of this latest Thayer
opinion. Space precludes its detailed treatment here. To quote
it, to analyze it, adequately to comment upon it would require

a book. Having now put the materials for detailed judgment at the disposal of readers, we are compelled to confine ourselves to a few brief observations. By what is left out and by what is put in, the uninformed reader of Judge Thayer's opinion would be wholly misled as to the real facts of the case. Speaking from a considerable experience as a prosecuting officer, whose special task for a time it was to sustain on appeal convictions for the Government, and whose scientific duties since have led to the examination of a great number of records and the opinions based thereon, I assert with deep regret, but without the slightest fear of disproof, that certainly in modern times Judge Thayer's opinion stands unmatched for discrepancies between what the record discloses and what the opinion conveys. His 25,000-word document cannot accurately be described otherwise than as a farrago of misquotations, misrepresentations, suppressions, and mutilations. The disinterested inquirer could not possibly derive from it a true knowledge of the new evidence that was submitted to him as the basis for a new trial. The opinion is literally honeycombed with demonstrable errors, and a spirit alien to judicial utterance permeates the whole. A study of the opinion in the light of the record led the conservative *Boston Herald,* which long held the view that the sentence against these men should be carried out, to a frank reversal of its position.

Dr. Morton Prince writes that any expert psychologist reading the Thayer opinion 'could not fail to find evidences that portray strong personal feeling, poorly concealed, that should have no place in a judicial document.' One or two illustrations must suffice. William G. Thompson is one of the leaders of the Boston bar. Yet Judge Thayer thus characterized Mr. Thompson's activities in behalf of these two Italians:—

Since the trial before the jury of these cases a new type of disease would seem to have developed. It might be called 'lego-psychic neurosis' or hysteria, which means: 'A belief in the existence of something which in fact and truth has no such existence.'

And this from a judge who gives meretricious authority to his self-justification by speaking of the verdict which convicted these men as 'approved by the Supreme Judicial Court of this Commonwealth.' The Supreme Court never approved the verdict; nor did it pretend to do so. The Supreme Court passed on technical claims of error, and, 'finding no error, the verdicts are to stand.' Judge Thayer knows this, but laymen may not. Yet Judge Thayer refers to the verdict as 'approved by the Supreme Judicial Court.'

No wonder that Judge Thayer's opinion has confirmed old doubts as to the guilt of these two Italians and aroused new anxieties concerning the resources of our law to avoid grave miscarriage of justice. The courageous stand taken by the *Boston Herald* has enlisted the support of some of the most distinguished citizens of Massachusetts. The *Independent* has thus epitomized this demand:—

Because of the increasing doubt that surrounds the question of the guilt of these men, springing from the intrinsic character of Judge Thayer's decision, and instanced by the judgment of the *Herald* editorial writer and other observers whose impartiality is unquestioned, we strongly hope that a new trial will be granted. It is important to note that the appeal is being made on the basis of new evidence never passed on before the Supreme Court.

No narrow, merely technical, question is thus presented. The Supreme Court of Massachusetts will be called upon to search the whole record in order to determine whether Judge Thayer duly observed the traditional standards of fairness and reason which govern the conduct of an Anglo-American judge, particularly in a capital case. This court has given us the requirements by which Judge Thayer's decision is to be measured and the tests which it will use in determining whether a new trial shall be granted:—

The various statements of the extent of the power and of limitations upon the right to grant new trials . . . must yield to the funda-

136   THE CULTURE OF THE TWENTIES

mental test, in aid of which most rules have been formulated, that
such motions ought not to be granted unless on a survey of the whole
case it appears to the judicial conscience and judgment that otherwise a miscarriage of justice will result.

Nor must a new trial be withheld where in justice it is called
for because thereby encouragement will be given to improper
demands for a new trial. For, as the Chief Justice of Massachusetts has announced, courts cannot close 'their eyes to injustice
on account of facility of abuse.'

With these legal canons as a guide, the outcome ought not to
be in doubt.

10 / BARTOLOMEO VANZETTI

"The Jury Were Hating Us"

Vanzetti's statement about why he should not be executed by the
Commonwealth of Massachusetts is an eloquent and human plea for
what he thought to be justice. In his powerful but broken English,
he described the emotional context and tonalities of his trial. In
order to understand why so many writers and intellectuals came to
his defense it is necessary to know something of the man, as well as
the ambiguities of his trial. This statement is the single best disclosure of Vanzetti as a human being.

Clerk WORTHINGTON.   Bartolomeo Vanzetti, have you anything to say why sentence of death should not be passed upon
you?

From "Statement by Bartolomeo Vanzetti," *The Sacco-Vanzetti Case*
(New York: Henry Holt and Co., 1929), V: 4896–4904. Text taken from
The Sacco-Vanzetti Case: Transcript of the Record (New York: Henry
Holt and Company, 1929). Testimony reprinted by permission of John P.
Concannon, Clerk of the Courts, Norfolk County, Commonwealth of
Massachusetts.

STATEMENT BY BARTOLOMEO VANZETTI

Yes. What I say is that I am innocent, not only of the Braintree crime, but also of the Bridgewater crime.* That I am not only innocent of these two crimes, but in all my life I have never stole and I have never killed and I have never spilled blood. That is what I want to say. And it is not all. Not only am I innocent of these two crimes, not only in all my life I have never stole, never killed, never spilled blood, but I have struggled all my life, since I began to reason, to eliminate crime from the earth.

Everybody that knows these two arms knows very well that I did not need to go in between the street and kill a man to take the money. I can live with my two arms and live well. But besides that, I can live even without work with my arm for other people. I have had plenty of chance to live independently and to live what the world conceives to be a higher life than not to gain our bread with the sweat of our brow.

My father in Italy is in a good condition. I could have come back in Italy and he would have welcomed me every time with open arms. Even if I come back there with not a cent in my pocket, my father could have give me a possession, not to work but to make business, or to oversee upon the land that he owns. He has wrote me many letters in that sense, and other well to do relatives have wrote me many letters in that sense that I can produce.

Well, it may be a boast. My father and my uncle can boast themselves and say things that people may not be compelled to believe. People may say they may be poor when I say that they are to consider to give me a position every time that I want to settle down and form a family and start a settled life. Well, but there are people maybe in this same court that could testify to

---

*Vanzetti was also charged with an armed robbery in Bridgewater. Sacco had a strong alibi for the day of this earlier crime, and thus was not charged.–Ed.

what I have say and what my father and my uncle have say to me is not a lie, that really they have the means to give me position every time that I want.

Well, I want to reach a little point farther, and it is in this,— that not only have I not been trying to steal in Bridgewater, not only have I not been in Braintree to steal and kill and have never steal or kill or spilt blood in all my life, not only have I struggled hard against crimes, but I have refused myself the commodity or glory of life, the pride of life of a good position, because in my consideration it is not right to exploit man. I have refused to go in business because I understand that business is a speculation on profit upon certain people that must depend upon the business man, and I do not consider that that is right and therefore I refuse to do that.

Now, I should say that I am not only innocent of all these things, not only have I never committed a real crime in my life —though some sins but not crimes—not only have I struggled all my life to eliminate crimes, the crimes that the official law and the official moral condemns, but also the crime that the official moral and the official law sanctions and sanctifies,—the exploitation and the oppression of the man by the man, and if there is a reason why I am here as a guilty man, if there is a reason why you in a few minutes can doom me, it is this reason and none else.

I beg your pardon. [Referring to paper.] There is the more good man I ever cast my eyes upon since I lived, a man that will last and will grow always more near and more dear to the people, as far as into the heart of the people, so long as admiration for goodness and for sacrifice will last. I mean Eugene Debs. I will say that even a dog that killed the chickens would not have found an American jury to convict it with the proof that the Commonwealth produced against us. That man was not with me in Plymouth or with Sacco where he was on the day of the crime. You can say that it is arbitrary, what we are saying, that he is good and he applied to the other his own goodness, that he is incapable of crime, and he believed that everybody is incapable of crime.

Well, it may be like that but it is not, it could be like that but it is not, and that man has a real experience of court, of prison and of jury. Just because he want the world a little better he was persecuted and slandered from his boyhood to his old age, and indeed he was murdered by the prison. He know, and not only he but every man of understanding in the world, not only in this country but also in the other countries, men that we have provided a certain amount of a record of the times, they all still stick with us, the flower of mankind of Europe, the better writers, the greatest thinkers of Europe, have pleaded in our favor. The scientists, the greatest scientists, the greatest statesmen of Europe, have pleaded in our favor. The people of foreign nations have pleaded in our favor.

Is it possible that only a few on the jury, only two or three men, who would condemn their mother for worldly honor and for earthly fortune; is it possible that they are right against what the world, the whole world has say it is wrong and that I know that it is wrong? If there is one that I should know it, if it is right or if it is wrong, it is I and this man. You see it is seven years that we are in jail. What we have suffered during these seven years no human tongue can say, and yet you see me before you, not trembling, you see me looking you in your eyes straight, not blushing, not changing color, not ashamed or in fear.

Eugene Debs say that not even a dog—something like that —not even a dog that kill the chickens would have been found guilty by American jury with the evidence that the Commonwealth have produced against us. I say that not even a leprous dog would have his appeal refused two times by the Supreme Court of Massachusetts—not even a leprous dog.

They have given a new trial to Madeiros for the reason that the Judge had either forgot or omitted to tell the jury that they should consider the man innocent until found guilty in the court, or something of that sort.* That man has confessed. The man was tried and has confessed, and the court give him another trial. We have proved that there could not have been another Judge on the face of the earth more prejudiced and more cruel than you have been against us. We have proven that. Still they refuse the new trial. We know, and you know in your heart, that you have been against us from the very beginning, before you see us. Before you see us you already know that we were radicals, that we were underdogs, that we were the enemy of the institution that you can believe in good faith in their goodness—I don't want to condemn that—and that it was easy on the time of the first trial to get a verdict of guiltiness.

We know that you have spoke yourself and have spoke your hostility against us, and your despisement against us with friends of yours on the train, at the University Club of Boston, on the Golf Club of Worcester, Massachusetts. I am sure that if the people who know all what you say against us would have the civil courage to take the stand, maybe your Honor—I am sorry to say this because you are an old man, and I have an old father—but maybe you would be beside us in good justice at this time.

When you sentenced me at the Plymouth trial you say, to the best of my memory, of my good faith, that crimes were in accordance with my principle,—something of that sort,—and you take off one charge, if I remember it exactly, from the jury. The jury was so violent against me that they found me guilty of both charges, because there were only two. But they would have found me guilty of a dozen of charges against your Honor's instructions. Of course I remember that you told them that there was no reason to believe that if I were the bandit I have intention to kill somebody, so that they will take off the indict-

_____

*A member of the Morelli gang of Providence, who in 1925 confessed that he and his gang had committed the Braintree crime. Vanzetti is referring to his retrial after conviction on a murder charge growing out of a bank robbery.—Ed.

ment of attempt to murder. Well, they found me guilty of what? And if I am right, you take out that and sentence me only for attempt to rob with arms,—something like that. But, Judge Thayer, you give more to me for that attempt of robbery than all the 448 men that were in Charlestown, all of those that attempted to rob, all those that have robbed, they have not such a sentence as you gave me for an attempt at robbery.

I am willing that everybody that does believe me that they can make commission, they can go over there, and I am very willing that the people should go over there and see whether it is true or not. There are people in Charlestown who are professional robbers, who have been in half the prisons of the United States, that they are steal, or hurt the man, shoot him. By chance he got better, he did not die. Well, the most of them guilty without trial, by self-confession, and by asking the aid of their own partner, and they got 8 to 10, 8 to 12, 10 to 15. None of them has 12 to 15, as you gave me for an attempt at robbery. And besides that, you know that I was not guilty. You know that my life, my private and public life in Plymouth, and wherever I have been, was so exemplary that one of the worst fears of our prosecutor Katzmann was to introduce proof of our life and of our conduct. He has taken it off with all his might and he has succeeded.

You know if we would have Mr. Thompson,* or even the brother McAnarney, in the first trial in Plymouth, you know that no jury would have found me guilty. My first lawyer has been a partner of Mr. Katzmann, as he is still now. My first lawyer of the defense, Mr. Vahey, has not defended me, has sold me for thirty golden money like Judas sold Jesus Christ. If that man has not told to you or to Mr. Katzmann that he know that I was guilty, it is because he know that I was not guilty. That man has done everything indirectly to hurt us. He has

---

*William G. Thompson was a prominent Massachusetts lawyer, one of the defense counsels for appeal of Sacco and Vanzetti's original conviction.—Ed.

made long speech with the jury about things that do matter nothing, and on the point of essence to the trial he has passed over with few words or with complete silence. This was a premeditation in order to give to the jury the impression that my own defender has nothing good to say, has nothing good to urge in defense of myself, and therefore go around the bush on little things that amount to nothing and let pass the essential points either in silence or with a very weakly resistance.

We were tried during a time that has now passed into history. I mean by that, a time when there was a hysteria of resentment and hate against the people of our principles, against the foreigner, against slackers, and it seems to me—rather, I am positive of it, that both you and Mr. Katzmann has done all what it were in your power in order to work out, in order to agitate still more the passion of the juror, the prejudice of the juror, against us. . . .

. . . But the jury were hating us because we were against the war, and the jury don't know that it makes any difference between a man that is against the war because he believes that the war is unjust, because he hate no country, because he is a cosmopolitan, and a man that is against the war because he is in favor of the other country that fights against the country in which he is, and therefore a spy, and he commits any crime in the country in which he is in behalf of the other country in order to serve the other country. We are not men of that kind. Katzmann know very well that. Katzmann know that we were against the war because we did not believe in the purpose for which they say that the war was done. We believe it that the war is wrong, and we believe this more now after ten years that we understood it day by day,—the consequences and the result of the after war. We believe more now than ever that the war was wrong, and we are against war more now than ever, and I am glad to be on the doomed scaffold if I can say to mankind, "Look out; you are in a catacomb of the flower of mankind. For what? All that they say to you, all that they have promised to you—it was a lie, it was an illusion, it was a cheat, it was a fraud, it was a crime. They promised you liberty. Where is liberty? They promised you prosperity. Where is prosperity? They have promised you elevation. What is the elevation?"

From the day that I went in Charlestown, the misfortune, the population of Charlestown has doubled in number. Where is the moral good that the War has given to the world? Where is the spiritual progress that we have achieved from the War? Where are the security of life, the security of the things that we possess for our necessity? Where are the respect for human life? Where are the respect and the admiration for the good characteristics and the good of the human nature? Never as now before the war there have been so many crimes, so many corruptions, so many degeneration as there is now. . . .

It was also said that the defense has put every obstacle to the handling of this case in order to delay the case. That sound weak for us, and I think it is injurious because it is not true. If we consider that the prosecution, the State, has employed one entire year to prosecute us, that is, one of the five years that the case has last was taken by the prosecution to begin our trial, our first trial. Then the defense make an appeal to you and you waited, or I think that you were resolute, that you had the resolute in your heart when the trial finished that you will refuse every appeal that we will put up to you. You waited a month or a month and a half and just lay down your decision on the eve of Christmas—just on the evening of Christmas. We do not believe in the fable of the evening of Christmas, neither in the historical way nor in the church way. You know some of our folks still believe in that, and because we do not believe in that, it don't mean that we are not human. We are human, and Christmas is sweet to the heart of every man. I think that you have done that, to hand down your decision on the evening of

Christmas, to poison the heart of our family and of our beloved. I am sorry to be compelled to say this, but everything that was said on your side has confirmed my suspicion until that suspicion has changed to certitude. So that you see that one year it has taken before trying us. . . .

What I want to say is this: Everybody ought to understand that the first of the defense has been terrible. My first lawyer did not stick to defend us. He has made no work to collect witnesses and evidence in our favor. The record in the Plymouth Court is a pity. I am told that they are almost one-half lost. So the defense had a tremendous work to do in order to collect some evidence, to collect some testimony to offset and to learn what the testimony of the State has done. And in this consideration it must be said that even if the defense take double time of the State without delay, double time that they delay the case it would have been reasonable, whereas it took less than the State.

Well, I have already say that I not only am not guilty of these two crimes, but I never commit a crime in my life,—I have never steal and I have never kill and I have never spilt blood, and I have fought against the crime, and I have fought and I have sacrified myself even to eliminate the crimes that the law and the church legitimate and sanctify.

This is what I say: I would not wish to a dog or to a snake, to the most low and misfortunate creature of the earth—I would not wish to any of them what I have had to suffer for things that I am not guilty of. But my conviction is that I have suffered for things that I am guilty of. I am suffering because I am a radical and indeed I am a radical; I have suffered because I was an Italian, and indeed I am an Italian; I have suffered more for my family and for my beloved than for myself; but I am so convinced to be right that if you could execute me two times, and if I could be reborn two other times, I would live again to do what I have done already.

I have finished. Thank you.

11 / WALTER LIPPMANN

Political Apathy

The retreat from politics, from public life, was frequently observed during the Twenties. The recoil from Wilson's manifold and manifest failures was one obvious explanation, but Walter Lippmann (1889–   ), journalist, leading liberal social critic, and political theorist (*A Preface to Politics*, 1913; *Public Opinion*, 1922; *Men of Destiny*, 1927; and *A Preface to Morals*, 1929), in the following article found a richer and more complex set of factors underlying depoliticization. The absence of truly national leaders, issues, and parties created both confusion and cynicism in voters, and the negative administration of Coolidge had, by calculation, encouraged political apathy. But it was the widespread if incomplete affluence of the time that permitted men to ignore politics. Without a genuine economic basis politics seemed to wither away, thanks in part to the new public relations skills of the modern capitalists. But, according to Lippmann, the American populace was vitally interested in the struggle between village and urban values, between old and new America, between the defenders and critics of this struggle's symptoms: Prohibition, xenophobia, and especially the anti-evolution issue. Lippmann believed that the resolution of this conflict would determine the direction of America's future.

I

The record shows that in the last campaign President Coolidge appealed twice to the voters. Once he asked them to vote, to go to the polls and vote, to mark ballots for somebody. And once he emerged from behind the veil of the official spokesman's unofficial and indirect discourse to plead with the people of Massachusetts for his friend and campaign manager, Senator Butler. This attitude was a fair sample of how the country felt about the election. A voter ought to vote. That was generally admitted in theory. But in practice the private citizen, like the President of the United States, was interested only in some one local election.

Mr. Coolidge was interested in Massachusetts. Mr. Smith was interested in New York; Mr. Ritchie was interested in Maryland. Nobody was very much interested in the nation. Investigation would show, I am told, that the Republican National Committee was never called into action during the campaign, and that most of its energies since 1924 have been devoted to celebrating the personal virtues of Mr. Coolidge and to repairing the deficiencies of Senator Butler in Massachusetts. The Republican Party in 1926 had neither national leadership nor platform nor strategy. It was not like Cæsar's wife, and it was all things to all men. Its component factions engaged in a series of local elections from which not only Mr. Coolidge, but the national organization as well, held aloof. The party as a national organ abdicated, and either the voter had to follow Mr. Coolidge's example and excite himself about a local issue or he had not to excite himself at all.

The principles of the Democratic Party were likewise determined by geography. This party, too, had no national policy whatever. It too conducted a series of local campaigns, which were not only independent one of the other, but contradictory. Mr. Wagner ran in New York as a wet Democrat and Mr. Wilson ran in Pennsylvania as a dry. Mr. Brookhart ran in Iowa as an antitrust Republican and Mr. Butler ran in Massachusetts as the devoted slave of all business everywhere. Mr. Brennan in Illinois had about as much in common with Mr. Barkley of Kentucky as Mr. Wadsworth of New York had with Mr. Willis of Ohio. The only difference between the Republicans and the

Democrats was that the Republicans were split apart and didn't know it, whereas the Democrats were split apart and knew it. They could not help knowing it after the convention of 1924 in Madison Square Garden.

In fact, as one contemplates the activities of politicians there is little doubt that, if only there were voters somewhere who wanted it, Republican and Democratic principles could be accommodated locally to polygamy, foot binding, or voodooism. The rule is simply this: anything which helps you to carry your state is the immortal principles of Abraham Lincoln and Thomas Jefferson.

It is not surprising, then, that national partisan politics should have come to mean so little to the ordinary voter. There are no parties, there are no leaders, there are no issues. There are parties only in the states, there are leaders only of sections, there are issues, but they are either evaded by national public men or carefully confined to the localities. There is nobody in American public life to-day who, like Roosevelt or Wilson, is really a leader in all parts of the country. Mr. Coolidge has enjoyed popularity and confidence for two years, but the record of his leadership of Congress shows that he is essentially the representative of the Eastern tariff-protected interests. Neither Western agriculture nor the Eastern exporting interests have ever laid much of a hold on his mind. Mr. Lowden, undoubtedly the most powerful figure in the background of Republican politics, is devoting himself wholly to that agricultural interest which Mr. Coolidge has ignored. Senator Borah has touched almost every question and has come to grips with none; with all his great promise and immense personal opportunity he has failed to transform an attractive provincial insurgency into any sort of coherent national policy. There is no need to dwell upon Messrs. Dawes, Watson, Johnson. On the Democratic side there is Governor Smith, idol of the urban Democrats of the Northeast, but as yet wholly unknown, untried, and unexpressed on national questions. There is Governor Ritchie in Maryland, who may fairly claim to have a set of Democratic national principles, but who has not as yet a Democratic national following. And there is Senator Reed of Missouri, who has at least got this far nationally: he has made himself a holy terror to Republicans and Democrats alike.

II

The effect of these political disharmonies is to bewilder the electorate and to make the voters feel that politics is an elaborate game which has no serious and immediate consequences. This bewilderment manifests itself as complacency or as cynicism. Since 1920 the country has witnessed brazen and expensive corruption. In the amount of money involved the corruption is without parallel in our history. In its sordidness it is surely as bad as and probably a little worse than the scandals of the Grant administration. This generation has known nothing so disgraceful as the carryings on of Fall, Daugherty, and Forbes, nor anything like the Smith primary in Illinois and the Pepper-Vare primary in Pennsylvania. Fall has just been brought to trial; Daugherty was brought to trial only three or four months ago because of the exceptional energy of United States Attorney Buckner; the primary scandals were never rebuked by the leader of the Republican Party. In their public speech public men have been as complacent as possible about it all; and privately they have been prepared to explain that 'Well—oh well, you know, politics is a dirty game.' Maybe it is. But only a few years ago the country was still naïve enough, was still sentimental enough, to have become violently indignant over a cabinet officer accused of bribery. Indignation of this sort we have not known during these last few years. That too perhaps helps to explain why the interest in politics is at such low ebb, and why voting is not looked upon as such a very high duty. The impression has gone out from the White House that there is no use caring too much whether public officials are honest or whether elections are bought.

This persistent dampening down of popular interest in popular government has been the calculated policy of Mr. Coolidge ever since he became President. The reason given for it is that nothing must be done to distract business. The other reason for it, not given, but perfectly well understood, is that it is good politics when you are in power to discourage all manifestations of discontent. Mr. Coolidge is not exactly an ardent spirit. He is contented with little things; he is hardly suited to large thoughts and large deeds. He has not attempted them. On the contrary he has devoted himself to encouraging the people to turn their eyes away from the government. In peaceful, prosperous times not much encouragement is needed. Public spirit is at best a fragile thing when it comes into competition with the urgent demands of our private lives for money, for power, and for pleasure. So it has not been difficult for Mr. Coolidge to persuade the country that it need not take a vivid interest in public affairs.

III

Yet neither the personality of Mr. Coolidge nor the very special political strategy which he adopted will by itself account for the lethargy of spirit which has prevailed during his administration. Under different circumstances the virtues of Mr. Coolidge would almost certainly have been looked upon as vices. Mr. Coolidge has been praised for failing to lead Congress, for failing to lead his party, for refusing to become indignant at abuses, for not having a positive policy and a constructive programme. He would not have received this praise had the country not been in the mood for a negative administration.

It is the fashion to explain this mood by saying that after all the tall talk heard under Roosevelt and Wilson the country was exhausted emotionally and needed a rest. It had had its fill of idealism, of prophecy, of adventure, and of public action. It needed to forget Washington and the White House and the President, and tend to its private affairs. There is something in this explanation, of course, as there is also in the theory that the war brought a deep disenchantment with politicians, policies, and with what used to be called 'progressivism.' But all these explanations are obviously incomplete. For when you have said that men were tired of public affairs you have still to explain why, being tired of public affairs, they are able to indulge themselves by neglecting public affairs.

With this question we come, I think, nearer to the root of the matter. The American people, since the industrial recovery of 1922, has enjoyed an amazing prosperity. Except here and there in a few spots there has been such a surplus of wealth that practically the whole people has raised its standard of life. It was obvious that the opportunities to make money were so ample that it was a waste of time to think about politics. Nothing a man could hope to gain by voting for politicians, and by agitating for laws, was likely to be half so profitable as what he could make by participating in the boom.

The interested motives which are the driving force of political agitation were diverted to direct profit making. Now progressivism, as we have known it in the past, has arisen out of the belief of the debtors, the employees, the consumers, the farmers, that they could by changing the laws obtain a larger share of the national income. With the stupendous surplus available these last years, it has seemed to most men quicker and easier to go out and make money than to work through the cumbersome indirect processes of political action. Thus there has been no political discontent, except in a few farming states where the new surplus of wealth was not available, and where in consequence the old progressive motives and traditions survived. The common people looked to Roosevelt and to Wilson (before 1914) for relief from poverty and economic servitude. They did not look to Mr. Coolidge for relief because they were finding it by themselves. I am not attempting to say, of course, how real or how permanent is this relief; the fact which counts is that from about 1922 on almost everybody has had the feeling that he had a lot of money in his pocket, and would soon have more. It was this feeling which robbed progressive idealism of its urgency, and made it appear abstract and unimportant.

Together with this diffused prosperity, I should set down as a fundamental cause of political indifference the rise of what may be called the New Capitalism. There is no doubt that the large corporations are now under the control of a very different kind of man than they were when Roosevelt and Bryan and LaFollette were on the warpath. The new executive has learned a great deal that his predecessor would have thought was tommyrot. His attitude toward labor, toward the public, toward his customers and his stockholders, is different. His behavior is different. His manner is different. His press agents are different. I am far from thinking he is perfect even now, but I am certain that he is vastly more enlightened and that he will take ever so much more trouble to please. He is no doubt as powerful as he ever was, but his bearing is less autocratic. He does not arouse the old antagonism, the old bitter-end fury, the old feeling that he has to be clubbed into a sense of public responsibility. He will listen to an argument where formerly he was deaf to an agitation.

Whatever may be the intrinsic good and evil of such things as the wide distribution of securities, however questionable may be some of the practices to which Professor Ripley has called attention in this magazine, the net result of the new attitude on the part of capital has been to create a new attitude on the part of the public. The press agents of the corporations have been told to woo the public, and their wooing has been successful. Suspicion has died down. Yet here again we must recognize that it would not have died down if capitalism as we know it were not making most people feel quite comfortably well off.

During the last four years the actual prosperity of the people, combined with the greater enlightenment of the industrial leaders, has removed from politics all serious economic causes of agitation. There has been no pressing reason for an alignment of 'haves' and of 'have nots,' and no reader of history needs to be told that when you remove economic discontent you remove what is certainly the greatest cause, if it is not the mainspring, of political activity. Politics carried on for justice, for liberty, for prestige, is never more than the affair of a minority. For the great majority of men political ideals are almost always based upon and inspired by some kind of economic necessity and ambition.

These circumstances account for the striking differences between European and American politics. The European finance ministers have had to struggle with deficits, ours with a surplus; they have had to impose taxes, ours to reduce taxes. The European nations have had to borrow, we to lend; they to devise means of payment, we to find ways of receiving payments. They have had to struggle to raise a low standard of living, and we to protect a high standard. They have had to reconstruct and restore; we have had only to perfect and expand. To Europeans, therefore, the American situation has seemed almost idyllic, and there has appeared a great literature in Europe which discusses the American economic system, often with admiration, sometimes with envy, always with the implication that it is one of the most extraordinary phenomena in history. Here in the United States during the last few years capitalism has worked in a way which confounds those who, like most educated Europeans, were brought up to think of it according to the socialistic formula, as an industrial system destined soon to be superseded by some kind of collectivism. Events have taken a wholly unexpected turn in the United States, and the advanced thinker here and abroad suddenly finds that he is no longer advanced. His descriptions, his analyses, his programmes, all assume a different course of evolution. The more or less unconscious and unplanned activities of business men are for once more novel, more daring, and in a sense more revolutionary, than the theories of the progressives. Action has moved faster than thought in these last few years, and practice is ahead of the programmes.

This lag in the development of theory has had a curious effect on political discussion. Public speakers, if they are conservative, will usually be found defending practices that their supposed clients are rapidly abandoning; if they are progressive, they will be found rather wearily and half-heartedly repeating the charges and the idealisms that were current a decade ago. The real industrial development of the day, with its momentous social consequences, hardly figures at all in public discussion. The philosophy of it is not yet understood; we have not yet learned how to talk about it. The good and the evil it contains have not yet been registered and assayed. And as a result most public controversy seems not so much like hot air as stale air. Without knowing just why, most of us feel, I think, that the current conservatism and progressivism are irrelevant. They do not satisfy our minds or grip our emotions.

IV

The questions which really engage the emotions of the masses of the people are of a quite different order. They manifest themselves in the controversies over prohibition, the Ku Klux Klan, Romanism, Fundamentalism, immigration. These, rather than the tariff, taxation, credit, and corporate control, are the issues which divide the American people. These are the issues men care about. They are just beneath the surface of political discussion. In theory they are not supposed to be issues. The party platforms and the official pronouncements deal with them obliquely, if at all. But they are the issues men talk about privately, and they are, above all, the issues about which men have deep personal feelings.

These questions are diverse, but they all arise out of the same general circumstances. They arise out of the great migration of the last fifty years, out of the growth of cities, and out of the spread of that rationalism and the deepening of that breach with tradition which invariably accompany the development of a metropolitan civilization. Prohibition, the Ku Klux Klan, Fundamentalism, and xenophobia are an extreme but authentic expression of the politics, the social outlook, and the religion of the older American village civilization making its last stand against what looks to it like an alien invasion. The alien invasion is in fact the new America produced by the growth and the prosperity of America.

The evil which the old-fashioned preachers ascribe to the Pope, to Babylon, to atheists, and to the Devil is simply the new urban civilization, with its irresistible economic and scientific and mass power. The Pope, the Devil, jazz, the bootleggers, are a mythology which expresses symbolically the impact of a vast and dreaded social change. The change is real enough. The language in which it is discussed is preposterous only as all mythology is preposterous if you accept it literally. The mythology of the Ku Klux Klan is a kind of primitive science, an animistic and dramatized projection of the fears of a large section of our people who have yet to accommodate themselves to the strange new social order which has arisen in their midst.

This new social order is dominated by metropolitan cities of which New York is the largest and most highly developed. Therefore New York has become the symbol of all that is most wicked and of all that is most alluring in modern America. But New York to-day is only what Chicago, St. Louis, Detroit, Cleveland, Jacksonville, and Miami expect to be to-morrow. It is the seat of a vast population, mixed in its origins, uncertain of its social status, rather vague about the moral code. In these metropolitan centres the ancient social bonds are loosened. The patriarchal family, the well-established social hierarchy, the old roots of belief, and the grooves of custom are all obscured by new human relationships based on a certain kind of personal independence, on individual experiment and adventure, which are yet somehow deeply controlled by fads and fashions and great mass movements.

The campaign in certain localities to forbid the teaching of 'Darwinism' is an attempt to stem the tide of the metropolitan spirit, to erect a spiritual tariff against an alien rationalism which threatens to dissolve the mores of the village civilization. To many of us the effort seems quixotic, as indeed it is, judged by the intellectual standards of metropolitan life. But if we look at the matter objectively, disregarding the petty mannerisms of the movement, there is a pathos about it which always adheres to the last struggle of an authentic type of human living. The anti-evolutionists are usually less charming than Don Quixote. Perhaps that is because they have not been transfigured by an artist. They are at any rate fighting for the memory of a civilization which in its own heyday, and by its own criteria, was as valid as any other.

The anti-evolution bills are, of course, a comparatively trivial symptom of this profound maladjustment. The overt struggle turns politically on two questions: on the Eighteenth Amendment and on the nomination of Governor Alfred E. Smith. The struggle over these two issues implicates all the antagonisms between the older America and the new. The Eighteenth Amendment is a piece of legislation embodied in the Constitution which attempts to impose the moral ideals of the villages upon the whole nation. The force behind the Eighteenth Amendment is the Anti-Saloon League, which is the political arm of the evangelical churches in the small communities. The financial and political strength of the Anti-Saloon League is derived from the members of these churches, chiefly

Methodist and Baptist, with other denominations divided but following these militant sects. And the strength of these sects in the last analysis arises from the spiritual isolation of communities which have not yet been radically invaded by the metropolitan spirit.

The defense of the Eighteenth Amendment has, therefore, become much more than a mere question of regulating the liquor traffic. It involves a test of strength between social orders, and when that test is concluded, and if, as seems probable, the Amendment breaks down, the fall will bring down with it the dominion of the older civilization. The Eighteenth Amendment is the rock on which the evangelical church militant is founded, and with it are involved a whole way of life and an ancient tradition. The overcoming of the Eighteenth Amendment would mean the emergence of the cities as the dominant force in America, dominant politically and socially as they are already dominant economically.

V

The alignment of the new cities against the older villages traverses the nominal political alignment of the two great parties. In New York State, for example, it has divided and broken the Republican Party as a state organization. There is much more community of thought and feeling between Republicans and Democrats in New York City, in Buffalo, Rochester, Syracuse, and Albany, than there is between the urban and the rural Republicans. The unity of the Republican Party in New York is like the unity of the Democrats in the nation: a unity of politicians interested in offices supplemented by the prestige of a name and a tradition. There is no unity of interest, of principle, or of programme.

A similar condition exists in almost every state where there are powerful cities—in Massachusetts for Boston, in Pennsylvania for Pittsburgh and Philadelphia, in Ohio for Cleveland and Cincinnati, in Illinois for Chicago, in New Jersey for that urban conglomeration known as Hudson County, in Missouri for St. Louis. Both parties are cracking under the strain. Both maintain the appearance of unity by political deals and the compromise of principles. The well-known fact that parties have become meaningless is due to this internal division. They dare not take definite positions for fear of alienating one or the other of their irreconcilable factions.

For reasons which are not altogether clear the conflict has first become overt in the Democratic Party. The convention of 1924 was the scene of the first great, though inconclusive, phase of the struggle. All the signs indicate that the next phase, in 1928, will be at least as sharp and perhaps more decisive. In 1924 the urban democracy rallied around Governor Smith of New York, the village democracy around Mr. McAdoo. The urban Democrats in 1924 controlled a little more than one third of that convention. Since 1924 they have gained in strength and by 1928 they should control at least half of the convention. This change of their position from a minority to a majority faction is not due to the personality or to the leadership of Governor Smith. It is due to a growth of self-consciousness which is developing the latent strength of the city electorates. They are beginning to feel their oats. They are throwing off their sense of inferiority. They are beginning to demand the recognition which is due their intrinsic importance.

The outcome of the struggle within the Democratic Party is, of course, obscure. One can be certain of nothing except that the rapid growth of the cities at the expense of the countryside is bound at last to result in the political domination of the cities. This may come soon. It may be somewhat delayed. It will come. The first great result may be the disunion of the Democratic Party and perhaps even the rupture of the Solid South. If that is the result the ascendancy of the Republicans may be temporarily confirmed, but it will be followed almost certainly by a realignment of Republicans as well as of Democrats.

For the two parties live by taking in each other's washing. The unity of the one is dependent upon the unity of the other. The grip of the Eastern industrial Republicans on the national organization rests at last on the fact that in the South there is a Republican machine but no Republican electorate. If ever the South should break away from the Democrats, a Republican Party would appear in the South. The appearance of a Republican Party in the South would make the South as unmanageable to the Republicans of the Northeast as the Republican Party of the West now is.

These prospects are not alluring to men whose lives are bound up with the existing party system. They promise nothing but trouble for them personally. They call for an effort of thought which is distressing, and they open up issues for which political leaders, trained between 1890 and 1910, are not prepared. It is not surprising, then, that our political leaders are greatly occupied in dampening down interest, in obscuring issues, and in attempting to distract attention from the realities of American life.

PART 3

RELIGIOUS FUNDAMENTALISM

The Monkey Trial

In the middle of a hot July 1925, in Dayton, Tennessee, a comparatively simple law suit turned into an important conflict between Fundamentalist religion and science. A local school teacher, John Scopes, had violated Tennessee law by teaching the theory of evolution. William Jennings Bryan (1860–1925), a distinguished Democratic politician, orator, and statesman, joined the prosecuting attorneys; Clarence Darrow (1857–1938), the nation's most powerful liberal attorney, joined the defense. With their appearance, and because of their respective reputations, the trial all but ignored Scopes (although he was finally convicted and fined $100); the highlight came on the afternoon of the seventh day when Darrow surprised everyone by calling Bryan to the stand in order to expose the intellectual weaknesses in Bryan's Fundamentalism. For about two hours the two men faced each other in their shirt-sleeves. The following document is a transcript of most of the proceedings of that afternoon, which were finally adjourned for the day when both men were shaking their fists at each other.

MR. DARROW—You have given considerable study to the Bible, haven't you, Mr. Bryan?

From "Mr. Darrow Questions Mr. Bryan," *Bryan and Darrow at Dayton*, ed. Leslie H. Allen (New York: Arthur Lee and Co., 1925), chap. XV, pp. 133–156.

Mr. Bryan—Yes, sir, I have tried to.

Mr. Darrow—Well, we all know you have; we are not going to dispute that at all. But you have written and published articles almost weekly, and sometimes have made interpretations of various things?

Mr. Bryan—I would not say interpretations, Mr. Darrow, but comments on the lesson.

Mr. Darrow—If you commented to any extent, those comments have been interpretations?

Mr. Bryan—I presume that any discussion might be to some extent interpretations, but they have not been primarily intended as interpretations.

Mr. Darrow—But you have studied that question, of course!

Mr. Bryan—Of what?

Mr. Darrow—Of interpretation of the Bible?

Mr. Bryan—On this particular question?

Mr. Darrow—Yes, sir.

Mr. Bryan—Yes, sir.

Mr. Darrow—Then you have made a general study of it?

Mr. Bryan—Yes, I have. I have studied the Bible for about fifty years, or some time more than that. I have studied it more as I have become older than when I was but a boy.

Mr. Darrow—Do you claim that everything in the Bible should be literally interpreted?

Mr. Bryan—I believe everything in the Bible should be accepted as it is given there. Some of the Bible is given illustratively. For instance: "Ye are the salt of the earth."[1] I would not insist that man was actually salt, or that he had flesh of salt, but it is used in the sense of salt as saving God's people.

Mr. Darrow—But when you read that Jonah swallowed the whale—or that the whale swallowed Jonah, excuse me, please—how do you literally interpret that?

[1]Matthew 5:13.

Mr. Bryan—When I read that a big fish swallowed Jonah—it does not say whale.[2]

Mr. Darrow—Doesn't it? Are you sure?

Mr. Bryan—That is my recollection of it, a big fish; and I believe it; and I believe in a God who can make a whale and can make a man, and make both do what He pleases.

Mr. Darrow—Mr. Bryan, doesn't the New Testament say whale?[3]

Mr. Bryan—I am not sure. My impression is that it says fish; but it does not make so much difference; I merely called your attention that to where it says fish, it does not say whale.

Mr. Darrow—But in the New Testament it says whale, doesn't it?

Mr. Bryan—That may be true; I remember in my own mind what I read about it.

Mr. Darrow—Now, you say, the big fish swallowed Jonah, and he remained—how long?—three days, and then he spewed him up on the land. You believe that the big fish was made to swallow Jonah?

Mr. Bryan—I am not prepared to say that. The Bible merely says it was done.

Mr. Darrow—You don't know whether it was the ordinary mine-run of fish or made for that purpose?

Mr. Bryan—You may guess; you evolutionists guess.

Mr. Darrow—But when we do guess, we have the sense to guess right.

Mr. Bryan—But you do not do it often.

Mr. Darrow—You are not prepared to say whether that fish was made specially to swallow a man or not?

Mr. Bryan—The Bible doesn't say so. I am not prepared to say.

[2]Jonah 1:17.
[3]Matthew 12:40.

MR. DARROW—But you believe He made them—that He made such a fish and that it was big enough to swallow Jonah?

MR. BRYAN—Yes, sir. Let me add: One miracle is just as easy to believe as another.

MR. DARROW—It is for me.

MR. BRYAN—It is for me.

MR. DARROW—Just as hard?

MR. BRYAN—It is hard to believe for you, but easy for me. A miracle is a thing performed beyond what man can perform. When you get beyond what man can do you get within the realms of miracles; and it is just as easy to believe the miracle of Jonah as any other miracle in the Bible.

MR. DARROW—Perfectly easy to believe that Jonah swallowed the whale?

MR. BRYAN—If the Bible said so. The Bible doesn't make as extreme statements as evolutionists do.

MR. DARROW—The Bible says Joshua commanded the sun to stand still for the purpose of lengthening the day, doesn't it, and you believe it?[4]

MR. BRYAN—I do.

MR. DARROW—Do you believe at that time the entire sun went around the earth?

MR. BRYAN—No, I believe that the earth goes around the sun.

MR. DARROW—Do you believe that the men who wrote it thought that the day could be lengthened or that the sun could be stopped?

MR. BRYAN—I don't know what they thought.

MR. DARROW—You don't know?

MR. BRYAN—I think they wrote the fact without expressing their own thoughts. . . .

MR. DARROW—Have you an opinion as to whether—who-

---

[4] Joshua 10:12, 13.

ever wrote the book, I believe it was Joshua—the Book of Joshua—thought the sun went around the earth or not?

MR. BRYAN—I believe that he was inspired.

MR. DARROW—Can you answer my question?

MR. BRYAN—When you let me finish the statement.

MR. DARROW—It is a simple question, but finish it.

MR. BRYAN—You cannot measure the length of my answer by the length of your question. [Laughter]

MR. DARROW—No, except that the answer will be longer. [Laughter]

MR. BRYAN—I believe that the Bible is inspired, and an inspired author, whether one who wrote as he was directed to write understood the things he was writing about, I don't know.

MR. DARROW—Do you think whoever inspired it believed that the sun went around the earth?

MR. BRYAN—I believe it was inspired by the Almighty, and He may have used language that could be understood at that time.

MR. DARROW—So . . . it might have been subject to construction, might it not?

MR. BRYAN—It might have been used in language that could be understood then.

MR. DARROW—That means it is subject to construction?

MR. BRYAN—That is your construction. I am answering your questions.

MR. DARROW—Is that correct?

MR. BRYAN—That is my answer to it.

MR. DARROW—Can you answer?

MR. BRYAN—I might say Isaiah spoke of God sitting upon the circle of the earth.[5]

MR. DARROW—I am not talking about Isaiah.

JUDGE RAULSTON—Let him illustrate, if he wants to, Mr.

[5]Isaiah 10:22.

Darrow. It is your opinion that passage was subject to construction?

MR. BRYAN—Well, I think anybody can put his own construction upon it, but I do not mean necessarily that it is a correct construction. I have answered the question.

MR. DARROW—Don't you believe that in order to lengthen the day it would have been construed that the earth stood still?

MR. BRYAN—I would not attempt to say what would have been necessary, but I know this, that I can take a glass of water that would fall to the ground without the strength of my hand, and to the extent of the glass of water I can overcome the law of gravitation and lift it up; whereas, without my hand, it would fall to the ground. If my puny hand can overcome the law of gravitation, the most universally understood, to that extent, I would not set power to the hand of Almighty God that made the universe.

MR. DARROW—I read that years ago. Can you answer my question directly? If the day was lengthened by stopping, either the earth or the sun, it must have been the earth?

MR. BRYAN—Well, I should say so: yes, but it was language that was understood at that time, and we now know that the sun stood still, as it was, with the earth.

MR. DARROW—We know also the sun does stand still?

MR. BRYAN—Well, it is relatively so, as Mr. Einstein would say.

MR. DARROW—I ask you, if it does stand still?

MR. BRYAN—You know as well as I know.

MR. DARROW—Better. You have no doubt about it?

MR. BRYAN—No, no.

MR. DARROW—And the earth moves around it?

MR. BRYAN—Yes. But I think there is nothing improper if you will protect the Lord against your criticism.

MR. DARROW—I suppose he needs it?

MR. BRYAN—He was using language at that time that the people understood.

MR. DARROW—And that you call "interpretative"?

MR. BRYAN—No, sir, I would not call it interpretation.

MR. DARROW—I say, you would call it interpretation at this time, to say it meant something else?

MR. BRYAN—You may use your own language to describe what I have to say, and I will use mine in answering.

MR. DARROW—Now, Mr. Bryan, have you ever pondered what would have happened to the earth if it had stood still?

MR. BRYAN—No.

MR. DARROW—You have not?

MR. BRYAN—No. The God I believe in could have taken care of that, Darrow.

MR. DARROW—I see. Have you ever pondered what would naturally happen to the earth if it stood still suddenly?

MR. BRYAN—No.

MR. DARROW—Don't you know it would have been converted into a molten mass of matter?

MR. BRYAN—You testify to that when you get on the stand. I will give you a chance.

MR. DARROW—Don't you believe it?

MR. BRYAN—I would want to hear expert testimony on that.

MR. DARROW—You have never investigated that subject?

MR. BRYAN—I don't think I ever had the question asked.

MR. DARROW—Or ever thought of it?

MR. BRYAN—I have been too busy on things that I thought were of more importance than that.

MR. DARROW—You believe the story of the flood[6] to be a literal interpretation? When was that flood?

MR. BRYAN—I wouldn't attempt to fix the date. The date is fixed, as suggested this morning.

MR. DARROW—About 4004 B.C.?

MR. BRYAN—That has been the estimate. I would not say it is accurate.

[6]Genesis 7.

Mr. Darrow—That estimate is printed in the Bible.

Mr. Bryan—Everybody knows that—at least I think most people know—that was the estimate given.

Mr. Darrow—But what do you think that the Bible itself says? Don't you know how it is arrived at?

Mr. Bryan—I never made a calculation.

Mr. Darrow—A calculation from what?

Mr. Bryan—I could not say.

Mr. Darrow—From the generations of man?

Mr. Bryan—I would not want to say that.

Mr. Stewart again objected to the examination of Mr. Bryan.

Mr. Darrow—He is a hostile witness.

Judge Raulston—I am going to let Mr. Bryan control.

Mr. Bryan—I want him to have all the latitude that he wants, for I am going to have some latitude when he gets through.

Mr. Darrow—You can have latitude and longitude. [Laughter]

Judge Raulston—Order. . . .

Mr. Bryan—These gentlemen have not had much chance. They did not come here to try this case. They came here to try revealed religion. I am here to defend it, and they can ask me any questions they please.

Judge Raulston—All right. [Applause]

Mr. Darrow—Great applause from the bleachers!

Mr. Bryan—From those whom you call "yokels."

Mr. Darrow—I have never called them yokels.

Mr. Bryan—That is, the ignorance of Tennessee, the bigotry.

Mr. Darrow—You mean who are applauding?

Mr. Bryan—Those are the people whom you insult.

Mr. Darrow—You insult every man of science and learning in the world because he does not believe in your fool religion.

Judge Raulston—I will not stand for that.

Mr. Darrow—For what he is doing?

JUDGE RAULSTON—I am talking to both of you. . . .

MR. DARROW—How long ago was the flood, Mr. Bryan?

MR. BRYAN—Let me see Usher's calculation about it.

MR. DARROW—Surely. [Handing a Bible to the witness]

MR. BRYAN—I think this does not give it.

MR. DARROW—It gives an account of Noah. Where is the one in evidence? I am quite certain it is there.

MR. BRYAN—Oh, I would put the estimate where it is, because I have no reason to vary it. But I would have to look at it to give you the exact date.

MR. DARROW—I would, too. Do you remember what book the account is in?

MR. BRYAN—Genesis. It is given here as 2348 years B.C.

MR. DARROW—Well, 2348 years B.C.

MR. DARROW—You believe that all the living things that were not contained in the ark were destroyed?

MR. BRYAN—I think the fish may have lived.

MR. DARROW—Outside of the fish?

MR. BRYAN—I cannot say.

MR. DARROW—You cannot say?

MR. BRYAN—No. I accept that just as it is. I have no proof to the contrary.

MR. DARROW—I am asking you whether you believe it.

MR. BRYAN—I do. I accept that as the Bible gives it, and I have never found any reason for denying, disputing or rejecting it.

MR. DARROW—Let me make it definite—2,348 years?

MR. BRYAN—I didn't say that. That is the time given [indicating a Bible], but I don't pretend to say that is exact.

MR. DARROW—You never figured it out, those generations, yourself?

MR. BRYAN—No, sir; not myself.

MR. DARROW—But the Bible you have offered in evidence says 2340 something, so that 4,200 years ago there was not a living thing on the earth, excepting the people on the ark and the animals on the ark, and the fishes?

MR. BRYAN—There had been living things before that?

MR. DARROW—I mean at that time?

MR. BRYAN—After that.

MR. DARROW—Don't you know there are any number of civilizations that are traced back to more than five thousand years?

MR. BRYAN—I know we have people who trace things back according to the number of ciphers they have. But I am not satisfied they are accurate.

MR. DARROW—You are not satisfied there is any civilization that can be traced back five thousand years?

MR. BRYAN—I would not want to say there is, because I have no evidence of it that is satisfactory.

MR. DARROW—Would you say there is not?

MR. BRYAN—Well, so far as I know, but when 306,000,000 years is their opinion, as to how long ago life came here, I want them to be nearer, to come nearer together, before they demand of me to give up my belief in the Bible.

MR. DARROW—Do you say that you do not believe that there were any civilizations on this earth that reach back beyond 5,000 years?

MR. BRYAN—I am not satisfied by any evidence that I have seen——

MR. DARROW—I didn't ask what you are satisfied with. I asked if you believed it.

MR. BRYAN—Will you let me answer it?

JUDGE RAULSTON—Go right on.

MR. BRYAN—I am satisfied by no evidence that I have found that would justify me in accepting the opinions of these men against what I believe to be the inspired Word of God.

MR. DARROW—And you believe every nation, every organization of men, every animal in the world, outside of the fishes——

Mr. Bryan—The fish, I want you to understand, is merely a matter of humor.

Mr. Darrow—I believe the Bible says so. Take the fishes in?

Mr. Bryan—Let us get together and look over this.

Mr. Darrow—Probably we would better. We will after we get through. You believe that all the various human races on the earth have come into being in the last four thousand years or four thousand two hundred years, whatever it is?

Mr. Bryan—No. It would be more than that.

Mr. Darrow—1237?

Mr. Bryan—Some time after creation, before the flood.

Mr. Darrow—1925 added to it?

Mr. Bryan—The flood is 2300 and something and creation, according to the estimate there, is further back than that.

Mr. Darrow—Then you don't understand me. If we don't get together on it, look at the book. This is the year of grace 1925, isn't it? Let us put down 1925. Have you got a pencil? [One of the defense attorneys hands Mr. Darrow a pencil.]

Mr. Bryan—Add to that 4,004?

Mr. Darrow—Yes——

Mr. Bryan—That is the date [referring to the Bible] given here on the first page, according to Bishop Usher, which I say I accept only because I have no reason to doubt it.

Mr. Darrow—One thousand nine hundred and twenty-five plus 4,004 is 5,929 years. Now, then, what do you subtract from that?

Mr. Bryan—That is the beginning.

Mr. Darrow—I was talking about the flood.

Mr. Bryan—Two thousand three hundred and forty-eight on that, we said.

Mr. Darrow—Less than that?

Mr. Bryan—No; subtract that from 4,000. It would be about 1,700 years.

Mr. Darrow—That is the same thing?

MR. BRYAN—No; subtracted, it is twenty-three hundred and something before the beginning of the Christian era, about 1,700 years after the creation.

MR. DARROW—If I add 2,300 years, that is the beginning of the Christian era?

MR. BRYAN—Yes, sir.

MR. DARROW—If I add 1925 to that I will get it, won't I?

MR. BRYAN—Yes, sir.

MR. DARROW—That makes 4,262 years?

MR. BRYAN—According to the Bible there was a civilization before that, destroyed by the flood.

MR. DARROW—Let me make this definite. You believe that every civilization on the earth and every living thing, except possibly the fishes, that came out of the ark, were wiped out by the flood?

MR. BRYAN—At that time.

MR. DARROW—At that time; and then, whatever human beings, including all the tribes that inhabited the world, and have inhabited the world, and who run their pedigree straight back, and all the animals have come on to the earth since the flood?

MR. BRYAN—Yes.

MR. DARROW—Within 4,200 years? Do you know a scientific man on the earth that believes any such thing?

MR. BRYAN—I cannot say, but I know some scientific men who dispute entirely the antiquity of man as testified to by other scientific men.

MR. DARROW—Oh, that does not answer the question. Do you know of a single scientific man on the face of the earth that believes any such thing as you stated, about the antiquity of man?

MR. BRYAN—I don't think I have even asked one the direct question.

MR. DARROW—Quite important, isn't it?

MR. BRYAN—Well, I don't know as it is.

MR. DARROW—It might not be?

Mr. Bryan—If I had nothing else to do except speculate on what our remote ancestors were and what our remote descendants have been, but I have been more interested in Christians going on right now, to make it much more important than speculations on either the past or the future.

Mr. Darrow—You do know that there are thousands of people who profess to be Christians who believe the earth is much more ancient and that the human race is much more ancient?

Mr. Bryan—I think there may be.

Mr. Darrow—And you never have investigated to find out how long man has been on the earth?

Mr. Bryan—I have never found it necessary. I do not expect to find out all those things. I do not expect to find out about races.

Mr. Darrow—I didn't ask you that. Now, I ask you, if you know, if it was interesting enough, or important enough for you, to try to find out, how old these ancient civilizations are?

Mr. Bryan—No. I have not made a study of it.

Mr. Darrow—Don't you know that the ancient civilizations of China are six or seven thousand years old, at the very least?

Mr. Bryan—No, but they would not run back beyond the creation, according to the Bible, six thousand years.

Mr. Darrow—You don't know how old they are, is that right?

Mr. Bryan—I don't know how old they are, but possibly you do. [Laughter]

Mr. Darrow—Have you any idea how old the Egyptian civilization is?

Mr. Bryan—No.

Mr. Darrow—Do you know of any record in the world, outside of the story of the Bible, which conforms to any statement that it is 4,300 years ago or thereabouts, that all life was wiped off the face of the earth?

Mr. Bryan—I think they have found records.

Mr. Darrow—Do you know of any?

MR. BRYAN—Records reciting the flood, but I am not an authority on the subject.

MR. DARROW—Mr. Bryan, don't you know that there are many old religions that describe the flood?

MR. BRYAN—No, I don't know. The Christian religion has satisfied me and I have never felt it necessary to look up some competing religion. . . .

MR. DARROW—Do you know how old the Confucian religion is?

MR. BRYAN—I can't give you the exact date of it.

MR. DARROW—Do you know how old the religion of Zoroaster is?

MR. BRYAN—No, sir.

MR. DARROW—Do you know they are both more ancient than the Christian religion?

MR. BRYAN—I am not willing to take the opinion of people who are trying to find excuses for rejecting the Christian religion.

MR. DARROW—Are you familiar with James Clark's book on the ten great religions?

MR. BRYAN—No.

MR. DARROW—You don't know how old they are, all these other religions?

MR. BRYAN—I wouldn't attempt to speak correctly, but I think it is much more important to know the difference between them than to know the age.

MR. DARROW—Not for the purpose of this inquiry, Mr. Bryan. Do you know about how many people there were on this earth at the beginning of the Christian era?

MR. BRYAN—No. I don't think I ever saw a census on that subject.

MR. DARROW—Do you know about how many people there were on this earth 3,000 years ago?

MR. BRYAN—No.

MR. DARROW—Did you ever try to find out?

Mr. Bryan—When you display my ignorance, could you not give me the facts so I would not be ignorant any longer?

Mr. Darrow—Can you tell me how many people there were when Christ was born? You know, some of us might get the facts and still be ignorant.

Mr. Bryan—Will you please give me that? You ought not to ask me a question that you don't know the answer to.

Mr. Darrow—I can make an estimate.

Mr. Bryan—What is your estimate?

Mr. Darrow—Wait until you get to me. Do you know anything about how many people there were in Egypt 3,500 years ago, or how many people there were in China 5,000 years ago?

Mr. Bryan—No.

Mr. Darrow—Have you ever tried to find out?

Mr. Bryan—No, sir; you are the first man I ever heard of who was interested in it. [Laughter]

Mr. Darrow—Mr. Bryan, am I the first man you ever heard of who has been interested in the age of human societies and primitive man?

Mr. Bryan—You are the first man I ever heard speak of the number of people at these different periods.

Mr. Darrow—Where have you lived all your life?

Mr. Bryan—Not near you. [Laughter and applause]

Mr. Darrow—Nor near anybody of learning?

Mr. Bryan—Oh, don't assume you know it all.

Mr. Darrow—Do you know there are thousands of books in your libraries on all those subjects I have been asking you about?

Mr. Bryan—I couldn't say, but I will take your word for it.

Mr. Darrow—Did you ever read a book on primitive man? Like Tyler's Primitive Culture or Boaz or any of the great authorities?

Mr. Bryan—I don't think I ever read the ones you have mentioned.

Mr. Darrow—Have you read any?

MR. BRYAN—Well, I have read a little from time to time. But I didn't pursue it, because I didn't know I was to be called as a witness.

MR. DARROW—You have never in all your life made any attempt to find out about the other peoples of the earth—how old their civilizations are, how long they have existed on the earth, have you?

MR. BRYAN—No, sir, I have been so well satisfied with the Christian religion that I have spent no time trying to find argument against it.

MR. DARROW—Were you afraid you might find some?

MR. BRYAN—No, sir; I am not afraid that you will show me any.

MR. DARROW—You remember that man who said—I am not quoting literally—that one could not be content though he rose from the dead. You suppose you could be content?

MR. BRYAN—Well, will you give me the rest of it, Mr. Darrow?

MR. DARROW—No.

MR. BRYAN—Why not?

MR. DARROW—I am not interested.

MR. BRYAN—Why scrap the Bible? "They have Moses and the Prophets."[7]

MR. DARROW—Who has?

MR. BRYAN—That is the rest of the quotation you didn't finish.

MR. DARROW—And you think if they have Moses and the Prophets, they don't need to find out anything else?

MR. BRYAN—That was the answer that was made there.

MR. DARROW—You don't care how old the earth is, how old man is, and how long the animals have been here?

MR. BRYAN—I am not so much interested in that.

[7]Luke 16:29–31.

Mr. Darrow—You have never made any investigation to find out?

Mr. Bryan—No, sir, I never have.

Mr. Darrow—You have heard of the Tower of Babel, haven't you?

Mr. Bryan—Yes, sir.

Mr. Darrow—That tower[8] was built under the ambition that they could build a tower up to Heaven, wasn't it? And God saw what they were at and to prevent their getting into Heaven, He confused their tongues?

Mr. Bryan—Something like that. I wouldn't say to prevent their getting into Heaven. I don't think it is necessary to believe that God was afraid they would get to Heaven.

Mr. Darrow—I mean that way?

Mr. Bryan—I think it was a rebuke to them.

Mr. Darrow—A rebuke to them trying to go that way?

Mr. Bryan—To build that tower for that purpose.

Mr. Darrow—Take that short cut?

Mr. Bryan—That is your language, not mine.

Mr. Darrow—Now, when was that?

Mr. Bryan—Give us the Bible.

Mr. Darrow—Yes, we will have strict authority on it—scientific authority?

Mr. Bryan—That was about 100 years before the flood, Mr. Darrow, according to this chronology. It was 2247—the date on one page is 2218 and on the other 2247, and it is described in here——

Mr. Darrow—That is the year 2247?

Mr. Bryan—2218 B.C. is at the top of one page, and 2247 at the other, and there is nothing in here to indicate the change.

Mr. Darrow—Well, make it 2218 then?

Mr. Bryan—All right, about.

---

[8]Genesis 11:4–9.

MR. DARROW—Then you add 1500 to that.

MR. BRYAN—No, 1925.

MR. DARROW—Add 1925 to that—that would be 4,143 years ago. Up to 4,143 years ago, every human being on earth spoke the same language?

MR. BRYAN—Yes, sir, I think that is the inference that could be drawn from that.

MR. DARROW—All the different languages of the earth, dating from the Tower of Babel,—is that right? Do you know how many languages are spoken on the face of the earth?

MR. BRYAN—No. I know the Bible has been translated into 500, and no other book has been translated into anything like that many.

MR. DARROW—That is interesting, if true. Do you know all the languages there are?

MR. BRYAN—No, sir, I can't tell you. There may be many dialects besides that and some languages, but those are all the principal languages.

MR. DARROW—There are a great many that are not principal languages?

MR. BRYAN—Yes, sir.

MR. DARROW—You haven't any idea how many there are?

MR. BRYAN—No, sir.

MR. DARROW—And you say that all those languages of all the sons of men have come on the earth not over 4,150 years ago?

MR. BRYAN—I have seen no evidence that would lead me to put it any farther back than that.

MR. DARROW—That is your belief anyway? That was due to the confusion of tongues at the Tower of Babel? Did you ever study philology at all?

MR. BRYAN—No, I have never made a study of it—not in the sense in which you speak of it.

MR. DARROW—You have used language all your life?

MR. BRYAN—Well, hardly all my life—ever since I was about a year old.

MR. DARROW—And good language, too; and you never took any pains to find anything about the origin of languages?

MR. BRYAN—I never studied it as a science.

MR. DARROW—Have you ever by any chance read Max Mueller?

MR. BRYAN—No.

MR. DARROW—The great German philologist?

MR. BRYAN—No.

MR. DARROW—Or any book on that subject?

MR. BRYAN—I don't remember to have read a book on that subject, especially, but I have read extracts, of course, and articles on philology.

MR. DARROW—Mr. Bryan, could you tell me how old the earth is?

MR. BRYAN—No, sir, I couldn't.

MR. DARROW—Could you come anywhere near it?

MR. BRYAN—I wouldn't attempt to. I could possibly come as near as the scientists do, but I had rather be more accurate before I give a guess.

MR. DARROW—You don't think much of scientists, do you?

MR. BRYAN—Yes, I do, sir. . . .

MR. DARROW—When was the last Glacial Age?

MR. BRYAN—I wouldn't attempt to tell you that.

MR. DARROW—Have you any idea?

MR. BRYAN—I wouldn't want to fix it without looking at some of the figures.

MR. DARROW—Do you know whether it was more than 6,000 years ago?

MR. BRYAN—I think it was more than 6,000 years.

MR. DARROW—Have you any idea how old the earth is?

MR. BRYAN—No.

MR. DARROW—The Book you have introduced in evidence tells you, doesn't it? [Referring to the Bible]

MR. BRYAN—I don't think it does, Mr. Darrow.

MR. DARROW—Let's see whether it does. Is this the one?

MR. BRYAN—That is the one, I think.

Mr. Darrow—It says B.C. 4004.

Mr. Bryan—That is Bishop Usher's calculation.

Mr. Darrow—Do you think the earth was made in six days?

Mr. Bryan—Not six days of twenty-four hours.

Mr. Darrow—Doesn't it say so?

Mr. Bryan—No, sir.

Mr. Stewart—What is the purpose of this examination?

Mr. Bryan—The purpose is to cast ridicule on everybody who believes in the Bible, and I am perfectly willing that the world shall know that these gentlemen have no other purpose than ridiculing every person who believes in the Bible.

Mr. Darrow—We have the purpose of preventing bigots and ignoramuses from controlling the education of the United States, and you know it, and that is all.

Mr. Bryan—I am glad to bring out that statement. I want the world to know that this evidence is not for the view. Mr. Darrow and his associates have filed affidavits here stating the purpose which, as I understand it, is to show that the Bible story is not true. . . .

. . . I am simply trying to protect the Word of God against the greatest atheist or agnostic in the United States. [Prolonged applause] I want the papers to know I am not afraid to get on the stand in front of him and let him do his worst. I want the world to know that agnosticism is trying to force agnosticism on our colleges and on our schools, and the people of Tennessee will not permit it to be done. [Prolonged applause]

Mr. Darrow—I wish I could get a picture of these claquers. . . .

Mr. Darrow—Mr. Bryan, do you believe that the first woman was Eve?

Mr. Bryan—Yes.

Mr. Darrow—Do you believe she was literally made out of Adam's rib?

Mr. Bryan—I do.

MR. DARROW—Did you ever discover where Cain got his wife?[9]

MR. BRYAN—No, sir; I leave the agnostics to hunt for her.

MR. DARROW—You have never found out?

MR. BRYAN—I have never tried to find.

MR. DARROW—You have never tried to find?

MR. BRYAN—No.

MR. DARROW—The Bible says he got one, doesn't it? Were there other people on the earth at that time?

MR. BRYAN—I cannot say.

MR. DARROW—You cannot say? Did that never enter into your consideration?

MR. BRYAN—Never bothered me.

MR. DARROW—There were no others recorded, but Cain got a wife. That is what the Bible says. Where she came from, you don't know. All right. Does the statement, "The morning and the evening were the first day" and "The morning and the evening were the second day" mean anything to you?[10]

MR. BRYAN—I do not think it means necessarily a twenty-four-hour day.

MR. DARROW—You do not?

MR. BRYAN—No.

MR. DARROW—What do you consider it to be?

MR. BRYAN—I have not attempted to explain it. If you will take the second chapter—let me have the book. [Examining Bible] The fourth verse of the second chapter (Genesis) says: "These are the generations of the heavens and of the earth, when they were created, in the day that the Lord God made the earth and the heavens." The word "day" there in the very next chapter is used to describe a period. I do not see that there is necessity for construing the words, "the evening and the

[9]Genesis 4:17.
[10]Genesis 1:5, 8.

morning" as meaning necessarily a twenty-four-hour day: "in the day when the Lord made the Heaven and the earth."

MR. DARROW—Then when the Bible said, for instance, "And God called the firmament Heaven. And the evening and the morning were the second day,"—that does not necessarily mean twenty-four hours?

MR. BRYAN—I do not think it necessarily does.

MR. DARROW—Do you think it does or does not?

MR. BRYAN—I know a great many think so.

MR. DARROW—What do you think?

MR. BRYAN—I do not think it does.

MR. DARROW—You think these were not literal days?

MR. BRYAN—I do not think they were twenty-four-hour days.

MR. DARROW—What do you think about it?

MR. BRYAN—That is my opinion—I do not know that my opinion is better on that subject than those who think it does.

MR. DARROW—Do you not think that?

MR. BRYAN—No. But I think it would be just as easy for the kind of God we believe in to make the earth in six days as in six years or in six million years or in six hundred million years. I do not think it important whether we believe one or the other.

MR. DARROW—Do you think those were literal days?

MR. BRYAN—My impression is they were periods, but I would not attempt to argue as against anybody who wanted to believe in literal days.

MR. DARROW—Have you any idea of the length of the periods?

MR. BRYAN—No, I don't.

MR. DARROW—Do you think the sun was made on the fourth day?

MR. BRYAN—Yes.

MR. DARROW—And they had evening and morning without the sun?

MR. BRYAN—I am simply saying it is a period.

MR. DARROW—They had evening and morning for four periods without the sun, do you think?

MR. BRYAN—I believe in creation, as there told, and if I am not able to explain it, I will accept it.

MR. DARROW—Then you can explain it to suit yourself. And they had the evening and the morning before that time for three days or three periods. All right, that settles it. Now, if you call those periods, they may have been a very long time?

MR. BRYAN—They might have been.

MR. DARROW—The creation might have been going on for a very long time?

MR. BRYAN—It might have continued for millions of years.

MR. DARROW—Yes, all right. Do you believe the story of the temptation of Eve by the serpent?

MR. BRYAN—I do.

MR. DARROW—Do you believe that after Eve ate the apple, or gave it to Adam—whichever way it was—God cursed Eve, and at that time decreed that all womankind thenceforth and forever should suffer the pains of childbirth in the reproduction of the earth?[11]

MR. BRYAN—I believe what it says, and I believe the fact as fully.

MR. DARROW—That is what it says, doesn't it?

MR. BRYAN—Yes.

MR. DARROW—And for that reason, every woman born of woman, who has to carry on the race,—the reason they have childbirth pains is because Eve tempted Adam in the Garden of Eden?

MR. BRYAN—I will believe just what the Bible says. I ask to put that in the language of the Bible, for I prefer that to your language. Read the Bible, and I will answer.

MR. DARROW—All right, I will do that: "And I will put en-

[11]Genesis 3.

mity between thee and the woman."[12] That is referring to the serpent?

MR. BRYAN—The serpent.

MR. DARROW (reading)—"And between thy seed and her seed; it shall bruise thy head, and thou shalt bruise his heel. Unto the woman He said, I will greatly multiply thy sorrow and thy conception; in sorrow thou shalt bring forth children; and thy desire shall be to thy husband, and he shall rule over thee." That is right, is it?

MR. BRYAN—I accept it as it is.

MR. DARROW—Do you believe that was because Eve tempted Adam to eat the fruit?

MR. BRYAN—I believe it was just what the Bible said.

MR. DARROW—And you believe that is the reason that God made the serpent to go on his belly after he tempted Eve?

MR. BRYAN—I believe the Bible as it is, and I do not permit you to put your language in the place of the language of the Almighty. You read that Bible and ask me questions, and I will answer them. I will not answer your questions in your language.

MR. DARROW—I will read it to you from the Bible: "And the Lord God said unto the serpent, Because thou hast done this, thou art cursed above all cattle, and above every beast of the field; upon thy belly shalt thou go, and dust shalt thou eat all the days of thy life." Do you think that is why the serpent is compelled to crawl upon its belly?[13]

MR. BRYAN—I believe that.

MR. DARROW—Have you any idea how the snake went before that time?

MR. BRYAN—No, sir.

MR. DARROW—Do you know whether he walked on his tail or not?

[12]Genesis 3:15, 16.
[13]Genesis 3:14.

Mr. Bryan—No, sir. I have no way to know. [Laughter]

Mr. Darrow—Now, you refer to the bow that was put in the heaven after the flood, the rainbow. Do you believe in that?

Mr. Bryan—Read it.

Mr. Darrow—All right, Mr. Bryan, I will read it for you.

Mr. Bryan—Your Honor, I think I can shorten this testimony. The only purpose Mr. Darrow has is to slur at the Bible, but I will answer his questions. I will answer it all at once, and I have no objection in the world. I want the world to know that this man, who does not believe in a God, is trying to use a court in Tennessee——

Mr. Darrow—I object to that.

Mr. Bryan—To slur at it, and, while it will require time, I am willing to take it.

Mr. Darrow—I object to your statement. I am examining you on your fool ideas that no intelligent Christian on earth believes.

13 / H. L. MENCKEN

Was Bryan Sincere?

Bryan died a few days after the close of the Scopes trial, and H. L. Mencken (1880–1956) noted the fact in a three-page editorial in *The American Mercury.* Mencken's reputation in the Twenties was enormous, based in part on his literary felicity, searing wit, and absolutely complete disdain for the country yokels, their spokesmen, their politics, and their way of life. He tried to represent the urbane, civilized man beset by all the crudeness and crassness of provincial America. Understanding the tension between urban and village America, Mencken found his perfect but dangerous fool in Bryan, as the following characterization of "The Great Commoner" will show.

Has it been marked by historians that the late William Jennings Bryan's last secular act on this earth was to catch flies? A curious detail, and not without its sardonic overtones. He was the most sedulous flycatcher in American history, and by long odds the most successful. His quarry, of course, was not *Musca domestica* but *Homo neandertalensis*. For forty years he tracked it with snare and blunderbuss, up and down the backways of the Republic. Wherever the flambeaux of Chautauqua smoked and guttered, and the bilge of Idealism ran in the veins, and Baptist pastors dammed the brooks with the saved, and men gathered who were weary and heavy laden, and their wives who were unyieldingly multiparous and full of Peruna— there the indefatigable Jennings set up his traps and spread his bait. He knew every forlorn country town in the South and West, and he could crowd the most remote of them to suffocation by simply winding his horn. The city proletariat, transiently flustered by him in 1896, quickly penetrated his buncombe and would have no more of him; the gallery jeered him at every Democratic national convention for twenty-five years. But out where the grass grows high, and the horned cattle dream away the lazy days, and men still fear the powers and principalities of the air—out there between the corn-rows he held his old puissance to the end. There was no need of beaters to drive in his game. The news that he was coming was enough. For miles the flivver dust would choke the roads. And when he rose at the end of the day to discharge his Message there would be such breathless attention, such a rapt and enchanted ecstasy, such a sweet rustle of amens as the world had not known since Johanan fell to Herod's headsman.

There was something peculiarly fitting in the fact that his last days were spent in a one-horse Tennessee village, and

---

"Editorial," *The American Mercury*, VI, 22 (October 1925), 158–160. From "Obituary of William Jennings Bryan" by H. L. Mencken. Reprinted by permission of *The American Mercury*, Box 1306, Torrance, California.

that death found him there. The man felt at home in such scenes. He liked people who sweated freely, and were not debauched by the refinements of the toilet. Making his progress up and down the Main street of little Dayton, surrounded by gaping primates from the upland valleys of the Cumberland Range, his coat laid aside, his bare arms and hairy chest shining damply, his bald head sprinkled with dust—so accoutred and on display he was obviously happy. He liked getting up early in the morning, to the tune of cocks crowing on the dunghill. He liked the heavy, greasy victuals of the farmhouse kitchen. He liked country lawyers, country pastors, all country people. I believe that this liking was sincere—perhaps the only sincere thing in the man. His nose showed no uneasiness when a hillman in faded overalls and hickory shirt accosted him on the street, and besought him for light upon some mystery of Holy Writ. The simian gabble of a country town was not gabble to him, but wisdom of an occult and superior sort. In the presence of city folks he was palpably uneasy. Their clothes, I suspect, annoyed him, and he was suspicious of their too delicate manners. He knew all the while that they were laughing at him—if not at his baroque theology, then at least at his alpaca pantaloons. But the yokels never laughed at him. To them he was not the huntsman but the prophet, and toward the end, as he gradually forsook mundane politics for purely ghostly concerns, they began to elevate him in their hierarchy. When he died he was the peer of Abraham. Another curious detail: his old enemy, Wilson, aspiring to the same white and shining robe, came down with a thump. But Bryan made the grade. His place in the Tennessee hagiocracy is secure. If the village barber saved any of his hair, then it is curing gall-stones down there today.

II

But what label will he bear in more urbane regions? One, I fear, of a far less flattering kind. Bryan lived too long, and de-

scended too deeply into the mud, to be taken seriously hereafter by fully literate men, even of the kind who write school-
books. There was a scattering of sweet words in his funeral
notices, but it was no more than a response to conventional
sentimentality. The best verdict the most romantic editorial
writer could dredge up, save in the eloquent South, was to the
general effect that his imbecilities were excused by his earnest-
ness—that under his clowning, as under that of the juggler of
Notre Dame, there was the zeal of a steadfast soul. But this
was apology, not praise; precisely the same thing might be said
of Mary Baker G. Eddy, the late Czar Nicholas, or Czolgosz.
The truth is that even Bryan's sincerity will probably yield to
what is called, in other fields, definitive criticism. Was he sincere when he opposed imperialism in the Philippines, or when
he fed it with deserving Democrats in Santo Domingo? Was he
sincere when he tried to shove the Prohibitionists under the
table, or when he seized their banner and began to lead them
with loud whoops? Was he sincere when he bellowed against
war, or when he dreamed of himself as a tin-soldier in uniform,
with a grave reserved among the generals? Was he sincere
when he denounced the late John W. Davis, or when he swallowed Davis? Was he sincere when he fawned over Champ
Clark, or when he betrayed Clark? Was he sincere when he
pleaded for tolerance in New York, or when he bawled for the
fagot and the stake in Tennessee?

This talk of sincerity, I confess, fatigues me. If the fellow
was sincere, then so was P. T. Barnum. The word is disgraced
and degraded by such uses. He was, in fact, a charlatan, a
mountebank, a zany without shame or dignity. What animated
him from end to end of his grotesque career was simply ambition—the ambition of a common man to get his hand upon the
collar of his superiors, or, failing that, to get his thumb into
their eyes. He was born with a roaring voice, and it had the
trick of inflaming half-wits. His whole career was devoted to
raising these half-wits against their betters, that he himself

might shine. His last battle will be grossly misunderstood if it is thought of as a mere exercise in fanaticism—that is, if Bryan the Fundamentalist Pope is mistaken for one of the bucolic Fundamentalists. There was much more in it than that, as everyone knows who saw him on the field. What moved him, at bottom, was simply hatred of the city men who had laughed at him so long, and brought him at last to so tatterdemalion an estate. He lusted for revenge upon them. He yearned to lead the anthropoid rabble against them, to set *Homo neandertalensis* upon them, to punish them for the execution they had done upon him by attacking the very vitals of their civilization. He went far beyond the bounds of any merely religious frenzy, however inordinate. When he began denouncing the notion that man is a mammal even some of the hinds at Dayton were agape. And when, brought upon Darrow's cruel hook, he writhed and tossed in a very fury of malignancy, bawling against the baldest elements of sense and decency like a man frantic—when he came to that tragic climax there were snickers among the hinds as well as hosannas.

Upon that hook, in truth, Bryan committed suicide, as a legend as well as in the body. He staggered from the rustic court ready to die, and he staggered from it ready to be forgotten, save as a character in a third-rate farce, witless and in execrable taste. The chances are that history will put the peak of democracy in his time; it has been on the downward curve among us since the campaign of 1896. He will be remembered, perhaps, as its supreme impostor, the *reductio ad absurdum* of its pretension. Bryan came very near being President of the United States. In 1896, it is possible, he was actually elected. He lived long enough to make patriots thank the inscrutable gods for Harding, even for Coolidge. Dulness has got into the White House, and the smell of cabbage boiling, but there is at least nothing to compare to the intolerable buffoonery that went on in Tennessee. The President of the United States doesn't believe that the earth is square, and that witches should be put to death, and that Jonah swallowed the whale. The Golden Text is not painted weekly on the White House wall, and there is no need to keep ambassadors waiting while Pastor Simpson, of Smithsville, prays for rain in the Blue Room. We have escaped something—by a narrow margin, but still safely.

III

That is, so far. The Fundamentalists continue at the wake, and sense gets a sort of reprieve. The legislature of Georgia, so the news comes, has shelved the anti-evolution bill, and turns its back upon the legislature of Tennessee. Elsewhere minorities prepare for battle—here and there with some assurance of success. But it is too early, it seems to me, to send the firemen home; the fire is still burning on many a far-flung hill, and it may begin to roar again at any moment. The evil that men do lives after them. Bryan, in his malice, started something that it will not be easy to stop. In ten thousand country towns his old heelers, the evangelical pastors, are propagating his gospel, and everywhere the yokels are ready for it. When he disappeared from the big cities, the big cities made the capital error of assuming that he was done for. If they heard of him at all, it was only as a crimp for real-estate speculators—the heroic foe of the unearned increment hauling it in with both hands. He seemed preposterous, and hence harmless. But all the while he was busy among his old lieges, preparing for a *jacquerie* that should floor all his enemies at one blow. He did the job competently. He had vast skill at such enterprises. Heave an egg out of a Pullman window, and you will hit a Fundamentalist almost anywhere in the United States today. They swarm in the country towns, inflamed by their pastors, and with a saint, now, to venerate. They are thick in the mean streets behind the gasworks. They are everywhere that learning is too heavy a burden for mortal minds, even the vague, pathetic learning on tap in little red schoolhouses. They march with the Klan, with the

Christian Endeavor Society, with the Junior Order of United American Mechanics, with the Epworth League, with all the rococo bands that poor and unhappy folk organize to bring some light of purpose into their lives. They have had a thrill, and they are ready for more.

Such is Bryan's legacy to his country. He couldn't be President, but he could at least help magnificently in the solemn business of shutting off the presidency from every intelligent and self-respecting man. The storm, perhaps, won't last long, as time goes in history. It may help, indeed, to break up the democratic delusion, now already showing weakness, and so hasten its own end. But while it lasts it will blow off some roofs and flood some sanctuaries.

14 / W. B. RILEY

The Fundamentalists' Point of View

Religious Fundamentalism was provincial America's most characteristic attribute during the Twenties. It was, as both its advocates and critics agreed, a folk movement, of the countryside and small towns. The sensational Scopes trial had emphasized some of the bitterness elicited by the confrontation of Fundamentalism and liberalism, but that trial was merely a dramatic moment in a continuing battle. The following selection by W. B. Riley, a pastor of the First Baptist Church of Minneapolis, a founder of the Anti-Evolution League, and president of the World's Christian Fundamentals Association, reveals the doctrinal and emotional pitch of this essentially provincial mentality. Riley wrote many books defending Fundamentalism, along with the following article, an unusually lucid and articulate assertion of this position. It was the position that Sinclair Lewis explored in *Elmer Gantry*, and the one that drove H. L. Mencken to

his most devastating prose. It was also the one that typified many
millions of Americans in virtually every non-urban area of the nation.

What is Fundamentalism? It would be quite impossible,
within the limits of a single article, so to treat the subject as to
satisfy all interested parties. There are too many features of this
Christian faith for one to attempt a delineation. But there are
at least three major propositions that must appear in any adequate reply, and they are these: It is the Christian Creed; it is
the Christian Character; it is the Christian Commission.

THE GREATER CHRISTIAN DOCTRINES

Fundamentalism undertakes to reaffirm the greater Christian
doctrines. Mark this phrase, "the greater Christian doctrines."
It does not attempt to set forth every Christian doctrine. It has
never known the elaboration that characterizes the great denominational confessions. But it did lay them side by side, and,
out of their extensive statements, elect nine points upon which
to rest its claims to Christian attention. They were and are as
follows:

1. We believe in the Scriptures of the Old and New Testa-
ments as verbally inspired by God, and inerrant in the original
writings, and that they are of supreme and final authority in
faith and life.
2. We believe in one God, eternally existing in three persons, Father, Son and Holy Spirit.
3. We believe that Jesus Christ was begotten by the Holy
Spirit, and born of the Virgin Mary, and is true God and true
man.
4. We believe that man was created in the image of God,
that he sinned and thereby incurred not only physical death,

From "The Faith of the Fundamentalists," *Current History*, XXVI, no. 3
(June 1927), 434–440.

but also that spiritual death which is separation from God; and that all human beings are born with a sinful nature, and, in the case of those who reach moral responsibility, become sinners in thought, word and deed.

5. We believe that the Lord Jesus Christ died for our sins according to the Scriptures as a representative and substitutionary sacrifice; and that all that believe in Him are justified on the ground of His shed blood.

6. We believe in the resurrection of the crucified body of our Lord, in His ascension into Heaven, and in His present life there for us, as High Priest and Advocate.

7. We believe in "that blessed hope," the personal, premillennial and imminent return of our Lord and Saviour, Jesus Christ.

8. We believe that all who receive by faith the Lord Jesus Christ are born again of the Holy Spirit and thereby become children of God.

9. We believe in the bodily resurrection of the just and the unjust, the everlasting felicity of the saved and the everlasting conscious suffering of the lost.

It would seem absolutely clear, therefore, that many of the liberal writers of recent years have never taken the pains to ask for the basis of our belief. . . .

Modernism when it comes to deal with the Fundamentals movement is suddenly possessed with a strange imagination. If you want to know what the movement is *not* and who its leaders are *not*, read their descriptions of both. Certainly as to what we believe, the above declaration leaves no doubt, and only the man ignorant of the Bible or utterly indifferent to its teachings, could ever call into question that these nine points constitute the greater essentials in the New Testament doctrinal system.

Fundamentalism insists upon the plain intent of Scripture-speech. The members of this movement have no sympathy whatever for that weasel method of sucking the meaning out of words and then presenting the empty shells in an attempt to palm them off as giving the Christian faith a new and another interpretation. The absurdities to which such a spiritualizing method may lead are fully revealed in the writings of Mary Baker Eddy and modernists in general. When one is permitted to discard established and scientific definitions and to create, at will, his own glossary, language fails to be longer a vehicle of thought, and inspiration itself may mean anything or nothing, according to the preference of its employer. . . .

"Forever Settled in Heaven"

There are men who would join us tomorrow if we omitted the seventh point from our doctrinal statement, and they marvel that we permit it to remain in our declaration, knowing its divisive effect. Our answer is: Fundamentalism insists upon the plain intent of Scripture-speech and knows no method by which it can logically receive the multiplied and harmonious teachings of the Book concerning one doctrine and reject them concerning another. The greater doctrines are not individual opinions that can be handled about at pleasure. In the judgment of the Fundamentalist they are "forever settled in heaven." "Holy men of God, who spake as they were borne along by the Holy Ghost," have told us the truth—God's truth —and truth is as unchangeable as imperishable. "Scripture cannot be broken." The "truth of the Lord endureth forever." . . . And it not only endures forever, but it remains forever the same—the same in words, the same in meaning, the same in spiritual intent. God's work is incapable of improvement. The sun is old, but the world needs no new or improved one!

Fundamentalism is forever the antithesis of modernist critical theology. It is made up of another and an opposing school. Modernism submits all Scripture to the judgment of man. According to its method he may reject any portion of the Book as uninspired, unprofitable, and even undesirable, and accept another portion as from God because its sentences suit him, or its teachings inspire him. Fundamentalism, on the contrary, makes the Bible "the supreme and final authority in faith and life." Its teachings determine every question upon which they have spoken with some degree of fullness, and its mandates are only disregarded by the unbelieving, the materialistic and the immoral. Fundamentalists hold that the world is illumined and the Church is instructed and even science itself is confirmed, when true, and condemned when false, by the clear teachings of the open Book, while Liberalism, as *The Nation* once said, "pretends to preach the higher criticism by interpreting the sacred writings as esoteric fables." In other words, the two have nothing in common save church membership, and all the world wonders that they do or can remain together; and the thinking world knows that but one tie holds them, and that is the billions of dollars invested.

Nine out of ten of those dollars, if not ninety-nine out of every hundred of them, spent to construct the great denominational universities, colleges, schools of second grade, theological seminaries, great denominational mission stations, the multiplied hospitals that bear denominational names, the immense publication societies and the expensive magazines, were given by Fundamentalists and filched by modernists. It took hundreds of years to collect this money and construct these institutions. It has taken only a quarter of a century for the liberal bandits to capture them, and the only fellowship that remains to bind modernists and Fundamentalists in one body, or a score of bodies, is the Irish fellowship of a free fight—Fundamentalists fighting to retain what they have founded, and modernists fighting to keep their hold on what they have filched. It is a spectacle to grieve angels and amuse devils; but we doubt not that even the devils know where justice lies, and the angels from heaven sympathize with the fight and trust that faithful men will carry on.

Creed alone is neither competent nor convincing. Creed, in

the abstract, is cold and dead, but creed incarnate constitutes Christianity as positively as the word incarnate constituted the Christ. Christianity roots in a creed and fruits in character. . . .

CREED AND CONDUCT

The man who combines an unshaken faith in the authority and integrity of the Bible with an aggressive uprightness in conduct, is the man who approaches, in some human measure, the perfect copy in the Christ life, for in His words the most watchful enemies were unable to catch Him and against His works no worthy objection was ever urged. . . .

The proofs of Fundamentalism, then, are not in words, but in deeds. This has been the conception of Fundamentalists from the first, for while the World's Christian Fundamentals Association, as an organization, is but nine years old, Christian Fundamentalism has back of it two thousand years of glorious history. It was Fundamentalism that produced the Book of Acts. You will find every essential feature of our creed in Peter's sermon at Pentecost, even to the Second Coming. It was Fundamentalism that conquered the Roman Empire, and in one hundred years revised the conduct of men and brought in and established laws of righteousness, including regard for the Sabbath, the rights of the Church in the State, and the recognition of law versus anarchy. It was Fundamentalism that challenged corrupt Rome in Martin Luther's time and called out a people whose clean and wholesome conduct became the condemnation of foul papal practices, and turned the thought of the general public from the coercive measures of a corrupt Church to the intelligent and voluntary service of the King of Glory. It was Fundamentalism that faced the heresy of Deism one hundred and forty years ago, and in an open and fair field fought the battle to the finish, and slew that infidel monster as effectually as Saint George was ever imagined to have trampled the dragon. And it was Fundamentalist evangelists who so uniformly led the common people back to the "faith once de-livered" as to bury atheism practically out of sight for one hundred years.

But to battling, Fundamentalism has forever added building. Of all the colleges that Congregationalism, of nearly one hundred years ago, contributed to America, commencing with Harvard in the East, dotting practically every State in the Union with at least one, Fundamentalism built the entire line. The same remark applies to the Baptist, Presbyterian and Methodist institutions known to the whole American continent. . . .

Of what value is our boasted accomplishment of mechanical and electrical and chemical discoveries, if, while they are contributing to our material prosperity, they are more rapidly still undermining our morals? The whole doctrine of evolution is not only lacking a single illustration in the processes of nature, but it is being disproven by the program of man, for mechanical invention resulting in moral decay, is not even progress, but degeneration instead. Babylon, Persia, Greece and Rome—each of them reached a climax of material development and then deliberately committed suicide by moral degeneracy. . . .

FUTURE OF FUNDAMENTALISM

The future of Fundamentalism is not with claims, but with conquests. Glorious as is our past, history provides only an adequate base upon which to build. Fundamentalists will never need to apologize for the part they have played in education; they have produced it; or for their relationship to colleges and universities and theological seminaries, and all forms of social service; they have created them! . . . Now that modernism has come in to filch from us these creations of our creed, we must either wrest them from bandit hands or begin and build again. In the last few years, in fact, since the modernist-highwaymen rose up to trouble the Church and snatch its dearest treasures, it has shown itself as virile as the promise of Christ, "The gates of hell shall not prevail against it," ever indicated. Today there are one hundred schools and colleges connected with our Fundamentalist Association, some of which have escaped the covetous clutches of modernism, but most of which have been brought into being as a protest against modernism itself. Their growth has been so phenomenal as to prove that the old tree is fruitful still, and that the finest fruit is to be found upon its newest branches, orthodox churches, Fundamentalist colleges, sound Bible training schools, evangelical publication societies, multiplied Bible conferences and stanch defenders of the faith in ever increasing numbers in each denomination. . . .

PLIGHT OF MODERNISM

The greatest menace to Fundamentalism today is not the outright modernist. It is that middle-of-the-roader who is milking his denomination with one hand and every wealthy Fundamentalist approachable with the other, in behalf of what he maintains will be "a new Fundamentalist theological seminary," but who, when once the bucket is filled, will walk away with it to turn it over, again, as has been so often done, to the enemies of Christ. It is this course, employed by not a few in the last five years, that makes it difficult for the sound Fundamentalist institutions to secure help from those who believe with them. . . .

Imagine a mission board willing to send out upon the foreign fields, and fight for their retention and maintenance there, men who deny that declaration in its entirety, disputing alike the atonement made by Christ and His victory over the grave. There is not a week but brings us some report from foreign fields of division on the field itself over the promulgation of "another gospel," "which is no gospel"; of foreign mission schools that scoff at Moses and exalt Darwin; that reduce Christ to the level of a man and degrade Him to the descendant of a monkey, and of mission secretaries that hold to scorn the precious blood He shed, and denominate the declaration of it, "the gospel of shambles."

"Epilepsy of Darwinism"

The tragedy of it all! However, it takes hold of the . . . believers as they think of "the cup of salvation" sent to the Japanese and learn that some man or woman has, while wearing the name of missionary, put into that cup the deadly poison of modernism and made it to effect for those who drink of it, no redemption, but an epilepsy of Darwinism. . . . Think of theological seminaries, endowed to the extent of millions, and still pleading with Fundamentalists to give them more, training the children of Trinitarian believers in the Unitarian philosophy, and sending them forth to pulpits at home and abroad! It is to this non-spiritual, anti-Christian and insane procedure that Fundamentalism objects. Holding absolutely to the authority and integrity of God's Word, it believes itself commissioned by the risen Christ to "teach all nations, baptizing them in the name of the Father and of the Son and of the Holy Ghost." . . .

The Christian commission is to make disciples and not denominationalists. A disciple is a man taught, an instructed believer. We properly translate our commission, "Go ye, therefore, and disciple all nations." The history of the rights of denominationalism might be an interesting study, but it would clearly demonstrate no divinity. There is nothing in the New Testament to advocate or even justify its existence. The Bible is not a book so difficult of understanding as to separate men into factions. The trouble is they have come to it with their prejudiced opinions, with their fixed philosophies and have tried to find in its sacred pages the differences of inherited heresies, and denominationalism has been the result. . . .

Strangest of all things, the very men who are now seeking to save denominationalism do not seem to realize that they have taken the very steps that lead the way to her destruction. The explosion of the Interchurch Movement was a blast that loosened every denominational foundation. By the wild attempt to combine in *one* people whose creeds were utterly antagonistic; to unite together those who held the Church authoritative, and those who held the Bible authoritative, and those who held their own inner conscience authoritative, they produced the elements that effected explosion. Just as chlorine and hydrogen exposed to light produce an instant and destructive blast, so this Darwin-conceived attempt to ignore the great fundamentals of the Christian faith, bind in one body Unitarian, Trinitarian and atheist, when the light of God's truth was turned upon it, exploded the whole machine erected for the production of this combination. While certain high officials have found soft ecclesiastical positions upon which to land, millions of dollars went up in that smoke and not one fragment has ever since been found. It is practically the same men, ecclesiastical potentates, who have put their heads together and have agreed upon the division of fields at home and abroad, the cooperation of laborers irrespective of what views they might hold or what gospel they might preach, reducing even the gospel itself to a negligible quantity and asking nothing other than a cooperative endeavor in drawing salaries, enjoying offices, thinking out programs, pulling off feasts, and fleecing the uninformed in behalf of a world-scheme that gave no promise to the world itself. In nature and character such a scheme is a thinly disguised enemy of the Gospel of God's grace and the true Church of Christ.

Some of us have seen enough! Our hearts are sick with the sight! We know that our denominationalism means nothing to us but a deception. It seems to bind into a brotherhood men that have nothing in common, but branding with the same name, when the great truth is that in every evangelical denomination, certainly, and as we profoundly believe, even in Rome herself, there are thousands, hundreds of thousands, and millions upon millions of men who are practically in faith and heart *one,* and who ought to, perhaps without longer delay, surrender up to the modernist-marauders these institutions, now so uniformly manned by unbelievers, as a liability and not an asset. As a new organization we could then go forth as brethren in the Lord, as poor, perhaps, as were the original disciples, but believing His Word and trusting His blood, declare afresh the mission of the Church of Christ and continue the task, undertaken by the apostles, twenty centuries ago, of preaching the gospel to every creature and hastening the day of the coming King.

Who are my brethren? Baptists? Not necessarily, and, in thousands of instances, no! My brethren are those who believe in a personal God, in an inspired Book, and in a redeeming Christ.

15 / SHELDON BISSELL

Mrs. McPherson's Sensual Debauch

Aimee Semple McPherson (1890–1944) was one of the remarkable phenomena of the Twenties. Arriving penniless on the west coast, she quickly built both her reputation and her personal fortune. An extraordinary revivalist, she founded the Angelus Temple in Los Angeles in 1923, bought an estate worth over a million dollars, and through radio, became the faith-healer-in-residence to the nation. Her power and aura faded after the details of a questionable relationship were disclosed and after she returned from a mysterious disappearance. There was widespread gossip that she had run off with her lover, although on her return she claimed to have been kidnapped.

This descriptive article, written by a Los Angeles minister, captures the feel and power of one of Sister's religious spectacles.

Take the Edendale car out of Los Angeles some Sunday afternoon toward five o'clock. Ride for a bit less than a half-hour and alight at Echo Park. Here are much shade, cool green water, pleasant grassy glades, and, beyond and above it all, looming stark, ugly, bloated, a huge gray concrete excrescence on this delightful bit of nature. It is Angelus Temple, citadel of Aimee Semple McPherson and the Four-Square Gospel.

At 6:15 the doors swing open. The Temple holds 5,300, and probably one-fourth of that number are in line at this time. Within fifteen minutes the huge auditorium with its two flaring balconies is completely filled. The interior is plain, the stained-glass windows garish, but the lighting is adequate, the opera chairs restful after your long stand in line, and the ventilation through scores of doors and transoms is satisfactory. The platform is arranged for an orchestra of fifty, and the "throne" of "Sister" McPherson on a dais just below the high organ loft, softly bathed in creamy light from overhead electrics. Behind the "throne" is a shell of flowers and greenery. The musicians, mostly young and all volunteers, come in at 6:30.

The service proper will not begin until seven, but with the entrance of the band it is seen that not a seat is vacant, and that hundreds are standing at the doors. When it is remembered that this is only a usual, unadvertised—Aimee carries no church notice in the dailies—Sunday night service, repeated fifty-two times in the year, it will be seen that here we have a phenomenon almost, if not quite, unique in American church life. We are reminded also that this is "Radio KFSG" by two microphones.

For half an hour the band dispenses such familiar secular and quasi-religious selections as Sousa's "Washington Post,"

"Vaudeville at Angelus Temple," *The Outlook,* CXLIX (May 23, 1928), 126–127, 158.

Sullivan's "Lost Chord," a waltz-time arrangement of "Mighty Lak a Rose," and a crashing number, announced by the leader as "Radiant Morn March." After each selection there is loud applause. But the performance must at least be tagged as dedicated to the Lord, so at the sound of an electric bell two uniformed young women workers appear on the platform with a banner, "Silent Prayer." Instantly the musicians kneel, a hush falls upon the thousands, and in utter stillness the great throng sits for the space of thirty seconds. Then the bell rings again, the banner is quickly removed, and the band bursts into a lively waltz tune.

Now, at five minutes to seven, the vested choir, half a hundred strong, enters from either side. There is a moment of tension and hushed expectancy. All is in readiness. The dramatic has surely not been neglected by this super-dramatist. Audience, workers, band, choir, even microphones—all are here. But the throne is still empty, bathed in its soft light. Suddenly through a door far up on the wall, opening out on her private grounds, appears Mrs. McPherson. She is clad in white, with a dark cloak thrown loosely around her shoulders; her rich auburn hair, with its flowing permanent wave, is heaped high on her head. In her left arm she carries a bouquet of roses and lilies of the valley, artfully planned to illustrate a point in her sermon (Canticles ii. 1), a description ignorantly applied by her to Jesus; on her face is the characteristic expansive, radiant McPherson smile. She is a beautiful woman, seen from the auditorium, with the soft spotlight shining upon her. Let no man venture to deny it. And, in fact, no man will. The writer has seen screen beauties in his day, and confesses to a slight clutch of the heart as he watched her superb entrance. Assisted to her "throne," she gracefully seats herself, turns to her audience—and her microphone—and is ready to begin.

Of the almost bewildering program which followed there is time and space to say little. The singing was stupendous, cataclysmic, overwhelming. "Jesus, Saviour, Pilot Me," "Stand Up,

Stand Up for Jesus," "Rock of Ages," and other favorites followed in swift succession, a stanza or two of each. The more
than five thousand voices so filled the temple that the ear-
drums were bruised and beaten by the thunderous concussion.
"Sister" led with voice and waving arm, though she had choir
and organ and trumpeters behind and around her. It is her
service, let no man forget that. Not for one moment does she
drop the reins. The hand-shaking, sandwiched in between two
hymns, was a clever device to create the illusion that all—
sinners, saints, workers, mere spectators—are one huge happy
family.

"Every one take the hand of five others all around, in front
and in back," shouts the beaming Aimee.

Humming confusion with laughter and motion follow, while
the five thousand stand up and stretch. The choir then sings,
and sings gloriously, the composition of California's own
Charles Wakefield Cadman, "The Builders." Little children file
onto the stage, and they sing, too—sing so that all in the temple can hear every word, sing as I have never heard a dozen
little tots sing in all my life. And the silent radio catches every
note and flings it out to listening thousands. Then Aimee prays,
a prayer liberally splashed with "Amens" from the crowd. A
small boy, eleven years old, enlivens the occasion by playing
on a guitar "made of solid silver," as "Sister" radiantly announces. Only one short encore is allowed the enraptured audience, which applauds until Aimee holds up her hand. Much is
coming yet, and the time element bulks large. Mrs. McPherson
carries a watch, and she never forgets to look at it.

Next, the audience must judge between the comparative
merits of some songs written by workers in the Temple, and
sung lustily to different popular tunes, such as "There's a Long,
Long Trail" and "Tramp, Tramp, Tramp, the Boys Are Marching." A stereopticon flashes the words on a big bare spot on
the left-hand wall, where all can see. Winning words, in the

estimation of the crowd, judged by the volume of applause, began thus,

> I was loaded down with sin,
> But my Saviour took me in.

They were sung to "Tramp, Tramp," and it was easy to see that they would be a prime favorite in the Temple thereafter. The prize-winner was called to the platform, and there graciously presented with her reward by Aimee herself. After a rather humorous song by the Male Four-Square Quartet and a piano solo ending with a tremendous crash of all the keys within reach, the platform was cleared for a wedding. The big organ boomed forth the stately chords of the "Lohengrin" march, and the wedding party was discerned crawling at a snail's pace up the long, long aisles. Attention was divided between the procession and the superb figure standing before her "throne" waiting their arrival. Two Temple workers were to be made one and sent forth to preach in a branch of the Four-Square Gospel. Being an ordained minister, "Sister" performed the ceremony, using the full Episcopal service, slipping and faltering once or twice as she read the words.

The microphone is very close here, for the grandmother of the little bride is listening in at Albuquerque, New Mexico, and after the service, which is concluded with a loud "Salute the bride" from Aimee and a shower of rice raining down from the laughing men and women in the choir, "Sister" lifts the microphone and in dulcet tones calls greetings to the listening grandmother.

And now she announces, "The offering will be taken," and is so busy giving orders to her handsome young major-domo at her side that she almost forgets such a minor matter as the prayer over the plates held patiently by the dozen ushers, until the oversight is hurriedly rectified by "Lord, accept the offering we have brought. Amen." The collection is not a copper or even a silver one predominantly. Many bills are heaped in the baskets, for Mrs. McPherson preaches the alabaster box of costly ointment more frequently than the widow's mite, and her followers are all tithers, to the last individual.

"Open all the windows, all the doors," commands "Sister." "We have a rule in the Temple that no one shall leave during the sermon, under any circumstance. I become utterly helpless if there is any motion before me. No one must stir. The ushers will enforce this, please."

Smilingly said, but the tone is that of Napoleon before battle. All settle down as the lights are lowered, and the sermon, the climax of this astonishing religious vaudeville, begins.

Aimee preaches with a beautiful white-leather Bible in her right hand. The book is open, and the leaves of her sermon are within it. She is rather closely bound to her notes, yet so deftly does she handle them that it almost seems as though she were preaching extempore. The sermon, from the theme "What Think Ye of Christ?" is crude, rambling, now and then artfully self-laudatory, a handful of proof-texts loosely strung together with commonplace illustrations. Summoning fanciful figures to her side with a vigorous hand-clap, she conducts a court of inquisition. Builder, banker, jeweler, architect, politician, schoolboy—on they come in fancy, with many others, and each is asked the question, "What think ye of Christ?" to be answered with an ecstatically uttered text of Scripture. "He is the door," said the builder. "The pearl of great price," said the banker. "The Prince of Peace," said the statesman. "The rose of Sharon and the lily of the valley," said the florist—it was here that Aimee's bouquet made effective entrance. Even the grocer had to bear his testimony, for Jesus was to him "the fuller's soap." With illustrations, almost all of them more or less improbable, these gentlemen with their testimonies were homiletically strung together. But it was reserved to the schoolboy to make the hit of the evening.

"Schoolboy," shouted Aimee, summoning him with a clap of her hand from the aisles of memory, "what think YE of Christ?"

"Oh, he is the elder brother!"

"Yes," shouts "Sister," "he is. See the poor little schoolboy going home from school. Behind that tree lurks a big, blustering bully. He pounces on the little boy and pummels him. But down the road comes the elder brother on a bicycle. He leaps on the bully, and has him down; he rubs his face in the dirt." The action is graphically illustrated by Aimee, and greeted by the excited laughter of the thousands. "He saves the schoolboy. Amen." "Amen," is echoed by all. "Oh, how often have I been like that schoolboy," she goes on, a note of pathos creeping into her voice. "No husband, no father, no brother—all alone in the world. The big bully, the devil, has me down. He is pummeling poor Sister. But suddenly down the road, on his bicycle of love and grace, comes the Lord Jesus Christ. Praise the Lord! He rescues me." Fervent ejaculations from her auditors.

It was hopeless as a sermon, but it was consummate preaching. She knew her audience. She knew what she was after, and she got it. She is a superb actress. Her rather harsh and unmelodious voice has yet a modulation of pitch which redeems it from utter disagreeableness. To her carefully manicured and polished finger-tips she is dramatic. In her pose, her gesture, her facial expression, her lifted eyebrows, her scintillating smile, her pathetic frown, Aimee is a perfect exponent of the art of how to say a platitude and delude her hearers into thinking that it is a brand-new truth, just minted by her. She sweeps her audience as easily as the harpist close beside her sweeps the wires in soft broken chords while she preaches. And not for one instant of time is Mrs. McPherson unmindful of that great unseen listening multitude "on the air." She moves the microphone from time to time. She rests her hand lovingly upon it. She never shifts her position one step away from it. All her climaxes are enhanced to the listening thousands throughout southern California and near-by States who regularly "tune-in" on Sunday nights. Radio KFSG is as dear to her as the five thousand and more in Angelus Temple.

At 9:25 to the dot the converts fill the platform. Just why they come is a question. But they are there, waiting for " 'Sister' to pray for them."

"Here they come, from all sides; down from the top gallery, up the aisles, here they come," she almost screams through the microphone. (There were perhaps thirty-five out of an audience of 5,500.) But each convert was guided and supported by a personal worker who seemed to spring from the ground by magic the instant a hand was raised. How many remained and sought baptism after being lifted by Aimee to the throne of grace is not known. Doubtless none slipped through the net who could be kept.

At 9:30 to the second she dismisses the multitude with the benediction, inviting all "first-niters" to stay and be shown around the Temple by official guides; to see the commissary department with its store of food and clothing for the destitute to whom the Temple ministers, the carpenter shop where are made the "sets" with which Aimee frequently garnishes her evening performances and the school where more than a thousand students are taught McPhersonism and the Four-Square Gospel, to go out later as evangelists. But it is over three hours since most of those present seated themselves in the opera chairs, and three hours is longer than any church audience in America save Aimee's can be held together night after night.

The vast concourse swarms to the street. Scores of waiting electric cars take all swiftly back to the big city, swallowing up this tiny leaven of 5,500 in a garish, blatant, heedless lump of over a million souls.

What shall be said? Aimee is Aimee, and there is none like her. A religious message utterly devoid of sound thinking, loose and insubstantial in its construction, preposterously inadequate in its social implications, but amazingly successful after five years of running, and still going strong, judging from statistics, the infallible appeal of churchmen. No American evangelist of large enough caliber to be termed National has ever sailed with such insufficient mental ballast. The power of McPhersonism resides in the personality of Mrs. McPherson. The woman is everything; the evangel nothing. There is no way to understand how a jejune and arid pulpit output has become a dynamic of literally National proportions but to hear and see the woman. To visit Angelus Temple, the home of the Four-Square Gospel, is to go on a sensuous debauch served up in the name of religion.

Normalcy: Broadway, North from Harrison, Shelbyville, Indiana, 1925

Mobility for the common man: Ford's Model T, 1926

Sacco and Vanzetti, handcuffed, about to enter the courthouse in Dedham, Massachusetts, 1921

Clarence Darrow takes the stand. Scopes Trial, Dayton, Tennessee, 1925

Klan march on Washington, 1926

Prohibition agent supervises confiscation of 500 cases of Scotch whisky from hold of fishing boat, mid-1920s

Alice White and Sally O'Neill in a scene from "Mad Hour," 1928

Culver Pictures, Inc.

Brown Brothers

The Vagabond Lover: Rudy Vallee, 1929

Windy day, New York, 1927

The common man relaxes: Coney Island, early 1920s

The uncommon man relaxes:
Al Capone in Miami, late 1920s

The Spirit of St. Louis, 1927

Modernity: Fifth Avenue, New York, 1928

PART 4

THE BUSINESS
OF AMERICA

16 / SINCLAIR LEWIS

"Boosters—Pep!"

Sinclair Lewis (1885–1951) mastered the style, rhythm, and feel of provincial America. Beginning with *Main Street* (1920), he continued to cover this terrain in a series of novels: *Babbitt* (1922), *Arrowsmith* (1925), *Elmer Gantry* (1927), and *Dodsworth* (1929). Awarded the Nobel Prize for literature in 1930, Lewis in his acceptance speech admitted what only a few critics had already seen: his own attitude toward the provincial American was not unmixed scorn. The dull country doctors, hicks who could easily be taken in, pathetic and earnest do-gooders, frenetic boosters, and the rest, were, for Lewis, the kind of folks he had known in his home town, Sauk Center, Minnesota. There was at least some affection softening his disdain. In *Babbitt*, however, Lewis introduced a word into our language, and George F. Babbitt has become the almost universal symbol of the provincial mentality. With his carefully standardized facade as the Solid Citizen, with his lapel pin proclaiming "Boosters— Pep!" and with his cliché-filled life as a real estate salesman, Babbitt was the citadel the advocates of change during the Twenties would have to conquer. The following passages should show how difficult such a victory would be.

CHAPTER I

I

The towers of Zenith aspired above the morning mist; austere towers of steel and cement and limestone, sturdy as cliffs

From *Babbitt* (New York: Grosset & Dunlap, 1922), Chap. I, pp. 1–13, Chap. V, pp. 52–58. From *Babbitt* by Sinclair Lewis, copyright 1922, by Harcourt, Brace & World, Inc., renewed, 1950, by Sinclair Lewis. Reprinted by permission of the publishers.

and delicate as silver rods. They were neither citadels nor churches, but frankly and beautifully office-buildings.

The mist took pity on the fretted structures of earlier generations: the Post Office with its shingle-tortured mansard, the red brick minarets of hulking old houses, factories with stingy and sooted windows, wooden tenements colored like mud. The city was full of such grotesqueries, but the clean towers were thrusting them from the business center, and on the farther hills were shining new houses, homes—they seemed—for laughter and tranquillity.

Over a concrete bridge fled a limousine of long sleek hood and noiseless engine. These people in evening clothes were returning from an all-night rehearsal of a Little Theater play, an artistic adventure considerably illuminated by champagne. Below the bridge curved a railroad, a maze of green and crimson lights. The New York Flyer boomed past, and twenty lines of polished steel leaped into the glare.

In one of the skyscrapers the wires of the Associated Press were closing down. The telegraph operators wearily raised their celluloid eye-shades after a night of talking with Paris and Peking. Through the building crawled the scrubwomen, yawning, their old shoes slapping. The dawn mist spun away. Cues of men with lunch-boxes clumped toward the immensity of new factories, sheets of glass and hollow tile, glittering shops where five thousand men worked beneath one roof, pouring out the honest wares that would be sold up the Euphrates and across the veldt. The whistles rolled out in greeting a chorus cheerful as the April dawn; the song of labor in a city built—it seemed—for giants.

II

There was nothing of the giant in the aspect of the man who was beginning to awaken on the sleeping-porch of a Dutch Colonial house in that residential district of Zenith known as Floral Heights.

His name was George F. Babbitt. He was forty-six years old now, in April, 1920, and he made nothing in particular, neither butter nor shoes nor poetry, but he was nimble in the calling of selling houses for more than people could afford to pay.

His large head was pink, his brown hair thin and dry. His face was babyish in slumber, despite his wrinkles and the red spectacle-dents on the slopes of his nose. He was not fat but he was exceedingly well fed; his cheeks were pads, and the unroughened hand which lay helpless upon the khaki-colored blanket was slightly puffy. He seemed prosperous, extremely married and unromantic; and altogether unromantic appeared this sleeping-porch, which looked on one sizable elm, two respectable grass-plots, a cement driveway, and a corrugated iron garage. Yet Babbitt was again dreaming of the fairy child, a dream more romantic than scarlet pagodas by a silver sea.

For years the fairy child had come to him. Where others saw but Georgie Babbitt, she discerned gallant youth. She waited for him, in the darkness beyond mysterious groves. When at last he could slip away from the crowded house he darted to her. His wife, his clamoring friends, sought to follow, but he escaped, the girl fleet beside him, and they crouched together on a shadowy hillside. She was so slim, so white, so eager! She cried that he was gay and valiant, that she would wait for him, that they would sail—

Rumble and bang of the milk-truck.

Babbitt moaned, turned over, struggled back toward his dream. He could see only her face now, beyond misty waters. The furnace-man slammed the basement door. A dog barked in the next yard. As Babbitt sank blissfully into a dim warm tide, the paper-carrier went by whistling, and the rolled-up *Advocate* thumped the front door. Babbitt roused, his stomach constricted with alarm. As he relaxed, he was pierced by the familiar and irritating rattle of some one cranking a Ford: snap-ah-ah, snap-ah-ah, snap-ah-ah. Himself a pious motorist,

Babbitt cranked with the unseen driver, with him waited through taut hours for the roar of the starting engine, with him agonized as the roar ceased and again began the infernal patient snap-ah-ah—a round, flat sound, a shivering cold-morning sound, a sound infuriating and inescapable. Not till the rising voice of the motor told him that the Ford was moving was he released from the panting tension. He glanced once at his favorite tree, elm twigs against the gold patina of sky, and fumbled for sleep as for a drug. He who had been a boy very credulous of life was no longer greatly interested in the possible and improbable adventures of each new day.

He escaped from reality till the alarm-clock rang, at seventwenty.

III

It was the best of nationally advertised and quantitatively produced alarm-clocks, with all modern attachments, including cathedral chime, intermittent alarm, and a phosphorescent dial. Babbitt was proud of being awakened by such a rich device. Socially it was almost as creditable as buying expensive cord tires.

He sulkily admitted now that there was no more escape, but he lay and detested the grind of the real-estate business, and disliked his family, and disliked himself for disliking them. The evening before, he had played poker at Vergil Gunch's till midnight, and after such holidays he was irritable before breakfast. It may have been the tremendous home-brewed beer of the prohibition-era and the cigars to which that beer enticed him; it may have been resentment of return from this fine, bold man-world to a restricted region of wives and stenographers, and of suggestions not to smoke so much.

From the bedroom beside the sleeping-porch, his wife's detestably cheerful "Time to get up, Georgie boy," and the itchy sound, the brisk and scratchy sound, of combing hairs out of a stiff brush.

He grunted; he dragged his thick legs, in faded baby-blue pajamas, from under the khaki blanket; he sat on the edge of the cot, running his fingers through his wild hair, while his plump feet mechanically felt for his slippers. He looked regretfully at the blanket—forever a suggestion to him of freedom and heroism. He had bought it for a camping trip which had never come off. It symbolized gorgeous loafing, gorgeous cursing, virile flannel shirts.

He creaked to his feet, groaning at the waves of pain which passed behind his eyeballs. Though he waited for their scorching recurrence, he looked blurrily out at the yard. It delighted him, as always; it was the neat yard of a successful business man of Zenith, that is, it was perfection, and made him also perfect. He regarded the corrugated iron garage. For the three-hundred-and-sixty-fifth time in a year he reflected, "No class to that tin shack. Have to build me a frame garage. But by golly it's the only thing on the place that isn't up-to-date!" While he stared he thought of a community garage for his acreage development, Glen Oriole. He stopped puffing and jiggling. His arms were akimbo. His petulant, sleep-swollen face was set in harder lines. He suddenly seemed capable, an official, a man to contrive, to direct, to get things done.

On the vigor of his idea he was carried down the hard, clean, unused-looking hall into the bathroom.

Though the house was not large it had, like all houses on Floral Heights, an altogether royal bathroom of porcelain and glazed tile and metal sleek as silver. The towel-rack was a rod of clear glass set in nickel. The tub was long enough for a Prussian Guard, and above the set bowl was a sensational exhibit of tooth-brush holder, shaving-brush holder, soap-dish, sponge-dish, and medicine-cabinet, so glittering and so ingenious that they resembled an electrical instrument-board. But the Babbitt whose god was Modern Appliances was not pleased. The air of the bathroom was thick with the smell of a heathen toothpaste. "Verona been at it again! 'Stead of sticking to Lilidol, like I've re-peat-ed-ly asked her, she's gone and gotten some confounded stinkum stuff that makes you sick!"

The bath-mat was wrinkled and the floor was wet. (His daughter Verona eccentrically took baths in the morning, now and then.) He slipped on the mat, and slid against the tub. He said "Damn!" Furiously he snatched up his tube of shaving-cream, furiously he lathered, with a belligerent slapping of the unctuous brush, furiously he raked his plump cheeks with a safety-razor. It pulled. The blade was dull. He said, "Damn—oh—oh—damn it!"

He hunted through the medicine-cabinet for a packet of new razor-blades (reflecting, as invariably, "Be cheaper to buy one of these dinguses and strop your own blades") and when he discovered the packet, behind the round box of bicarbonate of soda, he thought ill of his wife for putting it there and very well of himself for not saying "Damn." But he did say it, immediately afterward, when with wet and soap-slippery fingers he tried to remove the horrible little envelope and crisp clinging oiled paper from the new blade.

Then there was the problem, oft-pondered, never solved, of what to do with the old blade, which might imperil the fingers of his young. As usual, he tossed it on top of the medicine-cabinet, with a mental note that some day he must remove the fifty or sixty other blades that were also temporarily piled up there. He finished his shaving in a growing testiness increased by his spinning headache and by the emptiness in his stomach. When he was done, his round face smooth and streamy and his eyes stinging from soapy water, he reached for a towel. The family towels were wet, wet and clammy and vile, all of them wet, he found, as he blindly snatched them—his own face-towel, his wife's, Verona's, Ted's, Tinka's, and the lone bath-towel with the huge welt of initial. Then George F. Babbitt did a dismaying thing. He wiped his face on the guest-towel! It was a pansy-embroidered trifle which always hung there to indicate that the Babbitts were in the best Floral Heights society. No one had ever used it. No guest had ever dared to. Guests secretively took a corner of the nearest regular towel.

He was raging, "By golly, here they go and use up all the towels, every doggone one of 'em, and they use 'em and get 'em all wet and sopping, and never put out a dry one for me—of course, I'm the goat!—and then I want one and— I'm the only person in the doggone house that's got the slightest doggone bit of consideration for other people and thoughtfulness and consider there may be others that may want to use the doggone bathroom after me and consider—"

He was pitching the chill abominations into the bath-tub, pleased by the vindictiveness of that desolate flapping sound; and in the midst his wife serenely trotted in, observed serenely, "Why Georgie dear, what are you doing? Are you going to wash out the towels? Why, you needn't wash out the towels. Oh, Georgie, you didn't go and use the guest-towel, did you?"

It is not recorded that he was able to answer.

For the first time in weeks he was sufficiently roused by his wife to look at her.

IV

Myra Babbitt—Mrs. George F. Babbitt—was definitely mature. She had creases from the corners of her mouth to the bottom of her chin, and her plump neck bagged. But the thing that marked her as having passed the line was that she no longer had reticences before her husband, and no longer worried about not having reticences. She was in a petticoat now, and corsets which bulged, and unaware of being seen in bulgy corsets. She had become so dully habituated to married life that in her full matronliness she was as sexless as an anemic nun. She was a good woman, a kind woman, a diligent woman, but no one, save perhaps Tinka her ten-year-old, was at all interested in her or entirely aware that she was alive.

After a rather thorough discussion of all the domestic and social aspects of towels she apologized to Babbitt for his having an alcoholic headache; and he recovered enough to endure the search for a B.V.D. undershirt which had, he pointed out, malevolently been concealed among his clean pajamas.

He was fairly amiable in the conference on the brown suit.

"What do you think, Myra?" He pawed at the clothes hunched on a chair in their bedroom, while she moved about mysteriously adjusting and patting her petticoat and, to his jaundiced eye, never seeming to get on with her dressing. "How about it? Shall I wear the brown suit another day?"

"Well, it looks awfully nice on you."

"I know, but gosh, it needs pressing."

"That's so. Perhaps it does."

"It certainly could stand being pressed, all right."

"Yes, perhaps it wouldn't hurt it to be pressed."

"But gee, the coat doesn't need pressing. No sense in having the whole darn suit pressed, when the coat doesn't need it."

"That's so."

"But the pants certainly need it, all right. Look at them— look at those wrinkles—the pants certainly do need pressing."

"That's so. Oh, Georgie, why couldn't you wear the brown coat with the blue trousers we were wondering what we'd do with them?"

"Good Lord! Did you ever in all my life know me to wear the coat of one suit and the pants of another? What do you think I am? A busted bookkeeper?"

"Well, why don't you put on the dark gray suit to-day, and stop in at the tailor and leave the brown trousers?"

"Well, they certainly need— Now where the devil is that gray suit? Oh, yes, here we are."

He was able to get through the other crises of dressing with comparative resoluteness and calm.

His first adornment was the sleeveless dimity B.V.D. undershirt, in which he resembled a small boy humorlessly wearing a cheesecloth tabard at a civic pageant. He never put on B.V.D.'s without thanking the God of Progress that he didn't wear tight, long, old-fashioned undergarments, like his father-in-law and partner, Henry Thompson. His second embellishment was combing and slicking back his hair. It gave him a tremendous forehead, arching up two inches beyond the former hair-line. But most wonder-working of all was the donning of his spectacles.

There is character in spectacles—the pretentious tortoise-shell, the meek pince-nez of the school teacher, the twisted silver-framed glasses of the old villager. Babbitt's spectacles had huge, circular, frameless lenses of the very best glass; the ear-pieces were thin bars of gold. In them he was the modern business man; one who gave orders to clerks and drove a car and played occasional golf and was scholarly in regard to Salesmanship. His head suddenly appeared not babyish but weighty, and you noted his heavy, blunt nose, his straight mouth and thick, long upper lip, his chin overfleshy but strong; with respect you beheld him put on the rest of his uniform as a Solid Citizen.

The gray suit was well cut, well made, and completely undistinguished. It was a standard suit. White piping on the V of the vest added a flavor of law and learning. His shoes were black laced boots, good boots, honest boots, standard boots, extraordinarily uninteresting boots. The only frivolity was in his purple knitted scarf. With considerable comment on the matter to Mrs. Babbitt (who, acrobatically fastening the back of her blouse to her skirt with a safety-pin, did not hear a word he said), he chose between the purple scarf and a tapestry effect with stringless brown harps among blown palms, and into it he thrust a snake-head pin with opal eyes.

A sensational event was changing from the brown suit to the gray the contents of his pockets. He was earnest about these objects. They were of eternal importance, like baseball or the Republican Party. They included a fountain pen and a silver pencil (always lacking a supply of new leads) which belonged in the righthand upper vest pocket. Without them he would have felt naked. On his watch-chain were a gold pen-knife, silver cigar-cutter, seven keys (the use of two of which he had forgotten), and incidentally a good watch. Depending from the chain was a large, yellowish elk's-tooth—proclamation of his membership in the Benevolent and Protective Order of Elks. Most significant of all was his loose-leaf pocket note-book, that modern and efficient note-book which contained the addresses of people whom he had forgotten, prudent memoranda of postal money-orders which had reached their destinations months ago, stamps which had lost their mucilage, clippings of verses by T. Cholmondeley Frink and of the newspaper editorials from which Babbitt got his opinions and his polysyllables, notes to be sure and do things which he did not intend to do, and one curious inscription—D.S.S.D.M.Y.P.D.F.

But he had no cigarette-case. No one had ever happened to give him one, so he hadn't the habit, and people who carried cigarette-cases he regarded as effeminate.

Last, he stuck in his lapel the Boosters' Club button. With the conciseness of great art the button displayed two words: "Boosters—Pep!" It made Babbitt feel loyal and important. It associated him with Good Fellows, with men who were nice and human, and important in business circles. It was his V.C., his Legion of Honor ribbon, his Phi Beta Kappa key.

With the subtleties of dressing ran other complex worries. "I feel kind of punk this morning," he said. "I think I had too much dinner last evening. You oughtn't to serve those heavy banana fritters."

"But you asked me to have some."

"I know, but— I tell you, when a fellow gets past forty he has to look after his digestion. There's a lot of fellows that don't take proper care of themselves. I tell you at forty a man's a fool or his doctor—I mean, his own doctor. Folks don't give enough attention to this matter of dieting. Now I think— Course a man ought to have a good meal after the day's work, but it would be a good thing for both of us if we took lighter lunches."

"But Georgie, here at home I always do have a light lunch."

"Mean to imply I make a hog of myself, eating down-town? Yes, sure! You'd have a swell time if you had to eat the truck that new steward hands out to us at the Athletic Club! But I certainly do feel out of sorts, this morning. Funny, got a pain down here on the left side—but no, that wouldn't be appendicitis, would it? Last night, when I was driving over to Verg Gunch's, I felt a pain in my stomach, too. Right here it was—kind of a sharp shooting pain. I— Where'd that dime go to? Why don't you serve more prunes at breakfast? Of course I eat an apple every evening—an apple a day keeps the doctor away —but still, you ought to have more prunes, and not all these fancy doodads."

"The last time I had prunes you didn't eat them."

"Well, I didn't feel like eating 'em, I suppose. Matter of fact, I think I did eat some of 'em. Anyway— I tell you it's mighty important to— I was saying to Verg Gunch, just last evening, most people don't take sufficient care of their diges—"

"Shall we have the Gunches for our dinner, next week?"

"Why sure; you bet."

"Now see here, George: I want you to put on your nice dinner-jacket that evening."

"Rats! The rest of 'em won't want to dress."

"Of course they will. You remember when you didn't dress for the Littlefields' supper-party, and all the rest did, and how embarrassed you were."

"Embarrassed, hell! I wasn't embarrassed. Everybody knows I can put on as expensive a Tux. as anybody else, and I should worry if I don't happen to have it on sometimes. All a darn nuisance, anyway. All right for a woman, that stays around the house all the time, but when a fellow's worked like the dickens all day, he doesn't want to go and hustle his head off getting into the soup-and-fish for a lot of folks that he's seen in just reg'lar ordinary clothes that same day."

"You know you enjoy being seen in one. The other evening you admitted you were glad I'd insisted on your dressing. You said you felt a lot better for it. And oh, Georgie, I do wish you wouldn't say 'Tux.' It's 'dinner-jacket.' "

"Rats, what's the odds?"

"Well, it's what all the nice folks say. Suppose Lucile Mc-Kelvey heard you calling it a 'Tux.' "

"Well, that's all right now! Lucile McKelvey can't pull anything on me! Her folks are common as mud, even if her husband and her dad are millionaires! I suppose you're trying to rub in *your* exalted social position! Well, let me tell you that your revered paternal ancestor, Henry T., doesn't even call it a 'Tux.'! He calls it a 'bobtail jacket for a ringtail monkey,' and you couldn't get him into one unless you chloroformed him!"

"Now don't be horrid, George."

"Well, I don't want to be horrid, but Lord! you're getting as fussy as Verona. Ever since she got out of college she's been too rambunctious to live with—doesn't know what she wants— well, I know what she wants!—all she wants is to marry a millionaire, and live in Europe, and hold some preacher's hand, and simultaneously at the same time stay right here in Zenith and be some blooming kind of a socialist agitator or boss charity-worker or some damn thing! Lord, and Ted is just as bad! He wants to go to college, and he doesn't want to go to college. Only one of the three that knows her own mind is Tinka. Simply can't understand how I ever came to have a pair of shilly-shallying children like Rone and Ted. I may not be any Rockefeller or James J. Shakespeare, but I certainly do know my own mind, and I do keep right on plugging along in the office and— Do you know the latest? Far as I can figure out, Ted's new bee is he'd like to be a movie actor and— And here I've told him a hundred times, if he'll go to college and law-school and make good, I'll set him up in business and— Verona just exactly as bad. Doesn't know what she wants. Well, well, come on! Aren't you ready yet? The girl rang the bell three minutes ago."

V

Before he followed his wife, Babbitt stood at the westernmost window of their room. This residential settlement, Floral Heights, was on a rise; and though the center of the city was three miles away—Zenith had between three and four hundred thousand inhabitants now—he could see the top of the Second National Tower, an Indiana limestone building of thirty-five stories.

Its shining walls rose against April sky to a simple cornice like a streak of white fire. Integrity was in the tower, and decision. It bore its strength lightly as a tall soldier. As Babbitt stared, the nervousness was soothed from his face, his slack chin lifted in reverence. All he articulated was "That's one lovely sight!" but he was inspired by the rhythm of the city; his love of it renewed. He beheld the tower as a temple-spire of the religion of business, a faith passionate, exalted, surpassing common men; and as he clumped down to breakfast he whistled the ballad "Oh, by gee, by gosh, by jingo" as though it were a hymn melancholy and noble. . . .

[CHAPTER V]

II

As he drove he glanced with the fondness of familiarity at the buildings.

A stranger suddenly dropped into the business-center of Zenith could not have told whether he was in a city of Oregon or Georgia, Ohio or Maine, Oklahoma or Manitoba. But to Babbitt every inch was individual and stirring. As always he noted that the California Building across the way was three stories lower, therefore three stories less beautiful, than his own Reeves Building. As always when he passed the Parthenon Shoe Shine Parlor, a one-story hut which beside the granite and red-brick ponderousness of the old California Building resembled a bath-house under a cliff, he commented, "Gosh, ought to get my shoes shined this afternoon. Keep forgetting it." At the Simplex Office Furniture Shop, the National Cash Register Agency, he yearned for a dictaphone, for a typewriter which would add and multiply, as a poet yearns for quartos or a physician for radium.

At the Nobby Men's Wear Shop he took his left hand off the steering-wheel to touch his scarf, and thought well of himself as one who bought expensive ties "and could pay cash for 'em, too, by golly"; and at the United Cigar Store, with its crimson and gold alertness, he reflected, "Wonder if I need some cigars—idiot—plumb forgot—going t' cut down my fool smoking." He looked at his bank, the Miners' and Drovers' National, and considered how clever and solid he was to bank with so marbled an establishment. His high moment came in the clash of traffic when he was halted at the corner beneath the lofty Second National Tower. His car was banked with four others in a line of steel restless as cavalry, while the cross-town traffic, limousines and enormous moving-vans and insistent motor-cycles, poured by; on the farther corner, pneumatic riveters rang on the sun-plated skeleton of a new building; and out of this tornado flashed the inspiration of a familiar face, and a fellow Booster shouted, "H' are you, George!" Babbitt waved in neighborly affection, and slid on with the traffic as the policeman lifted his hand. He noted how quickly his car picked up. He felt superior and powerful, like a shuttle of polished steel darting in a vast machine.

As always he ignored the next two blocks, decayed blocks not yet reclaimed from the grime and shabbiness of the Zenith of 1885. While he was passing the five-and-ten-cent store, the Dakota Lodging House, Concordia Hall with its lodge-rooms and the offices of fortune-tellers and chiropractors, he thought of how much money he made, and he boasted a little and worried a little and did old familiar sums:

"Four hundred fifty plunks this morning from the Lyte deal. But taxes due. Let's see: I ought to pull out eight thousand net this year, and save fifteen hundred of that—no, not if I put up garage and— Let's see: six hundred and forty clear last month, and twelve times six-forty makes—makes—let see: six times twelve is seventy-two hundred and— Oh rats, anyway, I'll make eight thousand—gee now, that's not so bad; mighty few fellows pulling down eight thousand dollars a year—eight thousand good hard iron dollars—bet there isn't more than five per cent. of the people in the whole United States that make more than Uncle George does, by golly! Right up at the top of the heap! But— Way expenses are— Family wasting gasoline, and always dressed like millionaires, and sending that eighty a month to Mother— And all these stenographers and salesmen gouging me for every cent they can get—"

The effect of his scientific budget-planning was that he felt at once triumphantly wealthy and perilously poor, and in the midst of these dissertations he stopped his car, rushed into a small news-and-miscellany shop, and bought the electric cigar-lighter which he had coveted for a week. He dodged his conscience by being jerky and noisy, and by shouting at the clerk, "Guess this will prett' near pay for itself in matches, eh?"

It was a pretty thing, a nickeled cylinder with an almost silvery socket, to be attached to the dashboard of his car. It was not only, as the placard on the counter observed, "a dandy little refinement, lending the last touch of class to a gentleman's auto," but a priceless time-saver. By freeing him from halting the car to light a match, it would in a month or two easily save ten minutes.

As he drove on he glanced at it. "Pretty nice. Always wanted one," he said wistfully. "The one thing a smoker needs, too."

Then he remembered that he had given up smoking.

"Darn it!" he mourned. "Oh well, I suppose I'll hit a cigar once in a while. And— Be a great convenience for other folks.

Might make just the difference in getting chummy with some fellow that would put over a sale. And— Certainly looks nice there. Certainly is a mighty clever little jigger. Gives the last touch of refinement and class. I— By golly, I guess I can afford it if I want to! Not going to be the only member of this family that never has a single doggone luxury!"

Thus, laden with treasure, after three and a half blocks of romantic adventure, he drove up to the club.

III

The Zenith Athletic Club is not athletic and it isn't exactly a club, but it is Zenith in perfection. It has an active and smoke-misted billiard room, it is represented by baseball and football teams, and in the pool and the gymnasium a tenth of the members sporadically try to reduce. But most of its three thousand members use it as a café in which to lunch, play cards, tell stories, meet customers, and entertain out-of-town uncles at dinner. It is the largest club in the city, and its chief hatred is the conservative Union Club, which all sound members of the Athletic call "a rotten, snobbish, dull, expensive old hole—not one Good Mixer in the place—you couldn't hire me to join." Statistics show that no member of the Athletic has ever refused election to the Union, and of those who are elected, sixty-seven per cent. resign from the Athletic and are thereafter heard to say, in the drowsy sanctity of the Union lounge, "The Athletic would be a pretty good hotel, if it were more exclusive."

The Athletic Club building is nine stories high, yellow brick with glassy roof-garden above and portico of huge limestone columns below. The lobby, with its thick pillars of porous Caen stone, its pointed vaulting, and a brown glazed-tile floor like well-baked bread-crust, is a combination of cathedral-crypt and rathskellar. The members rush into the lobby as though they were shopping and hadn't much time for it. Thus did Babbitt enter, and to the group standing by the cigar-counter he whooped, "How's the boys? How's the boys? Well, well, fine day!"

Jovially they whooped back—Vergil Gunch, the coal-dealer, Sidney Finkelstein, the ladies'-ready-to-wear buyer for Parcher & Stein's department-store, and Professor Joseph K. Pumphrey, owner of the Riteway Business College and instructor in Public Speaking, Business English, Scenario Writing, and Commercial Law. Though Babbitt admired this savant, and appreciated Sidney Finkelstein as "a mighty smart buyer and a good liberal spender," it was to Vergil Gunch that he turned with enthusiasm. Mr. Gunch was president of the Boosters' Club, a weekly lunch-club, local chapter of a national organization which promoted sound business and friendliness among Regular Fellows. He was also no less an official than Esteemed Leading Knight in the Benevolent and Protective Order of Elks, and it was rumored that at the next election he would be a candidate for Exalted Ruler. He was a jolly man, given to oratory and to chumminess with the arts. He called on the famous actors and vaudeville artists when they came to town, gave them cigars, addressed them by their first names, and—sometimes—succeeded in bringing them to the Boosters' lunches to give The Boys a Free Entertainment. He was a large man with hair *en brosse*, and he knew the latest jokes, but he played poker close to the chest. It was at his party that Babbitt had sucked in the virus of to-day's restlessness.

Gunch shouted, "How's the old Bolsheviki? How do you feel, the morning after the night before?"

"Oh, boy! Some head! That was a regular party you threw, Verg! Hope you haven't forgotten I took that last cute little jack-pot!" Babbitt bellowed. (He was three feet from Gunch.)

"That's all right now! What I'll hand you next time, Georgie! Say, juh notice in the paper the way the New York Assembly stood up to the Reds?"

"You bet I did. That was fine, eh? Nice day to-day."

"Yes, it's one mighty fine spring day, but nights still cold."

"Yeh, you're right they are! Had to have coupla blankets last night, out on the sleeping-porch. Say, Sid," Babbitt turned to Finkelstein, the buyer, "got something wanta ask you about. I went out and bought me an electric cigar-lighter for the car, this noon, and—"

"Good hunch!" said Finkelstein, while even the learned Professor Pumphrey, a bulbous man with a pepper-and-salt cutaway and a pipe-organ voice, commented, "That makes a dandy accessory. Cigar-lighter gives tone to the dashboard."

"Yep, finally decided I'd buy me one. Got the best on the market, the clerk said it was. Paid five bucks for it. Just wondering if I got stuck. What do they charge for 'em at the store, Sid?"

Finkelstein asserted that five dollars was not too great a sum, not for a really high-class lighter which was suitably nickeled and provided with connections of the very best quality. "I always say—and believe me, I base it on a pretty fairly extensive mercantile experience—the best is the cheapest in the long run. Of course if a fellow wants to be a Jew about it, he can get cheap junk, but in the long *run*, the cheapest thing is—the best you can get! Now you take here just th' other day: I got a new top for my old boat and some upholstery, and I paid out a hundred and twenty-six fifty, and of course a lot of fellows would say that was too much—Lord, if the Old Folks— they live in one of these hick towns up-state and they simply can't get onto the way a city fellow's mind works, and then, of course, they're Jews, and they'd lie right down and die if they knew Sid had anted up a hundred and twenty-six bones. But I don't figure I was stuck, George, not a bit. Machine looks brand new now—not that it's so darned old, of course; had it less 'n three years, but I give it hard service; never drive less 'n a hundred miles on Sunday and, uh— Oh, I don't really think you got stuck, George. In the *long* run, the best is, you might say, it's unquestionably the cheapest."

"That's right," said Vergil Gunch. "That's the way I look at it. If a fellow is keyed up to what you might call intensive living, the way you get it here in Zenith—all the hustle and mental activity that's going on with a bunch of live-wires like the Boosters and here in the Z.A.C., why, he's got to save his nerves by having the best."

Babbitt nodded his head at every fifth word in the roaring rhythm; and by the conclusion, in Gunch's renowned humorous vein, he was enchanted:

"Still, at that, George, don't know's you can afford it. I've heard your business has been kind of under the eye of the gov'ment since you stole the tail of Eathorne Park and sold it!"

"Oh, you're a great little josher, Verg. But when it comes to kidding, how about this report that you stole the black marble steps off the post-office and sold 'em for high-grade coal!" In delight Babbitt patted Gunch's back, stroked his arm.

"That's all right, but what I want to know is: who's the real-estate shark that bought that coal for his apartment-houses?"

"I guess that'll hold you for a while, George!" said Finkelstein. "I'll tell you, though, boys, what I did hear: George's missus went into the gents' wear department at Parcher's to buy him some collars, and before she could give his neck-size the clerk slips her some thirteens. 'How juh know the size?' says Mrs. Babbitt, and the clerk says, 'Men that let their wives buy collars for 'em always wear thirteen, madam.' How's that! That's pretty good, eh? How's that, eh? I guess that'll about fix you, George!"

17 / *HERBERT HOOVER*

The Constructive Instinct

The celebration of business as the foundation of America's culture, ethic, and purpose became a virtual reflex in the 1920's. Provincial Rotarians, international industrialists, and presidents of the nation all agreed that business enterprise was the vitalizing force of the

United States. During this time of general though not uniform or universal affluence, rising real wages, and declining union membership, Americans took genuine pride in contemplating and supporting the nation's industrial plant and commercial growth. For Harding "normalcy" meant continued and unobstructed growth, and for Coolidge it meant the direction of politics by "sound business practices." The growth of advertising and installment buying brought the ostensible cornucopia closer to home, and familiarized growing numbers of Americans with business rhetoric and values. The idea of "individualism" was basic to such values.

No one in the United States was better prepared than Herbert Hoover (1874–1964) to articulate an apparently contemporary theory of individualism. As a mining engineer whose success had carried him to nations all over the world, and as the humanitarian who successfully administered food relief plans in Europe after the war, Hoover combined both practicality and social idealism. He held the key post of Secretary of Commerce from 1921 to 1928, and regularly argued that American business enterprise had entered a new era marked by the disappearance of the older cut-throat policies and by the appearance of a new spirit of cooperation, especially as shown in the trade association movement. In the following selection, Hoover, calmly and with conviction, presents his brief for the supposedly new ethic of restrained individualism, for personal self-expression within a cooperative system, and for a perception of the United States as a mobile, classless society in which merit would be rewarded. Although there is something of the Horatio Alger instinct in these pages, Hoover had shown in his own life that at least some roads to personal success were in fact open. The apparent health and strength of the national economy, in those relatively balmy days before the Crash, also tended to support this kind of national self-satisfaction and bone-deep optimism.

On the philosophic side we can agree at once that intelligence, character, courage, and the divine spark of the human soul are alone the property of individuals. These do not lie

"Philosophic Grounds," from *American Individualism* (Garden City, N.Y.: Doubleday, Page and Co., 1922), pp. 14–25. Reprinted by permission of the Herbert Hoover Foundation.

in agreements, in organizations, in institutions, in masses, or in groups. They abide alone in the individual mind and heart.

Production both of mind and hand rests upon impulses in each individual. These impulses are made of the varied forces of original instincts, motives, and acquired desires. Many of these are destructive and must be restrained through moral leadership and authority of the law and be eliminated finally by education. All are modified by a vast fund of experience and a vast plant and equipment of civilization which we pass on with increments to each succeeding generation.

The inherited instincts of self-preservation, acquisitiveness, fear, kindness, hate, curiosity, desire for self-expression, for power, for adulation, that we carry over from a thousand of generations must, for good or evil, be comprehended in a workable system embracing our accumulation of experiences and equipment. They may modify themselves with time—but in terms of generations. They differ in their urge upon different individuals. The dominant ones are selfish. But no civilization could be built or can endure solely upon the groundwork of unrestrained and unintelligent self-interest. The problem of the world is to restrain the destructive instincts while strengthening and enlarging those of altruistic character and constructive impulse—for thus we build for the future.

From the instincts of kindness, pity, fealty to family and race; the love of liberty; the mystical yearnings for spiritual things; the desire for fuller expression of the creative faculties; the impulses of service to community and nation, are moulded the ideals of our people. And the most potent force in society is its ideals. If one were to attempt to delimit the potency of instinct and ideals, it would be found that while instinct dominates in our preservation yet the great propelling force of progress is right ideals. It is true we do not realize the ideal; not even a single person personifies that realization. It is therefore not surprising that society, a collection of persons, a necessary maze of compromises, cannot realize it. But that it has ideals, that they revolve in a system that makes for steady advance of them is the first thing. Yet true as this is, the day has not arrived when any economic or social system will function and last if founded upon altruism alone.

With the growth of ideals through education, with the higher realization of freedom, of justice, of humanity, of service, the selfish impulses become less and less dominant, and if we ever reach the millennium, they will disappear in the aspirations and satisfactions of pure altruism. But for the next several generations we dare not abandon self-interest as a motive force to leadership and to production, lest we die.

The will-o'-the-wisp of all breeds of socialism is that they contemplate a motivation of human animals by altruism alone. It necessitates a bureaucracy of the entire population, in which, having obliterated the economic stimulation of each member, the fine gradations of character and ability are to be arranged in relative authority by ballot or more likely by a Tammany Hall or a Bolshevist party, or some other form of tyranny. The proof of the futility of these ideas as a stimulation to the development and activity of the individual does not lie alone in the ghastly failure of Russia, but it also lies in our own failure in attempts at nationalized industry.

Likewise the basic foundations of autocracy, whether it be class government or capitalism in the sense that a few men through unrestrained control of property determine the welfare of great numbers, is as far apart from the rightful expression of American individualism as the two poles. The will-o'-the-wisp of autocracy in any form is that it supposes that the good Lord endowed a special few with all the divine attributes. It contemplates one human animal dealing to the other human animals his just share of earth, of glory, and of immortality. The proof of the futility of these ideas in the development of the world does not lie alone in the grim failure of Germany, but it lies in the damage to our moral and social fabric from those who have sought economic domination in America, whether employer or employee.

We in America have had too much experience of life to fool ourselves into pretending that all men are equal in ability, in character, in intelligence, in ambition. That was part of the clap-trap of the French Revolution. We have grown to understand that all we can hope to assure to the individual through government is liberty, justice, intellectual welfare, equality of opportunity, and stimulation to service.

It is in maintenance of a society fluid to these human qualities that our individualism departs from the individualism of Europe. There can be no rise for the individual through the frozen strata of classes, or of castes, and no stratification can take place in a mass livened by the free stir of its particles. This guarding of our individualism against stratification insists not only in preserving in the social solution an equal opportunity for the able and ambitious to rise from the bottom; it also insists that the sons of the successful shall not by any mere right of birth or favor continue to occupy their fathers' places of power against the rise of a new generation in process of coming up from the bottom. The pioneers of our American individualism had the good sense not to reward Washington and Jefferson and Hamilton with hereditary dukedoms and fixtures in landed estates, as Great Britain rewarded Marlborough and Nelson. Otherwise our American fields of opportunity would have been clogged with long generations inheriting their fathers' privileges without their fathers' capacity for service.

That our system has avoided the establishment and domination of class has a significant proof in the present Administration in Washington. Of the twelve men comprising the President, Vice-President, and Cabinet, nine have earned their own way in life without economic inheritance, and eight of them started with manual labor.

If we examine the impulses that carry us forward, none is so potent for progress as the yearning for individual self-expression, the desire for creation of something. Perhaps the greatest human happiness flows from personal achievement. Here lies the great urge of the constructive instinct of mankind. But it can only thrive in a society where the individual has liberty and stimulation to achievement. Nor does the community progress except through its participation in these multitudes of achievements.

Furthermore, the maintenance of productivity and the advancement of the things of the spirit depend upon the ever-renewed supply from the mass of those who can rise to leadership. Our social, economic, and intellectual progress is almost solely dependent upon the creative minds of those individuals with imaginative and administrative intelligence who create or who carry discoveries to widespread application. No race possesses more than a small percentage of these minds in a single generation. But little thought has ever been given to our racial dependency upon them. Nor that our progress is in so large a measure due to the fact that with our increased means of communication these rare individuals are today able to spread their influence over so enlarged a number of lesser capable minds as to have increased their potency a million-fold. In truth, the vastly greater productivity of the world with actually less physical labor is due to the wider spread of their influence through the discovery of these facilities. And they can arise solely through the selection that comes from the free-running mills of competition. They must be free to rise from the mass; they must be given the attraction of premiums to effort.

Leadership is a quality of the individual. It is the individual alone who can function in the world of intellect and in the field of leadership. If democracy is to secure its authorities in morals, religion, and statesmanship, it must stimulate leadership from its own mass. Human leadership cannot be replenished by selection like queen bees, by divine right or bureaucracies, but by the free rise of ability, character, and intelligence.

Even so, leadership cannot, no matter how brilliant, carry progress far ahead of the average of the mass of individual units. Progress of the nation is the sum of progress in its individuals. Acts and ideas that lead to progress are born out of the womb of the individual mind, not out of the mind of the crowd. The crowd only feels: it has no mind of its own which can plan. The crowd is credulous, it destroys, it consumes, it hates, and it dreams—but it never builds. It is one of the most profound and important of exact psychological truths that man in the mass does not think but only feels. The mob functions only in a world of emotion. The demagogue feeds on mob emotions and his leadership is the leadership of emotion, not the leadership of intellect and progress. Popular desires are no criteria to the real need; they can be determined only by deliberative consideration, by education, by constructive leadership.

18 / BRUCE BARTON

Jesus as a Businessman

Perhaps the most remarkable performance in the service of business rhetoric was a book written by Bruce Barton (1886–1967), a one-time journalist and one of the founders and later chairman of the advertising agency Batten, Barton, Durstine, and Osborn. In *The Man Nobody Knows,* Barton set himself the task of proving that Jesus was not merely "the founder of modern business," but that His principles would be as effective in the twentieth as in the first century. A true understanding of Jesus' business acumen would result in hard cash and personal power for his latest disciples in American business and industry. Christian discipleship, according to Barton, was in fact the surest way to a healthy profit and loss statement. The obvious vulgarity of Barton's argument should not obscure the fact of its enormous contemporary popularity (it was a "best seller"), if not actual influence.

CHAPTER VI

THE FOUNDER OF MODERN BUSINESS

When Jesus was twelve years old his father and mother took him to the Feast at Jerusalem.

It was the big national vacation; even peasant families saved their pennies and looked forward to it through the year. Towns like Nazareth were emptied of their inhabitants except for the few old folks who were left behind to look after the very young ones. Crowds of cheerful pilgrims filled the highways, laughing their way across the hills and under the stars at night.

In such a mass of folk it was not surprising that a boy of twelve should be lost. When Mary and Joseph missed him on the homeward trip, they took it calmly and began a search among the relatives.

The inquiry produced no result. Some remembered having seen him in the Temple, but no one had seen him since. Mary grew frightened: where could he be? Back there in the city alone? Wandering hungry and tired through the friendless streets? Carried away by other travelers into a distant country? She pictured a hundred calamities. Nervously she and Joseph hurried back over the hot roads, through the suburbs, up through the narrow city streets, up to the courts of the Temple itself.

And there he was.

Not lost; not a bit worried. Apparently unconscious that the

From Chap. VI: "The Founder of Modern Business," *The Man Nobody Knows: A Discovery of the Real Jesus* (Indianapolis, Ind.: Bobbs-Merrill Co., 1925), pp. 159–172, 177–180, 188–192. From *The Man Nobody Knows* by Bruce Barton, copyright 1925 by The Bobbs-Merrill Company, Inc., 1952 by Bruce Barton, reprinted by permission of the publishers.

Feast was over, he sat in the midst of a group of old men, who were tossing questions at him and applauding the shrewd common sense of his replies. Involuntarily his parents halted— they were simple folk, uneasy among strangers and disheveled by their haste. But after all they *were* his parents, and a very human feeling of irritation quickly overcame their diffidence. Mary stepped forward and grasped his arm.

"Son, why hast thou thus dealt with us?" she demanded. "Behold thy father and I have sought thee sorrowing."

I wonder what answer she expected to receive. Did she ever know exactly what he was going to say: did any one in Nazareth quite understand this keen, eager lad, who had such curious moments of abstraction and was forever breaking out with remarks that seemed so far beyond his years?

He spoke to her now with deference, as always, but in words that did not dispel but rather added to her uncertainty.

"How is it that ye sought me?" he asked. "Wist ye not that I must be about my father's *business?*"

His father's business, indeed, as if that wasn't exactly where they wanted him to be. His father owned a prosperous carpenter shop in Nazareth, and that was the place for the boy, as he very well knew. She was on the point of saying so, but there was something in his look and tone that silenced her. She and Joseph turned and started out, and Jesus followed them— away from the temple and the city back to little Nazareth.

His hour of boyish triumph had not turned his head. He knew how thorough must be his preparation for any really successful work. A building can rise high into the air only as it has sunk its foundations deep into the earth; the part of a man's life which the world sees is effective in proportion as it rests upon solid work which is never seen. Instinctively he knew this. For eighteen years more he was content to remain in that country town—until his strength was at its summit; until he had done his full duty by his mother and the younger children. Until his hour had come.

But what interests us most in this one recorded incident of his boyhood is the fact that for the first time he defined the purpose of his career. He did not say, "Wist ye not that I must practice preaching?" or "Wist ye not that I must get ready to meet the arguments of men like these?" The language was quite different, and well worth remembering. "Wist ye not that I must be about my father's *business?*" he said. He thought of his life as *business*. What did he mean by business? To what extent are the principles by which he conducted his business applicable to ours? And if he were among us again, in our highly competitive world, would his business philosophy work?

On one occasion, you recall, he stated his recipe for success. It was on the afternoon when James and John came to ask him what promotion they might expect. They were two of the most energetic of the lot, called "Sons of Thunder," by the rest, being noisy and always in the midst of some sort of a storm. They had joined the ranks because they liked him, but with no very definite idea of what it was all about; and now they wanted to know where the enterprise was heading, and just what there would be in it for them.

"Master," they said, "we want to ask what plans you have in mind for us. You're going to need big men around you when you establish your kingdom; our ambition is to sit on either side of you, one on your right hand and the other on your left."

Who can object to that attitude? If a man fails to look after himself, certainly no one will look after him. If you want a big place, go ask for it. That's the way to get ahead.

Jesus answered with a sentence which sounds poetically absurd.

"Whosoever will be great among you, shall be your minister," he said, "and whosoever of you will be the chiefest, shall be servant of all."

A fine piece of rhetoric, now isn't it? Be a good servant and you will be great; be the best possible servant and you will occupy the highest possible place. Nice idealistic talk but utterly impractical; nothing to take seriously in a common sense world. That is just what men thought for some hundreds of years; and then, quite suddenly, Business woke up to a great discovery. You will hear that discovery proclaimed in every sales convention as something distinctly modern and up to date. It is emblazoned in the advertising pages of every magazine.

Look through those pages.

Here is the advertisement of an automobile company, one of the greatest in the world. And why is it greatest? On what does it base its claim to leadership? On its huge factories and financial strength? They are never mentioned. On its army of workmen or its high salaried executives? You might read its advertisements for years without suspecting that it had either. No. "We are great because of our service," the advertisements cry. "We will crawl under your car oftener and get our backs dirtier than any of our competitors. Drive up to our service stations and ask for anything at all—it will be granted cheerfully. We serve; therefore we grow."

A manufacturer of shoes makes the same boast in other terms. "We put ourselves at your feet and give you everything that you can possibly demand." Manufacturers of building equipment, of clothes, of food; presidents of railroads and steamship companies; the heads of banks and investment houses—*all* of them tell the same story. "Service is what we are here for," they exclaim. They call it the "spirit of modern business"; they suppose, most of them, that it is something very new. But Jesus preached it more than nineteen hundred years ago. . . .

"If you're forever thinking about saving your life," Jesus said, "you'll lose it; but the man who loses his life shall find it."

Because he said it and he was a religious teacher, because it's printed in the Bible, the world has dismissed it as high minded ethics but not hard headed sense. But look again! . . .

What did Henry Ford mean, one spring morning, when he tipped a kitchen chair back against the whitewashed wall of his tractor plant and talked about his career?

"Have you ever noticed that the man who starts out in life with a determination to make money, never makes very much?" he asked. It was rather a startling question; and without waiting for my comment he went on to answer it: "He may gather together a competence, of course, a few tens of thousands or even hundreds of thousands, but he'll never amass a really great fortune. But let a man start out in life to build something better and sell it cheaper than it has ever been built or sold before —let him have *that* determination, and give his whole self to it —and the money will roll in so fast that it will bury him if he doesn't look out.

"When we were building our original model, do you suppose that it was money we were thinking about? Of course we expected that it would be profitable, if it succeeded, but that wasn't in the front of our minds. We wanted to make a car so cheap that every family in the United States could afford to have one. So we worked morning, noon and night, until our muscles ached and our nerves were so ragged that it seemed as if we just couldn't stand it to hear any one mention the word automobile again. One night, when we were almost at the breaking point I said to the boys, 'Well, there's one consolation,' I said. 'Nobody can take this business away from us unless he's willing to work harder than we've worked.' And so far," he concluded with a whimsical smile, "nobody has been willing to do that." . . .

"Whosoever shall compel thee to go a mile," said Jesus, "go with him twain."

Which means, I take it, "do more than is required of you, do twice as much." Another startling bit of business advice. Where will a man ever get, you ask, if he delivers twice as much as he is paid to deliver? The answer is that unless he's a fool he will probably get to and stay at the top. I remember once traveling from Chicago to New York on the Twentieth Century Limited. We were due in the Grand Central Station at nine-forty, a nice leisurely hour, and three of us who were traveling together decided to make a comfortable morning of it. We got out of our berths at a quarter after eight, shaved and dressed and half an hour later were making our way back to the dining-car.

A door to one of the drawing-rooms was open, and as we walked by we could hardly keep from looking in. The bed in the room had been made up long since; a table stood between the windows, and at the table, buried in work, was a man whose face the newspapers have made familiar to every one. He had been Governor of New York, a Justice of the Supreme Court, a candidate for the Presidency of the United States, and was—at the time—practising law and reputed to be earning much more than a hundred thousand dollars a year.

My companions and I were young men; he was well along in middle life. We were poor and unknown; he was rich and famous. We were doing all that was required of us. We were up and dressed and would be ready for business when the train pulled in at a little before ten. But this man, of whom nothing was actually required, was doing far more. I thought to myself as we passed on to our leisurely breakfast, "That explains him; now I understand Hughes."

I have several times been in the offices of J. P. Morgan and Company after six o'clock in the evening. I remember vividly the mental picture which I once had of what such a private banking house must be—the partners coming down in limousines at eleven and leaving at three, after having given their nonchalant approval to a million dollar deal. But on the occasion of one of the visits to which I refer the offices were closed. The clerks, and assistants and even the elevator men had gone, leaving only night-watchmen. Night-watchmen, *and* some of the partners. There seem to be always lights in the partners' offices no matter what the hour. Of the office force it is required that they travel the one mile which lies between nine o'clock in the morning and five o'clock at night. But the partners travel the second mile; have always traveled it all their lives; and are partners *because* they have. . . .

So we have the main points of his [Jesus'] business philosophy:

1. Whoever will be great must render great service.
2. Whoever will find himself at the top must be willing to lose himself at the bottom.
3. The big rewards come to those who travel the second, undemanded mile.

Judas would have sneered at all this. Not a bad fellow at heart, he had the virtues and the weaknesses of the small bore business man. He was "hard-boiled," and proud of it; he "looked out for Number One." It was no easy job being treasurer for a lot of idealists, Judas would have you know. He held the bag and gave every cent a good tight squeeze before he let it pass. When the grateful woman broke her box of costly ointment over Jesus' feet the other disciples thought it was fine, but he knew better. "Pretty wasteful business," he grumbled to himself. The big talk of the others about "thrones" and "kingdoms" and "victory" did not fool him; he could read a balance sheet, and he knew that the jig was up. So he made his private little deal with the priests, probably supposing that Jesus would be arrested, reproved and warned not to preach in Jerusalem again. "I will get mine and retire," he said to himself. Said Jesus, "I, if I be lifted up (on the cross; that is to say, if I lose my life) will draw all men to me." Each made his decision and received his reward.

We have quoted some men of conspicuous success, but the same sound principles apply to every walk of life. Great progress will be made in the world when we rid ourselves of the idea that there is a difference between *work* and *religious work*. We have been taught that a man's daily business activities are selfish, and that only the time which he devotes to church meetings and social service activities is consecrated. Ask any ten people what Jesus meant by his "Father's business," and nine of them will answer "preaching." To interpret the words in this narrow sense is to lose the real significance of his life. It was not to preach that he came into the world; nor to teach; nor to heal. These are all departments of his Father's business, but the business itself is far larger, more inclusive. For if human life has any significance it is this—that God has set going here an experiment to which all His resources are committed. He seeks to develop perfect human beings, superior to circumstance, victorious over Fate. No single kind of human talent or effort can be spared if the experiment is to succeed. The race must be fed and clothed and housed and transported, as well as preached to, and taught and healed. Thus *all* business is his Father's business. All work is worship; all useful service prayer. And whoever works wholeheartedly at any worthy calling is a co-worker with the Almighty in the great surprise which He has initiated but which He can never finish without the help of men. . . .

The Gospel story puts the dramatic climax into a single sentence:

Jesus, therefore, perceiving that they were about to come and take him by force to make him king, withdrew again into the mountain himself alone.

In that hour of crisis he proved his right to be the silent partner in every modern business; to sit at the head of every directors' table. There is no mere theorizing in his words; he speaks out of what he himself has proved. If he says that a man's work is more eternally important than any title, he has a right to speak. He himself refused the highest title. If he says that there are things more vital than merely making money, let no one question his authority. He was handed the wealth of a nation and handed it back again. Idealist he is, but there is nothing in the whole hard world so practical as his ideals. "There is a success which is greater than wealth or titles," he says. "It comes through making your work an instrument of greater service, and larger living to your fellow men and women. *This* is my Father's business and he needs your help."

He told one business story which should be published every year in all magazines of business, all trade papers, all house organs. It concerned a certain rich man whose enterprises prospered beyond all his expectations. His land "brought forth plentifully," so much so that he said to himself: "What shall I do, because I have no room where to bestow my fruits?"

And he said: "This will I do; I will pull down my barns and build greater; and there will I bestow all my fruits and my goods."

And I will say to my soul, "Soul, thou hast much goods laid up for many years; take thine ease, eat, drink and be merry."

But God said, "Thou fool, this night thy soul shall be required of thee."

The poor fool had regarded his business as nothing but a means of escape from business. He had hoarded his wealth, denying every generous impulse; spent his health, forfeiting every chance for wholesome enjoyment; sacrificed the joy of living for a selfish satisfaction that he hoped was coming when he had made his pile. And Fate laughed in his face. He thought he had provided for every contingency, but the one great Event which is always unexpected came like a thief in the night and found him unprepared. . . .

With that business anecdote should be published another, which is also a tragedy. It concerns the little hotel in Bethlehem, "the inn."

The mother of Jesus of Nazareth knocked at its doors and could not come in. It might have sheltered the greatest event in human history, and it lost its chance.

Why? Why was Jesus born in a stable? Because the people

in the inn were vicious or hostile? Not in the least. The inn was full, that was all; every room was taken by folk who had affairs to attend to and money to spend. It was busy.

There was no "room in the inn."

Men's lives are sometimes like that inn.

You know a man whose heart is broken because his son is a fool. Yet deep within himself he knows that the fault is his own. All through the formative years of the boy's development, he never gave him any time. Not that he didn't love the boy; but he was busy. There was no room for family life; and his son is a fool.

You know men whose health is gone; men whose taste for reading and music and art is gone. Men who have literally no interests in life beyond the office which has become a mere treadmill whereon their days are ground away.

In the process of being successful they have sacrificed success. Never once forgetting themselves they have forgotten everything else. This is not Jesus' idea of what a life should be. He, who refused to turn aside from his business to become a king, was never too busy to turn aside for a sick man, a friend, a little child. He never forgot that one night his mother had stood on a threshold where there was no welcome.

The threshold of the little inn in Bethlehem. It was so busy that the greatest event in history knocked at its doors
—and could not come in.

PART 5

THE YOUNGER GENERATION

A Debate About Morality

The following survey of the morality of the nation's youth was conducted by *The Literary Digest* in May 1921. Already the battle lines had formed over the questions of skirt lengths and new dances like the shimmy. What emerges from this survey is a divergence of opinion over the question of whether the young of the Twenties were merely in conflict with their elders, as young people had always been, or whether their behavior was new, a new low in public display and private behavior. The distaste of the traditionalists, including some stolid college editors, is clear enough, as is something of the gaiety of those who failed to see a portent of doom in the shortening skirts. Appropriately concluding with the worry that a reaction might set in that would destroy all that the younger generation had worked and played for, this survey is a revealing social document of the early Twenties.

Is "the old-fashioned girl," with all that she stands for in sweetness, modesty, and innocence, in danger of becoming extinct? Or was she really no better nor worse than the "up-to-date" girl—who, in turn, will become "the old-fashioned girl" to a later generation? Is it even possible, as a small but impressive minority would have us believe, that the girl of to-day has

---

From "Is the Younger Generation in Peril?" *The Literary Digest*, LXIX, no. 7 (May 14, 1921), 9–12, 58, 61, 63–64, 66–67, 69–70, 72, 73.

certain new virtues of "frankness, sincerity, seriousness of purpose," lives on "a higher level of morality," and is on the whole "more clean-minded and clean-lived" than her predecessors?

From Pope Benedict's pronouncement against "the present immodesty and extravagance in women's dress," to the widely copied protests of a Brown University student-editor against girls who wear too few clothes and require too much "petting," the press of the world in general, and of America in particular, is having much to say about "the present relaxation of morals and manners among young men and women." College presidents, famous divines, prominent novelists, and grave professors of sociology have joined the controversy. Thus, Franklin H. Giddings, author and Professor of Sociology at Columbia University, emits a counterblast to the many indictments of present conditions in the perhaps extreme pronouncement that "whether girls wear their skirts long or short makes as much difference as whether a man parts his hair in the middle or on the side." He concludes that "our moral tone is no lower than it was in the days of our mothers or our grandmothers, or even in the days of our great-grandmothers." The Professor does not question, however, the generally exprest opinion that the young people of to-day live in a more "free-and-easy" social atmosphere than surrounded their mothers. "We can't have anything without having too much of it," said William James, and Alexander Black, the novelist, quotes his philosophy in admitting that, in specific times and places, we may be having "too much" of this relaxation. The point of greatest disagreement comes up with the question of morality in general. "Do modern modes in dressing, dancing, and social intercourse," as an Eastern college paper phrases the question, "really mean that the present generation is less moral than the preceding one?" The answers, as given by college and school authorities, religious editors, the editors of student magazines, and the general press seem to be fairly evenly divided between attack and defense. It has been called the most two-sided question of the hour.

In the midst of the discussion, pro and con, a good deal is being done to check the tendency toward laxity among boys and girls of high-school age, where, in the belief of many observers, the greatest danger, or the only real danger, lies. We are reminded that supervision is always necessary here, and even so convinced a champion of modern ideas in manners and morals as the New York *Morning Telegraph* is stirred to protests by a report from Chicago that co-educational institutions in Illinois will not be responsible for the moral conduct of their girls. *The Telegraph* objects:

> Girls, when away from home, should not be thrown upon their own resources at an age when their judgment is unripe and their ability to steer their own course at best undeveloped. We are further informed that hereafter college dances will be unchaperoned and that self-reliance will be preached instead. This may make it easy on the deans of women, but it also may result disastrously in particular cases. Parents will hesitate before committing their daughters to institutions which, in striving to be up to date, have overlooked one of the most obvious truths in nature.

Aside from the usual protective measures, however, a number of organizations are unusually active on the ground that there is an unusual amount of immodest dressing and conduct. The Y. W. C. A. is conducting a national campaign among high-school girls. . . . [It] is also, through its press department, supplying newspapers with material which appears under such suggestive head-lines as "Working Girls Responsive to Modesty Appeal"; "High Heels Losing Ground Even in France"; and "It Isn't What the Girl Does; It's Just the Way She Does It." Photographs, pointing morals in dress and conduct, are also supplied. . . .

. . . The Woman's Auxiliary of the Episcopal Church has entered upon a nation-wide campaign, reports the New York *Times,* and it has "definite progress to report." It is conducting a series of meetings for girls throughout the country, to discuss

the problem of "upholding standards." The Catholic Arch-
bishop of the Ohio diocese has issued a warning against the
"toddle" and "shimmy" and also against "bare female shoulders." A bill which has passed both the New York Assembly
and Senate gives the Commissioner of Licenses in New York
the right to act as a censor of dances. In a number of State
legislatures, bills have been introduced aiming at regulation
of women's dress, reports the New York *American:*

In Utah a statute providing fine and imprisonment for those who
wear on the streets skirts higher than three inches above the ankle is
pending. The Philadelphia "moral gown," with its seven and a half
inches of "see level," as one visitor called it, would cease to be moral
in Utah if this law goes through.

A bill is before the Virginia legislature which would raise the
décolletage—front and back. It provides that no woman shall be
permitted to wear a shirtwaist or evening gown displaying more
than three inches of her throat. She must not have skirts higher than
four inches above the ground or any garment of "diaphanous material."

In Ohio a bill has been drafted prescribing that no *décolleté* shall
be more than two inches in depth and that no garment composed of
any transparent material shall be sold, nor any "garment which un-
duly displays or accentuates the lines of the female figure."

"And no female over fourteen years of age," says this same measure, "shall wear a skirt which does not reach to that part of the foot
known as the instep."

Similar legislation, differing only in the inches above the ground
and the inches below the neck, has been offered in New Jersey,
South Carolina, Kansas, Iowa, Pennsylvania, and a full dozen other
States.

From the three bills actually cited it would seem that, were these
to become laws, the dress with its four-inch-high skirt which would
be moral in Virginia would be immodest in Utah, while both the
Utah and Virginia skirts would be wicked enough in Ohio to make
their wearers subject to fine or imprisonment. Undoubtedly, other
State laws would add to this confusion, and therefore a standardiza-

tion acceptable to all is something that might ultimately be welcomed by women.

In Philadelphia a Dress-Reform Committee of prominent citizens decided to attack the problem in a businesslike way, and settle from the mouths of the critics themselves, once and for all, just what is immodest dress. A questionnaire was sent to 1,160 clergymen of all denominations in and near Philadelphia. Replies were received from them all, but examination, we are told, revealed that the clergy "were absolutely at odds themselves. There was far from a unanimous verdict even on the preliminary query as to whether the modern extreme styles are harmful to the morals of the wearers and to masculine observers." The Dress Committee adopted the device of striking an average of the answers and building a dress upon these averages, after submitting specifications and sketches to the clergymen. The design . . . was accepted by the majority, "altho there still remained two fairly strong minority parties, one of which thought the dress was not yet conservative enough, while the other thought it was too conservative."

Denunciation and defense center more specially, however, about modern dances and the conditions that surround the associations of boys and girls at these affairs. Conditions are "appalling," declares one critic who may be expected to speak with authority, a dean of women in a Midwestern college. "There is nothing wrong with the girl of to-day," insists another dean of women, also stationed at a Midwestern college, and speaking on the basis of a wide acquaintance with practically the same set of conditions. It is the perennial case of the "youngsters *versus* the oldsters," a Princeton College wit remarks, but the line-up of opinion somewhat disarranges his idea, for many "oldsters" are found championing the new and freer ways of the present generation, while numerous uncompromising enemies of the modern dance, abbreviated clothes, and "relaxed morals and manners" are to be found among those whose years classify them with the youngsters. THE DIGEST, by way of gathering national sentiment on the whole question, lately addrest a circular letter to the religious editors of the country, to the presidents of colleges and universities, and to the editors of college papers, asking for their opinions upon the charges of "lax standards" which have been freely made throughout the country, and for remedial suggestions, in case conditions seemed to demand remedies. These replies have been correlated with material on the same subject collected from newspapers and magazines in THE DIGEST office.

The comment, as received from religious editors, editors of student papers, and college deans and presidents, shows a surprizingly even division of opinion between those who believe that conditions are unusually bad and those who believe that they are not. The editors of college papers, themselves distinctly to be classed with the youngsters, show a larger proportion of "moral alarmists," as one of their number calls the reformist element, than do the presidents and deans of colleges. In round numbers, 55 college student-editors believe that conditions are unusually bad as against 38 who believe that they are not. Of the college presidents and deans, the proportion stands 52 against 43. The religious press, as might have been expected, shows a larger ratio of condemnation. Fifty-three religious editors believe we are having something like an immorality wave, as against six who believe that we are not. Fifteen of the replies in this category are difficult to classify, unless the writers be placed with the defenders of modernity on the ground that they do not consider present conditions worse than usual. Allowance must be made in these replies for a considerable number of editors of denominations which oppose dancing in any form. In forty-two of the colleges whose presidents replied, dancing is prohibited. Of the total number of replies received, counting out those religious editors who condemn dancing *per se*, without expressing any opinion as to the present conditions, counting out also the college professors who reply merely that dancing is prohibited in their institutions, the writers divide on the question in the order of 130 to 102, the first figure representing those who believe that we are in the midst of a dangerous moral decline, especially as it affects the younger generation. Including all the opponents of dancing, the figures would stand 202 to 102. . . .

Dividing the replies roughly into those which attack and those which defend modern manners and morals, the student-editors of the country, most of them young men, are found to furnish quite as severe an indictment as is presented by their elders. The defense, while not numerically so well represented, is strongly presented by student-editors chiefly representing the larger colleges. The attack, which will be presented first, comes almost entirely from the smaller institutions. This, of course, raises the old question whether the big or the little college has the more brains and character, which is another story. The Hobart College *Herald* (Geneva, N. Y.) sums up the arguments of many of the attackers in this thoughtful fashion:

The outstanding objection to the modern dance is that it is immodest and lacking in grace. It is not based on the natural and harmless instinct for rhythm, but on a craving for abnormal excitement.

And what is it leading to? The dance in its process of its degradation has passed from slight impropriety to indecency, and now threatens to become brazenly shameless. From graceful coordination of movement it has become a syncopated embrace.

Even the most callous devotee of modern dancing can not think with unconcern of the danger involved in any further excess. For American morals have undoubtedly degenerated with the dance.

It can not be denied that many who indulge in modern dancing do not realize the nature of the incentive which leads them to do so. They like to dance; it becomes a habit, a fascinating obsession. Continual debauches of highly emotional character weaken the moral fiber. When a newer and more daring dance is introduced it is immediately accepted without question.

Were this thoughtless immodesty restricted to the ballroom the danger would be great enough, but it is unconsciously carried into every-day life. Truly, then, it is imperative that a remedy be sought to arrest the development of the modern dance before this perilous state gets beyond control.

In spite of the gallant remark of the Michigan Agricultural College *Holcad*, in an editorial entitled "Haven't We Gone a Bit too Far?" that "the men are just as much to blame as the girls," a great many student-editors, mostly, as one of them points out, men, avail themselves of the Adamic tradition to point an accusing finger. From the New York University *News* we quote the following:

Overlooking the physiological aspects of women's clothing, there is a strong moral aspect to this laxity of dress. When every dancing step discloses the entire contour of the dancer, it is small wonder that moralists are becoming alarmed. The materials, also, from which women's evening dresses are made are generally of transparent cobweb. There is a minimum of clothes and a maximum of cosmetics, head-decorations, fans, and jewelry. It is, indeed, an alarming situation when our twentieth-century débutante comes out arrayed like a South Sea Island savage. . . .

The University of Maryland *Review* finds some of the dances "mere animal exhibitions of agility and feeling. There is nothing of grace in them, and such dances serve as an excuse for actions that would be severely censored anywhere but on the modern dance floor." The Mercer University *Cluster* considers that "the young people who take part in them can not fail to lose their fine sense of decency and propriety. No boy who has high ideals would allow his sister to take part where such dances are tolerated." *The Round Up*, of the New Mexico College of Agriculture and Mechanic Arts, believes that dancing such as is being done there "will lead to certain degeneration of decent society, and it is our understanding that this part of the country is no worse than any other." The writer objects further:

To glide gracefully over a floor, keeping time to the rhythm and harmony of music, is a pleasant recreation and is pleasing to witness, but to jig and hop around like a chicken on a red-hot stove, at the same time shaking the body until it quivers like a disturbed glass of jell-o, is not only tremendously suggestive but is an offense against common decency that would not be permitted in a semirespectable road-house.

The University of Illinois *Siren* explains for these objectors: ". . . if bow legs and thick ankles won't curb the present patent indecency in women's dress, morality surely hasn't any chance."

This same publication, however, furnishes a vivid arraignment of the modern dance, in the comments of a musician who played for college dances. The musician decided, one day, that he would play for no more such dances, and he gives his reason in these words:

The girls—some of them, not all of them, of course—dance by me with their eyes closed, their cheeks inflamed, a little line of passion across their brows. They cling to their partners; they cling and clutch. They are like Madonnas, some of them, and yet they dance . . . that way. The men who use us for an audience are not capable—quite—of being terrible. They are exhibitors, rather. They show us the closed eyes and dusky-red cheeks of their partners— they wink at us, they turn their eyes heavenward, as if to say, "You birds will know me, I wager, when next you see me. See what a state this girl is in. Hasn't she fallen for me, tho? Look at her; look at her!" —then they toddle out of sight. . . .

. . . The Dartmouth *Jack-o'-Lantern* attacks the subject in this frivolous manner, somewhat characteristic of the more sophisticated student papers:

We're a dizzy people. The shimmy proves that, without the ghost of a need for further proof. We—any of us—will travel for miles on a black night through mud and rain, we will endure any discomfort, eventually to arrive at a place where the shimmy is being shaken. Young girls, pretty girls, vivacious girls trust themselves to come safely through the identical experiences many of their wartime sweethearts were enduring in France. They will shimmy for hours, indefinitely, undergoing the pangs of hunger and increasing bodily fatigue. The mental side probably is not very much taxed. The effect seems merely to be that next night and thereafter they are ready to shimmy wherever the shimmy is being vibrated. All this doesn't prove anything, except that we're a dizzy lot!

The Cornell *Widow*, known in the periodical world as one of the cleverest and best-edited of student publications, presents this rimed review of the changes that dancing has undergone:

Times have waxed and waned a lot, as old-timers can recall, and the dancing now is not what it used to be at all; only awkward rubes and hicks execute the bows and kicks that were clever parlor tricks when our *paters* threw a ball. Our progenitors took pleasure in a slow and solemn way; they would tread a stately measure that was anything but gay, and the orchestra would render sentimental stuff and tender which the folks of either gender wouldn't listen to to-day. With a flock of flutes and 'cellos, plus a harp and silver horn, these accomplished music fellows would play on till early morn; they could keep "Blue Danube" flowing without letting up or slowing, till the bantams started crowing and they'd leave to hoe the corn. . . .

And as for the maids of yesterday and of to-day, says *The Widow:*

They used to wrap their hair in knobs fantastic, high, and queer; but now they cut it short in bobs or curl it round their ear. The skirts they wore would scrape the street, and catch the dust and germs; they're now so far above their feet, they're not on speaking terms. The things they do and wear to-day, and never bat an eye, would make their fogy forebears gray, they'd curl right up and die. . . .

THE "FLAPPER PROBLEM" IN THE NEWSPAPERS

The same general moral, that the greatest danger is to be found among girls of high-school age, is pointed by a series of widely advertised full-page articles in the Boston *Sunday Advertiser*. "The girl of fourteen is the problem of to-day," we are told, in large, black-faced letters, in the introduction to one of the pages of exposure and criticism. Among the "modern conditions" assigned as causes of trouble are:

"1. Auto 'pickups.'
"2. Modern dances and commercialized dance halls.
"3. Modern fashions.
"4. The pocket-flask habit, an outgrowth of prohibition.
"5. The occasional unclean movie.

"But the first blame is being placed on the mother—the child-girl's first guardian." . . .

Perhaps half of the several hundred recommendations received are summed up in a letter from President Gaines, of Agnes Scott College, Decatur, Ga. He suggests as remedies:

First, the influence of the home. I am informed that in many places parents themselves indulge in modern dances. What can be expected of their daughters but to follow their example? I am also informed that frequently mothers approve of the way in which their daughters dress. Can we not secure the cooperation and influence of the home in correcting these deplorable evils?

My second suggestion is to secure the influence of the press.

My third suggestion is that the entire influence of religion shall be exerted against these great evils. I suggest that all church papers, the influence of the pulpits of all the churches, should be brought to bear against these evils.

My fourth suggestion is to enlist the colleges. In the colleges of the country are the future leaders. If they can be enlisted even while they are in college they may be able to begin a crusade against these evils which will be most effective. Especially should this be true of the colleges for women.

These four great centers of influence could do much toward creating a healthy public sentiment which would counteract the evils of which you speak—namely, the home, the press, the church, and the college.

The college press, by and large, consider it a hopeful sign that the movement for reform should come, as is the case in so many colleges, from the students themselves. The immediate methods may vary somewhat, but in scores of institutions, the student-editors testify, various student governing associations have been able to do away with suggestive dancing and clothing. The Oberlin College *Review* states that the objectionable dances have been banned by the influence of the recreational director and some of the students. The daily *Nebraskan* says that they have not been bothered much by "the Eastern dances," but does admit that "the knee-length dresses of the modern girl have cast modesty from the dictionary," and says that recently some of the girls in the upper classes, "who are by no means the prudes at this school," at a large mass-meeting "passed resolutions to the effect that an era of simple dress for co-eds should be launched at Nebraska University," and advises:

If our country is to return to normalcy again in regard to dress, we must not look on with a critic's eye and take on the guise of reformers, but we must wear sensible clothes ourselves. If we start this as the "fad" of the day, it will not be long until everybody is wearing simple garments because it is "being done." . . .

The Smith College *Monthly* writes that Smith College students have taken a decided stand in favor of dress reform and are conducting a vigorous campaign against immodest clothing. In an editorial in that paper an attempt is made to explain the "petting" youngsters in a way both kindly and keen:

So long as the older generation "views with alarm," so long will the younger generation glory in its naughtiness and invent prodigious reasons.

The real reason is, I believe, simply this: young people are forced by the exigencies, customs, and inventions of modern life—such as newspapers, magazines, "movies," telephones, and facilitated modes of travel—to be cognizant at an early age of the world about them. Formerly, the family was a child's world till he left it for the larger one of school or business; nowadays, he comes in contact with persons, facts, and problems not at all connected with family affairs almost as soon as he can read and can run about by himself. He has to make up his mind for himself by himself; and he early learns the value of experiment.

Young men and women discover and face the idea of love by themselves; they experiment in that as in other things—not reckless, as is commonly supposed, but cautious.

As for remedy—well, gone long ago are the days when an evil might be checked by crying "Wicked!" Passing now is the detracting influence of "Danger!" and coming soon, I hope, the days when the only warning necessary will be "Foolish!" The "wild young people of to-day" are not fools, and do not want to be considered so. They will change their ways as soon as they have proved to themselves that their ways are—not wrong, not dangerous, but—unnecessary.

"There Is Nothing Wrong with the Girl of To-day"

A thoroughgoing optimist appears, ready to try conclusions with practically every real pessimist on the girl question. "There is nothing wrong with the girl of to-day," asserts the Dean of Women of Northwestern University, and she finds plenty of authorities, with excellent opportunities for observation, who agree with her. Several critics, not satisfied with denying the allegation that we are experiencing "an immorality wave," declare that, in spite of much talk and certain appearances, the younger generation of to-day is actually better, "more clean-minded and clean-lived," than its predecessors. Such is the view of President Sills, of Bowdoin College, Brunswick, Maine, who writes:

Ever since the time of Horace at least each generation has thought the succeeding generation worse than anything that has gone before, in manners and morals, and in criticising the youth of the present day we ought, I think, to keep this in mind. It is my opinion that the influence, to quote from your letter, "exercised upon our young people by some of the new dances and the costumes worn by those attending them" is much more patent on the side of manners than on the side of morals. The undergraduate of the present day is, I am sure, as good as any of his predecessors, probably more clean-minded and clean-lived. If he can be taught to avoid what is vulgar and cheap, and also be made to see that some of the new dances are very silly, some good might result.

"There has been some gain for women in the newer modes of dress which give them greater freedom of action and tend to better health," President Wilbur, of Stanford University, points out. "The oncoming generation will have grown accustomed to the exposure of limbs and neck and will not react as does the passing generation." President Smith, of Washington and Lee University, Lexington, Va., after admitting that abuses of the freer modern manners may have occurred, presents the following considerations which, he says, "may serve to comfort those inclined to pessimism":

1. Ignorant innocence is not true purity nor is prudery true modesty. Freedom of intercourse and constant association of boys and girls does not increase but rather diminishes sex-consciousness and immorality. And I have long since come to the conclusion that the suggestiveness of any mode of dress disappears entirely as soon as we become thoroughly accustomed to it. To the orthodox Persian a woman's uncovered face is shamelessly indecent and suggestive.

2. I have spent a lifetime in constant association with young people, and I am fully convinced that, surprizing as it may seem, in view of present social laxity, the level of sexual morality is higher to-day than formerly in those localities with which I am familiar.

3. The present dancing mania and general social laxity is probably a passing 'craze,' due to exceptional present conditions, which is already awakening universal condemnation, and like most epidemics will prove temporary and self-limited. . . .

COLLEGE EDITORS IN DEFENSE OF THE MODERN GIRL

If some college student-editors have taken the lead in speaking harshly to and about the short-skirted, free-acting, free-talking girl of to-day, others of the youthful brotherhood present defenses equally pungent and pointed. Thus *The Tartan*, the newspaper of the Carnegie Institute of Technology at Pittsburgh, rises up to defend the girl of to-day:

Just at present it seems to be the custom for every college paper to take a slam at the girls. It would appear that the younger generation is going to rack and ruin unless a halt is called in the terrible downward trend of the fashions. No ray of hope lightens the gloom which is, in the minds of most of our contemporaries, descending upon our colleges in the form of an assurance that all the young women are going from bad to worse. They not only wear clothes which would shock the most sophisticated of a few years back, but they dance—well, they dance simply awful.

Of course girls are wearing shorter skirts than they have ever worn before. But what wholesome, clean-minded man would not rather see a woman in a sane, short skirt, with plenty of freedom to move as nature intended she should, than in one of the "sheath" creations which emphasized her every contour while hobbling her movements almost beyond endurance, sweeping the ground in an attempt to trip her at every step. And yet we are supposed to have become so much more immodest with the innovation of the sensible short skirt.

Yet the gentler sex must be reformed before it is too late, say our virtuous youth. We have attended several dances during the last week, and no shocking décolletées were noticed except possibly on matrons who should have known better. The débutantes were even conservative in their manner of covering the throat. . . .

The Columbia *Spectator*, of Columbia University, New York, speaks for the metropolitan college:

The day is past when trusting parents confine their offspring to convents and monasteries, bringing them forth in due season, mature, worldly innocent, unsophisticated, and still none the less educated. Living as the college student of to-day does, in the heart of New York, Chicago, Boston, or San Francisco, in direct touch with city life—in fact, a part and parcel of it—that the scholar should conduct himself any differently from those about him is impossible. . . .

The *Spectator's* colleague, the Columbia *Jester,* with the liberty traditionally permitted to cap and bells, declares that it stands—

Unequivocally and irrevocably for the continuance of "petting" as a national institution, in order to guarantee sufficient contributions to bring out one magazine a month. We fail to take a more serious view of the situation, because we feel that the situation exists largely in the minds of bloodthirsty reformers and copy-by-the-inch hounds. They always have and they always will—which refers to fretting as well as petting. . . .

Two of the largest and best-known women's colleges in the East, Wellesley and Bryn Mawr, reply that their own dances have given them little concern, since, in the words of Wellesley's director of publicity, "objectionable and extreme dances are so comparatively rare."

JOURNALISTS AND AUTHORS WHO SEE NO "MORAL DECLINE"

"Salvation this new generation doubtless needs—like every other. But it has its virtues and they are large ones, we are convinced—candor, frankness, sincerity, seriousness of purpose, for a few items." So an editorial writer in the New York *Tribune* takes issue with the present "prophets of evil" in the social world. . . .

. . . Gertrude Atherton, the novelist, writing in *The Forum,* is similarly indignant with traducers of the new social freedom. "Take it all in all, it seems to me that if the United States of America is conquered by internal or external enemies," she writes, "it will not be from bad morals but smug stupidity." An editorial writer in *The Nation* also has this fear that we will be injured, not by immorality growing out of relaxed manners, but rather by the reaction that is likely to follow our present little taste of frankness and naturalness in the social relationships. Taking a historical view, he says:

> The rank and file of the virtues have not greatly changed, so far as we can see, during the comparatively few years in the life of the race over which the memory of man runs. All that appears is a certain pendulum swing from one repression or indulgence to another, reaction setting in whenever the virtues or vices of an age begin to bore it. Instead of repining that the present generation is unmitigably naughty, we observe that drunkenness throughout the world is pretty certainly on the decline and that the improving status of women bids fair to make them able to look out for themselves—a condition which we candidly prefer to all the chivalry that ever was invented. What worries us is not the age itself but the fear that its hilarities portend a reaction in the direction of insipid, smug propriety.

20 / JOHN F. CARTER, JR.

The Overnight Realists

Lamenting the supposed degeneration of the young became a favorite indoor sport in the Twenties. There was supposed to be a "revolution in morals" leading to flagrant sexuality, full speakeasies, social and political irresponsibility, and, most important, a repudiation of the values which supposedly had sustained Western civilization since the beginning of the Christian era. The charges against the young people were constructed of the usual mixture of truth and hysteria, although it was reasonably clear that something was happening. The war was the key to the new mood, one composed of a new toughness of mind, a frank repudiation of the Victorian ethic, and a very deep distrust of the rhetorical flourishes of the successful economic and political leaders. The delicacy and prettiness of the older generation, the young said, led to the most horrible war in human history. As John F. Carter (1897–   ), a journalist, later an economic specialist with the State Department, and still later a radio commentator with NBC, explains in the following selection, written in the year he was graduated from Yale, the young inherited a ruined world from their elders. Who were these "experienced and mature" defenders of traditional morality to instruct the young? If the world were ever to be put back together, Carter writes, the young would have to do it. And they would do it themselves, if Carter and his peers would or could have their own way.

For some months past the pages of our more conservative magazines have been crowded with pessimistic descriptions of the younger generation, as seen by their elders and, no doubt, their betters. Hardly a week goes by that I do not read some indignant treatise depicting our extravagance, the corruption of our manners, the futility of our existence, poured out in stiff, scared, shocked sentences before a sympathetic and horrified audience of fathers, mothers, and maiden aunts—but particularly maiden aunts.

In the May issue of the *Atlantic Monthly* appeared an article entitled 'Polite Society,' by a certain Mr. Grundy, the husband of a very old friend of my family. In kindly manner he

> Mentioned our virtues, it is true,
> But dwelt upon our vices, too.

'Chivalry and Modesty are dead. Modesty died first,' quoth he, but expressed the pious hope that all might yet be well if the

From " 'These Wild Young People,' By One of Them," *The Atlantic Monthly*, CXXVI (September 1920), 301–304. Copyright © 1920 by The Atlantic Monthly Company, Boston, Massachusetts 02116. Reprinted with permission.

oldsters would but be content to 'wait and see.' His article is one of the best-tempered and most gentlemanly of this long series of Jeremiads against 'these wild young people.' It is significant that it should be anonymous. In reading it, I could not help but be drawn to Mr. Grundy personally, but was forced to the conclusion that he, like everyone else who is writing about my generation, has very little idea of what he is talking about. I would not offend him for the world, and if I apostrophize him somewhat brutally in the following paragraphs, it is only because I am talking of him generically; also because his self-styled 'cousin' is present.

For Mrs. Katharine Fullerton Gerould has come forward as the latest volunteer prosecuting attorney, in her powerful 'Reflections of a Grundy Cousin,' in the August *Atlantic*. She has little or no patience with us. She disposes of all previous explanations of our degeneration in a series of short paragraphs, then launches into her own explanation: the decay of religion. She treats it as a primary cause, and with considerable effect. But I think she errs in not attempting to analyze the causes for such decay, which would bring her nearer to the ultimate truth.

A friend of mine has an uncle who, in his youth, was a wild, fast, extravagant young blood. His clothes were the amazement of even his fastest friends. He drank, he swore, he gambled, bringing his misdeeds to a climax by eloping with an heiress, a beautiful Philadelphian seraph, fascinated by this glittering Lucifer. Her family disowned her, and they fled to a distant and wild country. He was, in effect, a brilliant, worthless, attractive, and romantic person. Now he is the sedate deacon of a Boston Presbyterian church, *very* strong on morality in every shape, a terror to the young, with an impeccable business career, and a very dull family circle. Mrs. Gerould must know of similar cases, so why multiply instances? Just think how moral and unentertaining *our* generation will be when we have emerged from the 'roaring forties'!—and rejoice. . . .

I would like to say a few things about my generation.

In the first place, I would like to observe that the older generation had certainly pretty well ruined this world before passing it on to us. They give us this Thing, knocked to pieces, leaky, red-hot, threatening to blow up; and then they are surprised that we don't accept it with the same attitude of pretty, decorous enthusiasm with which they received it, 'way back in the eighteen-nineties, nicely painted, smoothly running, practically fool-proof. 'So simple that a child can run it!' But the child couldn't steer it. He hit every possible telegraph-pole, some of them twice, and ended with a head-on collision for which *we* shall have to pay the fines and damages. Now, with loving pride, they turn over their wreck to us; and, since we are not properly overwhelmed with loving gratitude, shake their heads and sigh, 'Dear! dear! We were so much better-mannered than these wild young people. But then we had the advantages of a good, strict, old-fashioned bringing-up!' How intensely *human* these oldsters are, after all, and how fallible! How they always blame us for not following precisely in their eminently correct footsteps!

Then again there is the matter of outlook. When these sentimental old world-wreckers were young, the world was such a different place—at least, so I gather from H. G. Wells's picture of the nineties, in *Joan and Peter*. Life for them was bright and pleasant. Like all normal youngsters, they had their little tin-pot ideals, their sweet little visions, their naïve enthusiasms, their nice little sets of beliefs. Christianity had emerged from the blow dealt by Darwin, emerged rather in the shape of social dogma. Man was a noble and perfectible creature. Women were angels (whom they smugly sweated in their industries and prostituted in their slums). Right was downing might. The nobility and the divine mission of the race were factors that led our fathers to work wholeheartedly for a millennium, which they caught a glimpse of just around the turn of the century.

Why, there were Hague Tribunals! International peace was at last assured, and according to current reports, never officially denied, the American delegates held out for the use of poison gas in warfare, just as the men of that generation were later to ruin Wilson's great ideal of a league of nations, on the ground that such a scheme was an invasion of American rights. But still, everything, masked by ingrained hypocrisy and prudishness, seemed simple, beautiful, inevitable.

Now my generation is disillusionized, and, I think, to a certain extent, brutalized, by the cataclysm which *their* complacent folly engendered. The acceleration of life for us has been so great that into the last few years have been crowded the experiences and the ideas of a normal lifetime. We have in our unregenerate youth learned the practicality and the cynicism that is safe only in unregenerate old age. We have been forced to become realists overnight, instead of idealists, as was our birthright. We have seen man at his lowest, woman at her lightest, in the terrible moral chaos of Europe. We have been forced to question, and in many cases to discard, the religion of our fathers. We have seen hideous peculation, greed, anger, hatred, malice, and all uncharitableness, unmasked and rampant and unashamed. We have been forced to live in an atmosphere of 'to-morrow we die,' and so, naturally, we drank and were merry. We have seen the rottenness and shortcomings of all governments, even the best and most stable. We have seen entire social systems overthrown, and our own called in question. In short, we have seen the inherent beastliness of the human race revealed in an infernal apocalypse.

It is the older generation who forced us to see all this, which has left us with social and political institutions staggering blind in the fierce white light that, for us, should beat only about the enthroned ideal. And now, through the soft-headed folly of these painfully shocked Grundys, we have that devastating

wisdom which is safe only for the burned-out embers of griz-
zled, cautious old men. We may be fire, but it was they who
made us play with gunpowder. And now they are surprised
that a great many of us, because they have taken away our
apple-cheeked ideals, are seriously considering whether or no
their game be worth *our* candle.

But, in justice to my generation, I think that I must admit
that most of us have realized that, whether or no it be worth
while, we must all play the game, as long as we are in it. And
I think that much of the hectic quality of our life is due to that
fact and to that alone. We are faced with staggering problems
and are forced to solve them, while the previous incumbents
are permitted a graceful and untroubled death. All my friends
are working and working hard. Most of the girls I know are
working. In one way or another, often unconsciously, the great
burden put upon us is being borne, and borne gallantly, by
that immodest, unchivalrous set of ne'er-do-wells, so delight-
fully portrayed by Mr. Grundy and the amazing young Fitzgerald. A keen interest in political and social problems, and a
determination to face the facts of life, ugly or beautiful, characterizes us, as it certainly did not characterize our fathers. We
won't shut our eyes to the truths we have learned. We have
faced so many unpleasant things already,—and faced them
pretty well,—that it is natural that we should keep it up.

Now I think that this is the aspect of our generation that
annoys the uncritical and deceives the unsuspecting oldsters
who are now met in judgment upon us: our devastating and
brutal frankness. And this is the quality in which we really
differ from our predecessors. We are frank with each other,
frank, or pretty nearly so, with our elders, frank in the way we
feel toward life and this badly damaged world. It may be a
disquieting and misleading habit, but is it a bad one? We find
some few things in the world that we like, and a whole lot that
we don't, and we are not afraid to say so or to give our reasons.
In earlier generations this was not the case. The young men

yearned to be glittering generalities, the young women to act like shy, sweet, innocent fawns—toward one another. And now, when grown up, they have come to believe that they actually were figures of pristine excellence, knightly chivalry, adorable modesty, and impeccable propriety. But I really doubt if they were so. Statistics relating to, let us say, the immorality of college students in the eighteen-eighties would not compare favorably with those of the present. However, now, as they look back on it, they see their youth through a mist of muslin, flannels, tennis, bicycles, Tennyson, Browning, and the Blue Danube waltz. The other things, the ugly things that we know about and talk about, must also have been there. But our elders didn't care or didn't dare to consider them, and now they are forgotten. We talk about them unabashed, and not necessarily with Presbyterian disapproval, and so they jump to the conclusion that we are thoroughly bad, and keep pestering us to make us good.

The trouble with them is that they can't seem to realize that we are busy, that what pleasure we snatch must be incidental and feverishly hurried. We have to make the most of our time. We actually haven't got so much time for the noble procrastinations of modesty or for the elaborate rigmarole of chivalry, and little patience for the lovely formulas of an ineffective faith. Let them die for a while! They did not seem to serve the world too well in its black hour. If they are inherently good they will come back, vital and untarnished. But just now we have a lot of work, 'old time is still a-flying,' and we must gather rosebuds while we may.

Oh! I know that we are a pretty bad lot, but has not that been true of every preceding generation? At least we have the courage to act accordingly. Our music is distinctly barbaric, our girls are distinctly *not* a mixture of arbutus and barbed-wire. We drink when we can and what we can, we gamble, we are extravagant—but we work, and that's about all that we can be expected to do; for, after all, we have just discovered that we

are all still very near to the Stone Age. The Grundys shake
their heads. They'll *make* us be good. Prohibition is put through
to stop our drinking, and hasn't stopped it. Bryan has plans to
curtail our philanderings, and he won't do any good. A Draco-
nian code is being hastily formulated at Washington and
elsewhere, to prevent us from, by any chance, making any alter-
ation in this present divinely constituted arrangement of things.
The oldsters stand dramatically with fingers and toes and noses
pressed against the bursting dykes. Let them! They won't do
any good. They can shackle us down, and still expect us to
repair their blunders, if they wish. But we shall not trouble
ourselves very much about them any more. Why should we?
What have they done? They have made us work as they never
had to work in all their padded lives—but we'll have our cakes
and ale for a' that.

For now we know our way about. We're not babes in the
wood, hunting for great, big, red strawberries, and confidently
expecting the Robin Red-Breasts to cover us up with pretty
leaves if we don't find them. We're men and women, long before our time, in the flower of our full-blooded youth. We have
brought back into civil life some of the recklessness and ability
that we were taught by war. We are also quite fatalistic in our
outlook on the tepid perils of tame living. All may yet crash to
the ground for aught that we can do about it. Terrible mistakes
will be made, but *we* shall at least make them intelligently and
insist, if we are to receive the strictures of the future, on doing
pretty much as we choose now.

Oh! I suppose that it's too bad that we aren't humble, starry-
eyed, shy, respectful innocents, standing reverently at their side
for instructions, playing pretty little games, in which they no
longer believe, except for us. But we aren't, and the best thing
the oldsters can do about it is to go into their respective back-
yards and dig for worms, great big pink ones—for the Grundy
tribe are now just about as important as they are, and they will

doubtless make company more congenial and docile than 'these
wild young people,' the men and women of my generation.

21 / SAMUEL HOPKINS ADAMS

A Flapper's Mentality

In the following passage from his popular novel, *Flaming Youth*,
Samuel Hopkins Adams (1871–1958), a journalist, novelist, film
writer, playwright, and social historian, caught a number of characteristics of the mind of the flapper. The following selection is a
letter written to Mona Fentriss, Pat's already dead mother, by
Robert Osterhout, a family friend. He is protesting the decision to
send Pat to a "Sisterhood School," and submits this analysis of Pat's
mind, talents, and interests as the basis of his objection. Pat, in this
excerpt, is important because she is not unusual, because she was
not a mindless hedonistic millionaire's daughter; she was a somewhat
earnest and relatively mild-mannered young lady whose strengths
and weaknesses, according to Adams, were symptomatic of her time
and place.

"If I could find it in my heart, dearest one, to blame you for
anything, it would be for sending little Pat to the Sisterhood
School." (So wrote Robert Osterhout to Mona Fentriss.) "With
the best of intentions they wreck a mind as thoroughly as
house-wreckers gut a building. It was your choice and I dare
not change it. Even if I could persuade Ralph to take her out
of that environment and send her to Bryn Mawr or Vassar or
Smith, which is where she ought to be, she would rebel. She

From Chap. XII, *Flaming Youth* (New York: Boni & Liveright, 1923),
pp. 125–130. Copyright ℝ 1951, Liveright Publishing Corporation, New
York. Reprinted by permission.

has a contempt for 'those rah-rah girls,' a prejudice bred of the shallow and self-sufficient snobbery which is the basic lesson of her scholastic experience. To be sure, they have finished her in the outward attributes of good form, but most of that is a natural heritage which any daughter of yours would have. She can be, when on exhibition, the most impeccable little creature, sparkling, and easy and natural and charmingly deferential toward the older people with whom she comes in contact—when she chooses. For the most part she elects to be calmly careless, slovenly of speech and manner, or lightly impudent. To have good breeding at call but not to waste it on most people—that is the cachet of her set.

"But these are surface matters. It is the inner woman—yes, beloved—our little Pat is coming to conscious and dynamic womanhood—which concerns me now and would concern you could you be here. Appalls me, too. But perhaps that is because my standards are the clumsy man-standards. What is she going to get out of life for herself? What does all this meaningless preparation, aside from the polishing process, look to? If hers were just a stupid, satisfied mind, a pattern intellect like Constance's, it would not so much matter. Or if she had the self-discipline and control which Dee's athletics have given her, I should be less troubled. But Pat's is a strange little brain; hungry, keen and uncontrolled. It really craves food, and it is having its appetite blunted by sweets and drugs. Is there nothing that I can do? I hear you ask it. Yes; now that she is at home I can train her a little, but not rigorously, for her mind is too soft and pampered to set itself seriously to any real task. In the days of her childish gluttony I used to drive her into a fury by mocking her for her pimples, and finally, by excoriating her vanity, got her to adopt a reasonable diet. The outer pimples are gone. But if one could see her mind, it would be found pustulous with acne. And there can I do little against the damnable influence of the school which has taught her that a hard-trained, clean-blooded mind is not necessary. The other girls do not go in for it. Why be a highbrow? She is so easily a leader in the school, and, as she boasts, puts it over the teachers in any way she pleases. In the days before she became aware of herself it used to be hard to get her to brush her teeth. To-day I presume that her worthy preceptresses would expel her if she did not use the latest dentrifice twice a day. But they are quite willing to let her mind become overlaid with foul scum for want of systematic brushing up.

"Dynamite for that institution and all like it! Nothing else would serve. With all your luxuriousness, Mona, your love of excitement, your *carpe diem* philosophy of life (Pat, who has 'taken' Latin, does not know what *carpe diem* signifies), your eagerness for the immediate satisfactions of the moment, you never let your brain become softened and untrained and fat. The higher interests were just as much a part of the embellishment of life to you as were flowers or games, music or friends. What inner friends will little Pat have? Not literature. Shakespeare she knows because she must; the school course requires it. But he is a task, not a delight. Thackeray is slow and Dickens a bore. Poetry is a mechanical exercise; I doubt whether a single really beautiful line of Shelley or Keats or Coleridge remains in her memory, though she can chant R. W. Service and Walt Mason. Swinburne she has read on the sly, absorbing none of the luminousness of his flame; only the heat. Similarly, Balzac means to her the 'Contes Drolatiques,' also furtively perused. Conrad and Wells are vague names; something to save until she is older. But O. Henry she dutifully deems a classic and is quite familiar with his tight-rope performances; proud of it, too, as evincing an up-to-date erudition. As for 'the latest books of the day,' she is keen on them, particularly if they happen to be some such lewd and false achievement as the intolerable 'Arab.' Any book spoken of under the breath has for her the stimulus of a race; she must absorb it first and look knowing and demure when it is mentioned. The age of sex, Mona. . . . Her standards of casual reading are of like degree; she considers *Town Topics* an important chronicle and *Vanity Fair* a symposium of pure intellect.

"Yet she has been taking a course in Literature at the school!

"Science has no thrill for Pat; therefore she ignores it. Futile little courses in 'How to Know' things like flowers and birds and mushrooms have gone no deeper than the skin. No love of nature has been inculcated by them. She hardly knows the names of the great scientists. Einstein she recognises through having seen his travels chronicled and heard vaudeville jokes about him. But mention Pasteur or Metchnikoff and you would leave her groping; and she doubtless would identify Lister as one who achieved fame by inventing a mouth wash. However, she could at once tell you the name of the fashionable physician to go to for nervous breakdown.

"Her economics are as vague as her science. Politics are a blank. But to be found ignorant of the most recent trend of the movies or the names of their heroes, or not to know the latest gag of some unspeakable vulgarian of the revues—that would overwhelm her with shame. Her speech and thought are largely a reflection of the contemporary stage. Not the stage of Shaw and O'Neill, but of bedroom farce and trite musical comedy. Thus far she compares unfavourably in education with the average shop girl.

"In music and art the reckoning is better. But this again is largely inherited. If the sap-headed sisterhood have not fostered, they at least have not tainted her sound instincts in these directions. She has followed her own bent.

"As it is a professedly denominational school she has, of course, specialised or been specialised upon as a churchwoman. A very sound and correct churchwoman, but not much of a Godwoman. No philosophy and very little ethics are to be found in her religion. Worship is for her a bargain of which the other consideration is prayer. She gives to God certain praises and observances and asks in return special favours. 'I'll do this for you, God, and you do as much for me some day.' Her expectancy of assured returns she regards as a praiseworthy and pious quality known as faith. Blasphemy, of course. Not the poor child's. The sin, which is a sin of ignorance and loose thinking, is upon the sanctified sisterhood. They have classified the Deity for Pat: God as a social arbiter.

"The sisterhood are purists. Naturally. But purists only by negation. All the essential facts they dodge. True, there is a course in hygiene. It is conducted by a desiccated virgin who minces about the simple and noble facts of sex life as if she were afraid of getting her feet wet, and whose soul would shrivel within her could she overhear the casual conversation of the girls whom she purports to instruct. All that side of knowledge and conjecture they absorb from outside contacts. A worse medium would be hard to conceive. From what Pat indicates of the tittle-tattle of ingénues' luncheons, it would enlighten Rabelais and shock Pepys! And the current jokes between the girls and their boy associates of college age are chiefly innuendo and *double entente* based on sex. Pat cannot say 'bed' or 'leg' or 'skin' without an expectant self-consciousness. Some reechy sort of bedroom story has been lately going the rounds, the point of which is involved in the words 'nudge' and 'phone.' Every time either word is used in Pat's set, there are knowing looks and sniggers, and some nimble wit makes a quick turn of the context and gets his reward in more or less furtive laughter. It is not so much the moral side, it is the nauseous bad taste that sickens one. The mind decays in that atmosphere. Once Pat said to me: 'Bobs, you and Mr. Scott are the only clean-minded men I know.' Think of what that means, Mona! The viciousness of such an environment. Yet the youngsters themselves are not essentially vicious; not many of them. They are curious with the itchy curiosity of their explorative time of life, and they have no proper guidance. The girls are worse off than the boys who do gain some standards in college. But our finishing schools, churchly or otherwise! Hell is paved with their good intentions. Pat's is not worse than the others, I suppose. But the pity of it; the waste of it for her. Hers is such a vivid mind; such a brave, straightforward little mind; at war with that hungry, passionate temperament of hers, yet instinctively clean if it could be protected from befoulment. I have been talking biology with her and she absorbs it with such swift, sure appreciation. The day of trial for her will come when the lighter amusements pall and her brain demands something to feed on—unless before that time it becomes totally encysted. . . ."

22 / BEATRICE M. HINKLE

Against the Double Standard

A growing awareness of the changing roles of women during the 1920's was evident almost everywhere. It was not merely that now women could vote, or that they dared to bare their knees, although both facts were important. The change seemed to involve something basic; some writers suggested that an assault was being mounted against the very principle of masculine supremacy. The world of the Gibson girl was clearly a man's world, and many modern and emancipated women would have none of it. In the following article, Dr. Beatrice M. Hinkle (1872–1953), a psychoanalyst, argues that growing economic independence meant that women were newly free to reject the old double standard. Women who had broken away from economic servitude were evidently no longer willing to personify the morality which men had never lived up to. The freedom from men meant a freedom to discover what it meant to be an individual human being, one with a mind, an earning capacity, and a desire to repudiate not merely the faith of the fathers but the fathers themselves.

In the general discussions of morality which are the fashion just now, sex morality seems to occupy the chief place. Indeed,

---

"Women and the New Morality," *Our Changing Morality,* ed. Freda Kirchway (New York: Albert and Charles Boni, 1930), pp. 235–249.

judging from the amount of talk on this subject one would be inclined to think it the outstanding problem of our time. Certainly the whole of humanity is concerned in and vitally affected by the sexual aspect of life. Sexuality in its capacity as an agent of transformation is the source of power underlying the creativeness of man. In its direct expression, including its influence upon human relationships in general, it is woman's particular concern. The position of importance it is assuming seems, therefore, to be justified, regardless of the protests of the intellect and the wish of the ego to minimize its significance.

A general weakening of traditional standards of ethics and morals and their gradual loss of control over the conduct of individuals have long been observed in other activities—in business affairs and in the world of men's relations with each other. This has taken place so quietly and with so much specious rationalizing that sharp practices and shady conduct which formerly would have produced scandals, shame, and social taboos now scarcely cause a protest from society. These aspects of morality belong to the masculine world in particular and produce little agitation, while the upheaval in sex morals particularly affects the feminine world and by many people can scarcely be considered calmly enough for an examination. The changes in this field are the most recent and are being produced by women; they are taking place in full view of all with no apologies and with little hesitation. They appear, therefore, most striking and disturbing. It can be said that in the general disintegration of old standards, women are the active agents in the field of sexual morality and men the passive, almost bewildered accessories to the overthrow of their long and firmly organized control of women's sexual conduct.

The old sex morality, with its double standard, has for years been criticized and attacked by fair-minded persons of both sexes. It has been recognized that this unequal condition produced effects as unfortunate for the favored sex as for the restricted one, and that because of this it could not be maintained indefinitely by a psychologically developing people. As a matter of course, whenever the single standard was mentioned, the standard governing women was invariably meant, and the fact was ignored that it is easier to break down restrictions than to force them upon those who have hitherto enjoyed comparative freedom. Furthermore, it was not realized that a sex morality imposed by repression and the power of custom creates artificial conceptions and will eventually break down.

This forced morality is in fact at the present time quite obviously disintegrating. We see women assuming the right to act as their impulses dictate with much the same freedom that men have enjoyed for so long. The single standard is rapidly becoming a *fait accompli*, but instead of the standard identified with women it is nearer the standard associated with men. According to a universal psychological law, actual reality eventually overtakes and replaces the cultural ideal.

Although this overthrow of old customs and sex ideals must be chiefly attributed to the economic independence of women brought about through the industrialism of our age, it is safe to say that no man thought ahead far enough or understood the psychology of women sufficiently to anticipate the fruit of this economic emancipation. As long as women were dependent upon men for the support of themselves and their children there could be no development of a real morality, for the love and feelings of the woman were so intermingled with her economic necessities that the higher love impulse was largely undifferentiated from the impulse of self-preservation. True morality can only develop when the object or situation is considered for itself, not when it is bound up with ulterior and extraneous elements which vitiate the whole. The old morality has failed and is disintegrating fast, because it was imposed from without instead of evolving from within.

A morality which has value for all time and is not dependent upon custom or external cultural fashions can arise only from a high development of the psychological functions of thinking and feeling, with the developed individual as the determiner of values instead of general custom or some one else's opinion. The function of feeling and the realm of the emotions have been universally regarded as woman's special province; therefore it is women who are specially concerned with testing out moral values involving sexual behavior. Women have been reproached by men again and again as being only sexual creatures, and they have meekly accepted the reproach. Now, instead of examining the statement, they have accepted the sexual problem of men as though it were their own, and with it the weight of man's conflict and his articulateness. For sexuality as a problem and a conflict definitely belongs to man's psychology; it is he primarily who has been ashamed of his domination by this power and has struggled valiantly to free himself; his egotistic and sexual impulses have always been at war with each other. But whoever heard of women being ashamed of yielding to the power of love? Instead they gloried in the surrender of themselves and counted themselves blessed when love ruled. It is this need of man to escape from the power of the sensual appeal that has made him scorn sex and look upon the great creative power of life as something shameful and inferior, and in modern days treat it as a joke or with the indifferent superficiality which betrays emasculation and inadequacy.

One has only to "listen in" where any large group of men, young or old, are gathered together in easy familiarity (the army camps were recent examples on a large scale) to discover the degree to which sexuality still dominates the minds of men, even though its expression is confined so largely to the jocose and the obscene. Many men can corroborate this report from a military camp—"we have sexuality in all its dirty and infantile forms served daily for breakfast, lunch, and dinner." It is the inferior and inadequate aspect of masculine sexuality that has made it necessary for man to conceive it as something shameful and unclean, and to insist that woman must carry his purity for him and live the restrictions and suppression that rightly belonged to him. Woman on her part became an easy victim of his ideas and convictions, because of the very fact that the function of feeling and the emotions so largely dominate her psychology. The translation of feeling into thought-forms has been slow and difficult. About herself woman has been quite inarticulate and largely unconscious. This inarticulateness inevitably made her accept man's standards and values for her, for little directed thinking is achieved without form and words. Because of her sexual fertility and fruitfulness woman had no sexual conflict; therefore, man easily unloaded his psychological burden upon her, and claimed freedom for the satisfaction of his own desires.

Thus, woman was made a symbol or personification of man's morality. She had to live for him that which he was unable to live for himself. This was the reason for his indignation at moral transgressions on her part. She had injured the symbol and revealed his weakness to him. However, with the discovery by women that they could be economically independent of men, they commenced to find themselves interesting. As they have gradually come to think for themselves about fundamental questions, there has begun a tremendous activity and busyness in regard to the very subject which was previously taboo.

A recent writer boasts that men have changed their attitude regarding sexual problems very little and are not much concerned in the new interest of women. This is probably true, for man has contributed all he has to give to the subject. He has laid down his taboos and externalized his restrictions, chiefly applicable to the other sex, and he is finished with the subject —bored by having it thrust forward as an unfinished problem needing reconsideration. All of his knowledge or understanding of the sexual aspect of life—the aspect underlying human creativeness, the faulty development of which is responsible for a large part of his woes, "can be told in two hours to any intelligent sixteen year old boy," another writer recently stated. It is this youthful ignorance and assurance that the last word has been spoken on this subject that has awakened women, no longer dependent economically, to the fact that they must also become independent of men intellectually if they wish to gain expression for their knowledge or to form their own rules of conduct based on their psychology. In the true scientific spirit of the age they are now experimenting and using nature's method of trial and error to find out for themselves by conscious living experience what feeling has vaguely told them. This is the first step towards objectifying and clarifying woman's intuitive knowledge.

With the revolt of women against the old restrictions and the demand for freedom to experience for themselves, there has appeared a most significant phase of the changed morality—the new relation of women toward each other. The significance of this enormous change which has been taking place very quietly and yet very rapidly is scarcely appreciated. However, when one realizes that only a generation ago the newspapers were still publishing their funny paragraphs at the expense of women ("The dear creatures; how they love one another"), the great difference in their relations today becomes evident. The generally accepted distinction between the personal loyalties of the sexes can be summed up in the statement that women are loyal in love and disloyal in friendship, while men are loyal in friendship and disloyal in love. It is this attitude of women that is gradually disappearing with the awakening of a new sense of themselves as individuals. Their changed attitude towards each other—the recognition of their own values, and the growing realization that only in solidarity can any permanent impression be made on the old conception of woman as an inferior, dependent creature, useful for one purpose only—constitutes the most marked difference between their present social condition and that of the past.

As long as women remained psychologically unawakened,

their individual values were swallowed up in their biological value for the race. They were under the unconscious domination of their sexual fruitfulness and an enemy of themselves as individuals. Weininger gives as the chief difference between the masculine and feminine creeds that "Man's religion consists in a supreme belief in himself—woman's in a supreme belief in other people." These other people being men, the sex rivalry among women that has so long stood in the way of their further development is easily understood. It has been a vicious circle which could only be broken by women's gaining another significance in the eyes of the world and in their own eyes. This other significance is the economic importance which they have acquired in the world of men.

It makes little difference within the social structure how many individual women exist who have forged a position for themselves and have won a freedom and independence equal to that possessed by the ordinary man, so long as they are isolated phenomena having little understanding of the peculiar difficulties and problems of women as a whole, and no relation with each other. These women have always existed in all culture periods, but they have produced little effect upon the social condition or psychology of women in general. There was no group action because the majority of women were inarticulate. The woman who was different became abnormal in the eyes of the world.

This lack of an adequate self-consciousness among women, their general inability to translate feeling into form capable of being understood by the masculine mind, accounts for their acceptance of the statements made about them by men in an effort to understand creatures apparently so different from themselves. There is no doubt that woman's inarticulateness about herself, even when her feelings were very different from those she was told were normal, has been responsible for a vast amount of the nonsense written about her.

This passive acceptance of the opinions of others has been

most disastrous for woman's development. Her superior psychological processes consist of feelings and intuitions, and when these are stultified or violated by being forced into a false relation, or are inhibited from development, the entire personality is crippled. The inadequate development of the function of thought and the dominating rôle played by the function of feeling in the psychology of woman have produced an obviously one-sided effect and have caused men to postulate theories about her, which are given forth as though they were the last word to be said—fixed and unchangeable. Indeed the statement that women are incapable of change and that no growth is possible for them is one of the favorite assertions of the masculine writers upon the subject of women's psychology. As the present is the first time in our historical period in which there has been any general opportunity for women as a whole to think for themselves and to develop in new ways, the basis for this assertion does not exist, and it obviously conceals an unconscious wish that women should not change.

The effect of collective ideas and cultural traditions upon the personality is immeasurable. The greatest general change that is taking place today is the weakening of these ideas and the refusal of women to be bound by them. Women are for the first time demanding to live the forbidden experiences directly and draw conclusions on this basis. I do not mean to imply that traditional moral standards controlling woman's sexual conduct have never been transgressed in the past. They have very frequently been transgressed, but secretly and without inner justification. The great difference today lies in the open defiance of these customs with feelings of entire justification, or even a non-recognition of a necessity for justification. In other words, there has arisen a feeling of moral rightness in the present conduct, and wrongness in the former morality. Actually the condition is one in which natural, long-restrained desire is being substituted for collective moral rules, and individuals are largely becoming a law unto themselves. It is difficult to predict what will be the result of the revolt, but it is certain that this is the preceding condition which renders it possible for a new morality in the real sense to be born within the individual. It has already produced the first condition of all conscious psychic development—a moral conflict—and woman has gained a problem.

In the general chaos of conflicting feelings she is losing her instinctive adaptation to her biological rôle as race bearer, and is attempting adaptation to man's reality. She is making the effort to win for herself some differentiation and development of the ego function apart from her instinctive processes. This is the great problem confronting woman today; how can she gain a relation to both racial and individual obligations, instead of possessing one to the exclusion of the other? Must she lose that which has been and still is her greatest strength and value? I for one do not think so, although I am fully conscious of the tremendous psychic effort and responsibility involved in the changing standards. It is necessary that women learn to accept themselves and to value themselves as beings possessing a worth at least equal to that of the other sex, instead of unthinkingly accepting standards based on masculine psychology. Then women will recognize the necessity of developing their total psychic capacities just as it is necessary for men to do, but they will see that this does not involve imitation of men or repudiation of their most valuable psychic functioning. The real truth is that it has at last become apparent to many women that men cannot redeem them.

It is not the purpose of this article to deal with the practical issues involved in the new moral freedom. One thing however is clearly evident: Women are demanding a reality in their relations with men that heretofore has been lacking, and they refuse longer to cater to the traditional notions of them created by men, in which their true feelings and personalities were disregarded and denied. This is the first result of the new morality.

23 / *ANITA LOOS*

"Paris Is Devine"

The empty-headed, sometimes charming, indefatigable American flapper was definitively portrayed by Anita Loos (1893–   ) in the best-selling *Gentlemen Prefer Blondes*. Produced on Broadway in 1926, this work was soon followed by another, *But Gentlemen Marry Brunettes* (1928). The following passage from the diary of the innocent from Little Rock on the day when she first arrived in "devine" Paris requires neither introduction nor explanation. The classic dumb blonde can speak for herself. She speaks in the accent of the roaring, jazzy Twenties, dedicated to wealth in the gay pursuit of pleasure.

Paris is devine. I mean Dorothy and I got to Paris yesterday, and it really is devine. Because the French are devine. Because when we were coming off the boat, and we were coming through the customs, it was quite hot and it seemed to smell quite a lot and all the French gentlemen in the customs, were squealing quite a lot. So I looked around and I picked out a French gentleman who was really in a very gorgeous uniform and he seemed to be a very, very important gentleman and I gave him twenty francs worth of French money and he was very very gallant and he knocked everybody else down and took our bags right through the custom. Because I really think that twenty Francs is quite cheap for a gentleman

From Chap. IV: "Paris Is Devine," *Gentlemen Prefer Blondes* (New York: Boni & Liveright, 1925), pp. 93–100, 102. From *Gentlemen Prefer Blondes*, copyright ⓡ 1952, Anita Loos. Reprinted by permission of Liveright Publishing Corporation, New York.

that has got on at least $100 worth of gold braid on his coat alone, to speak nothing of his trousers.

I mean the French gentlemen always seem to be squealing quite a lot, especially taxi drivers when they only get a small size yellow dime called a 'fifty santeems' for a tip. But the good thing about French gentlemen is that every time a French gentleman starts in to squeal, you can always stop him with five francs, no matter who he is. I mean it is so refreshing to listen to a French gentleman stop squeaking, that it would really be quite a bargain even for ten francs.

So we came to the Ritz Hotel and the Ritz Hotel is devine. Because when a girl can sit in a delightful bar and have delicious champagne cocktails and look at all the important French people in Paris, I think it is devine. I mean when a girl can sit there and look at the Dolly sisters and Pearl White and Maybelle Gilman Corey, and Mrs. Nash, it is beyond worlds. Because when a girl looks at Mrs. Nash and realizes what Mrs. Nash has got out of gentlemen, it really makes a girl hold her breath.

And when a girl walks around and reads all of the signs with all of the famous historical names it really makes you hold your breath. Because when Dorothy and I went on a walk, we only walked a few blocks but in only a few blocks we read all of the famous historical names, like Coty and Cartier and I knew we were seeing something educational at last and our whole trip was not a failure. I mean I really try to make Dorothy get educated and have reverance. So when we stood at the corner of a place called the Place Vandome, if you turn your back on a monument they have in the middle and look up, you can see none other than Coty's sign. So I said to Dorothy, does it not really give you a thrill to realize that that is the historical spot where Mr. Coty makes all the perfume? So then Dorothy said that she supposed Mr. Coty came to Paris and he smelled Paris and he realized that something had to be done. So Dorothy will really never have any reverance.

So then we saw a jewelry store and we saw some jewelry in

the window and it really seemed to be a very very great bargain but the price marks all had francs on them and Dorothy and I do not seem to be mathematical enough to tell how much francs is in money. So we went in and asked and it seems it was only 20 dollars and it seems it is not diamonds but it is a thing called "paste" which is the name of a word which means imitations. So Dorothy said "paste" is the name of the word a girl ought to do to a gentleman that handed her one. I mean I would really be embarrassed, but the gentleman did not seem to understand Dorothy's english.

So it really makes a girl feel depressed to think a girl could not tell that it was nothing but an imitation. I mean a gentleman could deceeve a girl because he could give her a present and it would only be worth 20 dollars. So when Mr. Eisman comes to Paris next week, if he wants to make me a present I will make him take me along with him because he is really quite an inveteran bargain hunter at heart. So the gentleman at the jewelry store said that quite a lot of famous girls in Paris had imitations of all their jewelry and they put the jewelry in the safe and they really wore the imitations, so they could wear it and have a good time. But I told him I thought that any girl who was a lady would not even think of having such a good time that she did not remember to hang on to her jewelry.

So then we went back to the Ritz and unpacked our trunks with the aid of really a delightful waiter who brought us up some delicious luncheon and who is called Leon and who speaks english almost like an American and who Dorothy and I talk to quite a lot. So Leon said that we ought not to stay around the Ritz all of the time, but we really ought to see Paris. So Dorothy said she would go down in the lobby and meet some gentleman to show us Paris. So in a couple of minutes she called up on the telephone from the lobby and she said "I have got a French bird down here who is a French title nobleman, who is called a veecount so come on down." So I said "How did a Frenchman get into the Ritz." So Dorothy said "He came in to

get out of the rain and he has not noticed that it is stopped."
So I said "I suppose you have picked up something without
taxi fare as usual. Why did you not get an American gentleman
who always have money?" So Dorothy said she thought a
French gentleman had ought to know Paris better. So I said
"He does not even know it is not raining." But I went down.

So the veecount was really delightful after all. So then we
rode around and we saw Paris and we saw how devine it
really is. I mean the Eyefull Tower is devine and it is much
more educational than the London Tower, because you can
not even see the London Tower if you happen to be two blocks
away. But when a girl looks at the Eyefull Tower she really
knows she is looking at something. So I suppose that is the
real historical reason why they call it the Eyefull Tower.

So then we went to a place called the Madrid to tea and it
really was devine. I mean we saw the Dolley Sisters and Pearl
White and Mrs. Corey and Mrs. Nash all over again.

So then we went to dinner and then we went to Momart and
it really was devine because we saw them all over again. I
mean in Momart they have genuine American jazz bands and
quite a lot of New York people which we knew and you really
would think you were in New York and it was devine. So we
came back to the Ritz quite late. So Dorothy and I had quite a
little quarrel because Dorothy said that when we were looking
at Paris I asked the French veecount what was the name of the
unknown soldier who is buried under quite a large monument.
So I said I really did not mean to ask him, if I did, because
what I did mean to ask him was, what was the name of his
mother because it is always the mother of a dead soldier that
I always seem to think about more than the dead soldier that
has died.

So the French veecount is going to call up in the morning
but I am not going to see him again. Because French gentlemen are really quite deceeving. I mean they take you to quite
cute places and they make you feel quite good about yourself

and you really seem to have a delightful time but when you get home and come to think it all over, all you have got is a fan that only cast 20 francs and a doll that they gave you away for nothing in a restaurant. I mean a girl has to look out in Paris, or she would have such a good time in Paris that she would not get anywheres. So I really think that American gentlemen are the best after all, because kissing your hand may make you feel very very good but a diamond and safire bracelet lasts forever. Besides, 1 do not think that I ought to go out with any gentlemen in Paris because Mr. Eisman will be here next week and he told me that the only kind of gentlemen he wants me to go out with are intelectual gentlemen who are good for a girls brains. So I really do not seem to see many gentlemen around the Ritz who seem to look like they would be good for a girl's brains. So tomorrow we are going to go shopping and I suppose it would really be to much to expect to find a gentleman who would look to Mr. Eisman like he was good for a girls brains and at the same time he would like to take us shopping.

PART 6

THE WRITERS

Artistic Poseurs

This brief report which Hemingway (see Document 3) wrote for the *Toronto Star Weekly* in March 1922 is a revealing statement about the massive exodus of Americans to Europe, and especially to Paris, in the Twenties. Hemingway's obvious scorn is most clearly aimed at the fake artists, the fake writers and thinkers, who lived off the real world Hemingway actually did occupy. At the Cafe Rotonde, long a favorite Parisian watering-hole, the tourist-as-artist was a continual reminder to Hemingway that America was as ugly and meaningless, and as dangerous to his art, as he remembered.

PARIS, FRANCE.—The scum of Greenwich Village, New York, has been skimmed off and deposited in large ladlesful on that section of Paris adjacent to the Cafe Rotonde. New scum, of course, has risen to take the place of the old, but the oldest scum, the thickest scum and the scummiest scum has come across the ocean, somehow, and with its afternoon and evening levees has made the Rotonde the leading Latin Quarter show place for tourists in search of atmosphere.

"American Bohemians in Paris," *The Toronto Star Weekly*, March 25, 1922. "American Bohemians in Paris" is reprinted with the permission of Charles Scribner's Sons from *By-Line: Ernest Hemingway*, pages 23–25, edited by William White. Copyright © 1967 By-Line Ernest Hemingway, Inc.

It is a strange-acting and strange-looking breed that crowd the tables of the Cafe Rotonde. They have all striven so hard for a careless individuality of clothing that they have achieved a sort of uniformity of eccentricity. A first look into the smoky, high-ceilinged, table-crammed interior of the Rotonde gives the same feeling that hits you as you step into the bird house at the zoo. There seems to be a tremendous, raucous, many-pitched squawking going on broken up by many waiters who fly around through the smoke like so many black and white magpies. The tables are full—they are always full—someone is moved down and crowded together, something is knocked over, more people come in at the swinging door, another black and white waiter pivots between tables toward the door and, having shouted your order at his disappearing back, you look around you at individual people.

You can only see a certain number of individuals at the Rotonde at one night. When you have reached your quota you are quite aware that you must go. There is a perfectly definite moment when you know you have seen enough of the Rotonde inmates and must leave. If you want to know how definite it is, try and eat your way through a jug of soured molasses. To some people the feeling that you cannot go on will come at the first mouthful. Others are hardier. But there is a limit for all normal people. For the people who crowd together around the tables of the Cafe Rotonde do something very definite to that premier seat of the emotions, the stomach.

For the first dose of Rotonde individuals you might observe a short, dumpy woman with newly-blonde hair, cut Old Dutch Cleanser fashion, a face like a pink enameled ham and fat fingers that reach out of the long blue silk sleeves of a Chinese-looking smock. She is sitting hunched forward over the table, smoking a cigaret in a two-foot holder, and her flat face is absolutely devoid of any expression.

She is looking flatly at her masterpiece that is hung on the white plaster wall of the cafe, along with some 3,000 others, as part of the Rotonde's salon for customers only. Her master-piece looks like a red mince pie descending the stairs, and the adoring, though expressionless, painter spends every afternoon and evening seated at the table before it in a devout attitude.

After you have finished looking at the painter and her work you can turn your head a little and see a big, light-haired woman sitting at a table with three young men. The big woman is wearing a picture hat of the Merry Widow period and is making jokes and laughing hysterically. The three young men laugh whenever she does. The waiter brings the bill, the big woman pays it, settles her hat on her head with slightly un-steady hands, and she and the three young men go out to-gether. She is laughing again as she goes out of the door. Three years ago she came to Paris with her husband from a little town in Connecticut, where they had lived and he had painted with increasing success for ten years. Last year he went back to America alone.

Those are two of the twelve hundred people who jam the Rotonde. You can find anything you are looking for at the Ro-tonde—except serious artists. The trouble is that people who go on a tour of the Latin Quarter look in at the Rotonde and think they are seeing an assembly of the real artists of Paris. I want to correct that in a very public manner, for the artists of Paris who are turning out creditable work resent and loathe the Rotonde crowd.

The fact that there are twelve francs for a dollar brought over the Rotonders, along with a good many other people, and if the exchange ever gets back to normal they will have to go back to America. They are nearly all loafers expending the en-ergy that an artist puts into his creative work in talking about what they are going to do and condemning the work of all artists who have gained any degree of recognition. By talking about art they obtain the same satisfaction that the real artist does in his work. That is very pleasant, of course, but they in-sist upon posing as artists.

Since the good old days when Charles Baudelaire led a purple lobster on a leash through the same old Latin Quarter, there has not been much good poetry written in cafes. Even then I suspect that Baudelaire parked the lobster with the concierge down on the first floor, put the chloroform bottle corked on the washstand and sweated and carved at the Fleurs du Mal alone with his ideas and his paper as all artists have worked before and since. But the gang that congregates at the corner of the Boulevard Montparnasse and the Boulevard Raspail have no time to work at anything else; they put in a full day at the Rotonde.

25 / F. SCOTT FITZGERALD

"America Is So Decadent"

F. Scott Fitzgerald (1896–1940) was the unrivaled spokesman of that part of the Twenties appropriately called (by him, he said) "the Jazz Age." He wrote of the flapper and of the moment's glamor with an authority, a zeal, and an audience that no one else commanded. Born in St. Paul, Minnesota, and educated at Princeton, he always displayed at least something of both places in his writing. After the great success of his first book, *This Side of Paradise* (1920), he was the acknowledged chronicler of the flapper and her friends. Living his role, he and Zelda, his wife, became part of the international social whirl, and he tried to write his way out of debt, out of alcohol, and out of the stretches of inactivity that regularly seized him. *The Beautiful and the Damned* was published in 1921; *Tales of the Jazz Age* in 1922; *The Vegetable*, a play, in 1923; *The Great Gatsby* in 1925; and *All the Sad Young Men* in 1926. He regularly wrote for popular magazines, frequently as a result of his need for money. Underlying the froth and chic of his work was an uneasiness, sometimes a pessimism, appropriate to the decade. This mood, along with the other, is most explicit in some of his personal letters, a selection of which follow. To the president of Princeton, who had written complaining of Fitzgerald's treatment of the University in *This Side of Paradise*, Fitzgerald tried to explain his need to "overaccentuate the gayety" of the school. To Edmund Wilson (see Document 26) he explained his reaction to Europe; he requested Wilson to re-do an article on Fitzgerald that he thought made too much of his drinking; and he described his impressions of American women in Paris. To his editor, Maxwell Perkins, Fitzgerald explained why his work was going so slowly, and what he hoped to do about it. He tried to explain America to Marya Mannes, and to Ernest Hemingway he tried to present himself as the personification of the jazzy and roaring Twenties. The following letters display at least some of Fitzgerald's growing desperation, along with his continually excited and gay facade. His letters, too, are an integral part of the ambivalent voice of the Jazz Age.

> *Wakeman's*
> *Westport, Connecticut*
> [*June 3, 1920*]

My dear President Hibben:*

I want to thank you very much for your letter and to confess that the honor of a letter from you outweighed my real regret that my book gave you concern. It was a book written with the bitterness of my discovery that I had spent several years trying to fit in with a curriculum that is after all made for the average student. After the curriculum had tied me up, taken away the honors I'd wanted, bent my nose over a chemistry book and said "No fun, no activities, no offices, no Trian-

Reprinted with the permission of Charles Scribner's Sons from pages 461–463, 326–327, 330, 162–163, 488–489, and 302–303 of *The Letters of F. Scott Fitzgerald* edited by Andrew Turnbull. Copyright © 1963 Frances Scott Fitzgerald Lanahan.
*John Grier Hibben, president of Princeton.

gle trips—no, not even a diploma if you can't do chemistry"
—after that I retired. It is easy for the successful man in college, the man who has gotten what he wanted to say.

"It's all fine. It makes men. It made me, see"—
—but it seems to me it's like the captain of a company when he has his men lined up at attention for inspection. He sees only the tightly buttoned coat and the shaved faces. He doesn't know that perhaps a private in the rear rank is half crazy because a pin is sticking in his back and he can't move, or another private is thinking that his wife is dying and he can't get leave because too many men in the company are gone already.

I don't mean at all that Princeton is not the happiest time in most boys' lives. It is, of course—I simply say it wasn't the happiest time in mine. I love it now better than any place on earth. The men—the undergraduates of Yale and Princeton are cleaner, healthier, better-looking, better dressed, wealthier and more attractive than any undergraduate body in the country. I have no fault to find with Princeton that I can't find with Oxford and Cambridge. I simply wrote out of my own impressions, wrote as honestly as I could a picture of its beauty. That the picture is cynical is the fault of my temperament.

My view of life, President Hibben, is the view of the Theodore Dreisers and Joseph Conrads—that life is too strong and remorseless for the sons of men. My idealism flickered out with Henry Strater's anti-club movement at Princeton. "The Four Fists," latest of my stories to be published, was the first to be written. I wrote it in desperation one evening because I had a three-inch pile of rejection slips and it was financially necessary for me to give the magazine what they wanted. The appreciation it has received has amazed me.

I must admit however that *This Side of Paradise* does overaccentuate the gayety and country club atmosphere of Princeton. For the sake of the reader's interest that part was much overstressed, and of course the hero, not being average, reacted rather unhealthily I suppose to many perfectly normal phenomena. To that extent the book is inaccurate. It is the Princeton of Saturday night in May. Too many intelligent classmates of mine have failed to agree with it for me to consider it really photographic any more, as of course I did when I wrote it.

Next time I am in Princeton I will take the privilege of coming to see you.

I am, sir,

Very respectfully yours,
F. Scott Fitzgerald

Hotel Cecil
London, England
[May, 1921]

Dear Bunny [Edmund Wilson]:

. . . God damn the continent of Europe. It is of merely antiquarian interest. Rome is only a few years behind Tyre and Babylon. The negroid streak creeps northward to defile the Nordic race. Already the Italians have the souls of blackamoors. Raise the bars of immigration and permit only Scandinavians, Teutons, Anglo-Saxons and Celts to enter. France made me sick. Its silly pose as the thing the world has to save. I think it's a shame that England and America didn't let Germany conquer Europe. It's the only thing that would have saved the fleet of tottering old wrecks. My reactions were all philistine, anit-socialistic, provincial and racially snobbish. I believe at last in the white man's burden. We are as far above the modern Frenchman as he is above the Negro. Even in art! Italy has no one. When Anatole France dies French literature will be a silly jealous rehashing of technical quarrels. They're thru and done. You may have spoken in jest about New York as the capital of culture but in 25 years it will be just as London is now. Culture follows money and all the refinements of aestheticism can't stave off its change of seat (Christ! what a metaphor). We will be the Romans in the next generations as the English are now.

Alec sent me your article. I read it half a dozen times and think it is magnificent. I can't tell you how I hate you. I don't hate Don Stewart half as much (tho I find that I am suddenly and curiously irritated by him) because I don't really dread him. But *you!* Keep out my sight. I want no more of your articles! . . .

Paradise is out here. Of 20 reviews about half are mildly favorable, a quarter of them imply that I've read "*Sinister Street* once too often" and the other five (including *The Times*) damn it summarily as artificial. I doubt if it sells 1500 copies.

Mencken's first series of *Prejudices* is attracting attention here. Wonderful review in *The Times*. . . .

With envious curses and hopes of an immediate response,

F. Scott Fitzgerald—author of *Flappers and Philosophers* (juvenile)

626 Goodrich Avenue
St. Paul, Minnesota
[January, 1922]

Dear Bunny:

Needless to say I have never read anything with quite the uncanny fascination with which I read your article [about Fitzgerald in the *Bookman*]. It is, of course, the only intelligible and intelligent thing of any length which has been written about me and my stuff—and like everything you write it seems to me pretty generally true. I am guilty of its every stricture and I take an extraordinary delight in its considered approbation. I don't see how I could possibly be offended at anything in it—on the contrary it pleases me more to be compared to "standards out of time," than to merely the usual scapegoats of contemporary criticism. Of course I'm going to carp at it a little but merely to conform to convention. I like it, I think it's an unprejudiced diagnosis and I am considerably in your debt for the interest which impelled you to write it.

Now as to the liquor thing—it's true, but nevertheless I'm going to ask you take it out. It leaves a loophole through which I can be attacked and discredited by every moralist who reads the article. Wasn't it Bernard Shaw who said that you've either got to be conventional in your work or in your private life or get into trouble? Anyway the legend about my liquoring is terribly widespread and this thing would hurt me more than you could imagine—both in my contact with the people with whom I'm thrown—relatives and respectable friends—and, what is much more important, financially. . . .

> *Great Neck* [*Long Island*]
> [*Before April 16, 1924*]

Dear Max [Maxwell Perkins]:

A few words more, relative to our conversation this afternoon. While I have every hope and plan of finishing my novel [*The Great Gatsby*] in June, you know how those things often come out, and even if it takes me ten times that long I cannot let it go out unless it has the very best I'm capable of in it, or even, as I feel sometimes, something better than I'm capable of. Much of what I wrote last summer was good but it was so interrupted that it was ragged and, in approaching it from a new angle, I've had to discard a lot of it—in one case, 18,000 words (part of which will appear in the *Mercury* as a short story ["Absolution"]). It is only in the last four months that I've realized how much I've, well, almost *deteriorated* in the three years since I finished *The Beautiful and Damned*. The last four months of course I've worked but in the two years—over two years—before that, I produced exactly *one* play, *half a dozen* short stories and three or four articles—an average of about *one hundred* words a day. If I'd spent this time reading or traveling or doing anything—even staying healthy—it'd be different, but I spent it uselessly, neither in study nor in contemplation but only in drinking and raising hell generally. If I'd written *The B. and D.* at the rate of one hundred words a day, it would have taken me *4 years*, so you can imagine the moral effect the whole chasm had on me.

What I'm trying to say is just that I'll have to ask you to have patience about the book and trust me that at last, or at least for the first time in years, I'm doing the best I can. I've gotten in dozens of bad habits that I'm trying to get rid of

1. Laziness
2. Referring everything to Zelda—a terrible habit; nothing ought to be referred to anybody until it's finished
3. Word consciousness and self-doubt, etc., etc., etc., etc.

I feel I have an enormous power in me now, more than I've ever had in a way, but it works so fitfully and with so many bogeys because I've *talked so much* and not lived enough within myself to develop the necessary self-reliance. Also I don't know anyone who has used up so much personal experience as I have at 27. *Copperfield* and *Pendennis* were written at past 40, while *This Side of Paradise* was three books and *The B. and D.* was two. So in my new novel I'm thrown directly on purely creative work—not trashy imaginings as in my stories but the sustained imagination of a sincere yet radiant world. So I tread slowly and carefully and at times in considerable distress. This book will be a consciously artistic achievement and must depend on that as the first books did not.

If I ever win the right to any leisure again, I will assuredly

not waste it as I wasted this past time. Please believe me when
I say that now I'm doing the best I can.

> Yours ever,
> Scott F——

> *Paris*
> [*Spring, 1925*]

To Edmund Wilson:

. . . I looked up Hemingway. He is taking me to see Gertrude
Stein tomorrow. This city is full of Americans—most of them
former friends—whom we spend most of our time dodging,
not because we don't want to see them but because Zelda's only
just well and I've got to work; and they seem to be incapable
of any sort of conversation not composed of semi-malicious
gossip about New York courtesy celebrities. I've gotten to like
France. We've taken a swell apartment until January. I'm
filled with disgust for Americans in general after two weeks'
sight of the ones in Paris—these preposterous, pushing women
and girls who assume that you have any personal interest in
them, who have all (so they say) read James Joyce and who
simply adore Mencken. I suppose we're no worse than anyone,
only contact with other races brings out all our worst qualities.
If I had anything to do with creating the manners of the contemporary American girl I certainly made a botch of the
job. . . .

> Scott

> *14 rue de Tilsitt*
> *Paris, France*
> [*October, 1925*]

Dear Marya [Mannes]:

Thank you for writing me about *Gatsby*—I especially appreciate your letter because women, and even intelligent women,

haven't generally cared much for it. They do not like women to be presented as *emotionally* passive—as a matter of fact I think most women are, that their minds are taken up with a sort of second-rate and unessential bookkeeping which their apologists call "practicality"—like the French, they are cen-time-savers in the business of magic. (You see I am a Schopen-hauerian, not a Shavian.)

You are thrilled by New York—I doubt you will be after five more years when you are more fully nourished from within. I carry the place around the world in my heart but sometimes I try to shake it off in my dreams. America's great-est promise is that something is going to happen, and after awhile you get tired of waiting because nothing happens to people except that they grow old, and nothing happens to American art because America is the story of the moon that never rose. . . .

The young people in America are brilliant with second-hand sophistication inherited from their betters of the war genera-tion who to some extent worked things out for themselves. They are brave, shallow, cynical, impatient, turbulent and empty. I like them not. The "fresh, strong river of America!" My God, Marya, where are your eyes—or are they too fresh and strong to see anything but their own color and contour in the glass? America is so decadent that its brilliant children are damned almost before they are born. Can you name a single American artist except James and Whistler (who lived in En-gland) who didn't die of drink? If it is fresh and strong to be unable to endure or tolerate things-as-they-are, to shut your eyes or to distort and lie—then you're right, Marya Mannes, and no one has ever so misinterpreted the flowers of civiliza-tion, the Greek or Gallic idea, as

Your sincere admirer,
F. Scott Fitzgerald

Ellerslie
Edgemoor, Delaware
[*December, 1927*]

Dear Ernest [Hemingway]:

Perkins sent me the check for 800 bits (as we westerners say), indicating, I hope, that you are now comfortably off in your own ascetic way. I am almost through my novel, got short and had to do three *Post* stories but as I am now their pet exhibit . . . to the tune of 32,000 bits per felony it didn't take long to come to the surface.

(This tough talk is not really characteristic of me—it's the influence of *All the Sad Young Men Without Women in Love*.) Louis Golding stepped off the boat and said you and I were the hope of American Letters (if you can find them) but aside from that things look black, "old pard"—Brommy is sweeping the West, Edna Ferber is sweeping the East and Paul Rosenfeld is sweeping what's left into a large ornate waste-basket, a gift which any Real Man would like, to be published in November under the title, *The Real Leisure Class*, containing the work of one-story Balzacs and poets so thin-skinned as to be moved by everything to exactly the same degree of mild remarking.

Lately I've enjoyed *Some People*, *Bismarck* (Ludwig's), *Him* (in parts) and the *Memoirs* of Ludendorff. I have a new German war book, *Die Krieg Against Krieg*, which shows men who mislaid their faces in Picardy and the Caucasus—you can imagine how I thumb it over, my mouth fairly slithering with fascination.

If you write anything in the line of an "athletic" story please try the *Post* or let me try them for you, or Reynolds. You were wise not to tie up with *Hearst's*. They are absolute bitches who feed on contracts like vultures, if I may coin a neat simile.

I've tasted no alcohol for a month but Xmas is coming.

Please write me at length about your adventures—I hear you were seen running through Portugal in used B.V.D.s, chewing ground glass and collecting material for a story about boule players; that you were publicity man for Lindbergh; that you have finished a novel a hundred thousand words long consisting entirely of the word "balls" used in new groupings; that you have been naturalized a Spaniard, dress always in a wine-skin with "zipper" vent and are engaged in bootlegging Spanish Fly between St. Sebastian and Biarritz where your agents sprinkle it on the floor of the Casino. I hope I have been misinformed but, alas!, it all has too true a ring. For your own good I should be back there, with both of us trying to be good fellows at a terrible rate. Just before you pass out next time think of me.

This is a wowsy country but France is [illegible] and I hope to spend March and April, or April and May, there and elsewhere on the continent.

How are you, physically and mentally? Do you sleep? "Now I Lay Me" was a fine story—you ought to write a companion piece, "Now I Lay Her." Excuse my bawdiness but I'm oversexed and am having saltpeter put in my *Pâté de Foie Gras au Truffles Provençal.* . . .

> Always afftly,
> Scott

26 / EDMUND WILSON

The Literary Achievement

The reputation of the literature of the Twenties has been solid almost from the very beginning of the decade. Critics have talked about a literary renaissance, a golden age of literature, and the explosive freedom of the literary sensibility to do work of enduring importance. By now it is of course clear that many writers did in fact flourish and create in that atmosphere and it has now become necessary to include the literary mind in almost any analysis of the period. There were, and are, however, dissenting views. Edmund Wilson (1895–   ), a journalist, literary critic, novelist, and poet during the 1920's, attempted in the following article to take a calmer and more disinterested look at the period; this piece was written in June 1926 and appeared anonymously. He concluded, in general, that American writers, critics, and academics, for all their vitality and talent, had still failed to come up to "the full European stature." He argued that the preceding literary generation in America, although stodgier, had had a "sounder culture" and had produced writers steadier in their craft. By comparison, the Twenties seemed to a sensitive and contemporary observer, "polyglot, parvenu, hysterical, and often only semi-literate." Wilson softened these judgments in time, but this note that is sourer than is customary for the time effectively achieves a measure of perspective. It is simply a plea for standards and sanity, from whose application the Twenties have for too long been guarded.

The writer of this article is a journalist whose professional activities have been chiefly concerned with the American literary movement of the last fifteen years. He has written reviews of the productions of that movement and worked on magazines which were identified with it; he has lived constantly in its atmosphere. And he feels a certain human sympathy with all of its manifestations, even with those of which, artistically, he disapproves. It is to him a source of deep gratification that literature has been "sold" to the American public, and, on principle, in the face of alien attack, he will stand by even the least intelligent, the least disinterested, of its sales-

---

"The All-Star Literary Vaudeville," in *American Criticism,* ed. W. A. Drake (New York: Harcourt, Brace, 1926), pp. 337–358; reprinted in *The Shores of Light* (New York: Farrar, Straus & Young, Inc., 1952), pp. 229–247. Reprinted by permission of the author.

men: he has served in that army himself. But it has recently occurred to him that, when he comes to take stock and is perfectly honest with himself, he must admit to feeling only the mildest interest in most of the contemporary literary goods which now find so wide a market, and that he is disaffected to the point of disgust with the publicity service which has grown up in connection with them. He has to take account of the fact that it is scarcely possible nowadays to tell the reviews from the advertising: both tend to convey the impression that masterpieces are being manufactured as regularly as new models of motor-cars. In the early days of the present era, the reviews of H. L. Mencken, Francis Hackett, Floyd Dell and Louis Untermeyer set an example of honesty and boldness. Today these journalist critics, having got the kind of literature they want, are apparently quite content; and most of the reviews are now written by people who do not try to go beyond them. The present writers on American literature all have interests in one phase or another of it: either the authors know one another personally or they owe one another debts of gratitude or they are bound together by their loyalty to some stimulating common cause. And almost all forget critical standards in their devotion to the great common causes: the cause of an American national literature in independence of English literature, and the cause of contemporary American ideas as against the ideas of the last generation. Even Stuart P. Sherman, once so savage in the opposite camp, has become as benevolent as Carl Van Doren and now occupies what has perhaps become, from the popular point of view, the central desk of authority, to which each of the performers in the all-star circus, from Ben Hecht to Ring Lardner, steps up to receive his endorsement. The present writer has, therefore, for his own satisfaction, for the appeasement of his own conscience, made an attempt to draw up a balance-sheet of his opinions in regard to his contemporaries, not merely in disparagement of those whom he considers rather overrated but in justice to those he admires.

If he succeeds in disturbing one editor or reviewer, in an atmosphere where now for some time politeness and complacency have reigned, he will feel that he has not written in vain.

To begin with the contemporary American novel—which is commonly assumed to be our principal glory—I must confess that I have difficulty in reading our novelists. We compare our fiction with English fiction and conclude that we have been brilliantly successful in this field; but the truth is merely that the English novel is just now at a particularly low ebb. We have no novelist of the first importance, of the importance of James, Joyce or Proust; or of that of Balzac or Dostoevsky. Dreiser commands our respect; but the truth is he writes so badly that it is almost impossible to read him, and, for this reason, I find it hard to believe in his literary permanence. To follow the moral disintegration of Hurstwood in *Sister Carrie* is to suffer all the agonies of being out of work without being rewarded by the aesthetic pleasure which art is supposed to supply. Sinclair Lewis, with a vigorous satiric humor, has brought against certain aspects of American civilization an indictment that has its local importance, but, when one has been through *Main Street* and *Babbitt,* amusing though they certainly are, one is not left with any appetite to read further novels by Lewis: they have beauty neither of style nor of form and they tell us nothing new about life. Joseph Hergesheimer, though he knows how to tell a story, writes nearly as badly in a fancy way as Dreiser does in a crude one: the judgment of him that I most agree with is the remark attributed to Max Beerbohm: "Poor Mr. Hergesheimer, he wants so much to be an artist." Cabell, though a man of real parts, is, at his worst, a case of the same kind: *Beyond Life* I regard as one of the most obnoxiously written books I have ever read. *Jurgen* certainly had its merits: it was well-planned and curiously successful in the artificial evocation of the atmosphere of primitive folklore. But, except at Cabell's moments of highest imaginative intensity, which are neither very frequent nor very intense, he is likely to be simply insipid. His genealogies and maps of Poictesme bore me beyond description, and the whole Poictesme business strikes me as the sort of thing with which ingenious literary schoolboys sometimes amuse themselves. I dislike also Cabell's Southern sentimentality, which leaves him soft when he thinks he is most cynical. One cannot help feeling that, in the impression he gives of living and working in a vacuum, he furnishes a depressing illustration of the decay of the South since the Civil War. Willa Cather is a good craftsman, but she is usually rather dull. In spite of a few distinguished stories, she suffers from an anemia of the imagination and, like that other rather distinguished novelist, Zona Gale, is given to terrible lapses into feminine melodrama. As for Waldo Frank, he writes in a style—to me, never quite satisfactory—that combines James Joyce with the Hebrew prophets. At his best, he touches tragedy and, at his worst, embraces melodrama. He possesses a real poetic sensibility and is refreshing in so far as his vision is different from that of any one else; but, in his novels, where we hope to see him stage a drama, he is usually content to invoke an apocalypse. I consider Jean Toomer's *Cane* rather better in literary quality than Frank's somewhat similar *Holiday*. I feel more interest in John Dos Passos and F. Scott Fitzgerald than in any of the writers mentioned above: they are younger than the others, and one does not feel as yet that one knows exactly what to expect of them. Dos Passos is ridden by adolescent resentments and seems given to documenting life from the outside rather than knowing it by intimate experience; but, though, like Lewis, that other documentator, he is far too much addicted to making out cases against society, he is a better artist than Lewis and has steadily progressed in his art. Scott Fitzgerald, possessing from the first, not merely cleverness, but something of inspired imagination and poetic literary brilliance, has not until recently given the impression of precisely knowing what he was about;

but with *The Great Gatsby* and some of his recent short stories, he seems to be entering upon a development in the course of which he may come to equal in mastery of his material those novelists whom he began by surpassing by vividness in investing it with glamor. Besides these, there are the other fabricators of fantasy and the realists, satiric and plain; but the former, so far as I have read them, are either tawdry, like Ben Hecht, or awfully mild, like Carl Van Vechten; and the latter, though both in novel and drama they have learned to apply the formulas of naturalism to almost every phase of American life and have, therefore, a certain interest in the history of American culture, are otherwise especially uninteresting at a time when naturalism has run its course and everywhere except in America is either being transformed or discarded. And we have also had the Wellsian social novel, at various levels of mediocrity.

Sherwood Anderson is a different matter. In his novels, despite excellent pages, I invariably become exasperated, before I have got to the end of them, by the vagueness of the characters and the constant repetitiousness of the form. But his short stories and his symbolist prose-poems have a kind of artistic authenticity that neither Lewis's richer resources nor Miss Cather's technical efforts have been able to win for those writers. Without ever having learned the tricks of his trade, Sherwood Anderson, in the best of his stories, has shown an almost perfect instinct that fashions, from what seems a more intimate stratum of feeling and imagination than our novelists usually explore, visions at once fresh and naïve and of a slightly discomfiting strangeness. He could stand to learn something, however, from the methods both of Miss Cather and of Lewis: too much of his material has evaporated in his hands from his not knowing how to deal with it. It can probably be said that, in general, the newer American writers have so far been distinguishing themselves in the short story rather than the novel. The short stories of Sherwood Anderson, Ernest

Hemingway's *In Our Time* and Gertrude Stein's early *Three Lives,* to which should be added the best of Ring Lardner, constitute an impressive group and one quite free from the outworn conventions and the suggestion of second-rate imitation that make many of the novels unsatisfactory. It is interesting to note that all four of these writers have certain characteristics in common, that they may almost be said to form a school, and that, remote though they may seem from one another, there is a fairly close relationship between them. Thus, Anderson has read Gertrude Stein and seems to have been influenced by *Three Lives;* and Hemingway has evidently read and been influenced by all three of the others. Each of these four writers has developed what seems only a special branch of the same simple colloquial language, based directly on the vocabulary and rhythm of ordinary American speech; and, if there can be said to be an American school of writing, aside from American journalese or from the use of American slang in otherwise conventional English prose, these writers would seem to represent it. It is a genre that has already produced one masterpiece in Mark Twain's *Huckleberry Finn,* a work to which Anderson, Hemingway and Lardner are probably all indebted.

As for the dramatists, there is still only O'Neill, who, for all his efforts to break away from naturalism, remains a typical naturalistic dramatist of something under the very first rank. He is a writer of the same school as Hauptmann, with much the same kind of merits; but, where Hauptmann is as steady as Shakespeare, O'Neill is hysterically embittered. He forces his tragic catastrophes and, at the same time, fails to prepare them; and, despite the magnificent eloquence of which he is sometimes capable, especially when handling some form of the vernacular, he has grave deficiencies of literary taste which allow him to leave great areas of his dialogue either banal or bald. John H. Lawson has a wit and a fancy which have found their proper vehicle in the theater; but, even more than his ally, Dos Passos, he is given to adolescent grievances and adolescent enthusiasms.

We come now to literary criticism. In my opinion, H. L. Mencken (who is perhaps a prophet rather than a critic) is ordinarily underrated as a writer of English prose. Belonging himself to the line of Butler and Swift rather than to that of Pater and De Quincey, he cherishes a rustic reverence for the more "aesthetic" branch and is never tired of celebrating the elegances of such provincial fops as Lord Dunsany, Hergesheimer and Cabell, who have announced—it is, I think, Mr. Cabell's phrase—that they aim to "write beautifully about beautiful things." But although it is true that Mencken's style lends itself to excesses and vulgarities, especially in the hands of his imitators, who have taken over the Master's jargon without possessing his admirable literary sense, I believe that his prose is more successful in its way than that of these devotees of beauty usually is in theirs. The ideas themselves behind Mencken's writing are neither many nor subtle, and even in his most serious productions, even in *The American Language,* he overindulges an appetite for paradox. But some strain of the musician and poet has made it possible for Mencken to turn these ideas into literature: it is precisely through the color and rhythm of a highly personal prose that Mencken's opinions have become so infectious. He has now been repeating these opinions with the same pugnacious emphasis for fifteen or twenty years, and one has become rather tired of hearing them; yet he sustains a certain distinction and affords a certain satisfaction. Consider, for example, the leaflet he recently circulated on the adventures of the *American Mercury* with the Boston Watch and Ward Society: this statement, of no literary pretensions, in which he appears without war-paint or feathers, displays most attractive eighteenth-century qualities of lucidity, order and force, for lack of which the youngest of the younger literary generation, who have thrown Mencken overboard, have proved so far rather ineffective.

Paul Rosenfeld is another critic very unpopular with this youngest generation who seems to me an excellent writer. Though he, too, has his faults of style, which include a confusing weakness for writing French and German locutions in English, his command of a rich English vocabulary is one of the things that make him exceptional among recent American writers—who are not infrequently handicapped by not having at their disposal a large enough variety of English words, or, if they have them, by not knowing what they mean. Mr. Rosenfeld, at his worst, is given to overwriting: receiving in his soul the seed of a work by some such writer as Sherwood Anderson, himself one of the tenderer plants, he will cause it to shoot up and exfloreate into an enormous and rather rank "Mystic Cabbage-Rose." On these occasions, his prose seems sometimes rather coarse in quality and his colors a little muddy; but, at his best, Mr. Rosenfeld's writing is certainly among our soundest and his colors are both brilliant and true. He is sensitive, intelligent, well-educated and incorruptibly serious; and he is perhaps the only American critic of the generation since that of James Huneker who has written anything of any real value on the current artistic life of Europe. Van Wyck Brooks, who also writes excellent prose, though of quite a different sort, I propose to discuss in another connection.

George Jean Nathan is a wonderful humorous writer and a better critic of the theater than A. B. Walkley, in a recent article, gave him credit for being; but his writing, which superficially resembles Mencken's, is usually lacking in the qualities that give Mencken's its durable texture. Willard Huntington Wright, some years ago, gave the impression of being some one important; and Lewis Mumford now gives the impression of some one perhaps about to be. Gilbert Seldes, through his activities as an editor of the *Dial* and his cultivation of the popular arts, has filled a role of considerable importance; but his principal literary quality is a kind of undisciplined wit which figures too often in his writings at the expense of lucidity and taste. He has lately become addicted to aesthetic editorial writing, a department for which his alert and vivid but glancing and volatile mind, is perhaps not very well adapted. In my opinion, he is seen at his best in passages of straight description of some movie or vaudeville act which has aroused his imagination. Burton Rascoe has performed the astonishing and probably unprecedented feat of making literature into news. A master of all the tricks of newspaper journalism, which he has introduced into the Sacred Grove to the horror of some of its high priests, his career has yet been singularly honorable in its disregard of popular values; and the cause of letters has profited more from his activities than the proprietors of popular newspapers who have inevitably discovered in the long run that they would feel more comfortable with a literary editor who did not find books so exciting. Mr. Rascoe has always written respectably and, at his best, with much ease and point. Most of the younger generation of critics either are badly educated or have never learned to write, and many suffer from both disabilities. At best, we have produced no literary critic of the full European stature. The much-abused Paul Elmer More still figures as our only professional critic whose learning is really considerable and whose efforts are ambitious and serious. His prose is quite graceless and charmless, but always precise and clear; his point of view, though the Puritan rationalism of which it is a late product has imposed on it some rigid limitations, has the force of a deep conviction and the advantage of a definite formulation. Mr. More, although hopelessly inhibited in the exercise of his aesthetic sensibility, has become, insofar as is possible without the free range of this, a real master of ideas.

The new post-war method of biography, based on Strachey and psychoanalysis, has had many practitioners in America: Katherine Anthony, Van Wyck Brooks, Thomas Beer, M. R. Werner and others; but, though it has turned out a number of agreeable books, I have not seen any except Brooks's *Mark Twain* that seemed of first-rate importance. In the special departments of scholarly and expository writing, the general inferiority of the level of our culture to that of Great Britain or

France becomes inescapably plain. There are not many of our college professors who can command the attention of the reading public. Professor John Dewey writes much and his influence has been considerable, but he has not inherited with pragmatism William James's literary gift. Professor Morris Cohen, who does possess a literary gift, has so far published nothing but reviews, and not very many of them. In the classics, Professor Tenney Frank seems the only representative of a new generation; but Professor Frank, although competent in a literary way and bold in interpretation, appears to be rather indifferent to the literary interest of the classics. Professor Paul Shorey of Chicago is perhaps the only other scholar who writes readable books in this field. We have, in short, no university professor with a literary reputation equal to that of Garrod, of Gilbert Murray, of Mackail, of A. E. Housman, or of Whitehead or Bertrand Russell or Lowes Dickinson. I can remember no recent book by an American professor which has been widely read on its literary merits, except Professor Warner Fite's *Moral Philosophy* and Professor Samuel Morison's *Maritime History of Massachusetts*. In science, we have some readable popularizers in the rousing modern manner, but they are mostly undistinguished writers: Doctor Fishbein, Doctor De Kruif and Doctor Dorsey. Edwin Slosson is rapidly becoming a sort of William Lyon Phelps of scientific culture. The zoölogist William Beebe writes a prose that is shamelessly journalistic; but he is a man of some literary ability, who deserves to be read by writers. One of his assets is an extraordinary vocabulary, which blends scientific with literary language in such a way that his scientific words are imbued with a new life and color. I doubt, however, whether the cable to the *New York Times* is a very good school of writing. I am sorry not to be able to do justice to our recent political writers. I believe that in this department we are somewhat better off than elsewhere; but it is the one in which I have lately read least.

As for poetry, the new movement of twelve years ago seemed at the time to assume impressive proportions. But who can believe in its heroes now? Edgar Lee Masters did one creditable thing: *The Spoon River Anthology;* but, except for a single fine poem called *Silence,* I have seen nothing by him since that I could read. Vachel Lindsay's best poems, such as his *Bryan,* are spoiled by the incurable cheapness and looseness which are rampant in the rest of his work. Carl Sandburg, unlike Masters and Lindsay, has a genuine talent for language; with a hard-boiled vocabulary and reputation, he offers what is perhaps the most attractive surface of any of the men of the group. But, when we come to read him in quantity, we are disappointed to find him less interesting than we had hoped; his ideas seem rather obvious, his emotions rather meager. The work of Amy Lowell is like a great empty cloisonné jar; that of John Gould Fletcher a great wall of hard descriptive prose mistakenly presented as poetry. Conrad Aiken, except in a few of his lyrics, is one of those curious people, like William Vaughn Moody, who can turn out a rich-looking texture of words and who can make at first glance the impression of being true and highly gifted inheritors of the English tradition of the nineteenth century, but who leave us, on closer reading, with a feeling that they have not quite got the "afflatus" that their themes and their style imply. Robert Frost has a thin but authentic vein of poetic sensibility; but I find him excessively dull, and he certainly writes very poor verse. He is, in my opinion, the most generally overrated of all this group of poets. Ezra Pound, who deserves all honor as a champion and pioneer, has worked conscientiously and stubbornly as one who understands very well, and as few of his contemporaries do, in what the highest poetry consists, but who has rarely been able to affect us as the highest poets do. His cantos of a "poem of considerable length," so ambitious and so full of fine passages, passages that, standing by themselves, might lead us to believe them mere ornaments from a masterpiece on the great scale, seem entirely composed of such fragments; a mosaic which fails to reveal a pattern, a monument, in its lack of cohesion, its lack of driving force or a center, to a kind of poetic bankruptcy. The other poets of the literary Left, though, like Pound, they can often write, seem to suffer from a similar sterility. Marianne Moore, for example, is sometimes very fine, but as she herself has shrewdly noted in choosing a title for her collected verse, the bulk of her work answers better to the description of "Observations," than to that of poetry. From a slag of intellectual processes that has only a viscous flow, there emerge intense and vivid images that seem to have been invested with a sharp emotional meaning but that are rarely precipitated out in such a way as to make the piece a poem. H. D., like Carl Sandburg, writes well; but, like Sandburg, there is not much in her. Wallace Stevens has a fascinating gift of words that is not far from a gift of nonsense, rather like that of Edith Sitwell, and he is a charming decorative artist. Alfred Kreymborg has his dry distinction, but he tends fatally toward insipidity. I think I prefer the oddity of his early work, frankly prosaic and dry, to his later more pretentious sonnets. E. E. Cummings possesses, in some respects, a more remarkable lyric gift than any of the poets reviewed above; his feeling is always spontaneous, and his words run naturally into music. But, as in his rather limp line-drawings, the hand does not seem very firm: all sorts of ideas and images have come streaming into his head, and he doesn't know how to manipulate them to make them artistically effective. W. C. Williams and Maxwell Bodenheim I have tried my best to admire, but I have never been able to believe in them.*

Since these poets made their first reputations, the general

---

*It was at about this time that Maxwell Bodenheim described me in some such phrase as "a fatuous policeman, menacingly swinging his club." In rereading this essay—in which I have qualified or softened some of the original judgments—I have sometimes been reminded of this.

appetite for poetry seems to have somewhat abated. Among the younger poets, for example, even those of most brilliant promise are having difficulty in getting their poems printed, not by the publishers only, who have evidently come to the conclusion that poetry is bound to be unprofitable, but even by the magazines. The editors of the magazines, who have brought out, since the poetic revival, two or three crops of poets, seem content now to close the canon, and have no place for the poetry of unknown men—even if so obviously gifted as Phelps Putnam or Allen Tate—who cannot be found in Mr. Untermeyer's anthologies or among the original contributors to the *Dial.*

I have left aside the women lyric poets in order to discuss them as a group by themselves. On the average, though less pretentious, I think I find them more rewarding than the men: their emotion is likely to be more genuine and their literary instinct surer. Miss Lizette Woodworth Reese, the dean of the guild, astonishes one by continuing to write, not only with the same fine quality, but almost with the same freshness, as forty years ago. Sara Teasdale, the monotony of whose sobbing note caused her to become rather unfashionable when a more arrogant race of young women appeared, has made definite progress in her art since her earlier books of poems and has recently written some of her most charming lyrics. Miss Edna St. Vincent Millay has now, in turn, grown so popular that she, too, is in danger of becoming unfashionable; but she remains the most important of the group and perhaps one of the most important of our poets. Like Mencken, the prophet of a point of view, she has, like him, become a national figure; nor, as in the case of some other prophets, is her literary reputation undeserved. With little color, meager ornament and images often commonplace, she is yet mistress of deeply moving rhythms, of a music which makes up for the ear what her page seems to lack for the eye; and, above all, she has that singular boldness, which she shares with the greatest poets and which consists in taking just that one step beyond where one's fellows stop that, by making a new contact with moral reality, has the effect of causing other productions to take on an aspect of literary convention. Elinor Wylie, in the best of her verse and in her novel *Jennifer Lorn,* gives expression to a set of emotions quite different from those of Miss Millay, but one which has also its typical interest and its own kind of intensity. Her literary proficiency is immense: she is never at a loss for a clever rhyme, a witty reference or a brilliant image; she can command all the finest fabrics, the choicest works of art, the most luxurious sensations, the most amusing historical allusions and the most delicious things to eat. And, as a consequence, her inferior work is almost as well-written as her best; and her best work has both a style and a splendor of a kind very rare in America —where, even when these qualities do appear together, as they did to some extent in Amy Lowell, they too often remain hollow and metallic from the lack of a heart at the core. Edna Millay's inferior work has no such embroidery to deck it; and, save in her vein of classical austerity, she has for her best but the imagery of the sorrel or mullein stalk of the barren and rocky pastures, the purple wild sweet-pea dragging driftwood across the sand, the dead leaves in the city gutters, the gray snow in the city street, the kettle, the broom, the uncarpeted stairs and the dead father's old clothes—grown strange and disturbing now, to this reader's sense, at least, as the prison cell of Verlaine or Catullus's common crossroads. Louise Bogan plucked one low resounding theme on tensely strung steel strings, but it is now the vibrations of this rather than a further development that are ringing still in the air. Léonie Adams's *Those Not Elect* is a very remarkable book, of which the language, which seems to branch straight from the richest seventeenth-century tradition, strikes music from the calm summer starbreak, the bright-washed night after rain or the blue translucence of evening, where a gull or a pigeon that flies alone, seeking freedom in that space and clarity, is lost in a confusion of cloud and light. An anthology of these women poets should include, besides those named above, the *Cinquains* of the late Adelaide Crapsey and the best of Miss Genevieve Taggard, Miss Babette Deutsch and several others, of whom the younger Laura Gottschalk may turn out to be one of the most interesting and in whose company Dorothy Parker, long known as a humorous writer, has recently, it seems to me, fully proved her right to belong.

I have left to the last the two poets whom, among the men, I admire most: T. S. Eliot and E. A. Robinson. T. S. Eliot, though heavily infected with the Alexandrianism of the Left, has been able to imbue with a personal emotion, not only his inveterate literary allusions and his echoes of other poets, but even the lines that he has borrowed from them. He deserves, both as critic and as poet, his present position of influence. I deplore the fatigued and despondent mood that seems lately to have been drying up both his criticism and his poetry; but I cannot believe that a passion for poetry so serious and so intense can be permanently stifled or numbed. E. A. Robinson is the last and, artistically (leaving the happiest flashes of Emerson aside), the most important of the New England poets. Though he has recently run much into the sands of long and arid blank-verse narratives, I believe that he is one of the poets of our time most likely to survive as an American classic. He and Eliot both, though there are times when they disappoint us by the tendency of their motors to stall and times when they get on our nerves by a kind of hypochondria of the soul, have possessed the poetic gift and the artist's mastery of it.

The subject of Mr. Robinson may lead us to some more general observations. I have said that E. A. Robinson is the last of the New England poets, and it is true that he really belongs to an earlier period than the present and has little in common with the writers in whose company the anthologists now place him. (He is closer to Hawthorne and Henry James.) When we look back on the literary era which preceded the recent renasence, we are surprised, after all that has been written about its paleness, its tameness and its sterility, to take account of the high standard of excellence to which its best writers attained. When we consider Henry James, Stephen Crane and even such novelists of the second rank as George W. Cable and William Dean Howells, with such critics as Irving Babbitt, W. C. Brownell and Paul Elmer More, who belong essentially to the same era, we are struck with certain superiorities over our race of writers today. It may be said of these men, in general, that, though their ideas were less "emancipated," they possessed a sounder culture than we; and that, though less lively, they were better craftsmen. They were professional men of letters, and they had thoroughly learned their trade. Note the intense concentration, the incapacity for careless writing, of even Stephen Crane, who passed for a clever newspaper man and an outlaw to respectable literature, but whose work astonishes us now by an excellence of quality by no means incomparable—as how much of our present fiction is?—to the best European work in the same kind.

Another writer who, like Mr. Robinson, is bound closely, through her craftsmanship and her culture, to this earlier American tradition, but who, by reason of her critical point of view, makes a connecting link with our own, is Edith Wharton. Often described as an imitator of Henry James, she was really, in her important novels, a writer of a different kind. Henry James, except at very rare moments, was never a preacher or a bitter social satirist; but Mrs. Wharton was perhaps the first American to write with indignant passion *against* American values as they had come to present themselves by the end of the last century. Her recent books, since *The Age of Innocence*, have been of rather inferior interest; but, in her prime, she produced what I strongly believe are the best examples of this kind of fiction that we have had in the United States. She was soon followed by Van Wyck Brooks, who represented a similar reaction against a world either brutal and commercial or moribund and genteel. One of the prophets of the present generation, he belongs to the older and more sober tradition and has never, for better or for worse, learned any of the methods of the new.

Join these writers with the others I have mentioned and it will be seen that they make a remarkable group. They have provided both a picture and a criticism of one period of American life. The writing of our own age will hardly, I fear, present so dignified or so firm a front. We have the illusion of a stronger vitality and of a greater intellectual freedom, but we are polygot, parvenu, hysterical and often only semi-literate. When time shall have weeded out our less important writers, it is probable that those who remain will give the impression of a literary vaudeville: H. L. Mencken hoarse with preaching in his act making fun of preachers; Edna St. Vincent Millay, the soloist, a contralto with deep notes of pathos; Sherwood Anderson holding his audience with naïve but disquieting bedtime stories; Theodore Dreiser with his newspaper narrative of commonplace scandals and crimes and obituaries of millionaires, in which the reporter astonishes the readers by being rash enough to try to tell the truth; T. S. Eliot patching from many cultures a dazzling and variegated disguise for the shrinking and scrupulous soul of a hero out of Henry James. Let us remember, however, that vaudeville has always been an American specialty; and that the writers we value most highly in the pre-Civil War period have not in general been such as I have mentioned above as typical of the generation just before our own. Emerson, Whitman, Poe; *Walden* and *Moby Dick*: they are all independent one-man turns, and who can say that we may not find their peers among our present bill of comic monologuists, sentimental songsters and performers of one-act melodramas?

PART 7

THE
SOCIAL CRITICS

27 / HAROLD E. STEARNS

The American Mind

Many of the most acute and perceptive intellectuals of the Twenties
felt themselves besieged not so much by alternative or false ideas as
by a deadening atmosphere. The social condition of America was
often described as antipathetic to the life of the mind; Prohibition,
xenophobia, religious Fundamentalism, business dominance, and
provinciality in all of its other aspects, were all cited as evidence
that American society was so unfriendly to new ideas that intellectuals perceived themselves as something like resident aliens. It
is not surprising, therefore, that much of the intellectual work of
the decade took the form of social criticism.

In what has by now become almost a classic statement of the
reasons for America's intellectual aridity, Harold E. Stearns (1891–
1943), a freelance intellectual and the editor of a famous compen-
dium of opposition to American Culture (*Civilization in the United
States*, 1922), pointed his accusing finger at the pioneer and the
American woman. Because of the lingering legacy of the pioneer,
according to Stearns, Americans had been trained to deprecate non-
utilitarian and leisurely activities; pragmatism was merely a sophisticated rendering of this earlier anti-intellectualism. Because
American men were consumed by work, they traditionally turned
matters of culture over to women; so feminized did culture become
that a man's virility would be thrown into question by his interest
in this forbidden territory. The ladies produced a Victorian intellec-

tual anemia which was the heritage for the twentieth century. For the men who actually built America the life of the mind was useless, although it was thought to be an appropriate decoration for their women. This combination of masculine scorn along with the feminine domestication of ideas created the intellectual and moral background of the Twenties. Yet Stearns did not absolutely despair; he trusted his own kind, the younger generation which was in open rebellion—the young poets, artists, and thinkers who knew what they wanted and who were willing, presumably, to smash their way through convention and propriety in order to achieve the good life never even dreamed of either on the frontier or in the fashionable salon.

When Professor Einstein roused the ire of the women's clubs by stating that "women dominate the entire life of America," and that "there are cities with a million population, but cities suffering from terrible poverty—the poverty of intellectual things," he was but repeating a criticism of our life now old enough to be almost a *cliché*. Hardly any intelligent foreigner has failed to observe and comment upon the extraordinary feminization of American social life, and oftenest he has coupled this observation with a few biting remarks concerning the intellectual anæmia or torpor that seems to accompany it. Naturally this attitude is resented, and the indiscreet visitor is told that he has been rendered astigmatic by too limited observation. He is further informed that he should travel in our country more extensively, see more people, and live among us longer. The inference is that this chastening process will in due time acquaint him with a beauty and a thrilling intellectual vitality coyly hidden from the superficial impressionist.

Now the thesis of this paper is that the spontaneous judgment of the perceptive foreigner is to a remarkable degree cor-

"The Intellectual Life," *Civilization in the United States*, ed. Harold E. Stearns (New York: Harcourt, Brace & Co., 1922), pp. 135–150. From *Civilization in the United States: An Inquiry by Thirty Americans*. Reprinted by permisson of Harcourt, Brace & World, Inc.

rect. But it is a judgment which has to be modified in certain respects rather sharply. Moreover, even long residence in the United States is not likely to give a visitor as vivid a sense of the historical background that has so largely contributed to the present situation as is aroused in the native American, who in his own family hears the folklore of the two generations preceding him and to whom the pioneer tradition is a reality more imaginatively plausible than, say, the emanations of glory from English fields or the aura of ancient pomp enwrapping an Italian castle. The foreigner is too likely to forget that in a young country, precisely because it is young, traditions have a social sanction unknown in an older country where memory of the past goes so far back as to become shadowy and unreal. It is a paradox of history that from ancient cultures usually come those who "were born too soon," whereas from young and groping civilizations spring the panoplied defenders of conventions. It is usually when a tradition is fresh that it is respected most; it is only when it has been followed for years sufficient to make it meaningless that it can create its repudiators. America is a very young country—and in no respect younger than that of all Western nations it has the oldest form of established government; our naïve respect for the fathers is surest proof that we are still in the cultural awkward age. We have not sufficiently grown up but that we must still cling to our father and mother. In a word, we still *think* in pioneer terms, whatever the material and economic facts of a day that has already outgrown their applicability.

And it is the pioneer point of view, once thoroughly understood, which will most satisfactorily explain the peculiar development of the intellectual life in the United States. For the life of the mind is no fine flower of impoverishment, and if the beginnings of human reflection were the wayward reveries of seamen in the long watches of the night or of a shepherd lying on his back idly watching the summer clouds float past, as surely have the considered intellectual achievements of modern men been due to the commercial and industrial organization which, whether or not conducive to the general happiness, has at least made leisure possible for the few. But in the pioneer community leisure cannot exist, even for the few; the struggle is too merciless, the stake—life itself, possibly—too high. The pioneer must almost of necessity hate the thinker, even when he does not despise thought in itself, because the thinker is a liability to a community that can afford only assets; he is nonproductive in himself and a dangerously subversive example to others. Of course, the pioneer will tolerate the minister, exactly as primitive tribes tolerated medicine men—and largely for the same reasons. The minister, if he cannot bring rain or ward off pestilence as the medicine man at least pretended he could, can soften the hardness of the human lot and can show the road to a future kingdom that will amply compensate for the drudgery of the present world. He has, in brief, considerable utilitarian value. The thinker *per se*, however, has none; not only that, he is a reproach and a challenge to the man who must labour by the sweat of his brow—it is as if he said, "For what end, all this turmoil and effort, merely to live? But do you know if life is worth while on such terms?" Questions like these the pioneer must cast far from him, and for the very good reason that if they were tolerated, new communities might never become settled. Scepticism is an expensive luxury possible only to men in cities living off the fruit of others' toil. Certainly America, up to the end of the reconstruction period following the Civil War, had little practical opportunity and less native impulse for the cultivation of this tolerant attitude towards ultimate values, an atmosphere which is a talisman that a true intellectual life is flourishing.

Consider the terrible hardness of the pioneer's physical life. I can think of no better description of it than in one of Sherwood Anderson's stories, "Godliness," in his book, "Winesburg, Ohio." He is writing of the Bentley brothers just before the

Civil War: "They clung to old traditions and worked like driven animals. They lived as practically all of the farming people of the time lived. In the spring and through most of the winter the highways leading into the town of Winesburg were a sea of mud. The four young men of the family worked hard all day in the fields, they ate heavily of coarse, greasy food, and at night slept like tired beasts on beds of straw. Into their lives came little that was not coarse and brutal, and outwardly they were themselves coarse and brutal." Naturally, this intense concentration upon work is not the whole of the picture; there was gaiety and often there was romance in the early days of pioneering, it ran like a coloured thread through all the story of our *Drang nach Westen*. But on the whole the period from our confederation into a Union until the expanding industrial era following the Civil War—roughly the century from 1783 to 1883—was a period in which the cardinal command was, "Be active, be bold, and above all, work." In that century we subdued and populated a continent. There was no time for the distractions of art or the amenities of literature.

To be sure, a short-range perspective seems to belie this last generalization. The colonial times and the first part of the 19th century witnessed a valid and momentous literary and intellectual efflorescence, and it was then we contributed many names to the biography of greatness. Yet it was a culture centred almost wholly in New England and wholly East of the Alleghenies; it had its vitality because it was not self-conscious, it was frankly derivative from England and Europe, it made no pretensions to being intrinsically American. The great current of our national life went irresistibly along, ploughing, and tilling, and cutting down the trees and brush, making roads and bridges as it filled the valleys and the plains. That was the real America, a mighty river of life, compared with which, for instance, Emerson and the Transcendentalists seemed a mere backwater—not a stagnant or brackish one to be sure, often a pool of quietude in which the stars, like Emerson's sentences, might be reflected. But the real America was still in the heart of the pioneer. And in one sense, it still is to-day.

The "real America," I say, because I mean the America of mind and attitude, the inner truth, not the outer actuality. That outer actuality has made the fact of the pioneer almost grotesque. The frontier is closed; the nation is the most prosperous among the harassed ones of the earth; there is no need for the old perpetual preoccupation with material existence. In spite of trade depressions and wars and their aftermaths, we have conquered that problem. But we have not conquered ourselves. We must still go on in the old terms, as if the purpose of making money in order to make more money were as important as the purpose of raising bread in order to support life. The facts have changed, but we have not changed, only deflected our interests. Where the pioneer cleared a wilderness, the modern financier subdues a forest of competitors. He puts the same amount of energy and essentially the same quality of thought into his task to-day, although the practical consequences can hardly be described as identical.

And what have been those practical consequences? As the industrial revolution expanded, coincidently with the filling up of the country, the surplus began to grow. That surplus was expended not towards the enrichment of our life—if one omit the perfunctory bequests for education—but towards the most obvious of unnecessary luxuries, the grandiose maintenance of our women. The daughters of pioneer mothers found themselves without a real job, often, indeed, the chief instrument for advertising their husbands' incomes. For years the Victorian conception of women as ornaments dominated what we were pleased to call our "better elements"—those years, to put it brutally, which coincided with that early prosperity that made the conception possible. If the leisure of the landed gentry class of colonial times had been other than a direct importation, if there had ever been a genuine *salon* in our cultural history, or if our early moneyed aristocracy had ever felt itself really secure from the constant challenge of immigrant newcomers, this surplus might have gone towards the deepening and widening of what we could have felt to be an indigenous tradition. Or if, indeed, the Cavalier traditions of the South (the only offshoot of the Renaissance in America) had not been drained of all vitality by the Civil War and its economic and intellectual consequences, this surplus might have enhanced the more gracious aspects of those traditions. None of these possibilities existed; and when prosperity smiled on us we were embarrassed. We were parvenus—even to this day the comic series, "Bringing Up Father," has a native tang. We know exactly how Mr. Jiggs feels when Mrs. Jiggs drags him away to a concert and makes him dress for a stiff, formal dinner, when all his heart desires is to smoke his pipe and play poker with Dinty and the boys. Indeed, this series, which appears regularly in all the newspapers controlled by Mr. Hearst, will repay the social historian all the attention he gives it. It symbolises better than most of us appreciate the normal relationship of American men and women to cultural and intellectual values. Its very grotesqueness and vulgarity are revealing.

In no country as in the United States have the tragic consequences of the lack of any common concept of the good life been so strikingly exemplified, and in no country has the break with those common concepts been so sharp. After all, when other colonies have been founded, when other peoples have roved from the homeland and settled in distant parts, they have carried with them more than mere scraps of tradition. Oftenest they have carried the most precious human asset of all, a heritage of common feeling, which enabled them to cling to the substance of the old forms even while they adapted them to the new conditions of life. But with us the repudiation of the old heritages was complete; we deliberately sought a new way of life, for in the circumstances under which we came into national being, breaking with the past was synonymous with casting off oppression. The hopefulness, the eagerness, the enthusiasm of that conscious attempt to adjudge all things afresh found its classic expression in the eloquent if vague Declaration of Independence, not even the abstract phraseology of which could hide the revolutionary fervour beneath. Yet a few short years and that early high mood of adventure had almost evaporated, and men were distracted from the former vision by the prospect of limitless economic expansion, both for the individual and the nation as a whole. The Declaration symbolized only a short interlude in the pioneer spirit which brought us here and then led us forth to conquer the riches nature, with her fine contempt of human values, so generously spread before us. The end of the revolutionary mood came as soon as the signing of the Constitution by the States, that admirable working compromise in government which made no attempt to underscore democracy, as we understand it to-day, but rather to hold it in proper check and balance. Free, then, of any common heritage or tradition which might question his values, free, also, of the troublesome idealism of the older revolutionary mood, the ordinary man could go forth into the wilderness with singleness of purpose. He could be, as he still is to-day, the pioneer *toujours*.

Now when his success in his half-chosen rôle made it unnecessary for him to play it, it was precisely the lack of a common concept of the good life which made it impossible for him to be anything else. It is not that Americans make money because they love to do so, but because there is nothing else to do; oddly enough, it is not even that the possessive instincts are especially strong with us (I think the French, for instance, are naturally more avaricious than we), but that we have no notion of a definite type of life for which a small income is enough, and no notion of any type of life from which work has been consciously eliminated. Never in any national sense having had leisure, as individuals we do not know what to do with it when good fortune gives it to us. Unlike a real game, we must go on playing *our* game even after we have won.

But if the successful pioneer did not know what to do with his own leisure, he had naïve faith in the capacity of his women to know what to do with theirs. With the chivalric sentimentality that often accompanies the prosperity of the primitive, the pioneer determined that his good luck should bestow upon his wife and sisters and mother and aunts a gift, the possession of which slightly embarrassed himself. He gave them leisure exactly as the typical business man of to-day gives them a blank check signed with his name. It disposed of them, kept them out of his world, and salved his conscience—like a check to charity. Unluckily for him, his mother, his wife, his sisters, and his aunts were of his own blood and breeding; they were the daughters of pioneers like himself, and the daughters of mothers who had contributed share and share alike to those foundations which had made his success possible. Although a few developed latent qualities of parasitism, the majority were strangely discontented (strangely, that is, from his point of view) with the job of mere Victorian ornament. What more natural under the circumstances than that the unimportant things of life—art, music, religion, literature, the intellectual life—should be handed over to them to keep them busy and contented, while he confined himself to the real man's job of making money and getting on in the world? Was it not a happy and sensible adaptation of function?

Happy or not, it was exactly what took place. To an extent almost incomprehensible to the peoples of older cultures, the things of the mind and the spirit have been given over, in America, into the almost exclusive custody of women. This has been true certainly of art, certainly of music, certainly of education. The spinster school-marm has settled in the impressionable, adolescent minds of boys the conviction that the cultural interests are largely an affair of the other sex; the intellectual life can have no connection with native gaiety, with sexual curiosity, with play, with creative dreaming, or with adventure. These more genuine impulses, he is made to feel, are not merely distinguishable from the intellectual life, but actually at war with it. In my own day at Harvard the Westerners in my class looked with considerable suspicion upon those who specialized in literature, the classics, or philosophy —a man's education should be science, economics, engineering. Only "sissies," I was informed, took courses in poetry out in that virile West. And to this day for a boy to be taught to play the piano, for example, is regarded as "queer," whereas for a girl to be so taught is entirely in the nature of things. That is, natural aptitude has nothing to do with it; some interests are proper for women, others for men. Of course there are exceptions enough to make even the boldest hesitate at generalizations, yet assuredly the contempt, as measured in the only terms we thoroughly understand, money, with which male teachers, male professors (secretly), male ministers, and male artists are universally held should convince the most prejudiced that, speaking broadly, this generalization is in substance correct.

In fact, when we try to survey the currents of our entire national life, to assess these vagrant winds of doctrine free from the ingenuousness that our own academic experience or training may give us, the more shall we perceive that the dichotomy between the cultural and intellectual life of men and women in this country has been carried farther than anywhere else in the world. We need only recall the older women's clubs of the comic papers—in truth, the actual women's clubs of to-day as revealed by small-town newspaper reports of their meetings—the now deliquescent Browning Clubs, the Chautauquas, the church festivals, the rural normal schools for teachers, the women's magazines, the countless national organizations for improving, elevating, uplifting this, that, or the other. One shudders slightly and turns to the impeccable style, the slightly tired and sensuous irony of Anatole France (not yet censored, if we read him in French) for relief. Or if we are so fortunate as to be "regular" Americans instead of unhappy intellectuals educated beyond our environment, we go gratefully back to our work at the office. Beside the stilted artificiality of this world of higher ethical values the business world, where men haggle, cheat, and steal with whole-hearted devotion is at least real. And it is this world, the world of making money, in which alone the American man can feel thoroughly at home. If the French romanticists of the 18th century invented the phrase *la femme mécomprise,* a modern Gallic visitor would be tempted to observe that in this 20th century the United States was the land of *l'homme mécompris.*

These, then, are the cruder historical forces that have led directly to the present remarkable situation, a situation, of course, which I attempt to depict only in its larger outlines. For the surface of the contemporary social structure shows us suffrage, the new insights into the world of industry which the war gave so many women for the first time, the widening of professional opportunity, co-education, and, in the life which perhaps those of us who have contributed to this volume know best, a genuine intellectual camaraderie. Nevertheless, I believe the underlying thesis cannot be successfully challenged. Where men and women in America to-day share their intellectual life on terms of equality and perfect understanding, closer examination reveals that the phenomenon is not a sharing but a capitulation. The men have been feminized.

Thus far through this essay I have by implication rather than direct statement contrasted genuine interest in intellectual things with the kind of intellectual life led by women. Let me say now that no intention is less mine than to contribute to the old controversy concerning the respective intellectual capacities of the two sexes. If I use the adjective "masculine" to denote a more valid type of intellectual impulse than is expressed by the adjective "feminine," it is not to belittle the quality of the second impulse; it is a matter of definition. Further, the relative degree of "masculine" and "feminine" traits possessed by an individual are almost as much the result of acquired training as of native inheritance. The young, independent college girl of to-day is in fact more likely to possess "masculine" intellectual habits than is the average Y.M.C.A. director. I use the adjectives to express broad, general characteristics as they are commonly understood.

For a direct examination of the intellectual life of women —which, I repeat, is practically the intellectual life of the nation—in the United States shows the necessity of terms being defined more sharply. Interest in intellectual things is first, last, and all the time *disinterested;* it is the love of truth, if not exclusively for its own sake, at least without fear of consequences, in fact with precious little thought about consequences. This does not mean that such exercise of the native disposition to think, such slaking of the natural metaphysical curiosity in all of us, is not a process enwrapped—as truly as the disposition to make love or to get angry—with an emotional aura of its own, a passion as distinctive as any other. It merely means that the occasions which stimulate this innate intellectual disposition are of a different sort than those which stimulate our other dispositions. An imaginative picture of one's enlarged social self will arouse our instincts of ambition or a desire to found a family, whereas curiosity or wonder about the mystery of life, the meaning of death, the ultimate nature of God (objects of desire as truly as other objects) will arouse our intellectual disposition. These occasions, objects, hypotheses are of necessity without moral significance. The values inherent in them are the values of satisfied contemplation and not of practical result. Their immediate utility —although their ultimate, by the paradox that is constantly making mere common sense inadequate, may be very great —is only subjective. In this sense, they seem wayward and masculine; and, cardinal sin of all, useless.

Perhaps the meaning of the "feminine" approach to the in-

tellectual life may be made somewhat clearer by this preliminary definition. The basic assumption of such an approach is
that ideas are measured for their value by terms outside the
ideas themselves, or, as Mrs. Mary Austin recently said in a
magazine article, by "her [woman's] deep sense of social
applicability as the test of value." Fundamentally, in a word,
the intellectual life is an instrument of moral reform; the real
test of ideas lies in their utilitarian success. Hence it is hardly
surprising that the intellectual life, as I have defined it, of
women in America turns out on examination not to be an
intellectual life at all, but sociological activity. The best of
modern women thinkers in the United States—and there are
many—are oftenest technical experts, keen to apply knowledge and skill to the formulation of a technique for the better
solution of problems *the answers to which are already assumed.* The question of fundamental ends is seldom if ever
raised: for example, the desirability of the modern family, the
desirability of children glowing with health, the desirability of
monogamy are not challenged. They are assumed as ends desirable in themselves, and what women usually understand by
the intellectual life is the application of modern scientific methods to a sort of enlarged and subtler course in domestic science.

This attitude of contempt for mere intellectual values has
of course been strengthened by the native pioneer suspicion of
all thought that does not issue immediately in successful action.
The remarkable growth of pragmatism, and its sturdy offspring instrumentalism, where ideas become but the lowly
handmaidens of "getting on," has been possible to the extent to
which we see it to-day precisely because the intellectual
atmosphere has been surcharged with this feminized utilitari-
anism. We are deeply uncomfortable before introspection,
contemplation, or scrupulous adherence to logical sequence.
Women do not hesitate to call these activities cold, impersonal,
indirect—I believe they have a phrase for them, "the poobah
tradition of learning." With us the concept of the intellect

as a soulless machine operating in a rather clammy void has acquired the force of folklore because we have so much wished to strip it of warmth and colour. We have wanted to discredit it in itself; we have respected it only for what it could do. If its operations lead to better sanitation, better milk for babies, and larger bridges over which, in Matthew Arnold's phrase, we might cross more rapidly from one dismal, illiberal city to another dismal, illiberal city, then those operations have been justified. That the life of the mind might have an emotional drive, a sting or vibrancy of its own, constituting as valuable a contribution to human happiness as, say, the satisfied marital felicity of the bacteria-less suburbanite in his concrete villa has been incomprehensible. Every science must be an *applied* science, the intellect must be *applied* intellect before we thoroughly understand it. We have created an environment in which the intellectual impulses must become fundamentally social in quality and mood, whereas the truth of the matter is that these impulses, like the religious impulse, in their pristine spontaneity are basically individualistic and capricious rather than disciplined.

But such individualism in thought, unless mellowed by contact with institutions that assume and cherish it and thus can, without patronizing, correct its wildnesses, inevitably turns into eccentricity. And such, unfortunately, has too often been the history of American intellectuals. The institutional structure that might sustain them and keep them on the main track of the humanistic tradition has been too fragile and too slight. The university and college life, the educational institutions, even the discipline of scholarships, as other essays in this volume show us, have been of very little assistance. Even the church has provoked recalcitrance rather than any real reorientation of religious viewpoint, and our atheists—recall Ingersoll—have ordinarily been quite conventional in their intellectual outlook. With educated Englishmen, for example, whatever their religious, economic, or political views, there has been a certain common tradition or point of departure and understanding, i.e., the classics. Mr. Balfour can speak the same language as Mr. Bertrand Russell, even when he is a member of a government that puts Mr. Russell in gaol for his political opposition to the late war. But it really is a strain on the imagination to picture Mr. Denby quoting Hume to refute Mr. Weeks, or Vice-President Coolidge engaging in an epistemological controversy with Postmaster-General Hays. There is no intellectual background common to President Harding and Convict Debs or to any one person and possibly as many as a hundred others—there are only common social or geographical backgrounds, in which the absence of a real community of interests is pathetically emphasized by grotesque emphasis upon fraternal solidarity, as when Mr. Harding discovered that he and his chauffeur belonged to the same lodge, regarding this purely fortuitous fact as a symbol of the healing power of the Fathers and of American Democracy!

In such an atmosphere of shadowy spiritual relationships, where the thinness of contact of mind with mind is childishly disguised under the banner of good fellowship, it might be expected that the intellectual life must be led not only with that degree of individualistic isolation which is naturally necessary for its existence, but likewise in a hostile and unintelligent environment of almost enforced "difference" from the general social type. Such an atmosphere will become as infested with cranks, fanatics, mushroom religious enthusiasts, moral prigs with new schemes of perfectability, inventors of perpetual motion, illiterate novelists, and oratorical cretins, as a swamp with mosquitoes. They seem to breed almost overnight; we have no standard to which the wise and the foolish may equally repair, no criterion by which spontaneously to appraise them and thus, by robbing them of the breath of their life, recognition, reduce their numbers. On the contrary, we welcome them all with a kind of Jamesian gusto, as if every fool, like every citizen, must have his right to vote. It is a kind of intellectual enfranchisement that produces the same sort of leadership which, in the political field of complete suffrage, we suffer under from Washington and our various State capitals. Our intellectual life, when we judge it objectively on the side of vigour and diversity, too often seems like a democracy of mountebanks.

Yet when we turn from the more naïve and popular experiments for finding expression for the baulked disposition to think, the more sophisticated *jeunesse dorée* of our cultural life are equally crippled and sterile. They suffer not so much from being thought and being "queer"—in fact, inwardly deeply uncomfortable at not being successful business men, they are scrupulously conventional in manner and appearance —but from what Professor Santayana has called, with his usual felicity, "the genteel tradition." . . . Real thinkers do not make this ascetic divorce between the passions and the intellect, the emotions and the reason, which is the central characteristic of the genteel tradition. Thought is nourished by the soil it feeds on, and in America to-day that soil is choked with the feckless weeds of correctness. Our sanitary perfection, our material organization of goods, our muffling of emotion, our deprecation of curiosity, our fear of idle adventure, our horror of disease and death, our denial of suffering—what kind of soil of life is that?

Surely not an over-gracious or thrilling one; small wonder that our intellectual plants wither in this carefully aseptic sunlight.

Nevertheless, though I was tempted to give the sub-title "A Study in Sterility" to this essay, I do not believe that our soil is wholly sterile. Beneath the surface barrenness stirs a germinal energy that may yet push its way through the weeds and the tin-cans of those who are afraid of life. If the genteel tradition did not succumb to the broad challenge of Whitman, his invitations have not been wholly rejected by the second generation following him. The most hopeful thing of intellectual promise in America to-day is the contempt of the younger people for their elders; they are restless, uneasy, disaffected. It is not a disciplined contempt; it is not yet kindled by any real love of intellectual values—how could it be? Yet it is a genuine and moving attempt to create a way of life free from the bondage of an authority that has lost all meaning, even to those who wield it. Some it drives in futile and pathetic expatriotism from the country; others it makes headstrong and reckless; many it forces underground, where, much as in Russia before the revolution of 1905, the *intelligentsia* meet their own kind and share the difficulties of their common struggle against an environment that is out to destroy them. But whatever its crudeness and headiness, it is a yeast composed always of those who *will not* conform. The more the pressure of standardization is applied to them the sharper and keener— if often the wilder—becomes their rebellion against it. Just now these non-conformists constitute a spiritual fellowship which is disorganized and with few points of contact. It may be ground out of existence, for history is merciless and every humanistic interlude resembles a perilous equipoise of barbaric forces. Only arrogance and self-complacency give warrant for assuming that we may not be facing a new kind of dark age. On the other hand, if the more amiable and civilized of the generation now growing up can somehow consolidate their scattered powers, what may they not accomplish? For we have a vitality and nervous alertness which, properly channelled and directed, might cut through the rocks of stupidity with the precision and spaciousness with which our mechanical inventions have seized on our natural resources and turned them into material goods. Our cup of life is full to the brim.

I like to think that this cup will not all be poured upon the sandy deltas of industrialism . . . we have so much to spare! Climb to the top of the Palisades and watch the great city in the deepening dusk as light after light, and rows of lights after rows, topped by towers of radiance at the end of the island, shine through the shadows across the river. Think, then, of the miles of rolling plains, fertile and dotted with cities, stretching behind one to that other ocean which washes a civilization that was old before we were born and yet to-day gratefully accepts our pitiful doles to keep it from starvation, of the millions of human aspirations and hopes and youthful eagernesses contained in the great sprawling, uneasy entity we call our country—must all the hidden beauty and magic and laughter we know is ours be quenched because we lack the courage to make it proud and defiant? Or walk down the Avenue some late October morning when the sun sparkles in a clear and electric air such as can be found nowhere else in the world. The flashing beauty of form, the rising step of confident animalism, the quick smile of fertile minds—must all these things, too, be reduced to a drab uniformity because we lack the courage to proclaim their sheer physical loveliness? Has not the magic of America been hidden under a fog of ugliness by those who never really loved it, who never knew our natural gaiety and high spirits and eagerness for knowledge? They have the upper hand now—but who would dare to prophesy that they can keep it?

Perhaps this is only a day-dream, but surely one can hope that the America of our natural affections rather than the present one of enforced dull standardization may some day snap the shackles of those who to-day keep it a spiritual prison. And as surely will it be the rebellious and disaffected who accomplish the miracle, if it is ever accomplished. Because at bottom their revolt, unlike the aggressions of the standardizers, is founded not on hate of what they cannot understand, but on love of what they wish all to share.

28 / *JOHN DEWEY*

Intellectual Illiberality

In *The New Republic* of May 10, 1922, John Dewey (1859–1952) used William Jennings Bryan's campaign against evolution as the occasion to analyze something of the national mood. Dewey was already a distinguished educator and philosopher, whose books through the Twenties included *The Influence of Darwin on Philosophy*, 1910; *German Philosophy and Politics*, 1915; *Democracy and Education*, 1916; *Reconstruction in Philosophy*, 1920; *Human Nature and Conduct*, 1922; *Experience and Nature*, 1925; *The Public and Its Problems*, 1927; and *The Quest for Certainty*, 1929. In the brief compass of the following article, Dewey explained many of his attitudes about America. For Dewey, Bryan personified the prosperous, provincial Midwestern American's coupling of political liberalism and intellectual illiberalism. The evangelical churches, although perhaps declining in direct power since the beginning of the nineteenth century, steadily increased their control of thought. The substitution of morality for thought had deadened the American mind, and had produced public leaders like Bryan, Theodore Roosevelt, and Woodrow Wilson—moral crusaders, not men of insight and intelligence. Dewey's own discontent about his early enthusiastic support of Wilson and the war had already turned to the disillusionment so characteristic of the decade.

The campaign of William Jennings Bryan against science and in favor of obscurantism and intolerance is worthy of serious study. It demands more than the mingled amusement and irritation which it directly evokes. In its success (and it is meet-

---

"The American Intellectual Frontier," *The New Republic*, XXX, 388 (May 10, 1922); reprinted in *Characters and Events*, ed. Joseph Ratner (New York: Henry Holt & Co. 1929), II, pp. 447–452.

ing with success) it raises fundamental questions about the quality of our democracy. It helps us understand the absence of intellectual radicalism in the United States and the present eclipse of social and political liberalism. It aids, abets and gives comfort to the thoroughgoing critics of any democracy. It gives point to the assertion of our Menckens that democracy by nature puts a premium on mediocrity, the very thing in human nature that least stands in need of any extraneous assistance.

For Mr. Bryan is a typical democratic figure. There is no gainsaying that proposition. Economically and politically he has stood for and with the masses, not radically but "progressively." The most ordinary justice to him demands that his usefulness in revolt against privilege and his rôle as a leader in the late progressive movement—late in every sense of the word, including deceased—be recognized. His leadership in antagonism to free scientific research and to popular dissemination of its results cannot therefore be laughed away as a personal idiosyncrasy. There is a genuine and effective connection between the political and the doctrinal directions of his activity, and between the popular responses they call out.

What we call the middle classes are for the most part the church-going classes, those who have come under the influence of evangelical Christianity. These persons form the backbone of philanthropic social interest, of social reform through political action, of pacifism, of popular education. They embody and express the spirit of kindly goodwill toward classes which are at an economic disadvantage and toward other nations, especially when the latter show any disposition toward a republican form of government. The "Middle West," the prairie country, has been the centre of active social philanthropies and political progressivism because it is the chief home of this folk. Fairly well to do, enough so at least to be ambitious and to be sensitive to restrictions imposed by railway and financial corporations, believing in education and better opportunities for its own children, mildly interested in "culture," it has formed the solid element in our diffuse national life and heterogeneous populations. It has been the element responsive to appeals for the square deal and more nearly equal opportunities for all, as it has understood equality of opportunity. It followed Lincoln in the abolition of slavery, and it followed Roosevelt in his denunciation of "bad" corporations and aggregations of wealth. It also followed Roosevelt or led him in its distinctions between "on the one hand and on the other hand." It has been the middle in every sense of the word and in every movement. Like every mean it has held things together and given unity and stability of movement.

It has never had an interest in ideas as ideas, nor in science and art for what they may do in liberating and elevating the human spirit. Science and art as far as they refine and polish life, afford "culture," mark stations on an upward social road, and have direct useful social applications, yes: but as emancipations, as radical guides to life, no. There is nothing recondite or mysterious or sinister or adverse to a reputable estimate of human nature in the causes of this state of mind. Historians of thought point out the difference between the fortunes of the new ideas of science and philosophy in the eighteenth century in England and France. In the former, they were accommodated, partially absorbed; they permeated far enough to lose their own inherent quality. Institutions were more or less liberalized, but the ideas were lost in the process. In France, the opposition was entrenched in powerful and inelastic institutions. The ideas were clarified and stripped to fighting weight. They had to fight to live, and they became weapons. What happened in England happened in America only on a larger scale and to greater depths. The net result is social and political liberalism combined with intellectual illiberality. Of the result Mr. Bryan is an outstanding symbol.

The fathers of our country belonged to an intellectual aristocracy; they shared in the intellectual enlightenment of the eighteenth century. Franklin, Jefferson, John Adams, in their beliefs and ideas were men of the world, especially of the contemporary French world. Their free-thinking ideas did not prevent their being leaders. A generation later and it is doubtful if one of them could have been elected town selectman, much less have become a powerful political figure. When Mr. Taft was a candidate for President, a professor of modern languages in a southern college was dismissed from his position because he remarked to a friend in private conversation that he did not think that the fact that Mr. Taft was a Unitarian necessarily disqualified him for service as President. The incident is typical of the change wrought in a century, a change which became effective, however, quite early in the century. There are histories of the United States written from almost every point of view; but the social and political consequences of the popular evangelical movement which began in the early years of the nineteenth century do not seem to have received the attention they deserve. A large part of what is attacked under the name of Puritanism has next to nothing to do with historic Puritanism and almost everything to do with that second "Great Awakening" which began in the border, southern and western frontier states in the first decade of the last century.

It is not without significance that Andrew Jackson, the first "church-going" President, was also the first political representative of the democratic frontier, the man who marks the change of the earlier aristocratic republic into a democratic republic. The dislike of privilege extended itself to fear of the highly educated and the expert. The tradition of higher education for the clergy was surrendered in the popular denominations. Religion was popularized, and thought, especially free-thought which impinged adversely upon popular moral conceptions, became unpopular, too unpopular to consist with political success. It was almost an accident that even Lincoln could be elected President. Nominal tribute, at least, has had to be paid to the beliefs of the masses. When popular education was extended and colleges and "universities" were scattered towards the frontier, denominational agencies alone had sufficient social zeal to take part. When state universities were founded they were open to the suspicion of ungodliness; and generally protected themselves by some degree of conformity to the expectations imposed by the intellectual prejudices of the masses. They could go much further than denominational colleges, but they could not go so far as to cultivate the free spirit. There were reserves, reticences and accommodations.

The churches performed an inestimable social function in frontier expansion. They were the rallying points not only of respectability but of decency and order in the midst of a rough and turbulent population. They were the representatives of social neighborliness and all the higher interests of the communities. The tradition persisted after the incoming of better schools, libraries, clubs, musical organizations and the other agencies of "culture." There are still thousands of communities throughout the country where the church building is the natural meeting-house for every gathering except a "show." The intensity of evangelical life toned down, and the asperities of dogmatic creeds softened. But the association of the church with the moral and the more elevated social interests of the community remained. The indirect power of the church over thought and expression increased as its direct power waned. The more people stopped going to church, the more important it became to maintain the standards for which the church stood. As the frontier ceased to be a menace to orderly life, it persisted as a limit beyond which it was dangerous and unrespectable for thought to travel.

What the frontier was to western expansion, slavery was for the South. After a period of genuine liberalism among the southern clergy, the church became largely a bulwark of support to the peculiar institution, especially as the battle took a sectional form. The gentry became at least nominally attached to the church in the degree in which clericalism attached itself to the support of slavery. The church was a natural outlet and consolation for the poor whites. It was upon the whole the most democratic institution within their horizon. It is notorious that the most reactionary theological tendencies have their home in the South. The churches there can thank God that they at least have not contaminated their theology with dangerous concessions to modern thought. In the South the movements to withhold public funds from public educational institutions which permit the teaching of evolution have their greatest success.

Mr. Bryan can have at best only a temporary triumph, a *succés d'estime*, in his efforts to hold back biological inquiry and teaching. It is not in this particular field that he is significant. But his appeals and his endeavors are a symptom and a symbol of the forces which are most powerful in holding down the intellectual level of American life. He does not represent the frontier democracy of Jackson's day. But he represents it toned down and cultivated as it exists in fairly prosperous villages and small towns that have inherited the fear of whatever threatens the security and order of a precariously attained civilization, along with pioneer impulses to neighborliness and decency. Attachment to stability and homogeneity of thought and belief seem essential in the midst of practical heterogeneity, rush and unsettlement. We are not Puritans in our intellectual heritage, but we are evangelical because of our fear of ourselves and of our latent frontier disorderliness. The depressing effect upon the free life of inquiry and criticism is the greater because of the element of soundness in frontier fear, and because of the impulses of good will and social aspiration which have become entangled with its creeds. The forces which are embodied in the present crusade would not be so dangerous were they not bound up with so much that is necessary and good. We have been so taught to respect the beliefs of our neighbors that few will respect the beliefs of a neigh-

bor when they depart from forms which have become associated with aspiration for a decent neighborly life. This is the
illiberalism which is deep-rooted in our liberalism. No account
of the decay of the idealism of the progressive movement in
politics or of the failure to develop an intelligent and enduring
idealism out of the emotional fervor of the war, is adequate
unless it reckons with this fixed limit to thought. No future
liberal movement, when active liberalism revives, will be permanent unless it goes deep enough to affect it. Otherwise we
shall have in the future what we have had in the past, revival-
ists like Bryan, Roosevelt and Wilson, movements which embody moral emotions rather than the insight and policy of
intelligence.

29 / JOSEPH WOOD KRUTCH

The End of Spiritual Comfort

Of all the dirges composed for the death of the once-familiar human
spirit, *The Modern Temper* by Joseph Wood Krutch (1893–   )
was the most gentle, persuasive, immensely sad, and influential.
Krutch had already published *Our Changing Morals* in 1925 and a
study of Poe in 1926, when the following article was published in
The Atlantic Monthly; this piece was expanded to book length in
1929. Krutch's basic premise was the assertion that the modern
world enforced a radical discontinuity upon men. Science replaced
poetry and myth, as reality replaced illusion, as experience replaced
innocence. No longer was there any rational basis for tradition,
ethics, or standards, with the consequence that any continuation of
belief was the result of "the temporary suspension of disbelief."
That the despair of the Twenties was not merely localized, not
merely a response to concrete events such as the war or Versailles
or provinciality, is proved best by Krutch's radical and cosmic

anguish. Reduced to a schizoid as his reason and education diverged, man, Krutch believed, was now reduced to mocking "his torn and divided soul." Only the reason could rejoice in science, so that, finally, Krutch concluded: "What man knows is everywhere at war with what he wants." This lament over the corpse of humanism was one response to modernity, a transitional response between the confidences of Victorian America and the later recognition that man's isolation was possibly a new kind of freedom. Occupying that fragile position between two worlds, Krutch's essay cogently argues the case for the Twenties.

I

It is one of Freud's quaint conceits that the baby in its mother's womb is the happiest of living creatures. Into his consciousness no conflict has yet entered, for he knows no limitations to his desires and the universe is exactly as he wishes it to be. All his needs are satisfied before even he becomes aware of them, and if his awareness is dim, that is but the natural result of a complete harmony between the self and the environment, since, as Spencer pointed out in a remote age, to be omniscient and omnipotent would be to be without any consciousness whatsoever. The discomfort of being born is the first warning which he receives that any event can be thrust upon him; it is the first limitation of his omnipotence which he perceives, and he is cast upon the shores of the world wailing his protest against the indignity to which he has been subjected. Years pass before he learns to control the expression of enraged surprise which arises within him at every unpleasant fact with which he is confronted, and his parents conspire so to protect him that he will learn only by very slow stages how far is the world from his heart's desire.

The cradle is made to imitate as closely as may be the conditions, both physical and spiritual, of the womb. Of its occupant no effort is demanded, and every precaution is taken to anticipate each need before it can arise. If, as the result of any unforeseen circumstance, any unsatisfied desire is born, he need only raise his voice in protest to cause the entire world in so far as he knows it—his nurse or his parents—to rush to his aid. The whole of his physical universe is obedient to his will and he is justified by his experience in believing that his mere volition controls his destiny. Only as he grows older does he become aware that there are wills other than his own or that there are physical circumstances rebellious to any human will. And only after the passage of many years does he become aware of the full extent of his predicament in the midst of a world which is in very few respects what he would wish it to be.

As a child he is treated as a child, and such treatment implies much more than the physical coddling of which Freud speaks. Not only do those who surround him coöperate more completely than they ever will again to satisfy his wishes in material things, but they encourage him to live in a spiritual world far more satisfactory than their own. He is carefully protected from any knowledge of the cruelties and complexities of life; he is led to suppose that the moral order is simple and clear, that virtue triumphs, and that the world is, as the desires of whole generations of mankind have led them to try to pretend that it is, arranged according to a pattern which would seem reasonable and satisfactory to human sensibilities. He is prevented from realizing how inextricably what men call good and evil are intertwined, how careless is Nature of those values called mercy and justice and righteousness which men have come, in her despite, to value; and he is, besides, encouraged to believe in a vast mythology peopled with figments that range all the way from the Saints to Santa Claus and that represent projections of human wishes which the adult has come to recognize as no more than projections, but which he is willing that the child, for the sake of his own happiness, should believe real. Aware how different is the world which experience reveals from the world which the spirit desires, the mature, as though afraid that reality could not be endured unless the mind had been gradually inured to it, allow the child to become aware of it only by slow stages, and little by little he learns, not only the limitations of his will, but the moral discord of the world. Thus it is, in a very important sense, true that the infant does come trailing clouds of glory from that heaven which his imagination creates, and that as his experience accumulates he sees it fade away into the light of common day.

Now races as well as individuals have their infancy, their adolescence, and their maturity. Experience accumulates not only from year to year but from generation to generation, and in the life of each person it plays a little larger part than it did in the life of his father. As civilization grows older it too has more and more facts thrust upon its consciousness and is compelled to abandon one after another, quite as the child does, certain illusions which have been dear to it. Like the child, it has instinctively assumed that what it would like to be true is true, and it never gives up any such belief until experience in some form compels it to do so. Being, for example, extremely important to itself, it assumes that it is extremely important to the universe also. The earth is the centre of all existing things, man is the child and the protégé of those gods who transcend and who will ultimately enable him to transcend all the evils which he has been compelled to recognize. The world and all that it contains were designed for him, and even those things which seem noxious have their usefulness only temporarily hid. Since he knows but little he is free to imagine, and imagination is always the creature of desire.

II

The world which any consciousness inhabits is a world made up in part of experience and in part of fancy. No experience, and hence no knowledge, is complete, but the gaps which lie between the solid fragments are filled in with shadows. Connections, explanations, and reasons are supplied by the imagination, and thus the world gets its patterned completeness from material which is spun out of the desires. But as time goes on and experience accumulates there remains less and less scope for the fancy. The universe becomes more and more what experience has revealed, less and less what imagination has created, and hence, since it was not designed to suit man's needs, less and less what he would have it be. With increasing knowledge his power to manipulate his physical environment increases, but in gaining the knowledge which enables him to do so he surrenders insensibly the power which in his ignorance he had to mould the universe. The forces of nature obey him, but in learning to master them he has in another sense allowed them to master him. He has exchanged the universe which his desires created, the universe made for man, for the universe of nature of which he is only a part. Like the child growing into manhood, he passes from a world which is fitted to him into a world for which he must fit himself.

If, then, the world of poetry, mythology, and religion represents the world as man would like to have it, while science represents the world as he gradually comes to discover it, we need only compare the two to realize how irreconcilable they appear. For the cozy bowl of the sky arched in a protecting curve above him he must exchange the cold immensities of space, and, for the spiritual order which he has designed, the chaos of nature. God he had loved *because* God was anthropomorphic, because He was made in man's own image, with purposes and desires which were human and hence understandable. But Nature's purpose, if purpose she can be said to have, is no purpose of his and is not understandable in his terms. Her desire merely to live and to propagate in innumerable forms, her ruthless indifference to his values, and the blindness of her irresistible will strike terror to his soul, and he comes in the fullness of his experience to realize that the ends which he proposes to himself—happiness and order and reason—are ends which he must achieve, if he achieve them at all, in her despite. Formerly he had believed in even his darkest moments that the universe was rational if he could only grasp its rationality, but gradually he comes to suspect that rationality is an attribute of himself alone and that there is no reason to suppose that his own life has any more meaning than the life of the humblest insect that crawls from one annihilation to another. Nature, in her blind thirst for life, has filled every possible cranny of the rotting earth with some sort of fantastic creature, and among them man is but one—perhaps the most miserable of all, because he is the only one in whom the instinct of life falters long enough to enable it to ask the question 'Why?' As long as life is regarded as having been created, creating may be held to imply a purpose, but merely to have come into being is, in all likelihood, merely to go out of it also.

Fortunately, perhaps, man, like the individual child, was spared in his cradle the knowledge which he could not bear. Illusions have been lost one by one. God, instead of disappearing in an instant, has retreated step by step and surrendered gradually his control of the universe. Once he decreed the fall of every sparrow and counted the hairs upon every head; a little later he became merely the original source of the laws of nature, and even to-day there are thousands who, unable to bear the thought of losing him completely, still fancy that they can distinguish the uncertain outlines of a misty figure. But the rôle which he plays grows less and less, and man is left more and more alone in a universe to which he is completely alien. His world was once, like the child's world, three quarters myth and poetry. His teleological concepts moulded it into a form which he could appreciate and he gave to it moral laws which would make it meaningful, but step by step the outlines of nature have thrust themselves upon him, and for the dream which he made is substituted a reality devoid of any pattern which he can understand.

In the course of this process innumerable readjustments have been made, and always with the effort to disturb as little as possible the myth which is so much more full of human values than the fact which comes in some measure to replace it. Thus, for example, the Copernican theory of astronomy, removing the earth from the centre of the universe and assigning it a very insignificant place among an infinitude of whirling motes, was not merely resisted as a fact, but was, when finally accepted, accepted as far as possible without its implications. Even if taken entirely by itself and without the whole system of facts of which it is a part, it renders extremely improbable the assumption, fundamental in most human thought, that the universe has man as its centre and is hence understandable in her terms, but this implication was disregarded just as, a little later, the implications of the theory of evolution were similarly disregarded. It is not likely that if man had been aware from the very beginning that his world was a mere detail in the universe, and himself merely one of the innumerable species of living things, he would ever have come to think of himself, as he even now tends to do, as a being whose desires must be somehow satisfiable and whose reason must be matched by some similar reason in nature. But the myth, having been once established, persists long after the assumptions upon which it was made have been destroyed, because, being born of desire, it is far more satisfactory than any fact.

Unfortunately, perhaps, experience does not grow at a constant, but at an accelerated, rate. The Greeks who sought knowledge, not through the study of nature, but through the examination of their own minds, developed a philosophy which was really analogous to myth, because the laws which determined its growth were dictated by human desires, and they discovered few facts capable of disturbing the pattern which they devised. The Middle Ages retreated still further

into themselves, but with the Renaissance man began to surrender himself to nature, and the sciences, each nourishing the
other, began their iconoclastic march. Three centuries lay between the promulgation of the Copernican theory and the
publication of the *Origin of Species,* but in sixty-odd years
which have elapsed since that latter event the blows have
fallen with a rapidity which left no interval for recovery. The
structures which are variously known as mythology, religion,
and philosophy, and which are alike in that each has as its
function the interpretation of experience in terms which have
human values, have collapsed under the force of successive
attacks and shown themselves utterly incapable of assimilating
the new stores of experience which have been dumped upon
the world. With increasing completeness science maps out the
pattern of nature, but the latter has no relation to the pattern
of human needs and feelings.

Consider, for example, the plight of ethics. Historical criticism having destroyed what used to be called by people of
learning and intelligence 'Christian Evidences,' and biology
having shown how unlikely it is that man is the recipient of any
transcendental knowledge, there remains no foundation in
authority for ideas of right and wrong; and if, on the other
hand, we turn to the traditions of the human race, anthropol-
ogy is ready to prove that no consistent human tradition has
ever existed. Custom has furnished the only basis which ethics
have ever had, and there is no conceivable human action which
custom has not at one time justified and at another condemned.
Standards are imaginary things, and yet it is extremely doubtful if man can live well, either spiritually or physically, without
the belief that they are somehow real. Without them society
lapses into anarchy and the individual becomes aware of an
intolerable disharmony between himself and the universe. Instinctively and emotionally he is an ethical animal. No known
race is so low in the scale of civilization that it has not attributed a moral order to the world, because no known race is so

little human as not to suppose a moral order so innately desirable as to have an inevitable existence. It is man's most fundamental myth, and life seems meaningless to him without it. Yet, as that systematized and cumulative experience which is called science displaces one after another the myths which have been generated by need, it grows more and more likely that he must remain an ethical animal in a universe which contains no ethical element.

III

Mystical philosophers have sometimes said that they 'accepted the universe.' They have, that is to say, formed of it some conception which answered the emotional needs of their spirit and which brought them a sense of being in harmony with its aims and processes. They have been aware of no needs which Nature did not seem to supply and of no ideals which she too did not seem to recognize. They have felt themselves one with her because they have had the strength of imagination to make her over in their own image, and it is doubtful if any man can live at peace who does not thus feel himself at home. But as the world assumes the shape which science gives it, it becomes more and more difficult to find such emotional correspondences. Whole realms of human feeling, like the realm of ethics, find no place for themselves in the pattern of nature and generate needs for which no satisfaction is supplied. What man knows is everywhere at war with what he wants.

In the course of a few centuries his knowledge, and hence the universe of which he finds himself an inhabitant, have been completely revolutionized, but his instincts and his emotions have remained, relatively at least, unchanged. He is still, as he always was, adjusted to the orderly, purposeful, humanized world which all peoples unburdened by experience have figured to themselves, but that world no longer exists. He has the same sense of dignity to which the myth of his descent from the gods was designed to minister, and the same innate purposefulness which led him to attribute a purpose to Nature, but he can no longer think in terms appropriate to either. The world which his reason and his investigation reveal is a world which his emotions cannot comprehend.

Casually he accepts the spiritual iconoclasm of science, and in the detachment of everyday life he learns to play with the cynical wisdom of biology and psychology, which explain away the awe of emotional experience just as earlier science explained away the awe of conventional piety. Yet, under the stress of emotional crises, knowledge is quite incapable of controlling his emotions or of justifying them to himself. In love, he calls upon the illusions of man's grandeur and dignity to help him accept his emotions, and faced with tragedy he calls upon illusion to dignify his suffering; but lyric flight is checked by the rationality which he has cultivated, and in the world of metabolism and hormones, repressions and complexes, he finds no answer for his needs. He is feeling about love, for example, much as the troubadour felt, but he thinks about it in a very different way. Try as he may, the two halves of his soul can hardly be made to coalesce, and he cannot either feel as his intelligence tells him that he should feel or think as his emotions would have him think, and thus he is reduced to mocking his torn and divided soul. In the grip of passion he cannot, as some romanticist might have done, accept it with a religious trust in the mystery of love, nor yet can he regard it as a psychiatrist, himself quite free from emotion, might suggest— merely as an interesting specimen of physical botany. Man *qua* thinker may delight in the intricacies of psychology, but man *qua* lover has not learned to feel in its terms; so that, though complexes and ductless glands may serve to explain the feelings of another, one's own still demand all these symbols of the ineffable in which one has long ceased to believe.

Time was when the scientist, the poet, and the philosopher

walked hand in hand. In the universe which the one perceived the other found himself comfortably at home. But the world of modern science is one in which the intellect alone can rejoice. The mind leaps, and leaps perhaps with a sort of elation, through the immensities of space, but the spirit, frightened and cold, longs to have once more above its head the inverted bowl beyond which may lie whatever paradise its desires may create. The lover who surrendered himself to the Implacable Aphrodite or who fancied his foot upon the lowest rung of the Platonic ladder of love might retain his self-respect, but one can neither resist nor yield gracefully to a carefully catalogued psychosis. A happy life is a sort of poem, with a poem's elevation and dignity, but emotions cannot be dignified unless they are first respected. They must seem to correspond with, to be justified by, something in the structure of the universe itself; but though it was the function of religion and philosophy to hypostatize some such correspondence, to project a humanity upon Nature, or at least to conceive of a humane force above and beyond her, science finds no justification for such a process and is content instead to show how illusions were born.

The most ardent love of truth, the most resolute determination to follow Nature no matter to what black abyss she may lead, need not blind one to the fact that many of the lost illusions had, to speak the language of science, a survival value. Either individuals or societies whose life is imbued with a cheerful certitude, whose aims are clear, and whose sense of the essential rightness of life is strong, live and struggle with an energy unknown to the skeptical and the pessimistic. Whatever the limitations of their intellects as instruments of criticism, they possess the physical and emotional vigor which is, unlike critical intelligence, analogous to the processes of nature. They found empires and conquer wildernesses, and they pour the excess of their energy into works of art which the intelligence of more sophisticated peoples continues to admire even though it has lost the faith in life which is requisite for the building of a Chartres or the carving of a Venus de Milo. The one was not erected to a law of nature or the other designed to celebrate the *libido*, for each presupposed a sense of human dignity which science nowhere supports.

Thus man seems caught in a dilemma which his intellect has devised. Any deliberately managed return to a state of relative ignorance, however desirable it might be argued to be, is obviously out of the question. We cannot, as the naïve proponents of the various religions, new and old, seem to assume, believe one thing and forget another merely because we happen to be convinced that it would be desirable to do so; and it is worth observing that the new psychology, with its penetrating analysis of the influence of desire upon belief, has so adequately warned the reason of the tricks which the will can play upon it that it has greatly decreased the possibility of beneficent delusion and serves to hold the mind in a steady contemplation of that from which it would fain escape. Weak and uninstructed intelligences take refuge in the monotonous repetition of once living creeds, or are even reduced to the desperate expedient of going to sleep amid the formulæ of the flabby pseudo-religions in which the modern world is so prolific. But neither of these classes affords any aid to the robust but serious mind which is searching for some terms upon which it may live.

And if we are, as by this time we should be, free from any teleological delusion, if we no longer make the unwarranted assumption that every human problem is somehow of necessity solvable, we must confess it may be that for the sort of being whom we have described no survival is possible in any form like that which his soul has now taken. He is a fantastic thing that has developed sensibilities and established values beyond the nature which gave him birth. He is of all living creatures the one to whom the earth is the least satisfactory. He has arrived at a point where he can no longer delude himself as to the extent of his predicament, and should he either become modified or disappear the earth would continue to spin and the grass to grow as it has always done. Of the thousands of living species the vast majority would be as unaware of his passing as they are unaware now of his presence, and he would go as a shadow goes. His arts, his religions, and his civilizations —these are fair and wonderful things, but they are fair and wonderful to him alone. With the extinction of his poetry would be extinguished also the only sensibility for which it has any meaning, and there would remain nothing capable of feeling a loss. Nothing would be left to label the memory of his discontent 'divine,' and those creatures who find in nature no lack would resume their undisputed possession of the earth.

Anthropoid in form some of them might continue to be, and possessed as well of all of the human brain that makes possible a cunning adaption to the conditions of physical life. To them nature might yield up subtler secrets than any yet penetrated; their machines might be more wonderful and their bodies more healthy than any yet known—even though there had passed away, not merely all myth and poetry, but the need for them as well. Cured of his transcendental cravings, content with things as they are, accepting the universe as experience had shown it to be, man would be freed of his soul and, like the other animals, either content or at least desirous of nothing which he might not hope ultimately to obtain.

Nor can it be denied that certain adumbrations of this type have before now come into being. Among those of keener intellect there are scientists to whom the test tube and its contents are all-sufficient, and among those of coarser grain, captains of finance and builders of mills, there are those to whom the acquirement of wealth and power seems to constitute a life in which no lack can be perceived. Doubtless they are not new types; doubtless they have always existed; but may they not be the strain from which Nature will select the coming race? Is not their creed the creed of Nature, and are they not bound to triumph over those whose illusions are no longer potent because they are no longer really believed? Certain philosophers, clinging desperately to the ideal of a humanized world, have proposed a retreat into the imagination. Bertrand Russell in his popular essay, *A Free Man's Worship,* Unamuno and Santayana *passim* throughout their works, have argued that the way of salvation lay in a sort of ironic belief, in a determination to act as though one still believed the things which once were really held true. But is not this a desperate expedient, a last refuge likely to appeal only to the leaders of a lost cause? Does it not represent the last, least substantial phase, of fading faith, something which borrows what little substance it seems to have from a reality of the past? If it seems half real to the sons of those who lived in the spiritual world of which it is a shadow, will it not seem, a little further removed, only a faint futility? Surely it has but little to oppose to those who come armed with the certitudes of science and united with, not fleeing from, the nature amid which they live.

And if the dilemma here described is itself a delusion it is at least as vividly present and as terribly potent as those other delusions which have shaped or deformed the human spirit. There is no significant contemporary writer upon philosophy, ethics, or æsthetics whose speculations do not lead him to it in one form or another, and even the less reflective are aware of it in their own way. Both our practical morality and our emotional lives are adjusted to a world which no longer exists. In so far as we adhere to a code of conduct, we do so largely because certain habits still persist, not because we can give any logical reason for preferring them, and in so far as we indulge ourselves in the primitive emotional satisfactions,—romantic love, patriotism, zeal for justice, and so forth,—our satisfaction is the result merely of the temporary suspension of our disbelief in the mythology upon which they are founded. Traditionalists in religion are fond of asserting that our moral codes are flimsy because they are rootless; but, true as this is, it is perhaps not so important as the fact that our emotional lives are root-less too.

If the gloomy vision of a dehumanized world which has just been evoked is not to become a reality, some complete read-justment must be made, and at least two generations have found themselves unequal to the task. The generation of Thomas Henry Huxley, so busy with destruction as never ade-quately to realize how much it was destroying, fought with such zeal against frightened conservatives that it never took time to do more than assert with some vehemence that all would be well, and the generation that followed either danced amid the ruins or sought by various compromises to save the remains of a few tottering structures. But neither patches nor evasions will serve. It is not a changed world but a new one in which man must henceforth live if he lives at all, for all his premises have been destroyed and he must proceed to new conclusions. The values which he thought established have been swept away along with the rules by which he thought they might be attained.

To this fact many are not yet awake, but our novels, our poems, and our pictures are enough to reveal that a generation aware of its predicament is at hand. It has awakened to the fact that both the ends which its fathers proposed to them-selves and the emotions from which they drew their strength seem irrelevant and remote. With a smile, sad or mocking, according to individual temperament, it regards those works of the past in which were summed up the values of life. The romantic ideal of a world well lost for love and the classic ideal of austere dignity seem equally ridiculous, equally meaningless when referred, not to the temper of the past, but to the temper of the present. The passions which swept through the once major poets no longer awaken any profound response, and only in the bleak, torturous complexities of a T. S. Eliot does it find its moods given adequate expression. Here disgust speaks with a robust voice and denunciation is confident, but ecstasy, flickering and uncertain, leaps fitfully up only to sink back among the cinders. And if the poet, with his gift of keen perceptions and his power of organization, can achieve only the most momentary and unstable adjustments, what hope can there be for those whose spirit is a less powerful instrument?

And yet it is with such as he, baffled, but content with nothing which plays only upon the surface, that the hope for a still humanized future must rest. No one can tell how many of the old values must go or how new the new will be. Thus, while under the influence of the old mythology the sexual instinct was transformed into romantic love and tribal solidarity into the religion of patriotism, there is nothing in the modern consciousness capable of effecting these transmutations. Neither the one nor the other is capable of being, as it once was, the raison d'être of a life or the motif of a poem which is not, strictly speaking, derivative and anachronistic. Each is fading, each becoming as much a shadow as devotion to the cult of purification through self-torture. Either the instincts upon which they are founded will achieve new transformations or they will remain merely instincts, regarded as having no particular emotional significance in a spiritual world which, if it exists at all, will be as different from the spiritual world of, let us say, Robert Browning as that world is different from the world of Cato the Censor.

As for this present unhappy time, haunted by ghosts from a dead world and not yet at home in its own, its predicament is not, to return to the comparison with which we began, unlike the predicament of the adolescent who has not yet learned to orient himself without reference to the mythology amid which his childhood was passed. He still seeks in the world of his experience for the values which he had found there, and he is aware only of a vast disharmony. But boys—most of them, at least—grow up, and the world of adult consciousness has always held a relation to myth intimate enough to make readjustment possible. The finest spirits have bridged the gulf, have carried over with them something of a child's faith, and only the coarsest have grown into something which was no more than finished animality. To-day the gulf is broader, the adjustment more difficult, than ever it was before, and even the possibility of an actual human maturity is problematic. There impends for the human spirit either extinction or a readjustment more stupendous than any made before.

30 / WALDO FRANK

The Perception of Power

The emerging technological and economic power of the United States was an external phenomenon, according to Waldo Frank (1889–   ), a critic and novelist. He said that Americans had made their new power into a god and had worshipped it in a proliferating number of cults. At last, however, the new industrial, technological, and scientific power of the nation would not help ordinary people to live with themselves, and the new mechanized deities might actually impede self-knowledge. Presumably secure in their new skyscraper temples, the directors of technology were merely re-affirming most of the provincial strands in the American mind. Waldo Frank's list of the new gods and cults is an inventory of vulgarity that was accepted, more or less, by most of the writers and intellectuals of the last years of the Twenties.

1

The American gods of Power have a temple. It is the best we can show as formal articulation of what we are and what

From Chap. VIII: "Gods and Cults of Power," *The Re-Discovery of America* (New York: Charles Scribner's Sons, 1929), pp. 90–105. Reprinted with permission of Charles Scribner's Sons from *The Re-Discovery of America*, pages 90–105, by Waldo Frank. Copyright 1929 Charles Scribner's Sons; renewal copyright © 1957 Waldo Frank.

we love. We call it the Skyscraper. Fifty stories heaped alike one atop another express a herd; even as the Romanesque bespoke an integrating, the Gothic an integrated, the Renaissance Baroque a distintegrating people. We are a mass rigidly compressed into a simple structure; our rank is equalitarian, our aim is eminence, our dynamics is addition, our clearest value is the power of the bulk of ourselves. So the house that stands for us has immensity for its aim, and for its method the monotonous piling of sameness upon sameness.

When the skyscraper aspires beyond these real traits, it becomes a hypocrite. The will to beauty begets the archæological lies that our ambitious architects smear over our steel structures. The skyscraper is a simple frame in which stones are laid like stuffing; as befits a false democracy the individual stones lack structural importance. In the Gothic, the stress of every separate block upholds the vault: each stone like each soul is indispensable. Yet it is the booty of such constrasting forms that one finds pilfered and stuck about our buildings. Thus, the crass splendour of the American cliff-dwelling is concealed beneath some wistful need of the American soul.

In most rituals of our gods of Power, you will find a like hypocrisy. And in most commentaries on our way of life, one of two equal errors: either the pretense is taken at its face value, or it is sneered at. The truth is in neither camp. We are not a cultural people, nor are we primitives. We are neo-primitives. The memory of our cultural past colours our quest of values beyond those which our actual lives distil. The dissolution of the Mediterranean Whole lives in us, not as mere decay, but as *ferment*. This ferment it is which stirs us into make-believes of "truth" and "beauty." Our hypocrisy is like the normal process of the child, aping the man. Without it, we should be hopeless.

A realtor blowing "service" into inane speculations, Rotarians shouting brotherhood at lunch-time, Henry Ford justifying his flivver on the ground that it made better roads, the

ad writer prating of æsthetics, the politician mouthing God—
are signs not of mere emptiness, but of an emptiness that
would be full. Our business seems to provide no adequate flesh
for our ideals, hence the abyss between what we do and what
we say we are doing. But merely to strip our acts of the gorgeous names we call them is as sterile as to take the names for
granted. The skyscraper may express the herd, but the motifs
on its façade filched from Chartres or Gizeh express the need
of the herd to be a herd no longer.

Let us not forget this as we proceed in our scrutiny of American life. *The pretense is quite as real as the fact.* Pretense is
misplaced desire. It may be dynamic (consider the boy who
plays the man); to the psychologist it is always of importance.
The American lives in a pantheon of Power; but he has filled
his world with highfalutin phrases that prove how intolerable
to himself his world must be. He is something better than an
honest savage: he is a savage in transition. But the problem is
hard; transition is a dangerous age. Being imaginative and
having behind him a vast lineage of dualistic thought, the
American may render bearable his intolerable world, not by
transfiguring it, but by perfecting an anæsthetic system of
substitutes to hide it. If so, his world will not grow; and he
eventually, lost in his anæsthesia, will perish. For all the
"good" lies cannot alter an essential want of opportunities for
creative living. The way out is severely to dissociate our fact
from our pretense: to determine the values that reside in both,
and to bring *these* together.

2

In this spirit, we isolate the Power-fact in a few of our pretentious practices and cults:

SUCCESS: to Americans, success is an exercise of power visible
to the world. If some one else can't see it, it is not success. The
end of riches, popularity, public repute, not their content,

makes success. This means that American success is a surface: what lies behind that surface may be bad or good or even noble: it is irrelevant to success.

THE MACHINE: our household idol, as we have found, because it supplies the explicit objective for the American's self-adoration. Creature of his need of power action, it sensuously displays the means of his own ideal of behaviour. He loves it autoerotically. Its body of surfaces must shine, as if it were the body of the beloved. It must gleam with oil as with ointment, glide silently as in soft raiment. Much of the male American's emotion (which American women need to become women) goes to the machine.

EFFICIENCY AND SERVICE: the machine-ideal in these cults is clear in that their "values" are conceived as working externally and for some particular end related to success. No American is "efficient" because of work done within himself or within others: nor is he "of service" because he raises the level of mankind. "Service" is a particularly hideous cult, because it is the bare hypocrisy of Power.

THE CORPORATION: an idol which combines the values of success and the machine. The individual is held within an organisation that approaches the machine in action and that stands for success. The individual may or may not share in the material profits, he does share in the atmosphere of power. His loyalty is commanded to the company's success, so that he vicariously lives success. This sharing is called "service." Note that the business of the corporation is not really a value to him: it does not, like a church, subsist on his own spiritual increase or salvation. The corporation feeds him and physically "protects" him. But he would be the first to deny that these were ends proportionate with such terms as loyalty and service. The organisation is a fictitious receptacle for his devotion as a social, even religious being; and its true function is just this: to enable him, lacking a divine object, to "serve"; lacking a love object, to be loyal. This is possible, only because of the individual's unconscious cult of power and love of the machine as an instrument of power. He adores the corporation for what it is, believing it to be what he adores. In this strange ritual, there is no true difference between employer and employee. They receive money for their job in varying degree, but both bring to it a cult that has no relevance to money. The corporation is an irrational means for worship to president and office-boy alike: both need it, both lack a better. Therefore, the magnate who at the company's annual love-feast orates to his employees of the "common cause" is telling the truth despite himself. What capitalist and "wage slave" share in the corporation is far deeper than the discrepancy of what they earn.[1]

THE FRATERNAL ORGANISATION: an essential analogue of the commercial company, as are the Boy Scout movement and the State itself, in so far as these also command loyalty beyond their possible intrinsic spiritual content.

POPULAR LITERATURE AND ART: in no country is there more rife devotion, than in ours, to the arts and to their makers. The full reason for this will become more clear when we consider the American cult of comfort, as a corollary of the cult of Power. Here it is to be observed that our arts appeal in the extent that they approach the nature of the machine, and indoctrinate success. The vogue of the radio is almost independent of what comes over the air. The values to the "fan" of radio-art are: (1) the mechanism that does the work, (2) the thrill of success in getting the connection and (3) gregarious satisfaction in the contact with the body and heads of the herd. The American short-story and motion-picture must be mechanical in their precision; originality and truth are readily sacrificed to the urgency of the *formula*. Such art may even be endlessly repetitious without suffering in approval, since its value is its mechanical form. What this form conveys is of

[1]When our communists and socialists, with many of whose aims I am in profound sympathy, learn such truths as this, there will be more cogency to the American revolutionary movement.

course a vicarious success. American art is a "success-machine." The message, the fate of the characters, the atmosphere of the artist must all mechanically converge to this indoctrination. Efficiency, speed, regularity, become habiliments of an art whose end is to enhance the sense of Power. It need not be pointed out how antithetical all this is to the true æsthetic function.

SPORT: also a combination cult of the machine and success. Man individually or in a team is organised mechanically for a success which is the spectacular specific display of Power. Note that American athletics *as a cult* is intrinsically empty. It is not practised (despite the inherited palaver) for the joy of exercise, for physical improvement, as service to a physical god, *or even as the expression of rivalry.* It is watched distantly from a vast stadium in the depths of which the athletes shrink to the size of symbols: or it is read about: or it is followed on the radio and ticker. It has no inner kinship with Greek gymnastics, the Corybantic dance, or the English game. For the sportsman, the end is notoriety and money: for the public, it is the thrill of mechanical perfection, violence, hero-worship, vicarious power.

POLITICS: the analogy between our politics and professional baseball is almost perfect. In both, there are numberless bush-leagues—local bodies which play the game for town and county. Above are the minor leagues—state clubs which feed the Majors. In both, participate a class of specialists and professionals, who, beyond their skill in their game, are in no direct touch with American life; who seal the game to themselves and who serve chiefly as symbols for the rivalries and passions of a dispossessed public. Both politics and baseball are machines. Of course, the politician who holds office fulfils certain organisational functions, so that his utility is different from the sportsman's. Such offices, however, could be filled far better by technicians. The higher political offices are necessary for American life, for the same reason that such phenomena as Babe Ruth are necessary: as means of vicarious Power. The politician is in the game for Power; and the public wants him to play big and to look big, in order to feel big through him.

CRIME: a cult so potent and popular that it outdoes politics and vies with sport in its rank in the public prints. Crime is an expression of Power peculiarly appealing, because it is violent, spectacular, more sportsmanlike than sport, and—in America—almost as successful. It touches the heart of the American atom, who, being compressed into the herd by economy, law and habit, conceives of liberty as an explosion. The American is not intellectual enough to know of revolution or of ideal rebellion. Crime is more within his means: it is the wistful ethos of American self-assertion. Of course, this idolatry cannot be admitted in a jungle so thick with moral relics. So the crowd creates a huge professional class of criminals—entertainers who grow yearly more self-conscious of their "mission." To cooperate with them in their trials and exploits there is an almost equally large group of crime-reporters. Both news accounts of actual trials and fiction about crime conform with our mechanical ideal of art. The process of trial law is a machine, and the good detective tale is a machine as well. The extent to which we rationalise the cult of Crime was revealed to me recently in the editorial of a detective magazine. It recommended that schools subscribe to it on the ground that children, taught by reading its tales how crimes are committed, would be more likely to "go straight."

SEX: as a cult, like that of sport and crime, it is vicarious. It has naught to do with the clean, open ecstasy of sexual play. It flourishes among the masses in whom economic pressure and regimentation of ideas have destroyed that liberty of thought and movement without which sex play is as impossible as singing without air. Its stuffy temple is the tabloid, the movie, or the Broadway show. It is not, in the mind of its adherents, distinguished from crime; and this puts the proper mark on it. America regards sex, as it does crime, as an explosion. (There is, however, a healthy reaction throughout the land against this blear-eyed vicarious cult of Sex, on the part of the flapper and her boy. . . .)

LEGISLATION: a popular cult. Our faith in statutes as an expression of social virtue reveals the classic lineaments of Power: externality, force, display. A law, making men pure, is visible to all, is applicable from the outside, is hence satisfactory in creating that surface of purity which Power alone discerns. Any statute, moreover, is a power-action, and any vice is a pretext for Power to suppress it. Whether such legislation renders pure is, of course, a nugatory matter.

HUMANITARIANISM, OFFICIAL CHARITY, etc.: these with us are cults of Power, and peculiarly vicious. In no other country are they made so much of. They are parasites of the cult of Success. Organised charity is the spectacular means of keeping your less fortunate neighbour in your power, and your conscience in trim. To practise it in Drives and "Federations" is an oblique way of placarding your (financial) goodness. Humanitarianism is a reverse of humanism. It connotes a complacent condescension to your fellows: you wish men well (so long as they do not outstrip you). But humanism wishes men well, only in so far as they aspire to an exalted standard. In a herd without hierarchic values, all men as potential rivals are turned against all men. The salve of this coarse obsession is humanitarianism. If you are so fortunate as to beat your neighbour, publicly you shake his hand: if you are beaten, you disguise the fact by shaking his hand still harder. This is the essence of the thing. It will go any length—within the realm of gesture. A recent example is the "good-will" flight of Colonel Lindbergh to Latin-American lands which we are in the process of devouring.

PURITANISM: the Puritan's metamorphosis in American life from religiosity to acquisition, and his relation with pioneer

ideals, have received much notice in our critical letters.[2] But
we have overlooked the danger of associating historic Puritanism with the force that takes this name to-day. Our Puritanism
is very distinct, not alone from that of Milton, of Roger Williams, of Jonathan Edwards, but as well from that which
inspired Mormonism and Abolition. Mr. Irving Babbitt's definition of Puritanism as "the inner check upon the expansion of
natural impulse" says too little and too much. Too little, because it does not give the motives that bring about this check;
too much, because it does not allow for the natural impulse of
acquisition and of Power, in favour of which Puritanism merely
checked other, to it less important, natural desires. Puritanism
as an ideal gave no single word on slavery, liquor, sex, religious
or political dogma. There were Puritans who drank good
liquor, preached free love, denied the dogmatic authority
even of their private preachers, despised property, believed in
communism, etc. The historic motive behind the Puritans' behaviour had a mystical and economic element: the post-mediæ-
val attitude towards religion as an experience *adumbrating
from the personal will,* and their rationalisation, through Scripture, of their own rise as a Chosen People within the "Egypt"
whose economic feudal fabric oppressed them. This economic
rationalisation shifted in America to the pioneers' need of
eschewing certain enjoyments in order to conquer the wilds.
Finally, this motive evaporated altogether, as did the attitude
towards Scripture from which they built their theocratic notions. What remained was the bare conditioned Puritan behaviour: the will-to-power through insistence on personal
regulation. But since the religious values of Puritanism were
gone, the tendency of this power-expression was to become
exclusively external. Puritan self-rule for ideal ends turned

---

[2]See the works of Randolph Bourne, Van Wyck Brooks, my "Our
America," Lewis Mumford's "The Golden Day," André Siegfried's "Les
Etats-Unis d'Aujourd'hui," and the little known, important volume of
William Carlos Williams, "In the American Grain."

into rule of "the other fellow," still along moral lines, for sheer purposes of power. Puritanism's past of social antagonism, together with its dualistic philosophy of good and bad conditioned it, so that it still sees the world as a divided camp with itself (the good) in the minority. Whatever the numerical fact, modern Puritanism must behave as if it were on the defensive against odds. In this way, it rationalises its need of saying No. And it must say No, since it no longer has any positive values to say Yea to. There is in Tennessee no intellectual horror of Darwin; the farmer wives of Kansas have no articulate theory about alcohol and cigarettes; nor do the Nordics of Vermont *think* themselves superior to the Italians. But evolution, wine and Latin blood are badges of opposing camps. "All Power to us. Suppress 'em!"

SPIRITUALISM, CHRISTIAN SCIENCE, etc.: these are offshoots of the old Puritanism which still had ideal values, modern cults in which the modern habit of Puritan negation takes an ideal form. Spiritualism tends to deny the reality of a painful terrestrial life. It is a demon worship. The mediums are magicians who have a certain power over departed spirits, and deflect this power for the usually material benefit of the believers. Christian Science is no less of a power-plant. From dimly surviving strains of Platonism, neo-Platonism, Gnosticism, Manicheism, it concocts a means of overcoming pain and evil by denying them. That alone is real, it says, which benefits *you*. To the childish power principle, everything is sacrificed *which hurts*. These are significant ideal symptoms of the social disease of Power.

THEOSOPHY, etc.: as the Mediterranean dogmas grow worn with use, the peace and power hungering soul looks farther afield. America, moving west, comes to the east. So India sends patches of her glorious truth to be woven into modern comforters. The weak soul which cannot master the chaos of our world will be tempted to deny it altogether. If one way is too close, in its associations, to the world of our fathers, another—

remoter, more esoteric, must be found. Paths and Methods are offered, with precise specifications, for reaching Truth. And Truth means Success, if not here, then hereafter. The mental and human science of the East is dogmatised into mechanical salvation. Breathe *thus,* think *so*—and you will outstrip mankind in the race to Glory or Nirvana. Thus Hinduism is bereft of its organic meanings, indissoluble with Indian social and psychic forms; and supplies power systems for impotent Americans. Many of our eastern cults are for dull people; but not all.

PSYCHOANALYSIS: the empiric method and hypotheses of Freud are probably as important to psychology as were the analogous geneticisms of Darwin and Marx to biology and economics. To the growth of this discipline, America has contributed very little; in the extent that it has been practised here by competent analysts for therapeutic ends, it does not concern us. But small intellectual groups have turned the technics of Vienna and Zurich into a cult. This has been done by setting up the "causes" "under" our consciousness as god, the jargon that describes these "causes" as the one critical language, and the search of these "causes" in oneself as the Way of life. The empiric theory is, that the neurotic should "solve" his problem in the hermetic symbol-relation with the analyst, in order to be able to go forth better equipped to solve it in real life. What actually happens is that the patient is placed in an infantile relationship under some single individual who lacks even the vicarious wisdom of a church or a race tradition to make him worthy. This relation, called "transference," reveals the Power element, in the peculiarly dangerous disguise of science. The victim who seeks Power always falls into the power of another. Of course, in cure of a disease, such a power relationship with a physician is temporarily needed— even as a man may have to put himself into the power of a surgeon. As a means of "learning to live," of solving problems of spiritual adjustment, psychoanalysis is a menace—a short-cut not to life, but to life's avoidance. Often this practice of self-analysis is found more desirable than actual living and permanently replaces it; the relation with the analyst drains the need of relations with the rough-and-tumble world. When this is the effect, psychoanalysis is a full-fledged power-cult; and as such it has been rife with a peculiarly sensitive and intellectual class of American woman. It is worthy of mention here, because it shows how the *élite* parallel the way of the less sophisticate with their ancient doctrines, by twisting modern theories into means of Power.

3

Our list need not be extended. These practices, devotions, cults of Power, have a common trait: they are not what they seem, so that we bring to them a hope which they do not fulfil. Our success does not make happy, our loyalty to State or Corporation does not enlarge, our cult of sport does not invigorate, our cult of crime does not release; our education does not educate, our politicians do not govern, our arts do not recreate, our beauty does not nourish, our religions do not make whole. Yet it is our energy that feeds these practices and cults. With our spirit, we give them life and blood, in order that they should fulfil us. *And they do not touch us.*

PART 8

TECHNOLOGY

The Goddess Electricity

In the following short scene from his little-known play, *Dynamo*, Eugene O'Neill (1888–1953) captured the excitement and mystery of the new technology. The pagan religiosity of Reuben's approach to the dynamo recalls the more traditional religiosity of Henry Adams' use of the Virgin as an earlier unifying counterforce to the dynamo, also Adams' symbol for modernity.

O'Neill became America's best playwright after he flunked out of Princeton and spent years first as a common seaman and later as a journalist. *Bound East for Cardiff* was produced in 1916, and three of his major works in the Twenties each won a Pulitizer Prize: *Beyond the Horizon*, 1920; *Anna Christie*, 1922; and *Strange Interlude*, 1927. He won the Nobel Prize for Literature in 1936. *Emperor Jones* was published in 1921, *The Hairy Ape* in 1922, *Desire Under the Elms* in 1924, and *Dynamo* in 1929. In this last play O'Neill was not at his creative or theatrical best, but he did illuminate the question of contemporaneity that also absorbed many of the other writers and intellectuals of the decade. Feeling betrayed by the women in his life, Reuben, the play's protagonist, leaves home and the religion of his Reverend father and mother. He finally returns as an atheist, devout only in the presence of the new era's god, electricity. Devoted to the dynamo, his new Mistress, Reuben completely abandons the love of a human woman, commits murder, and electrocutes himself in the dangerous coils of his new altar. O'Neill, even in this very short scene, tells us something of his view of the necessary dehumanization of the new technicized era, of the insuperable barriers between people, and of the fundamental irrelevance of traditional attitudes and reflexes. In freeing himself from the past, after all, Reuben kills himself in and by means of the present.

ACT TWO; SCENE THREE: . . . *Exterior of the Light and Power Company's hydro-electric plant about two miles from the town. The plant is comparatively a small one. The building is red brick. The section on the left, the dynamo room, is much wider than the right section but is a story less in height. An immense window and a big sliding door are in the lower part of the dynamo-room wall, and there is a similar window in the upper part of the section on right. Through the window and the open door of the dynamo room, which is brilliantly lighted by a row of powerful bulbs in white globes set in brackets along both walls, there is a clear view of a dynamo, huge and black, with something of a massive female idol about it, the exciter set on the main structure like a head with blank, oblong eyes above a gross, rounded torso.*

Through the upper window of the right section of the building, in the switch galleries, by a dim light, one gets a glimpse of the mathematically ordered web of the disconnecting switches, double busses, and other equipment stretching up through the roof to the outgoing feeders leading to the transmission towers.

The air is full of sound, a soft overtone of rushing water from the dam and the river bed below, penetrated dominantly by the harsh, throaty, metallic purr of the dynamo.

REUBEN *comes in from the right and approaches until he is opposite the open doorway. He stands there staring at the dynamo and listening to it.*

REUBEN

[*After a pause—fascinatedly*]
It's so mysterious . . . and grand . . . it makes you feel things . . .
you don't need to think . . . you almost get the secret . . . what
electricity is . . . what life is . . . what God is . . . it's all the same
thing . . .

[*A pause—then he goes on in the same fascinated tone*]

It's like a great dark idol . . . like the old stone statues of gods people
prayed to . . . only it's living and they were dead . . . that part on
top is like a head . . . with eyes that see you without seeing you . . .
and below it is like a body . . . not a man's . . . round like a woman's
. . . as if it had breasts . . . but not like a girl . . . not like Ada . . .
no, like a woman . . . like her mother . . . or mine . . . a great, dark
mother! . . . that's what the dynamo is! . . . that's what life is! . . .

[*He stares at it raptly now*]

Listen to her singing . . . that beats all organs in church . . . it's the
hymn of electricity . . . "always singing about everything in the
world" . . . if you could only get back into that . . . know what it
means . . . then you'd know the real God!

[*Then longingly*]

There must be some way! . . . there must be something in her song
that'd tell you if you had ears to hear! . . . some way that she'd teach
you to know her . . .

[*He begins to hum, swaying his body—then stops when he can't
catch the right tone*]

No, you can't get it! . . . it's as far off as the sky and yet it's all
around you! . . . in you! . . .

[*Excitedly*]

I feel like praying now! . . . I feel there is something in her to pray
to! . . . something that'll answer me! . . .

[*He looks around him and moves to the right out of the square of
light from the open doorway*]

Supposing any one saw me . . . they'd think I was nutty . . . the old prayer stuff! . . .

[*Then arguing tormentedly with himself*]

But I feel it's right . . . I feel Mother wants me to . . . it's the least I can do for her . . . to say a prayer . . .

[*He gets down on his knees and prays aloud to the dynamo*]

Oh, Mother of Life, my mother is dead, she has passed back into you, tell her to forgive me, and to help me find your truth!

[*He pauses on his knees for a moment, then gets slowly to his feet. There is a look of calm and relief on his face now. He thinks reverentially*]

Yes, that did it . . . I feel I'm forgiven . . . Mother will help me . . . I can sleep . . . I'll go home . . .

[*He walks slowly off right*]

CURTAIN

32 / CHARLES A. BEARD

The Civilization
of the Machine

The bruised sensibilities of Joseph Wood Krutch (see Document 29) were in part a result of his inability to cheer the new industrial and scientific order. For tougher if coarser minds, Krutch's lament became a paean. Charles A. Beard (1874–1948), an eminent and prolific historian (among his major works were *The Economic Basis of Politics*, 1910; *An Economic Interpretation of the Constitution*, 1913; *Economic Origins of Jeffersonian Democracy*, 1915; and, in collaboration with his wife, *The Rise of American Civilization*,

1927), denied every one of the usual charges made against a machine civilization in his introduction to *Whither Mankind*, which he edited. Arguing that technology was not inherently ugly, materialistic, or antihumanitarian, Beard accepted the present and future with a willingness that would probably only have convinced Krutch that the new barbarians had come to stay.

All over the world, the thinkers and searchers who scan the horizon of the future are attempting to assess the values of civilization and speculating about its destiny. Europe, having just passed through a devastating war and already debating the hour for the next explosion, wonders whether the game is worth the candle or can be played to the bitter extreme without inviting disaster so colossal as to put an end to civilization itself. In America, where Europeans have renewed their youth, conquered a wilderness, and won wealth and leisure in the sweat of their brows, the cry ascends on all sides: "Where do we go from here?" *Vivere deinde philosophari*—the stomach being full, what shall we do next? Far away in Japan, the younger generation, still able to see with their own eyes vestiges of a feudal order abandoned by their elders, are earnestly inquiring whether they must turn back upon their path or lunge forward with renewed energy into the age of steel and electricity. So for one reason or another, the intellectuals of all nations are trying to peer into the coming day, to discover whether the curve of contemporary civilization now rises majestically toward a distant zenith or in reality has already begun to sink rapidly toward a nadir near at hand.

On casual thought, names of anxious inquirers from every land come to mind: Ku Hung Ming and Hu Shih in China; Gandhi and Tagore in India; Yusuke Tsurumi and the late Arishima in Japan; Ferrero and Croce in Italy; Spengler and

From "Introduction," *Whither Mankind,* ed. Charles A. Beard (New York: Longmans, Green, & Co., 1928), pp. 1–3, 4–5, 14–15, 20–24. Used by permission of David McKay Company, Inc.

Keyserling in Germany; Fabre-Luce, Demangeon, and Georges Batault in France; Wells, Chesterton, Belloc, Shaw, and Dean Inge in England; Unamuno in Spain; Trotzsky in Russia; Ugarte in Argentina. The very titles of the books having a challenging ring: "The Decline of the West," "Mankind at the Crossroads," "The Rising Tide of Color," "The Revolt of the Unfit," "The Tragic Sense of Life," "The Decline of Europe," "War the Law of Life," and "The Destiny of a Continent."

It is not alone the philosophers who display anxiety about the future. The policies of statesmen and the quest of the people in circles high and low for moral values reveal a concern about destiny that works as a dynamic force in the affairs of great nations. In Italy, the Fascisti repudiate both democracy and socialism, bring about the most effective organization of capital and labor yet accomplished in any country, and prepare the way for the cooperation of these two forces or for a class war all the more terrible on account of the social equipment of the contending parties. In Russia, the Bolsheviki join the Italians in rejecting democracy but attempt to create a communist state which, if a success, would be a standing menace to all the governments of the world founded on different principles. Germany writhes and turns, torn by an inner *Zerrissenheit*, with Nationalists cursing international capitalism and longing for buried things, with Socialists and Communists still active if shorn of their former confidence, and with the mass of the people once more absorbed in the routine of the struggle for existence, yet dimly aware that the Faustian age may not be closed after all. In an hour of victory, France reckons the terrible cost and stirs restlessly, wondering about the significance of the ominous calm. Likewise triumphant, England sits as of yore enthroned amid her Empire, with all her old goods intact and valuable additions made; but the self-governing dominions assert an unwonted independence; top-heavy capitalism, having devoured domestic agriculture, feverishly searches for new markets among the half-civilized and backward races of the earth, hoping to keep its machinery turning and its profits flowing, while American and German competition in the same enterprise presses harder and harder upon the merchants of London, Manchester, and Liverpool.

Apparently secure between two seas, and enriched by the fortunes of the European war, America reaches out ever more vigorously, huckstering and lending money, evidently hoping with childlike faith that sweet things will ever grow sweeter; but critics, foreign and domestic, disturb the peace of the new Leviathan. Einstein frankly sneers at American intelligence; Siegfried finds here sounding brass, tinkling cymbals, noise, and materialism. If many are inclined to discount the aspersions of the alien, they are immediately confronted by a host of domestic scoffers. The appearance and success of the *American Mercury*, the weekly, nay, almost daily, blasts of H. L. Mencken, so deeply stir the Rotarians and Kiwanians that one of the richest chemical companies buys space in his magazine to make fun of the editor. In a milder vein, but perhaps still more ruinous to the counsels of perfection, the *Saturday Review of Literature*, edited by H. S. Canby, steadily undermines naïve valuations of every sort, bringing artistic judgments ever nearer to the test of realism. And still more ruthless in dealing with moss-grown conventions, V. F. Calverton, with too much assurance perhaps, slashes at the preciosities of American art and thought, threatening them all with the cruel touch of economic appraisal. The age of Victorian complacency has closed everywhere; those who are whistling to keep up their courage and deceive their neighbors merely succeed in hoodwinking themselves. . . .

[Beard surveys here some of the more routinely political and cultural challenges to civilization.—Ed.]

Even if Europe could resolve her conflicts and let the war of the books over civilization die away there in peace and prosperity, the rise of the United States would perhaps keep the old question still open to debate. The passage of America from a provincial, agricultural status to the position of the premier capitalist power in international politics, with a navy hardly second to that of England, is itself an inescapable fact for those who speculate on cultural destinies. American civilization, the full flower of the machine apotheosized, with few traces of feudalism in its make-up, even more than Russia challenges the contemporary régime of Europe, particularly the Latin countries. If once the peasants, farmers, and laborers of the Old World should get it into their heads that more material goods would flow from machinery, science, efficiency and capitalism triumphant, the result would be the abandonment of whole provinces of the ancient heritage, even in remote districts. . . .

What is called Western or modern civilization by way of contrast with the civilization of the Orient or mediæval times is at bottom a civilization that rests upon machinery and science as distinguished from one founded on agricultural or handicraft commerce. It is in reality a technological civilization. It is only about two hundred years old, and, far from shrinking in its influence, is steadily extending its area into agriculture as well as handicrafts. If the records of patent offices, the statistics of production, and the reports of laboratories furnish evidence worthy of credence, technological civilization, instead of showing signs of contraction, threatens to overcome and transform the whole globe.

Considered with respect to its intrinsic nature, technological civilization presents certain precise characteristics. It rests fundamentally on power-driven machinery which transcends the physical limits of its human directors, multiplying indefinitely the capacity for the production of goods. Science in all its branches—physics, chemistry, biology, and psychology—is the servant and upholder of this system. The day of crude invention being almost over, continuous research in the natural sciences is absolutely necessary to the extension of the machine and its market, thus forcing continuously the creation of new goods, new processes, and new modes of life. As the money for learning comes in increasing proportions from taxes on industry and gifts by captains of capitalism, a steady growth in scientific endowments is to be expected, and the scientific curiosity thus aroused and stimulated will hardly fail to expand—and to invade all fields of thought with a technique of ever-refining subtlety. Affording the demand for the output of industry are the vast populations of the globe; hence mass production and marketing are inevitable concomitants of the machine routine.

For the present, machine civilization is associated with capitalism, under which large-scale production has risen to its present stage, but machine civilization is by no means synonymous with capitalism—that ever-changing scheme of exploitation. . . . The kind of servile revolt that was so often ruinous in Greece and Rome is hardly possible in a machine civilization, even if economic distress were to pass anything yet experienced since the eighteenth century. The most radical of the modern proletariat want more of the good things of civilization—not a destruction of technology. If the example of Russia be pressed as relevant, the reply is that Russia possessed not a machine, but an agricultural civilization of the crudest sort; peasant soldiers supplied the storm troops of the November revolution, and the Bolsheviki are straining every nerve to maintain their position by promising the peasants and urban dwellers that the benefits of a machine order will surely come. There will be upheavals in machine civilizations, no doubt, and occasional dictatorships like that in the United States between 1861 and 1865, but the triumph of a party dedicated to a deliberate return to pre-machine agriculture with its low standards of life, its diseases, and its illiteracy is beyond the imagination.

Finally, we must face the assertion that wars among the various nations of machine civilization may destroy the whole order. Probably terrible wars will arise and prove costly in blood and treasure, but it is a strain upon the speculative faculties to conceive of any conflict that could destroy the population and mechanical equipment of the Western world so extensively that human vitality and science could not restore economic prosperity and even improve upon the previous order. According to J. S. Mill, the whole mechanical outfit of a capitalistic country can be reproduced in about ten years. Hence the prospect of repeated and costly wars in the future need not lead us to the pessimistic view that suicide is to be the fate of machine civilization. We may admit the reality of the perils ahead without adopting the counsel of despair. If Europe and America were absolutely devastated, Japan with her present equipment in libraries, laboratories, and technology could begin the work of occupying the vacant areas, using the machine process in the operation.

For the reasons thus adduced it may be inferred: that modern civilization founded on science and the machine will not decline after the fashion of older agricultural civilizations; that analogies drawn from ages previous to technology are inapplicable; that according to signs on every hand technology promises to extend its area and intensify its characteristics; that it will afford the substance with which all who expect to lead and teach in the future must reckon.

Such appears to be the promise of the long future, if not the grand destiny of what we call modern civilization—the flexible framework in which the human spirit must operate during the coming centuries. Yet this view by no means precludes the idea that the machine system, as tested by its present results, presents shocking evils and indeed terrible menaces to the noblest faculties of the human race. By the use of material standards for measuring achievement, it is in danger of developing a kind of ignorant complacency that would make Phidias, Sophocles, Horace, St. Augustine, Dante, Michelangelo, Shakespeare, Lord Bacon, Newton, Goethe, Ruskin, and Emerson appear to be mere trifling parasites as compared with Lord

Beaverbrook, Hugo Stinnes, John Pierpont Morgan, and Henry Ford. To deny the peril that lies in any such numerical morality would be a work of supererogation. More perilous still is the concentration on the production of goods that will sell quickly at the best price the traffic will bear and fall to pieces quickly —mass production of cheap goods—rather than concentration on the manufacture and exchange of commodities with the finest intrinsic values capable of indefinite endurance. What the creed of "give as little as you can for as much as you can get" will do to the common honesty of mankind, if followed blindly for centuries, can readily be imagined. Finally, it must be admitted that the dedication of the engines of state, supported by a passionate and uninformed chauvinism, to the promotion and sale of machine-made goods is creating zones of international rivalry likely to flame up in wars more vast and destructive than any yet witnessed.

To consider for the moment merely the domestic aspects of the question, the machine civilization is particularly open to attack from three sides.

On æsthetic grounds, it has been assailed for nearly a hundred years, England, the classical home of the industrial revolution, being naturally enough the mother of the severest critics—Ruskin, Carlyle, Kingsley, and Matthew Arnold. The chief article in their indictment, perhaps, is the contention that men who work with machinery are not creative, joyous, or free, but are slaves to the monotonous routine of the inexorable wheel. In a sense it is true that, in the pre-machine age, each craftsman had a certain leeway in shaping his materials with his tools and that many a common artisan produced articles of great beauty.

Yet the point can be easily overworked. Doubtless the vast majority of mediæval artisans merely followed designs made by master workmen. This is certainly true of artisans in the Orient today. With respect to the mass of mankind, it is safe to assume that the level of monotony on which labor is conducted under the machine regime is by and large not lower but higher than in the handicraft, servile, or slave systems in the past. Let anyone who has doubts on this matter compare the life of laborers on the latifundia of Rome or in the cities of modern China with that of the workers in by far the major portion of machine industries. Those who are prepared to sacrifice the standard of living for the millions to provide conditions presumably favorable to the creative arts must assume a responsibility of the first magnitude.

Indeed, it is not certain, so primitive as yet are the beginnings of machine civilization, that there can be no substitute for the handicrafts as æsthetic stimulants, assuming that mechanical industry is not favorable to the creative life. The machine régime does not do away with the necessity for designing or reduce the opportunities for the practice of that craft: it transfers the operation from the shop to the laboratory; and it remains to be seen whether great æsthetic powers will not flourish after the first storm of capitalism has passed. In any case, it must be admitted that the "cheap and nasty" character of machine-made goods, so marked everywhere, may really be due to the profit-making lust and the desire of the multitude to have imitations of the gew-gaws loved by the patricians, not to the inherent nature of machine industry. Possibly what is lost in the merits of individual objects of beauty may be more than offset by city and community planning, realizing new types of æsthetic ideals on a vast, democratic basis. Certainly the worst of the æsthetic offences created by the machine—the hideous factory town—can be avoided by intelligent co-operative action, as the garden-city movement faintly foreshadows. In a hundred years the coal-consuming engine may be as obsolete as the Dodo and the Birminghams, Pittsburghs, and Essens of the modern world live only in the records of the historians. However this may be, the æsthetes of the future will have to work within the limitations and opportunities created by science and the machine, directed, it may be hoped, by a more intelligent economy and nobler concepts of human values.

Frequently affiliated with æsthetic criticism of the machine and science is the religious attack. With endless reiteration, the charge is made that industrial civilization is materialistic. In reply, the scornful might say, "Well, what of it?" But the issue deserves consideration on its merits, in spite of its illusive nature. As generally used, the term "materialistic" has some of the qualities of moonshine; it is difficult to grasp. It is the fashion of certain Catholic writers to call Protestantism materialistic, on account of its emphasis on thrift and business enterprise—a fashion which some radicals have adopted: Max Weber in Germany and R. H. Tawney in England, for example. With something akin to the same discrimination, Oswald Spengler calls all England materialistic, governed by pecuniary standards—as contrasted with old Prussia where "duty," "honor," and "simple piety" reigned supreme. More recently, André Siegfried, following a hundred English critics, with Matthew Arnold in the lead, has found materialism to be one of the chief characteristics of the United States, as contrasted with the richer and older civilizations of Europe, particularly France. And Gandhi consigns every one of them—England, Prussia, France, and America—to the same bottomless pit of industrial materialism. When all this verbiage is sifted, it usually means that the charge arises from emotions that have little or no relation to religion or philosophy—from the quarrels of races, sects, and nations.

If religion is taken in a crude, anthropomorphic sense, filling the universe with gods, spirits, and miraculous feats, then beyond question the machine and science are the foes of religion. If it is materialistic to disclose the influence of technology and environment in general upon humanity, then perhaps the machine and science are materialistic. But it is one of the ironies of history that science has shown the shallowness of the old battle between materialist and spiritist and through the mouths of physicists has confessed that it does not know what matter and force are. Matter is motion; motion is matter; both elude us, we are told. Doubtless science does make short shrift of a thousand little mysteries once deemed as essential to Christianity as were the thousand minor gods to the religion of old Japan, but for these little mysteries it has substituted a higher and sublimer mystery.

To descend to the concrete, is the prevention of disease by sanitation more materialistic than curing it by touching saints' bones? Is feeding the multitude by mass production more materialistic than feeding it by a miracle? Is the elimination of famines by a better distribution of goods more materialistic than prevention by the placation of the rain gods? At any rate, it is not likely that science and machinery will be abandoned because the theologian (who seldom refuses to partake of their benefits) wrings his hands and cries out against materialism. After all, how can he consistently maintain that Omnipotent God ruled the world wisely and well until the dawn of the modern age and abandoned it to the Evil One because Henry VIII or Martin Luther quarrelled with the Pope and James Watt invented the steam engine?

Arising, perhaps, from the same emotional source as æsthetic and religious criticisms, is the attack on the machine civilization as lacking in humanitarianism. Without commenting on man's inhumanity to man as an essential characteristic of the race, we may fairly ask on what grounds can anyone argue that the masses were more humanely treated in the agricultural civilization of antiquity or the middle ages than in the machine order of modern times. Tested by the mildness of its laws (brutal as many of them are), by its institutions of care and benevolence, by its death rate (that tell-tale measurement of human welfare), by its standards of life, and by every conceivable measure of human values, machine civilization, even in its present primitive stage, need fear no comparison with any other order on the score of general well-being.

Under the machine and science, the love of beauty, the sense of mystery, and the motive of compassion—sources of æsthetics, religion, and humanism—are not destroyed. They remain essential parts of our nature. But the conditions under which they must operate, the channels they must take, the potentialities of their action are all changed. These ancient forces will become powerful in the modern age just in the proportion that men and women accept the inevitability of science and the machine, understand the nature of the civilization in which they must work, and turn their faces resolutely to the future.

33 / LEWIS MUMFORD

The Esthetic of the Machine

The architectural and esthetic logic of the machine, if honestly and imaginatively applied, could free America from the esthetic tyranny of Europe. This was the argument used by Lewis Mumford (1895–), historian, architectural and social critic, and author, in the Twenties, of *The Story of Utopias,* 1922; *Sticks and Stones,* 1924; *The Golden Day,* 1926; *Herman Melville,* 1929; and *American Taste,* 1929. If Americans would take up the challenge of the contemporary, they would necessarily develop new and distinctively national cultural forms, as they had already done in the designs of automobiles and bathroom fixtures. Mumford believed that the attempt to hide America's technological mastery behind traditional European forms would necessarily result in a further debasement of American taste. Unless American artists faced up to the opportunities and challenges of applied science, they would remain imitators and plagiarists. Technology could function as America's declaration of esthetic independence only if Americans had the courage to be themselves.

. . . During the nineties American taste was faced with a critical alternative. It could either accept the forces of its own age, and seek to humanize them and turn them to aesthetic ends, as Richardson, Sullivan, and Frank Lloyd Wright were doing in architecture; or it would shirk the problem of contemporary taste altogether, neglecting the lessons to be drawn from engineering and the sciences, neglecting all the vital impulses of the American scene itself—and take refuge in the taste and products of other periods and other cultures, no matter how remote or dissimilar they were.

The first path was the path of adventure. Its foundations were sunk in the powerful ugliness of contemporary design; those who followed it recognized and did not flinch from the turbid industrial environment of the railroad age; and sought to take from this environment the materials and forms that were capable of sustaining the growth of the arts, mixing them with the general human heritage from the past, so that the raw and formidable forces of modern existence might be transformed into new cultural forms. Enough artists set forth on this path to assure us, by their achievements, that it was not a blind alley. Perhaps the most successful expression of this effort was the shingled cottages first designed by Richardson. With their full windows, their broad roofs, their rich harmonies in russet, green, and black, they were as native to the seaboard as sumach, wild aster, and goldenrod; they were American in a much deeper sense than our eighteenth-century Georgian mixtures ever were.

In the Middle West, a little later, there was a similar efflorescence of fresh, indigenous designs. The low-lying, many-windowed, wide-roofed, horizontally spacious country houses designed by Mr. Wright were as much a part of the prairies as the cornfields themselves; moreover, the design was carried

---

From *American Taste* (San Francisco: The Westgate Press, 1929), pp. 16–22, 27–31, 34. Reprinted by permission of the author.

through in every detail, in the furniture, in the lighting fixtures, in the delicate tracery and iridescence of Mr. Wright's windows. In houses such as those of Sullivan and Wright and the more adept of their followers it was impossible to think of reviving periods or imitating certified brands of European or early American culture; these buildings were too thoroughly a part of their own day to be disguised in borrowed clothes and threadbare costumes.

Had American taste been sufficiently adventurous, as it was originally in Chicago—or sufficiently sure of itself—to follow the trail marked out by these artists and designers we might have created a milieu in which all the arts could have flourished on a parity. At the very least, we should have been spared the whited sepulchres that began to parade as the seal and hallmark of sound aesthetics, the dull porticoes, the feeble massive pillars that support nothing and express nothing, the half-timbered work that is backed by steel, the French chateau in New England and the Spanish palace in the midst of the prairie—all these fatuities might never have existed. What is more, we should have wasted no time in gutting European palaces or in imitating, by machinery, the great productions of a vanished handicraft. Unfortunately, we lacked both the spirit of adventure and confidence; and in the nineties the scaffold of taste collapsed again.

We took the easier way. Horrified by the ugliness around us, and unable to command the forces that were producing it, American taste retreated from the contemporary stage, and sought to build up little ivory towers of "good taste" by putting together the fragments of the past. The architects led this retreat, particularly the successful Eastern architects; but they were anticipated by the great patrons of art, like Mrs. Jack Gardner; and presently our homes and our buildings ceased to have any fundamental relation to the American scene: they became fragments of the museum. This retreat into the past did not, however, preserve even the temporary and artificial unity that was fostered by the seventeenth-century interest in classical culture; here it lifted a building from a colonial seaport, fitted to the needs of a merchant captain; there it took over bodily a Florentine palace or a chateau from the Loire region; in another place it copied a church by Wren. Art was reduced to tit-bits; plagiarism became an emblem of reputability.

Needless to say, in touching on these large ventures in adaptation and reproduction I am discussing only the works of the very well-to-do; but the middle classes followed at a distance, possessed by the same mood, if unable to translate their desires so grandly into actual houses, furnishings, paintings. A walk through almost any suburban street, or a tour of the furniture section of a department store will give one a more concrete notion of the weird medley of designs produced by this attempt to stamp the present with the counterfeit image of the past.

There have been much uglier periods of design than the last twenty years; for the habit of stylicizing our decorations swept out automatically large quantities of maleficent bric-a-brac and junk; in the negative sense there is now much less to offend the eye in the typical American home than there has been, perhaps, at any other time since 1830. But I doubt if any period has ever exhibited so much spurious taste as the present one; that is, so much taste derived from hearsay, from imitation, and from the desire to make it appear that mechanical industry has no part in our lives and that we are all blessed with heirlooms testifying to a long and prosperous ancestry in the Old World. Our taste, to put it brutally, is the taste of parvenus. The last touch of absurdity to this hunt for antiques was given in a government bulletin which suggested that every American house should have at least one "early American" room. Splendid advice for a population a hundred times as numerous as that of the Thirteen Colonies! . . .

If our anaemic taste excludes the contemporary imaginative artist on one hand, it is equally inhospitable to the industrial arts on the other: the greatest achievement of the modern American building is to exclude or stick in a corner any suggestion of the precise machinery and the delicate apparatus upon which a great part of our life now depends. I do not refer to such manifest idiocies as dolls' dresses to cover telephones—fortunately one does not see many of these; but radio sets made to look like Florentine or Georgian cabinets are examples of this habit of mind; while the rest of our furniture, instead of being adapted to machine construction and simplified in line and detail to the last degree, is frequently cheapened in the things that make for true quality—the excellence of the wood, the seasoning of the stock, the close setting of joints—while the exterior design is elaborated in machine-carved curlycues, in imported marquetry, in feebly painted flowers, or in imitations of age and use, in a fashion that annuls all economies and beauties effected by the machine.

This contempt for the quality of machine work and for the necessary lines fostered by machine-production would be bad enough in itself; it becomes even more contemptible when we consider that none of our arty decorations and adaptations can approach for sheer beauty of line and color a modern automobile or a simple tiled bathroom or the fixtures of a modern kitchen. In motors and in porcelain bathroom fixtures we have, by designing steadily for beauty through the imaginative modification of useful instruments, produced objects of art which stand on the same plane as the handicraft productions of earlier ages.

If our taste were well-formed our chief effort would be to make all our interior fittings—our furniture, our walls, our carpets, our lamps—with the same spirit as we design our automobiles and bathtubs. We would use the machine not to counterfeit handicraft, but to produce its equivalent by another method. This does not necessarily mean complete standardization; for machine-tools now turn out a bewildering variety of "styles," and if the design of our furniture were really adapted to modern methods of production, and to our modern feeling for line and color, there is no inherent reason why it should produce but a single pattern. Here and there, in the design of textiles for instance, we are moving haltingly away from our subservience to ancient styles; but there is a perpetual danger, in the present infirmity of our taste, of a retrogression: every year I tremble lest a distinguished collector of antiques in Detroit should attempt to turn out an "early American" motor car; and at a recent exhibition of the Architectural League in New York I must record with regret the appearance of a stylicized bathroom, with various arty and retrospective notes in its fittings. An occasional exhibition of expensive furniture in le style moderne is not very reassuring, either; for honest machine work is not hopelessly expensive; and our American designers, instead of designing directly for our needs and tastes, are now prepared to copy French modernism, if it becomes fashionable, just as they habitually copy antiques. In short, we shrink from the logic of the machine; yet without accepting it we cannot achieve new beauties, nor can we incorporate human purpose into the fabric of our present civilization.

On this point, European taste is now relatively cultivated; while American taste, by a paradox, has become antipathetic to machinery and tearfully sentimental about ages which did not boast our technical resources. Since the nineties our taste and art have been the product of a divided mind. On one hand we wanted labor-saving devices, we wanted machine production, we wanted the telephone, the auto, the radio; in particular we wanted the profits and dividends that could be derived from exploiting these technological ingenuities. Once we achieved these financial rewards, however, we turned an ostrich head to the process and all its contrivances: we use the means we have acquired to counterfeit, by hook or crook, the environment of the candle, the link-boy, the town-crier, and the log fire. . . .

. . . Clean, devoid of archaic ornament, polished, efficient, carefully adapted to every human need, humane, friendly, a new sort of architecture has already begun to raise its head again in America, throwing off the tedious compromises and the pseudo-culture of the museum. With a little candor and a little sincerity such buildings and such art will perhaps flourish more widely, except where the antagonistic canons of finance and the desire for "conspicuous waste" exert more urgent claims.

PART 9

EPILOGUE

34 / NANCY EVANS

A Revolt Against Defeat

From the vantage point of the early years of the Depression, the Twenties often seemed a gay interregnum. The decade was sharply delimited by the Armistice and the Crash, and the power of the social symbols tended to obscure the multifaceted nature of the time. Babe Ruth, Lindbergh, the flapper, and Capone each represented something significant. But the dispossessed farmer, struggling immigrant, and millions of ordinary workers who were touched by neither the supposed roaring of the Twenties nor the jazz of the age, receded almost beyond historical vision. Even the obvious and celebrated features of the Twenties became somewhat discolored with the knowledge of the Depression. The Twenties produced, or helped to produce, the worst depression in history; an increasing number of analysts began to de-emphasize the supposed integrity of the decade as a result of their knowledge of its miserable culmination. It was too much to say that Americans were developing a tragic sense, but it seemed right to say that at least they were losing the crassest form of optimism that had made Babbitt what he was.

The Depression tended to re-politicize Americans. The relatively sudden reinvigoration of social thought showed that some of the behavior in the Twenties was sometimes petulant, massively narcissistic, and a bad model for the young in the Thirties. There was often a new zest in work as the deepening personal anguish of the Twenties was made to seem merely indulgent in the context of material privation, hunger, and the possibility—theoretical, at least—

of genuine revolution. As America turned its back on the Twenties, a reassertion of traditional values could be expected, as the following short selection shows; but the Twenties had done its work sufficiently well so that some of the results of its rebellion would remain even when the rebellion was itself denied, as this selection also shows. Now, according to Nancy Evans (a Greenwich Village refugee from Ohio since 1924, a free lance writer and business woman), the emancipation of women would lead away from bohemia and free love toward a home, marriage, and children. But the significance of the Twenties can be seen in the fact that emancipation itself was not even questioned.

Being in New York is rather a responsibility; Margaret, for example, always assumes that I move in an artistic, vaguely intellectual paradise. She refers to me as a free spirit and she has a mind's picture of me exotically gowned and surrounded by famous people (chiefly men). In this rare aura epigrams are commonplace and gallantry is unnecessary. I am supposed to be doing important work and it is a matter of course that I am making money. And so, despite my careful efforts to present an exact picture, a letter from Ohio addressed in Margaret's up-hill script makes me feel a hypocrite.

The latest letter was much like the others except for a new phrase that stopped me; Margaret spoke several times of the "demands of domesticity." The complaining tone was unmistakable and there was too much about artists and beauty and freedom. It was hopelessly naïve and I realized that Margaret was still living in our college world of 1923 when we spent long afternoons reading Harriet Monroe's "New Poetry," "Janet March," "Crome Yellow," and "The Triumph of the Egg." We believed quite blandly in sophistication and the arts. To be sure, Margaret found that she loved "funny, old-fashioned Tom" after all; she married and she had two sons, but she

From "Good-by, Bohemia," *Scribner's Magazine*, LXXXIX, no. 6 (June 1931), 643, 645–646.

probably still thought she could write and she still had a secret desire for Bohemia. And now she was dramatizing herself and she was appealing to me as to one who would understand her frustration. I resolved to sit down and destroy her illusions about Greenwich Village, the ways of the artists, and freedom in general before they could do further damage.

Most of the writers and painters have fled New York anyway, and if they haven't, their lives are as regular as they are expensive, and as respectable as they are hard-working. Yes, certainly, bohemianism and defiance are outmoded. Perhaps they never were very satisfactory; Floyd Dell says that even in the old days, in 1913, when the Village was beginning to be a credo, various people he knew were secretly married though apparently living in sin. Such is social pressure! They had, of course, started without benefit of clergy, but after a time emotion got the upper hand and they wanted to insure themselves to each other. And now, just eighteen years later, the cult of bohemianism is dead, gone entirely, as an intellectual movement. . . .

By the time Greenwich Village was accepted, merely living there had become an intellectual pose. But the young believed and they came to find fulfilment; only a few were talented enough to win against the heavy odds of overexcitement and intrusion. The others went back to their homes, or they remained and went in for sophistication. The ones that remained and compromised are department-store executives, greeting-card artists, copywriters and stylists; and they may be seen nightly, prosperous and older, along Eighth Street.

The popularization of Bohemia was one result of a national rush for ready-made liberalism. In 1913 free love was sinister, by 1923 monogamy was shamefaced; and now in 1931 the circle is completed, marriage is respectable, and it is smart to be feminine—even in behavior!

The past eighteen years of experimentation have produced their results—some fortunate and others sad. The young of 1920 had the worst of it, and if they belonged to the smart set (either in New York or Newtonville), their lives were pretty well thrown away. They may have had lovers, they may have been married, but if they believed in freedom and the devil take the rest, they had ample opportunity to theorize themselves out of happiness. There are many women in New York who are prosperous and suave, but thirty and alone; very often they have a child or children whom they are supporting properly, and they confide that if they had known as much as they know now, their husbands would have had a chance to be faithful.

The young people of to-day, those who are just leaving college, have the benefit of the situation. They may choose their loyalties and be blameless. If they like the consequences, they may be modern à la 1920; or they may, if they are not afraid to risk believing, be modern à la 1931. Or they may choose the in-between despair that emerged about 1925 when the results of taking things apart were found to be less than might be desired. The ideas that became serious about this time were expressed only too well by Joseph Wood Krutch in his "The Modern Temper," published about four years later. Mr. Krutch offered very little hope for the reinstatement of the ancient nobility of mankind, but now we are beginning to see that he reckoned without the persuasion of the sun (or moon) and the inevitable tides of reaction.

On all hands people are searching for new values and restating the old ones. Man's conception of his universe and himself has changed; science is here to stay, but philosophy and metaphysics point their claims. This balancing of forces, a sort of revolt against defeat, does not mean that the battle for honesty is off, that it has been quietly lost. Nothing of the sort; it merely indicates that the roads are open and that a modicum of victory is lying around for the asking. Agnosticism does not make one a social pariah, and it is admitted that man is not always heroic. Main Street has accepted as much of the iconoclasm of H. L. Mencken as it needs, and in Montgomery, Ala., it declared a truce by electing him to the Rotary Club. The word sex is not a solecism and lip-stick is not the emblem of a fallen woman. It is considered rational to be interested in ideas, and an artist is not necessarily a libertine.

Greenwich Village did not quite eliminate the home, and romantic love is more firmly instated than ever before. It is expected that a girl will marry the man of her choice, and that she will be an intelligent human being both before and after. To be sure, many young women may have as much difficulty in getting back into the home on self-respecting terms as their sisters of a decade ago had in breaking away; but in any case, they may admit that they do not have everything they want without marriage and children.

35 / *F. SCOTT FITZGERALD*

History's Most Expensive Orgy

It is appropriate that the last word about the Twenties should go to its poet laureate, F. Scott Fitzgerald (see Document 25). In this recollection of his time of glory, Fitzgerald's easy style and confident tone persist, even when he points to the weaknesses and disabilities of the decade. The nostalgia in this obituary to an era is clear, as is his tentative desire to hang on for perhaps just a little while longer. But Fitzgerald was already somewhat older, sadder, and more responsible. So was his country.

It is too soon to write about the Jazz Age with perspective, and without being suspected of premature arteriosclerosis.

"Echoes of the Jazz Age," *Scribner's Magazine*, XC, no. 5 (November 1931), 459–465. From F. Scott Fitzgerald, *The Crack-Up*. Copyright 1931 by Charles Scribner's Sons; 1945 by New Directions Publishing Corporation. Reprinted by permission of New Directions Publishing Corporation.

Many people still succumb to violent retching when they happen upon any of its characteristic words—words which have since yielded in vividness to the coinages of the underworld. It is as dead as were the Yellow Nineties in 1902. Yet the present writer already looks back to it with nostalgia. It bore him up, flattered him and gave him more money than he had dreamed of, simply for telling people that he felt as they did, that something had to be done with all the nervous energy stored up and unexpended in the War.

The ten-year period that, as if reluctant to die outmoded in its bed, leaped to a spectacular death in October, 1929, began about the time of the May Day riots in 1919. When the police rode down the demobilized country boys gaping at the orators in Madison Square, it was the sort of measure bound to alienate the more intelligent young men from the prevailing order. We didn't remember anything about the Bill of Rights until Mencken began plugging it, but we did know that such tyranny belonged in the jittery little countries of South Europe. If goose-livered business men had this effect on the government, then maybe we had gone to war for J. P. Morgan's loans after all. But, because we were tired of Great Causes, there was no more than a short outbreak of moral indignation, typified by Dos Passos' "Three Soldiers." Presently we began to have slices of the national cake and our idealism only flared up when the newspapers made melodrama out of such stories as Harding and the Ohio Gang or Sacco and Vanzetti. The events of 1919 left us cynical rather than revolutionary, in spite of the fact that now we are all rummaging around in our trunks wondering where in hell we left the liberty cap—"I know I *had* it"—and the moujik blouse. It was characteristic of the Jazz Age that it had no interest in politics at all.

It was an age of miracles, it was an age of art, it was an age of excess, and it was an age of satire. A Stuffed Shirt, squirming to blackmail in a lifelike way, sat upon the throne of the United States; a stylish young man hurried over to represent to us the throne of England. A world of girls yearned for the young Englishman; the old American groaned in his sleep as he waited to be poisoned by his wife, upon the advice of the female Rasputin who then made the ultimate decision in our national affairs. But such matters apart, we had things our way at last. With Americans ordering suits by the gross in London, the Bond Street tailors perforce agreed to moderate their cut to the American long-waisted figure and loose-fitting taste, something subtle passed to America, the style of man. During the Renaissance, Francis the First looked to Florence to trim his leg. Seventeenth-century England aped the court of France, and fifty years ago the German Guards officer bought his civilian clothes in London. Gentleman's clothes—symbol of "the power that man must hold and that passes from race to race."

We were the most powerful nation. Who could tell us any longer what was fashionable and what was fun? Isolated during the European War, we had begun combing the unknown South and West for folkways and pastimes and there were more ready to hand.

The first social revelation created a sensation out of all proportion to its novelty. As far back as 1915 the unchaperoned young people of the smaller cities had discovered the mobile privacy of that automobile given to young Bill at sixteen to make him "self-reliant." At first petting was a desperate adventure even under such favorable conditions, but presently confidences were exchanged and the old commandment broke down. As early as 1917 there were references to such sweet and casual dalliance in any number of the *Yale Record* or the *Princeton Tiger.*

But petting in its more audacious manifestations was confined to the wealthier classes—among other young people the old standards prevailed until after the War, and a kiss meant that a proposal was expected, as young officers in strange cities sometimes discovered to their dismay. Only in 1920 did the veil finally fall—the Jazz Age was in flower.

Scarcely had the staider citizens of the republic caught their breaths when the wildest of all generations, the generation which had been adolescent during the confusion of the War, brusquely shouldered my contemporaries out of the way and danced into the limelight. This was the generation whose girls dramatized themselves as flappers, the generation that corrupted its elders and eventually overreached itself less through lack of morals than through lack of taste. May one offer in exhibit the year 1922! That was the peak of the younger generation, for though the Jazz Age continued, it became less and less an affair of youth.

The sequel was like a children's party taken over by the elders, leaving the children puzzled and rather neglected and rather taken aback. By 1923 their elders, tired of watching the carnival with ill-concealed envy, had discovered that young liquor will take the place of young blood, and with a whoop the orgy began. The younger generation was starred no longer.

A whole race going hedonistic, deciding on pleasure. The precocious intimacies of the younger generation would have come about with or without prohibition—they were implicit in the attempt to adapt English customs to American conditions. (Our South, for example, is tropical and early maturing—it has never been part of the wisdom of France and Spain to let young girls go unchaperoned at sixteen and seventeen.) But the general decision to be amused that began with the cocktail parties of 1921 had more complicated origins.

The word jazz in its progress toward respectability has meant first sex, then dancing, then music. It is associated with a state of nervous stimulation, not unlike that of big cities behind the lines of a war. To many English the War still goes on because all the forces that menace them are still active—

Wherefore eat, drink and be merry, for to-morrow we die. But different causes had now brought about a corresponding state in America—though there were entire classes (people over fifty, for example) who spent a whole decade denying its existence even when its puckish face peered into the family circle. Never did they dream that they had contributed to it. The honest citizens of every class, who believed in a strict public morality and were powerful enough to enforce the necessary legislation, did not know that they would necessarily be served by criminals and quacks, and do not really believe it to-day. Rich righteousness had always been able to buy honest and intelligent servants to free the slaves or the Cubans, so when this attempt collapsed our elders stood firm with all the stubbornness of people involved in a weak case, preserving their righteousness and losing their children. Silver-haired women and men with fine old faces, people who never did a consciously dishonest thing in their lives, still assure each other in the apartment hotels of New York and Boston and Washington that "there's a whole generation growing up that will never know the taste of liquor." Meanwhile their granddaughters pass the well-thumbed copy of "Lady Chatterly's Lover" around the boarding-school and, if they get about at all, know the taste of gin or corn at sixteen. But the generation who reached maturity between 1875 and 1895 continue to believe what they want to believe.

Even the intervening generations were incredulous. In 1920 Heywood Broun announced that all this hubbub was nonsense, that young men didn't kiss but told anyhow. But very shortly people over twenty-five came in for an intensive education. Let me trace some of the revelations vouchsafed them by reference to a dozen works written for various types of mentality during the decade. We begin with the suggestion that Don Juan leads an interesting life ("Jurgen," 1919); then we learn that there's a lot of sex around if we only knew it ("Winesburg, Ohio," 1920), that adolescents lead very amorous lives

("This Side of Paradise," 1920), that there are a lot of neglected Anglo-Saxon words ("Ulysses," 1921), that older people don't always resist sudden temptations ("Cytherea," 1922), that girls are sometimes seduced without being ruined ("Flaming Youth," 1922), that even rape often turns out well ("The Sheik," 1922), that glamorous English ladies are often promiscuous ("The Green Hat," 1924), that in fact they devote most of their time to it ("The Vortex," 1926), that it's a damn good thing too ("Lady Chatterly's Lover," 1928), and finally that there are abnormal variations ("The Well of Loneliness," 1928, and "Sodome and Gomorrhe," 1929).

In my opinion the erotic element in these works, even "The Sheik" written for children in the key of "Peter Rabbit," did not one particle of harm. Everything they described, and much more, was familiar in our contemporary life. The majority of the theses were honest and elucidating—their effect was to restore some dignity to the male as opposed to the he-man in American life. ("And what is a 'He-man'?" demanded Gertrude Stein one day. "Isn't it a large enough order to fill out to the dimensions of all that 'a man' has meant in the past? A '*He*-man'!") The married woman can now discover whether she is being cheated, or whether sex is just something to be endured, and her compensation should be to establish a tyranny of the spirit, as her mother may have hinted. Perhaps many women found that love was meant to be fun. Anyhow the objectors lost their tawdry little case, which is one reason why our literature is now the most living in the world.

Contrary to popular opinion the movies of the Jazz Age had no effect upon its morals. The social attitude of the producers was timid, behind the times and banal—for example no picture mirrored even faintly the younger generation until 1923, when magazines had already been started to celebrate it and it had long ceased to be news. There were a few feeble splutters and then Clara Bow in "Flaming Youth"; promptly the Hollywood hacks ran the theme into its cinematographic grave.

Throughout the Jazz Age the movies got no farther than Mrs. Jiggs, keeping up with its most blatant superficialities. This was no doubt due to the censorship as well as to innate conditions in the industry. In any case the Jazz Age now raced along under its own power, served by great filling stations full of money.

The people over thirty, the people all the way up to fifty, had joined the dance. We graybeards (to tread down F.P.A. [Franklin P. Adams]) remember the uproar when in 1912 grandmothers of forty tossed away their crutches and took lessons in the Tango and the Castle-Walk. A dozen years later a woman might pack the Green Hat with her other affairs as she set off for Europe or New York, but Savonarola was too busy flogging dead horses in Augean stables of his own creation to notice. Society, even in small cities, now dined in separate chambers, and the sober table learned about the gay table only from hearsay. There were very few people left at the sober table. One of its former glories, the less sought-after girls who had become resigned to sublimating a probable celibacy, came across Freud and Jung in seeking their intellectual recompense and came tearing back into the fray.

By 1926 the universal preoccupation with sex had become a nuisance. (I remember a perfectly mated, contented young mother asking my wife's advice about "having an affair right away," though she had no one especially in mind, "because don't you think it's sort of undignified when you get much over thirty?") For a while bootleg negro records with their phallic euphemisms made everything suggestive, and simultaneously came a wave of erotic plays—young girls from finishing-schools packed the galleries to hear about the romance of being a Lesbian and George Jean Nathan protested. Then one young producer lost his head entirely, drank a beauty's alcoholic bath-water and went to the penitentiary. Somehow his pathetic attempt at romance belongs to the Jazz Age, while his contemporary in prison, Ruth Snyder, had to be hoisted into it by the tabloids—she was, as *The Daily News* hinted deliciously to gourmets, about "to cook, *and sizzle, AND FRY!*" in the electric chair.

The gay elements of society had divided into two main streams, one flowing toward Palm Beach and Deauville, and the other, much smaller, toward the summer Riviera. One could get away with more on the summer Riviera, and whatever happened seemed to have something to do with art. From 1926 to 1929, the great years of the Cap d'Antibes, this corner of France was dominated by a group quite distinct from that American society which is dominated by Europeans. Pretty much of anything went at Antibes—by 1929 at the most gorgeous paradise for swimmers on the Mediterranean no one swam any more, save for a short hang-over dip at noon. There was a picturesque graduation of steep rocks over the sea and somebody's valet and an occasional English girl used to dive from them but the Americans were content to discuss each other in the bar. This was indicative of something that was taking place in the homeland—Americans were getting soft. There were signs everywhere: we still won the Olympic games but with champions whose names had few vowels in them— teams composed, like the fighting Irish combination of Notre Dame, of fresh overseas blood. Once the French became really interested the Davis Cup gravitated automatically to their intensity in competition. The vacant lots of the Middle-Western cities were built up now—except for a short period in school we were not turning out to be an athletic people like the British after all. The hare and the tortoise. Of course if we wanted to we could be in a minute; we still had all those reserves of ancestral vitality, but one day in 1926 we looked down and found we had flabby arms and a fat pot and couldn't say boop-boop-a-doop to a Sicilian. Shades of Van Bibber!—no utopian ideal, God knows. Even golf, once considered an effeminate game, had seemed very strenuous of late—an emasculated form appeared and proved just right.

By 1927 a wide-spread neurosis began to be evident, faintly signalled, like a nervous beating of the feet, by the popularity of cross-word puzzles. I remember a fellow expatriate opening a letter from a mutual friend of ours, urging him to come home and be revitalized by the hardy, bracing qualities of the native soil. It was a strong letter and it affected us both deeply, until we noticed that it was headed from a nerve sanitarium in Pennsylvania.

By this time contemporaries of mine had begun to disappear into the dark maw of violence. A classmate killed his wife and himself on Long Island, another tumbled "accidentally" from a skyscraper in Philadelphia, another purposely from a skyscraper in New York. One was killed in a speak-easy in Chicago; another was beaten to death in a speak-easy in New York and crawled home to the Princeton Club to die; still another had his skull crushed by a maniac's axe in an insane asylum where he was confined. These are not catastrophes that I went out of my way to look for—these were my friends; moreover, these things happened not during the depression but during the boom.

In the spring of '27, something bright and alien flashed across the sky. A young Minnesotan who seemed to have had nothing to do with his generation did a heroic thing, and for a moment people set down their glasses in country clubs and speak-easies and thought of their old best dreams. Maybe there was a way out by flying, maybe our restless blood could find frontiers in the illimitable air. But by that time we were all pretty well committed; and the Jazz Age continued; we would all have one more.

Nevertheless, Americans were wandering ever more widely —friends seemed eternally bound for Russia, Persia, Abyssinia and Central Africa. And by 1928 Paris had grown suffocating. With each new shipment of Americans spewed up by the boom the quality fell off, until toward the end there was something sinister about the crazy boatloads. They were no longer the simple pa and ma and son and daughter, infinitely superior in their qualities of kindness and curiosity to the corresponding class in Europe, but fantastic neanderthals who believed something, something vague, that you remembered from a very cheap novel. I remember an Italian on a steamer who promenaded the deck in an American Reserve Officer's uniform picking quarrels in broken English with Americans who criticised their own institutions in the bar. I remember a fat Jewess, inlaid with diamonds, who sat behind us at the Russian ballet and said as the curtain rose, "Thad's luffly, dey ought to baint a bicture of it." This was low comedy but it was evident that money and power were falling into the hands of people in comparison with whom the leader of a village Soviet would be a gold-mine of judgment and culture. There were citizens travelling in luxury in 1928 and 1929 who, in the distortion of their new condition, had the human value of pekinese bivalves, cretins, goats. I remember the Judge from some New York district who had taken his daughter to see the Bayeux Tapestries and made a scene in the papers advocating their segregation because one scene was immoral. But in those days life was like the race in "Alice in Wonderland," there was a prize for every one.

The Jazz Age had had a wild youth and a heady middle age. There was the phase of the necking parties, the Leopold-Loeb murder (I remember the time my wife was arrested on Queensborough Bridge on the suspicion of being the "Bob-haired Bandit") and the John Held Clothes. In the second phase such phenomena as sex and murder became more mature, if much more conventional. Middle age must be served and pajamas came to the beach to save fat thighs and flabby calves from competition with the one-piece bathing-suit. Finally skirts came down and everything was concealed. Everybody was at scratch now. Let's go——

But it was not to be. Somebody had blundered and the most expensive orgy in history was over.

It ended two years ago, because the utter confidence which was its essential prop received an enormous jolt and it didn't take long for the flimsy structure to settle earthward. And after two years the Jazz Age seems as far away as the days before the War. It was borrowed time anyhow—the whole upper tenth of a nation living with the insouciance of grand ducs and the casualness of chorus girls. But moralizing is easy now and it was pleasant to be in one's twenties in such a certain and unworried time. Even when you were broke you didn't worry about money, because it was in such profusion around you. Toward the end one had a struggle to pay one's share; it was almost a favor to accept hospitality that required any travelling. Charm, notoriety, mere good manners, weighed more than money as a social asset. This was rather splendid but things were getting thinner and thinner as the eternal necessary human values tried to spread over all that expansion. Writers were geniuses on the strength of one respectable book or play; just as during the War officers of four months' experience commanded hundreds of men, so there were now many little fish lording it over great big bowls. In the theatrical world extravagant productions were carried by a few second-rate stars, and so on up the scale into politics where it was difficult to interest good men in positions of the highest importance and responsibility, importance and responsibility far exceeding that of business executives but which paid only five or six thousand a year.

Now once more the belt is tight and we summon the proper expression of horror as we look back at our wasted youth. Sometimes, though, there is a ghostly rumble among the drums, an asthmatic whisper in the trombones that swings me back into the early twenties when we drank wood alcohol and every day in every way grew better and better, and there was a first abortive shortening of the skirts, and girls all looked alike in sweater dresses, and people you didn't want to know said "Yes, we have no bananas," and it seemed only a question of a few years before the older people would step aside and let the world be run by those who saw things as they were—and it all seems rosy and romantic to us who were young then, because we will never feel quite so intensely about our surroundings any more.

Index